The Politics of Human Rights in Southeast Asia

The divide between the West and Southeast Asia seems to be nowhere more apparent than in debates about human rights. Within these diverse geographical, political and cultural climates, human rights seem to have become relative, and the quest for absolutes seems unattainable.

In this new book Philip Eldridge seeks to question this stalemate. He argues that full participation in Unted Nations' human rights treaties by both western and Southeast Asian countries could be the common ground that bridges the gap. Eldridge uses topical case studies and primary research from Malaysia, Indonesia and Australia, to compare the effectiveness of United Nations' human rights directives on local democracies.

This study presents insightful research into a hotly debated topic. As such it will be a thought-provoking resource for students of human rights, politics and international relations.

Philip J. Eldridge is Honorary Research Associate at the School of Government, University of Tasmania.

Politics in Asia series
Edited by Michael Leifer
London School of Economics

**ASEAN and the Security of
South-East Asia**
Michael Leifer

**China's Policy towards
Territorial Disputes**
The case of the South China sea islands
Chi-kin Lo

India and Southeast Asia
Indian perceptions and policies
Mohammed Ayoob

Gorbachev and Southeast Asia
Leszek Buszynski

Indonesian Politics under Suharto
Order, development and pressure for
change
Michael R. J. Vatikiotis

**The State and Ethnic Politics in
Southeast Asia**
David Brown

**The Politics of Nation Building and
Citizenship in Singapore**
Michael Hill and Lian Kwen Fee

Politics in Indonesia
Democracy, Islam and the ideology of
Tolerance
Doughlas E. Ramage

**Communitarian Ideology and
Democracy in Singapore**
Beng-Huat Chua

The Challenge of Democracy in Nepal
Louise Brown

Japan's Asia Policy
Wolf Mendl

**The International Politics of the
Asia-Pacific, 1945–1995**
Michael Yahuda

Political Change in Southeast Asia
Trimming the Banyan Tree
Michael R. J. Vatikiotis

Hong Kong
China's Challenge
Michael Yahuda

Korea versus Korea
A case of contested legitimacy
B. K. Gills

Taiwan and Chinese Nationalism
National identity and status in
International society
Christopher Hughes

Managing Political Change in Singapore
The elected presidency
Kevin Y. L. Tan and Lam Peng Er

Islam in Malaysian Foreign Policy
Shanti Nair

Political Change in Thailand
Democracy and participation
Kevin Hewison

The Politics of Human Rights in Southeast Asia

Philip J. Eldridge

London and New York

First published 2002
by Routledge
11 New Fetter Lane, London EC4P 4EE

Simultaneously published in the USA and Canada
by Routledge
29 West 35th Street, New York, NY 10001

Routledge is an imprint of the Taylor & Francis Group

Typeset in Times New Roman by
Newgen Imaging Systems (P) Ltd.
Printed and bound in Great Britain by
Biddles Ltd, Guildford and King's Lynn

British Library Cataloguing in Publication Data
A catalogue record for this book is available
from the British Library

Library of Congress Cataloging-in-Publication Data
Eldridge, Philip J. (Philip John)
    The politics of human rights in Southeast Asia / Philip J. Eldridge.
        p. cm.
    Includes bibliographical references and index.
    ISBN 0-415-21429-7
    1. Human rights–Asia, Southeastern. 2. Democratization–Asia, Southeastern.
3. Asia, Southeastern–Economic conditions. I. Title.

JC599.A785 E45 2002
323'.0959–dc21   2001048183

Contents

Preface and Acknowledgements

Southeast Asia has experienced a period of sustained upheaval since research for this project began in 1995. Assumptions underlying the work and the empirical foundations on which they are based have experienced corresponding turbulence. The human and political as well as economic impact of the regional crisis, beginning in 1997, has been profound. A major regime change in Indonesia and the emergence of East Timor as an independent state have been among the more dramatic developments. Currently, the resignation or impeachment of President Wahid appear highly probable. Intensifying struggles for democratic reform in Malaysia, major constitutional change in Thailand and enlargement of ASEAN membership may prove of equally long term significance to regional human rights development.

This account explores diffuse interactions between democracy, human rights and economic development in Southeast Asian regional and domestic politics, with parallel accounts of ASEAN states' strategies in balancing national sovereignty priorities and pressures to conform with international human rights law, as articulated in United Nations covenants and conventions. The original country focus on Indonesia and Malaysia is reflected in specialised chapters. Together with Singapore, these countries were the most articulate advocates of relativist cum Asian values approaches in regional human rights debates before 1997. These themes have retained their salience, although changing forms since the economic crisis. Subsequently, the work has been expanded to include, though unevenly, all ten ASEAN countries.

Australia combines western history and Asian geography, and is of necessity closely engaged with the region. Comparison of Australia's bilateral relations with ASEAN states indicates a pragmatic approach to integrating human rights policies with regional diplomacy and considerations of national sovereignty, security and economic interest. Accounts of internal debates draw out often overlooked tensions between western-style democracy and universal human rights. As Southeast Asian countries democratise, and therefore societies as well as governments interact more closely, human rights are becoming increasingly part of such engagement. In the short term at least, democratisation in Indonesia and East Timor's secession, coinciding with populist re-directions in Australia's regional policy, have worsened relations at both societal and elite levels.

Networks of scholars have been researching notions of dialogue, interdependence and inclusiveness of human rights for many years. But false polarisation between civil and political as against economic, social and cultural rights, together with inflexible understandings of national sovereignty, still frustrate their efforts. This study supports the universalist rather than relativist side of the human rights debate, but takes pains to argue that means for accommodating the region's diffuse cultural traditions are provided within the existing framework of international human rights law.

While universal values are unlikely to be agreed in an absolute sense, UN human rights instruments can be seen as representing the highest level of normative consensus achieved at any given stage by the international community, recognising that this is a continuing process. Most importantly, they provide an operational framework of *a priori* moral equality and mutual accountability.

Sharp differences between Southeast Asian governments and non-government organisations (NGOs), in the context of a global and regional UN-sponsored consultation in 1993, focused attention on the UN context at an early stage of this research. An international conference at La Trobe University, Melbourne, in July 1995, coordinated by Professor Joseph Camilleri, to celebrate the United Nations fiftieth birthday, provided further encouragement in this direction. I also acknowledge earlier exposure to 'humane governance' themes at the Centre for Developing Societies and Lokayan, Delhi, thanking especially Rajni Kothari, D. L. Sheth, Smitu Kothari and Harsh Sethi.

The study's time frame centres on the 1990's, with excursions into earlier history as appropriate. The manuscript has been finalised in late May 2001. Inevitably, problems have been encountered during the final stages in keeping abreast of diffuse, continuously breaking developments in several countries bearing on the work's main themes. The reader's understanding is, therefore, requested for some uneven depth and coverage plus sometimes uncertain use of tenses. However, key themes and arguments, as stated in the Introduction and Conclusion have remained consistent.

Thanks are due to the University of Tasmania Office for Research and Arts Faculty for research travel support, and to the School of Government (previously Department of Political Science) both before and after my retirement from full time academic employment in November 1997, when I was appointed as Honorary Research Associate, for collegial and infrastructure support, including excellent internet and document delivery facilities. Former Head of Department, James Cotton, provided continuing encouragement and insights during the early stages of research. Exchanges with David Jones (Government) and Simon Philpott (Asian Studies/Languages) are also appreciated.

Thanks are due to the Australian Department of Foreign Affairs and Trade for financing a Research Fellowship in Australia–Southeast Asia Relations for nine months at the Institute of Southeast Asian Studies (ISEAS), Singapore, from August 1995 to May 1996. I revisited ISEAS for six weeks in January–February 1997 and briefly in May 1998. I visited Malaysia and Indonesia from ISEAS between September–December 1995 and February–March 1996, with follow-up fieldwork from April to June 1998. Contact with developments has been maintained through the internet and through fieldwork and conferences in Canberra, Melbourne and Sydney at regular intervals during the whole period of research.

At ISEAS, thanks are due to the former Director, Prof. Chan Heng Chee, Administration Secretary, Mrs. Y. Lee, Triena Ong and other Library and Administrative staff and academic colleagues, notably Tania Li, Caroline Gates, Peou Sorpong, John Funston, Diana Wong and Tin Maung Maung Than for providing a stimulating and supportive environment. At a critical stage, the late Michael Leifer, Professor of International Relations at London School of Economics, a regular visitor to ISEAS and Editor of Routledge's Politics in Asia Series, encouraged me in broadening the focus of my work, subsequently commenting on various drafts. Leo Suryadinata, Department of Politics, National University of Singapore, provided incisive commentary on regional, especially Indonesian politics. Exchanges with Hari Singh in that Department are also appreciated.

In Melbourne, I am indebted to the School of Sociology, Anthropology and Politics, La Trobe University, for a Study Fellowship in Governance which provided support in the later stages of my work. Exchange of ideas with Anthony Jarvis is appreciated, as is administrative assistance by School Secretary, Liz Byrne. Institutional and collegial support was also provided by the Asia Institute and Politics Department, Monash University. Thanks are due to Susan Blackburn and David Goldsworthy. Arief Budiman and Gerry van Klinken, variously encountered in Australia and Indonesia, provided background insights on many issues.

Community Aid Abroad and the Overseas Service Bureau provided salient points of contact with the NGO sector. The Human Rights office of the Australian Council for Overseas Aid (ACFOA), particularly its Director Pat Walsh, as in previous work, provided a wealth of resources and insights. Alan Matheson in the international section of the Australian Council of Trade Unions (ACTU) provided important information and insights, plus a network of regional contacts. These included the Asian regional office of the International Confederation of Free Trade Unions based in Singapore and the International Labour Organisation (ILO) regional office in Bangkok. The Australian Chamber of Commerce and Industry (ACCI), through its Director, Brian Noakes, provided parallel business insights and contacts, notably with the Indonesia–Australian Business Council in Jakarta.

In Sydney, I consulted with the Human Rights and Equal Opportunity Commission (HREOC), Australian Legal Resources, which acts as the funding arm of the International Commission of Jurists in Indonesia, and the Human Rights Council of Australia. Thanks are due to Kieran Fitzpatrick, Liz Biok and Andre Frankovits.

In periodic visits to Canberra, the Department of Political and Social Change, Australian National University, provided an institutional base and collegial support. Warm thanks are due to Harold Crouch for exchange on both Indonesia and Malaysia. Edward Aspinall assisted my understanding of developments in the

Indonesian student movement. The National Library provided a solid resource base throughout my work.

Thanks are due to many desk and section officers in the Department of Foreign Affairs and Trade, Defence and Intelligence Organisation (DIO), Australian Agency for International Development (AUSAID), and their counterparts in Australian embassies in Jakarta, Singapore, Kuala Lumpur and Bangkok for providing high quality information and resources. Margaret Svieringa, Secretary to the Human Rights Subcommittee of the Parliamentary Joint Standing Committee on Foreign Affairs, Defence and Trade also provided extensive information and insights. Among NGOs, assistance is acknowledged from Michael Curtoti (Australian Forum of Human Rights Organisations), Janet Hunt (Australian Council for Overseas Aid) and Patrick Kilby (Community Aid Abroad).

The Centre of Strategic and International Studies (CSIS), as my main academic base in Jakarta, provided a supportive, collegial environment. Its library provided an excellent press cuttings service. Particular thanks are due to Yusuf Wanandi and Hadi Soesastro. Thanks are also due to Ikrar Bhakti, Dewi Fortuna Anwar and Rifki Muna (Indonesian Institute of Sciences – LIPI) for wide-ranging exchanges.

At Gajah Mada University, Yogyakarta, Lukman Sutrisno (Rural Development Studies Centre) has been a continuing source of energy and ideas. The Social and Political Science Faculty hosted periodic visits. Thanks are due to Yahya Muhaimin, Afan Gafar and other Faculty members for lively exchange – also to visiting Australian lecturers Herbert Feith and Lance Castles. The Centre for Strategic and Policy Studies (linked to the Institute of Indonesian Muslim Intellectuals) offered an additional resource base.

Exchanges with activists and associated intellectuals in human rights and related fields in Jakarta and Yogyakarta included Gustav Dupe (Indonesian People for a Humanitarian Community); Bonar Tigor Naipospos and Eko Dananjaya (Information Centre and Action Network for Democratic Reform); Achmad Taufik (Alliance of Independent Journalists); Dita Sari (Centre for Indonesian Labour Struggles); Abdul Hakim Nusantara, (Institute of Policy Research and Advocacy); Asmara Nababan and Maria Pakpahan (International Forum for Indonesian Development); Buyung Nasution, Mulya Lubis, Budi Santoso and Fauzi Abdullah (Indonesian Legal Aid Institute); Poncke Princen (Institute for the Defence of Human Rights); M. Billah (Community for Participatory Social Management); B. J. Marbun (National Human Rights Commission); Tati Krisnawati (Women's Solidarity); Dadang Juliantoro (Lappera); Adi Sasono (ICMI); Nurcholish Madjid (Yayasan Wakaf Paramadina); the late Fr. Romo Mangunwijaya (Kanisius Foundation); Mansour Fakih (Institute for Social Transformation); Sabam Siagian (Jakarta Post Director and former Ambassador to Australia). I also enjoyed the privilege of an interview in December 1995 with Indonesia's current President, Abdurrachman Wahid, who was then Chairman of Nahdlatul Ulama.

In Malaysia, thanks are due to Jomo Sundaram and Farish Noor (University of Malaya); A. B. Shamsul (Malaysian National University); Loh Kok Wah, Khoo

Boo Teik and Johan Saravanamuttu (Social Science Faculty, University Sains, Penang); Harun Mahmud Hashim and Ahmed Ibrahim (International Islamic University); Noor Sopie, Balakrishnan and Munirah Alatas (Institute for Strategic and International Studies); Wan Mohd Nor Wan Daud (International Institute of Islamic Thought and Civilization). Thanks are also due to the Politics and Information Section, Ministry of Foreign Affairs, for briefing on Malaysian external affairs priorities.

Professional, NGO and other activists contacted in Kuala Lumpur and Penang included Puan Hendon and Cecil Rajendra (Malaysian Bar Council); P. G. Lim (Regional Centre for Arbitration); Sivarasa Rasiah and Elizabeth Wong (Voice of Malaysia); P. Rama, 'Sam' Loh Kok Wah (Aliran Kesadaran Negara); Chandra Muzaffar (Just World Trust); Mary Assunta (Consumers' Association Penang); Thayalan Muniandy (legal adviser to Consumers' Association Penang and Friends of the Earth Malaysia); Tan Beng Hui and Zaitun Kassim (All Women's Action Society of Malaysia); Zaina Anwar and Norani Othman (Sisters in Islam); Irene Fernandez (Tenaganita); Ahmad Azam (Movement in Defence of Malaysian Islam); Gurmit Singh, (Environmental Protection Society); Fan Yew Teng (Centre for Peace); T. Rajamoorthy (Third World Network); Gopal and Rajasekaran (Malaysian Trade Union Council). Musa Hitam, Former Deputy Prime Minister and United Nations Human Rights Commissioner also provided important comparative perspectives.

In Bangkok, thanks are due to Prof. Suchit Bunbongkarn and other staff of the Department of Political Science, Chulalungkorn University, for valuable exchange during my visit in January 1996. Also to Thongbai Thongpao, veteran human rights lawyer and activist, for wide-ranging information and insights.

Sincere apologies are offered to many who gave generously of their time and ideas, who may have been omitted involuntarily from these acknowledgements, due to the effluxion of time and information overload on an ageing scholar. Many others encountered in the course of travels, without contributing in a direct academic sense, added to the general enjoyment and conviviality gained from this research.

Finally, I thank my wife, Inna, for invaluable cross-cultural 'reality checks' besides much other support.

Responsibility for interpretation, errors and omissions remains my own.

Philip Eldridge
Hobart, Australia
25 May 2001

Abbreviations

ABIM	Movement in Defence of Malaysian Islam (Angkatan Bela Islam Malaysia)
ABRI	Armed forces of the Republic of Indonesia (Angkatan Bersenjata Republik Indonesia)
ACCI	Australian Chambers of Commerce and Industry
ACFOA	Australian Council for Overseas Aid
ACTU	Australian Council of Trade Unions
ADF	Australian Defence Forces
AFHRO	Australian Forum of Human Rights Organisations
AFTA	ASEAN Free Trade Area
AHRC	Asian Human Rights Commission
AJI	Independent Journalists' Alliance (Alliansi Jurnalis Independen) (Indonesia)
AMDA	Association of Medical Doctors of Asia
ANCP	AusAID-NGO Cooperation Program
ANZ	Australia and New Zealand
APEC	Asia-Pacific Economic Cooperation
APFNHRI	Asia-Pacific Forum of National Human Rights Institutions
APHR-FT	Asia Pacific Human Rights (NGOs) Facilitating Team
ARF	ASEAN Regional Forum
ARMM	Autonomous Region of Moslem Mindanao
ASEAN	Association of Southeast Asian Nations
ASEM	Asia-Europe Meeting
ASIET	Action for Solidarity with Indonesia and East Timor (Australia)
AusAID	Australian Agency for International Development
AWAM	All Women's Action Society of Malaysia
BA	Alternative Front (Barisan Alternatif) (Malaysia)
BAPPENAS	National Planning Board (Badan Perencanaan Pembangunan Nasional) (Indonesia)
BDLP	Buddhist Liberal Democratic Party (Thailand)
BN	National Front (Barisan Nasional) (Malaysia)
BSPP	Burma Socialist Programme Party
CAA	Community Aid Abroad
CAP	Consumers' Association of Penang
CAT	Convention against Torture and other Cruel, Inhuman or Degrading Treatments or Punishments

CDA	Constitution Drafting Assembly (Thailand)
CDI	Centre for Democratic Institutions (Australia)
CE	Christian Era
CEDAW	Convention on the Elimination of All Forms of Discrimination against Women
CENPEACE	Centre for Peace (Malaysia)
CERD	Convention on the Elimination of All Forms of Racial Discrimination
CGI	(World Bank) Consortium Group for Indonesia
CNRT	National Resistance Council for Independent East Timor
COHCHR	Cambodian Office of the High Commissioner for Human Rights
CPC	(Malaysian) Criminal Procedure Code
CPF	(Singapore) Central Provident Fund
CPP	Cambodian People's Party
CROC	Convention on the Rights of the Child
DAC	Development Assistance Committee (of the OECD)
DAP	Democratic Action Party (Malaysia)
DFAT	Department of Foreign Affairs and Trade (Australia)
DIFF	Development Import Finance Facility (Australia)
DIMA	Department of Immigration and Multicultural Affairs (Australia)
DPR	House of Representatives (Dewan Perwakilan Rakyat) (Indonesia)
EAEC	East Asian Economic Caucus
ECOSOC	(United Nations) Economic and Social Council
EPSM	Environmental Protection Society of Malaysia
FORERI	Forum for Reconciliation in Irian Jaya
FPDA	Five Power Defence Arrangements
FSBI	All-Indonesia Workers' Federation (Federasi Serikat Buruh Indonesia)
FUNCINPEC	National United Front for an Independent, Neutral, Peaceful and Cooperative Cambodia
GAM	Free Aceh Movement (Gerakan Aceh Merdeka)
GBHN	Guidelines of State Policy (Garis-Garis Besar Haluan Negara) (Indonesia)
GDP	Gross Domestic Product
GNP	Gross National Product
HAKAM	National Association for Human Rights (Persatuan Kebangsaan Hak Asasi Manusia) (Indonesia)
HDI	Human Development Index
HRCA	Human Rights Council of Australia
HREOC	Human Rights and Equal Opportunity Commission (Australia)
ICCPR	International Covenant on Civil and Political Rights
ICESCR	International Covenant on Economic, Social and Cultural Rights
ICMI	Institute of Indonesian Muslim Intellectuals (Institut Cendekiawan Muslim Se-Indonesia)
ICFTU	International Confederation of Free Trade Unions
ILO	International Labour Organisation
IMF	International Monetary Fund
INDOC	Indonesian Documentation and Information Centre
INFID	International Forum for Indonesian Development
INGI	International Non-Government Group for Indonesia
INTERFET	International Force for East Timor
IRI	International Republican Institute (USA)
JIOG	Joint International Observers' Group (for Cambodian elections)

JSCFADT	Joint Standing Committee on Foreign Affairs, Defence and Trade (Australia)
KBL	New Society Movement (Philippines)
KIPP	Independent Committee to Monitor Elections (Komite Independen Pemantau Pemilu) (Indonesia)
KISDI	Indonesian Committee for Solidarity with the Islamic World (Komite Indonesia untuk Solidaritas Dunia Islam)
KLSE	Kuala Lumpur Stock Exchange
KNP	Khmer Nation Party (Cambodia)
Komnas HAM	National Human Rights Commission (Komite Nasional untuk Hak Asasi Manusia) (Indonesia)
LEMHAMNAS	National Defence Institute (Lembaga Hankam Nasional) (Indonesia)
LP3ES	Social and Economic Research, Education and Information Institute (Lembaga Penelitian Pendidikan, Penerangan Ekonomi Dan Sosial) (Indonesia)
MAF	Malaysian Action Front
MIC	Malaysian Indian Congress
MILF	Moro Islamic Liberation Front (Philippines)
MIUK	Indonesian People for a Humanitarian Community (Masyarakat Indonesia Untuk Kemanusiaan – MIUK)
MNLF	Moro National Liberation Front (Philippines)
MPR	People's Deliberative Council (Majelis Pemusyawaratan Rakyat) (Indonesia)
NAMFREL	National Movement for Free Elections (Philippines)
NCW	National Council of Women (Malaysia)
NDP	New Development Policy (Malaysia)
NEP	New Economic Policy (Malaysia)
NGO	Non-government organisation
NIEO	New International Economic Order
NLD	National League for Democracy (Burma/Myanmar)
NPA	New People's Army (Philippines)
NTT	East Nusa Tenggara (Nusa Tenggara Timur) (Indonesia)
NU	Association of Religious Scholars (Nahdlatul Ulama) (Indonesia)
NUPW	National Union of Plantation Workers (Malaysia)
ODA	Overseas Development Assistance
OECD	Organisation for Economic Cooperation and Development
OHCHR	Office of the (United Nations) High Commissioner for Human Rights
OIC	Organisation of Islamic Countries
OPM	Free Papua Organisation (Organisasi Papua Merdeka)
PAN	National Mandate Party (Partai Amanat Nasional) (Indonesia)
PAP	People's Action Party (Singapore)
PAS	Islamic Party (Malaysia)
PARMUSI	Indonesian Islamic Party (Partai Muslim Indonesia)
PBS	United Sabah Party (Partai Bersatu Sabah) (Malaysia)
PDI	Indonesian Democratic Party (Partai Demokrasi Indonesia)
PDI-P	Indonesian Democratic Party of Struggle (Partai Demokrasi Indonesia Perjuangan)
PDR	Centre for People's Democracy (Pusat Demokrasi Rakyat) (Indonesia)
PGI	Indonesian Communion of Churches (Persekutuan Gereja–Gereja Indonesia)

PIJAR	Information Centre and Action Network for Democratic Reform (Pusat Informasi dan Jaringan Aksi untuk Reformasi) (Indonesia)
PKB	National Awakening Party (Partai Kebangkitan Bangsa) (Indonesia)
PKI	Indonesian Communist Party (Partai Komunis Indonesia)
PKK	Family Welfare Association (Pembinaan Kesejahteraan Keluarga) (Indonesia)
PNG	Papua-New Guinea
PPBI	Centre for Indonesian Labour Struggles (Pusat Perjuangan Buruh Indonesia)
PPP	Development Unity Party (Partai Persatuan Pembangunan) (Indonesia)
PRD	People's Democratic Party (Partai Rakyat Demokrasi) (Indonesia)
PRM	Malaysian People's Party (Partai Rakyat Malaysia)
PSI	Indonesian Socialist Party (Partai Sosialis Indonesia)
PUDI	Indonesian United Democratic Party (Partai Uni Demokrasi Indonesia)
PWI	Indonesian Journalists' Association (Persatuan Wartawan Indonesia)
RAM	Reform of the Armed Forces Movement (Philippines)
RDA	Racial Discrimination Act (Australia)
RTD	United Nations Declaration on the Right to Development
SAHRDC	South Asia Human Rights Documentation Center
SAL	Structural Adjustment Loan
SAM	Friends of the Earth (Sahabat Alam) (Malaysia)
SBSI	Indonesian Labour Welfare Association (Serikat Buruh Sejahtera Indonesia)
SLORC	State Law and Order Restoration Committee (Burma/Myanmar)
SP	Women's Solidarity (Solidaritas Perempuan) (Indonesia)
SPDC	State Peace and Development Council (Burma/Myanmar)
SPRIM	Indonesian Peoples' Solidarity Struggle with the Maubere People (Solidaritas Perjuangan Rakyat Indonesia dengan Maubere)
SPSI	All Indonesian Workers' Union (Serikat Pekerja Seluruh Indonesia)
SUARAM	Voice of Malaysia (Suara Malaysia)
SUHAKAM	Human Right Commission of Malaysia (Suruhanjaya Hak Asasi Manusia Malaysia)
TNI	Indonesian National Army (Tentara Nasional Indonesia)
TRC	Truth and Reconciliation Commission (Indonesia)
UDHR	Universal Declaration of Human Rights
UK	United Kingdom (of Great Britain and Northern Ireland)
UMNO	United Malays' National Organisation (Malaysia)
UN	United Nations
UNAMET	United Nations Mission for East Timor
UNDP	United Nations Development Programme
UNCHR	United Nations Commission for Human Rights
UNHCR	United Nations High Commission for Refugees
UNTAET	United Nations Temporary Administration in East Timor
UNTAC	United Nations Transitional Administration of Cambodia
USA	United States of America
USDA	Union Solidarity and Development Association (Burma/Myanmar)
USSR	Union of Soviet Socialist Republics
VDPA	Vienna Declaration and Programme of Action
WTO	World Trade Organisation
YLBHI	Foundation of Indonesian Legal Aid Institutions (Yayasan Lembaga Bantuan Hukum Indonesia)
YPMD	Institute for Rural Development (Yayasan Pengembangan Masyarakat Desa) (Indonesia)

Introduction

Political conflict surrounding human rights in Southeast Asia has intensified since the end of the Cold War, especially since the recent regional economic crisis. Conceptions of human rights are inevitably controversial, as they reach to the heart of a society's cultural and political identity. This book explores key themes influencing policy and discourse in a contextualised study linking international, regional and domestic politics across the ten Association of Southeast Asian Nations (ASEAN) countries plus Australia. States' responses to international human rights law expressed via United Nations (UN) human rights instruments provide a primary frame of reference.

Key themes relate to the universality or relativity of human rights, tensions between national sovereignty and international human rights law, and comparing approaches to integrating human rights, democracy and economic development. Complexities of democratic transition in Southeast Asia and the political fallout from the regional economic crisis also feature strongly. The impact of religious ideas on human rights is taken up in selected country contexts.

Both the concept and application of universal human rights have been extensively challenged in Southeast Asia. Some governments see them as potentially threatening their national sovereignty, unity and stability, and emphasis on civil and political aspects of human rights in international discourse as tending to downgrade the priority they accord to economic development. Their concerns were articulated in the early 1990s through 'Asian values' and 'Asian democracy' paradigms. These deny universality and assert the relative nature of human rights, based on countries' unique culture, institutions and history. Such ideas have in turn been challenged by civil society groups, as legitimising authoritarian rule. Most groups nevertheless reject exclusion of social and economic rights in western neo-liberal formulations.

The politics of human rights in Southeast Asia entail a complex balance between diffuse domestic and external pressures. Post-colonial ASEAN governments, though historically resistant to universalist discourse based on international human rights law, have been increasingly obliged since the end of the Cold War to incorporate human rights into their objectives, policy frameworks and conceptions of national interest. Resulting inconsistencies are drawn out in the narrative. Civil society groups, though often championing human rights, are also inconsistent in their enthusiasm and emphasis, depending on their particular agendas.

UN human rights regimes, integral to any study of human rights, serve to strengthen understanding of key debates in this field. For example, ASEAN states' stress on economic development relative to democratic freedom will be shown as imitating but distorting UN assertions of 'indivisibility' between major streams of rights. However, there is no intention to impose UN regimes as a blanket explanatory framework. These are carefully located in their respective contexts, with comparable weight given to individual states' society and politics, perceptions of national and regional interests.

Despite many convolutions and points of resistance, there appears to be a gradual trend towards participating in UN human rights regimes by ASEAN states. This is reflected in piecemeal institutionalisation of international human rights law, as part of more general global convergence towards common codes of practice. UN regimes offer potentially the most effective multilateral, inclusive and legitimate framework for dialogue and dispute resolution in this highly contentious area. Norms of mutual accountability and peer review can also reduce affronts to sovereignty from uninvited bilateral criticisms. On the other hand, the growing legitimacy of UN human rights instruments, while encouraging formal adherence, may lead to new patterns of evasion in practice. Some governments also seek to weaken UN regimes by demanding consensus processes giving them effective veto powers.

Australia's role is treated somewhat differently compared with ASEAN countries, in that the focus is more on regional policy and interactions than domestic human rights practice – though this is included. Australia's proximity, and geo-cultural uniqueness as an economically developed and historically western-oriented country, offer a potentially valuable contrasting mirror to the conduct of human rights politics in Southeast Asia. Engagement is effectively compelled by Australia's growing, though uneven economic and strategic integration into the region. While Australia's stance is often the object of strong criticism, there has also been cooperation and even convergence with ASEAN states on human rights issues. Australia also illustrates difficulties experienced by fully-fledged liberal democratic states in conforming with UN regimes, and is not averse to invoking similar sovereignty concerns as Southeast Asian countries.

Realist international relations theory has historically assumed that a world order based on universal values can only be imposed by some form of world government possessing legal authority and force. This currently appears a far distant and not widely endorsed prospect. However, there is no reason why normal processes of cooperation, competition, and conflict in domestic and international political arenas should not co-exist within an overall framework of international human rights law, continually re-negotiated and adjusted to changing needs and circumstances. Conceptions of universal rights will thereby be rendered less abstract and unattainable. Though by no means infallible 'tablets of stone', UN human rights instruments represent the highest measure of normative and practical consensus achieved by the international community at any given time.

Democratisation processes are central to current human rights debates in Southeast Asia, linked to both internal and external pressures for reform. Democracy must nevertheless be distinguished from human rights. While free representative democracy is a major component of human rights, its necessarily majoritarian principles do not guarantee and may override rights of minorities. This reality, long evident in South Asia, will become clearer as more Southeast Asian countries institutionalise western-style electoral processes. Thus communal and religious conflict, linked to high levels of criminality and corruption, have been aggravated in several states undergoing turbulent democratic transitions. The challenge, therefore, is to develop a more deep-rooted human rights culture across both civil society and state structures.

Debates over economic policy are closely woven into the account, although space allows only minimal discussion of conflicting policy prescriptions or development philosophies from which they derive. As all protagonists assert better overall living standards as their ultimate goal, particular approaches cannot be categorised as *a priori* more human rights friendly than others. Means and ends are comparatively closer in relation to many aspects of civil and political rights. Nevertheless, approaches most urgently concerned with economic human rights focus on outcomes which provide a basic physical quality of life in areas of health, nutrition, clean drinking water, sanitation and shelter, with a strong focus on education and literacy, and embracing gender equality, rights of minorities and environmental sustainability. Labour human rights and the right to work are integral to both human dignity and economic rights. Approaches which treat such issues as the by-product of market forces or postpone outcomes for the majority too far into the future can be regarded as indifferent or inimical to economic human rights. This is implicit in injunctions in the International Covenant on Economic, Social and Cultural Rights (ICESCR) to 'respect, protect and promote' such rights.

Human rights concepts are diffused across a range of cross-cutting discourses and contexts, including international relations, globalisation, nation-building, democratisation, governance, social and economic development. They are contested across many disciplines, sub-disciplines and theoretical frameworks, embracing liberal and social democratic, marxist and neo-marxist, conservative cum organic state theory and post-modernism, to name the most obvious. Feminist and ecological perspectives provide important counter-discourses to those deriving from longer established streams of theory, as do writings concerning 'humane governance' initiated via the 'World Order Models Project' (Falk 1995). While Chapter 1 offers a basic outline of contending theories, the book's focus is on the implications of ideologies and values for politics and public policy rather than textual genealogies or theoretical explanation for its own sake.

Two opposite trends are evident in explaining the role of culture in society and politics. Both liberals and marxists have viewed culture as subordinate to economic, technological and, in the case of marxists, class forces. For liberals, culture represents an aspect of consumer choice, changing with society and economy, or relegated to the private and domestic spheres. Marxists view culture as a tool manipulated to legitimate the interests of dominant classes. Conversely, culture can be seen in various reified forms, as serving to integrate diffuse social elements, yet retaining its own autonomous existence. Organic state theories whether of the conservative Durkheimian or more totalitarian kind derived from Hegelian thought, draw heavily on such ideas.

None of these perspectives can account for the extent of cross-cultural borrowing and adaptation occurring within a context of rapid globalisation. Individuals and groups, particularly within urban contexts, increasingly operate within milieus of multiple and competing influences, with cultural boundaries obscured by 'seepage of a global cosmopolitan civilisation' (Vincent 1986: 54). Culture is thus not statically fixed in time or place, and is both contested and negotiable.

Diffuse post-modernist theories converge in denying the validity of overarching explanations of history and society. Universal human rights is one such 'grand narrative' naturally identified as a prime target for 'deconstruction'. While many historians and social scientists are sceptical of overarching explanations on empirical grounds, post-modernists go further in posing the social and cultural orientation of the observer as an insuperable obstacle to valid empirical observation, comparison or value judgments. The problem is by no means new to philosophers, but achievement of some kind of shared values and understanding remains essential to building a peaceful and stable world.

Superficially, post-modernist thought and notions of cultural relativism converge in opposing universalist frameworks. Yet there is something odd about characterising Lee Kuan Kew or Mahathir Mohamad, two of the most forceful advocates of relativist Asian values, as post-modernists, in view of their commitment to rapid technological modernisation. In reality, cultural relativists have their own grand narratives, both when engaged in ideological battles with western countries and in constructing identity for purposes of nation building.

Max Weber, the nineteenth century German sociologist, offers a potential middle way, by integrating a systematic view of ideas, which retain their autonomy though located within specific social, economic and political contexts. There is obviously no need to accept Weber's specific conclusions on the relationship between religion and capitalist development. In that context, pitfalls of 'ethnocentrism' and 'orientalism' pointed out by Edward Said (1995: 259) can at least be reduced, if not entirely eliminated, by including a wide range of both Southeast Asian and western, official and non-official perspectives. Foucault notwithstanding, while dominant discourses obviously represent tools of the powerful, this need not lead to a reductionist view of values and ideas, which can spring from every level of society, motivating popular sentiment and action.

The role of religion is relevant, both specifically to human rights discourse and overall interaction between 'east' and 'west'. Despite charges of ethnocentrism levelled more or less exclusively against supposedly western Christianity, particularly its Protestant variety, most religions in practice claim universality for their cosmic outlook and claims to truth, although their specific practices manifest many local variants and counter-traditions. Even Hinduism, and Buddhism, which emphasise plurality and relativity of truth as central to their belief systems, operate within an identifiable framework of ideas.

Many religious leaders and adherents in Asia, though vigorously refuting what they perceive as claims of western cultural or other kinds of hegemony, also reject their governments' claims to define some exclusive 'Asian way' and monopolise definitions of national culture. Some actively pursue the path of 'inter-civilisational' dialogue, both within the Asian region and across 'East–West' boundaries. The creative potential of this enterprise could offer a powerful counter to Samuel Huntington's 'clash of civilisations' thesis. However, the nature of any consensus which emerges will determine whether such dialogue will have positive or negative implications for universal human rights.

Chapter outline

Chapter 1 explores the concept of human rights in relation to common themes in international relations discourse.

In principle, universal rights must be intrinsic and not socially or culturally contingent. The author concurs with Donnelly's position in seeing the substance of the Universal Declaration of Human Rights (UDHR) and other major UN human rights instruments as evidence of in principle normative consensus (Donnelly 1989). Understanding of human rights also evolves in the light of new knowledge and challenges. But if relativism is rejected, can cultural differences be accommodated within a universalist framework? UN norms, and to some extent the texts of covenants and conventions, allow for a 'margin of appreciation' in interpretation and application. While dialogue can assist in extracting universal elements from cultural and religious particularities, acceptance of lowest common denominators of agreement must be avoided if universal rights are not to be subverted.

The case for indivisibility is supported by textual analysis indicating that links between the two main streams of rights – civil-political and economic-social-cultural – pervade all major UN covenants and declarations. Distinctions between 'negative' and 'positive' rights are correspondingly unsustainable. While problems of reconciling or prioritising particular rights – for example, between women's rights and freedom of religion – are acknowledged, principles of universality provide the best pointers to their resolution.

Rights and obligations are linked in almost all philosophical, religious and popular thought. However, there is a clear difference between liberal notions of everyone having rights by virtue of being human, with mutual obligations to respect and protect those rights, and communitarian outlooks which make rights dependent on fulfilling obligations defined by the state and society. As Donnelly points out, most traditional societies are based on the second idea. Totalitarian, military and one party states have developed it more systematically.

While relations between states are still based on formal principles of absolute national sovereignty, none can avoid the necessity for cooperation and accommodation. National boundaries are similarly porous with regard to ideas and networking between civil society groups. Human rights issues thus cannot be ignored by governments, although they may seek to coopt and domesticate them. Violations can also threaten domestic and even external stability if not addressed. International human rights law thus provides both a challenge and opportunity to states. While means of enforcement are lacking at this stage, it also provides leverage and legitimacy for domestic advocacy.

Discussion of globalisation draws particularly on models of David Held (1995) and Richard Falk (1995) concerning 'international cosmopolitan democracy' and 'humane governance'. While other authors are cited affirming the continuing salience of states in determining law and policy directions, the trans-national nature of many new sites of contestation is constantly re-shaping the nature of human rights struggles. Many standard dualisms between state and civil society, public and private sectors also need reviewing.

The last sections of Chapter 1 draw out interactions between human rights, democracy and development, central to discussion in later chapters. Principles underlying the ICESCR and the UN Declaration on the Right to Development (RTD) are compared, together with differences between UN concepts of economic and social rights and dominant development paradigms promoted by Southeast Asian governments. It is concluded that notions of indivisibility both support and challenge their stance on universal human rights.

Chapter 2 seeks to apply understandings of relationships between democracy, development and human rights developed in Chapter 1, to Southeast Asia. The first section maps an environment unfavourable to incorporating universal rights into official discourse and policy frameworks. However, trends in both intellectual thought and popular mobilisation potentially converge with understandings of universal human rights based on principles of indivisibility and interdependence.

Probing of 'Asian values' and 'Asian democracy' paradigms identifies many inconsistencies. But some variants appear receptive to cross-cultural dialogue concerning universal values, providing democratic concerns are linked with issues of social and economic justice and flexible concerning cultural forms. Many civil society groups nevertheless experience tensions between liberal and communitarian values, with most reacting negatively to neo-liberal critiques of their societies. Even so, more groups now incorporate UN human rights instruments into their advocacy programmes.

Comparative evidence indicates an unclear relationship between countries' economic performance and systems of government. Debates surrounding the post-1997 regional crisis have tended to shed more heat than light on this aspect. While some softening of Asian values rhetoric has been evident, in face of both a more popular democratic temper and external financial pressures, anti-western resentment has also risen.

These various issues and trends are further drawn out in case studies covering Singapore, Philippines and Thailand. The latter two countries have travelled a broadly democratic road over the past 10–15 years. Though both, especially Philippines, have strong traditions of popular mobilisation, they confront entrenched oligarchies in both civil society and bureaucracy, linked to military interests. Criminality, electoral corruption and violence also pose continuing threats to democratic processes. However, strong institutional frameworks built into their respective constitutions have so far proved resilient. Singapore, by contrast, has maintained relatively authoritarian, or illiberal forms of democracy, though buttressed by strong 'rule of law' and meritocracy principles. Widely shared economic prosperity and social harmony provide a strong case in support of authoritarian government as a vehicle for economic development. However, Singapore's example also refutes ideas of economic success necessarily leading to liberal democracy, despite various trends towards greater openness.

The chapter concludes by applying Larry Diamond's tests of democratic consolidation (Diamond 1999) to ASEAN countries covered in this chapter and foreshadowed in later chapters. These tests stress respect for and commitment to constitutional processes at all levels of government, among politicians and parties and throughout civil society. Institutional reforms, though essential, do not automatically eradicate deep-rooted practices of corruption or establish a democratic culture. Although economic performance cannot be easily tied to particular political systems, it is nevertheless important in determining popular support.

Chapter 3 focuses on regional and international aspects of human rights in Southeast Asia. The chapter begins with an overview of regional perspectives towards UN regimes, extending discussion of Asian values and democracy discourse from Chapter 2. The global and regional UN consultation process in 1993 and its aftermath provide a focal point, with issues of universalism and relativism, rights and responsibilities prominent.

The outlook of the five permanent UN Security Council members towards key UN human rights treaties is outlined in order to provide a comparative benchmark. The survey indicates substantial deficiencies in their adherence to UN regimes, weakening any claims they may have to act as human rights role models for Southeast Asia. ASEAN countries' stance towards the ten human rights treaties specified at the beginning of Chapter 1 is then compared, drawing out issues for individual states in complying with particular treaties, linked to analysis in Chapters 2 (Singapore, Philippines, Thailand), 4 (Malaysia) and 5 (Indonesia). Two major sections are devoted to Myanmar (Burma) and Cambodia. While Myanmar has been the focus of intense conflict between ASEAN and western countries, Cambodia has had a uniquely close interaction with UN human rights regimes. While Myanmar has adopted a defiant and Cambodia a conciliatory stance towards the international community, both have manifested great tenacity in asserting national sovereignty. Though extreme human rights abuses in both countries have embarrassed ASEAN, successful integration of each into ASEAN has proved the highest priority. Official mantras of 'constructive engagement', designed to counter western pressures for intervention, have proved largely devoid of content.

The UN's lack of a regional human rights arm has left no obvious framework for engagement. Emerging national human rights institutions, (NHRIs) encouraged by the United Nations Commission for Human Rights (UNCHR), are intended to act both as catalysts for domestic change and vehicles for regional human rights networking. Their impact has been greatly influenced by their relative autonomy from governments. This is greatest where constitutionally entrenched, as in Thailand and the Philippines. Also, their human rights mandates do not in all cases fully reflect universal principles, but rather the extent of their governments' conformity with UN instruments.

Overall ASEAN participation in UN human rights regimes, though more positive than much official rhetoric, remains uneven and characterised by many reservations, reflecting diverse priorities, domestic and external balances. Adherence to international human rights law also broadly correlates with relative democratisation trends.

Chapter 4 is devoted to Malaysia, which does not fit easily into any standard categories of political or economic development. Its politics are dominated by two major imperatives. The first is to reconcile national unity and development with pre-eminence of the Malay race, language and religion. The second is that only dissent which does not seriously challenge key power holders can be tolerated. Extensive security legislation and concentration of executive powers are required to sustain these objectives, which entail ambivalence and often hostility towards universal human rights.

Up to 1998, the 'semi-democratic' tag applied by several scholars seemed plausible in terms of the idiosyncrasies of Malaysia's political system and the nature of its nation-building project. Their balance has been upset, less by the economic crisis, from which Malaysia appears to have recovered strongly, than by political fallout from the dubious arrest and trial processes of former Deputy Prime Minister, Anwar Ibrahim. Personal concentration of power in the Prime Minister's hands and systematic suppression of dissent, employing draconian security legislation, following opposition gains at November 1999 elections, have rendered any remaining democracy highly 'illiberal'.

Despite limited democratic space, Malaysian non-government organisations, labour, women's and other civil society groups have achieved a significant measure of pluralism, cross-community coalition and advocacy. While groups increasingly incorporate universal human rights goals, sharp divisions have emerged between liberal and communitarian approaches. Anwar Ibrahim's detention has nevertheless forged significant unity among them.

Malaysian politics is dominated by a powerful nexus between Islam and Malay ethnicity. Discourse is consequently distorted by bitter battles between the United Malays National Organisation (UMNO), the leading government party, and the Islamic Party (PAS), which currently dominates the opposition alliance. Islamic scholarship, as distinct from the reactionary stance of many clerics, identifies important convergences between Islamic and universal human rights principles. However, potential here is obscured by conflict between official uses of the religion to promote national objectives and PAS' objective of imposing *Shariah* law. Issues of freedom of religion in relation to Islam are as yet inadequately articulated.

Currently, Malaysia asserts sweeping reservations on the only three human rights treaties it has ratified, in terms of priorities of religion and inter-communal harmony.

Establishment of the Malaysian Human Rights Commission could provide a vehicle for domestic reform, not least by addressing obstacles to ratifying major UN instruments reported over many years. However, lack of transparency in its establishment, limited autonomy and restrictive definitions of human rights have so far weakened confidence in the Commission's capacities.

Chapter 5 surveys Indonesia's democratic transformation since President Suharto's fall in 1998. Changes include dismantling of regulatory infrastructure controlling Indonesian media; openly conducted parliamentary elections; election of the President by a new Parliament, and a reformed Constitution limiting presidential powers, promoting regional devolution and entrenching a charter of human rights.

Democratic consolidation has been set back by resistance from military and political elites loyal to former President Suharto; sidetracking of reforms by parliamentary focus on impeaching President Wahid; religious and ethnic disorder; separatist demands in Aceh and Irian Jaya; inter-linked problems of poverty, economic crisis, corruption, failure to implement financial and administrative reforms and loss of investor confidence. Constitutional balance between presidential and parliamentary systems remains uncertain, with no clear distinction between government and opposition supporters in a multi-party Parliament. Reforms to Indonesia's judiciary are crucial to public confidence in the 'rule of law'.

The military remains strong at regional and local levels, despite erosion of its formal political powers. Inaction and collusion in outbreaks of communal disorder have been widely condemned. But apart from disunity, indiscipline and possible intent to undermine democratic reforms, military leaders face contradictory demands both to withdraw from politics and play stabilising police roles.

Similar patterns of reform and resistance are evident on the human rights front. The work of the National Human Rights Commission (Komnas HAM) has been applauded in many quarters. However, structural weaknesses are evident, while links with the UN human rights system need strengthening. Ratification of new instruments appears to have stalled since President Habibie left office. Operation of new human rights courts has been frustrated by politics surrounding their establishment and problems of retrospectivity.

Issues of political culture underlie interpretation and practice of democracy and human rights. Ideological ground rules for newly democratic Indonesia have yet to be firmly established as between communitarian and liberal-democratic outlooks. Inheritances here are identified from Indonesia's post-independence history, with reference to both civil society and formal governmental and political spheres. Pancasila's five principles, which stress values of harmony, tolerance and national unity, remains Indonesia's national ideology, through losing its monopoly status. Pancasila potentially allows both pro- and anti-democratic interpretations. Islamic discourse also commands attention, in view of its importance in shaping Indonesia's current directions.

Chapter 6 covers the popular consultation process in East Timor, including widespread killings and destruction before and after the 30 August 1999 ballot. Sharp polarisation within Indonesia is evident between 'democratic internationalist' and 'military-nationalist' outlooks. Each reflects domestic agendas broadly supportive or negative towards democratisation, with the latter seeking to exploit resentment against western pressures for political and economic reforms.

Rival Indonesian and UN investigations identified extensive military and militia violence. But recommended prosecutions have been obstructed by government inaction and political infighting. The special tribunal finally established in April 2001 will only have powers to try alleged violations occurring after the ballot. International condemnation is also directed against continuing Indonesian failure to end militia control of refugee camps in West Timor, thereby denying a free choice to refugees whether to return home. The murder of three aid workers caused the UN to withdraw all personnel.

A review of issues relating to East Timor's transition to nationhood, the UNs' role and relations with Indonesia indicates deep-rooted problems of economic and social reconstruction, political stability and national security.

Coverage of Australia's regional human rights role in Chapter 7 offers a counterpoint to Southeast Asian perspectives. While strategic priorities dictate a realist approach, strong domestic pressures have forced human rights on to Australia's regional diplomatic agendas. But dissonance is evident between Australia's official stance and more critical civil society messages projected into Southeast Asia.

Australia–ASEAN relations have their own unique characteristics, despite Australia sharing many western European and north American perspectives. Geographical proximity and networks of strategic and economic interest entail comparatively closer and more sustained engagement. However, this no longer entails exaggerated claims to be 'part of Asia', which tend to both embarrass ASEAN states and elicit counter-productive domestic reactions. There are nevertheless legitimate concerns that engaging with Southeast Asia should not entail conformity or muffling dissenting voices.

Australian governments have shifted from 'realist' approaches which marginalised human rights from practical policy-making to incorporating them within frameworks of national interest, expressed through dialogue and 'practical' assistance in improving regional governance. While much useful work has been achieved in legal and judicial training and exchange, and supporting national human rights commissions, inevitable tensions between human rights, economic and diplomatic goals tend to be glossed over in official discourse. Balance is maintained by strong civil society networking.

Australia formally complies with all ten UN human rights instruments compared in this survey. But compliance has been uneven. For example, recent policies breach convention requirements relating to refugees and racial equality. When pressed, Australian governments tend to reflect Southeast Asian counterparts in invoking national sovereignty arguments. Australia's federal system is also regularly invoked, despite clear international law principles asserting national governments' sole responsibility for implementing treaties. Requirements of electoral democracy, asserting the supremacy of popular will via elected legislatures, demonstrate that democracy is a necessary but not sufficient condition for realising universal human rights. Finally, Australia's legal system, based on English common law, cannot easily adapt to principles of international human rights law. A Bill of Rights is a possible, though at present unlikely compromise.

The latter part of the chapter explores the role of human rights in bilateral relations with all ASEAN states except Laos and Brunei. No obvious correlation emerges between human rights engagement and diplomatic cordiality or conflict. Thus, there has been little such engagement with either Singapore, with which Australia has good relations, or Malaysia, with which relations have been strained over many years. Greatest levels of activity have been in Cambodia, Myanmar and Indonesia, where human rights violations are greatest. While relations with Cambodia have been positive, they have ranged from cool to hostile with Myanmar (Burma), and swung to both extremes with Indonesia. Australia has worked closely with the UN in relation to Cambodia, Myanmar and East Timor, in the latter case causing serious deterioration in relations with Indonesia.

As a small to medium power, Australia poses no threat, and can potentially persuade ASEAN states of a shared stake in international law as counterweight to great power politics. Peer review through mutual commitment to UN human rights treaties would support this objective. However, trends towards asserting 'Australian values' undermine such a prospect, as does their use as a blanket defence against UN criticism of Australia's domestic performance, linked to generalised attacks on UNCHR processes.

The work concludes by accepting Southeast Asian states' goals of integrating democracy, human rights and economic development but rejecting communitarian and relativist understandings of human rights, and Asian values cum democracy discourse supporting them. Such goals are better served by applying universalist norms of international human rights law, linked to principles of indivisibility between different streams of rights.

Comparative evidence shows improving but uneven participation in UN treaties by ASEAN states, broadly correlating with levels of democratisation. While security and developmentalist concerns dominate national agendas, universal human rights provide a pervasive challenge. Forces of globalisation pose many challenges to national sovereignty, though not all models are supportive of universal human rights. Nation states are likely to survive as key actors, but efforts to maintain total autonomy and immunity from external scrutiny cannot be sustained. While pessimistic scenarios abound, institutionalisation of human rights and momentum for change in the region may soon become self sustaining.

1 International human rights

Theory and practice

Nature and scope of human rights

The foundation UN human rights document is the 1948 Universal Declaration of Human Rights (UDHR). This was developed in greater detail in two major conventions adopted in 1966 – the International Covenant on Civil and Political Rights (ICCPR) and the International Covenant on Economic, Social and Cultural Rights (ICESCR). These three instruments are known collectively as the International Bill of Rights. They are supplemented by many specialised conventions, including the Convention on the Elimination of All Forms of Racial Discrimination (CERD), the Convention against Torture and other Cruel, Inhuman or Degrading Treatments or Punishments (CAT), the Convention on the Elimination of All Forms of Discrimination against Women (CEDAW), the Convention on the Rights of the Child (CROC), the Convention relating to the Status of Refugees and the Convention on the Prevention and Punishment of the Crime of Genocide. There are also two optional protocols to the ICCPR, which can be adopted by states which have ratified the main Covenant. The first allows individuals or groups which have exhausted their state's internal processes to bring complaints of alleged violation directly to the United Nations Commission for Human Rights (UNCHR). Under the second, states agree to abolish the death penalty. These ten treaties provide a continuing frame of reference throughout this work.

Universalist theories of human rights derive from western concepts of natural law originating from the Roman Empire, evolving in face of many challenges through the Renaissance and Enlightenment periods into the contemporary industrial and post-industrial age (Vincent 1986: 19–36). Human, as distinct from citizens' or other rights derived from membership of specific communities, are claimed on no other grounds than human identity, and are to be enjoyed equally by everyone. On this basis, Jack Donnelly (1989: 1–19) defines the human rights project as translating rights which everyone has into enjoyment and legal codification of their actual substance. This assumes arrangement of legal and political systems so that human rights are paramount, 'trumping' all other systems of law and administration (Dworkin 1977). Paradoxically, to the extent that this is achieved, consciousness of their universal nature can be lost (Donnelly 1989: 17–19).

Despite its strong intuitive appeal, natural law is highly problematic as a basis for rights claims, as there is no universally agreed account of human nature, which contains base as well as ethical characteristics. The normative nature of the universal human rights project must, therefore, be frankly acknowledged. Even so, emphasis on *rights* indicates far more than mere aspiration or a morally desirable state of affairs. Rights imply entitlements which everyone must be accorded, whatever their status or situation.

The notion of universal entitlement raises questions of obligation since, if everyone has rights, each person has an obligation to ensure their fulfilment. Donnelly asserts that liberal rights theories have historically recognised this nexus, despite characterisations of rampant individualism by critics – though he acknowledges their validity in relation to unfettered promotion of property rights in contemporary neo-liberal theory. Donnelly claims that only the liberal-democratic formulation asserts rights as equal, inalienable and intrinsic, as a basis for powerful claims against the state. Obligations derive both from one's own and others' rights. Opposing communitarian formulations, whether of the marxist, corporatist-authoritarian or traditional variety, grant rights on the basis of social roles and performance of duties, as defined by custom or the relevant authorities.

Donnelly further claims that, apart from rights to self-determination, UN texts refer overwhelmingly to individual rather than group rights. Though embedded in socio-political contexts, groups such as families essentially act as intermediate social groups protecting individual family members. Therefore, families may not deny freedom of religion, rights of political participation or discriminate on grounds of gender (Donnelly 1989: 19–21).

Acknowledging the inconclusiveness of previous attempts to find either a moral or anthropological account of human nature which would command general consent, he claims that there is nevertheless a 'remarkable international normative consensus', supporting in principle if not in practice the list of rights contained in the International Bill of Rights. Continuing reaffirmation over time serves to de-legitimise violations (Donnelly 1989: 22–3, 42). However, many Asian leaders reject the basic idea of universality with regard to both meaning and application. Donnelly responds that formulation of rights in these texts should for that reason not be regarded as fixed, but as evolving in relation to changes in technology, society and notions of human dignity.

The latter depend on how they are understood within different societies, religions and cultures. While universality cannot be claimed *a priori*, too strenuous attempts to find consensus are likely to result in a lowest common denominator approach. Normative claims can be further asserted in terms of Kant's principle that what ought to be cannot be justified merely by purely anthropological reference to what is, and the consequent need to strive for a 'public law of mankind' (Vincent: 1986: 39, 118–19). Merely recognising that notions of human dignity can be identified in most, and probably all major world religions, leads only to obligations to respect, as distinct from recognising them as a basis of rights (Donnelly 1989: 49–50).

Key issues in categorising and prioritising rights include:

1   the possibility of extracting core or basic rights from the extensive list of rights in the various UN covenants and conventions;

2   the relationship between so called civil and political as against economic, social and cultural rights.

The idea of a short list of rights which should be regarded as paramount and universal has received support from both western and non-western sources, with even dedicated anti-universalists such as former Singapore Prime Minister, Lee Kuan Yew, supporting outlawing of genocide, torture and racial discrimination (Acharya 1995: 172). Fouad Ajami adds food security, which he claims as defensible as within state capacities in a context of widespread violations (Donnelly 1989: 41–2). Cranston implicitly supports the short list concept, with pleas that 'universal, paramount, categorical moral rights' should not be trivialised by marginal claims for paid holidays and similar contingent, often unrealisable rights (Donnelly 1989: 24). However, lack of consensus on core rights is illustrated by Cranston's exclusion of economic and social rights, which he regards as neither universal, practical nor of paramount importance, by contrast with the fundamental nature of rights to life, liberty and property (Donnelly 1989: 31–4). Conversely, Vincent (1986: 143–50), argues that only the limited goal of placing subsistence and security against violence, as conditions for all other rights, at the centre of international relations agendas, can have a reasonable prospect of gaining consensus.

Conservatives tend to see 'basic needs' agendas as entailing extensive and undesirable interventions in international markets and management. Acknowledging interdependence will lengthen the list of basic rights. Liberals object that this least common denominator approach will allow power holders discretion to define and limit universal standards, also implying that other human rights are not basic and may be sacrificed as need arises (Donnelly 1989: 37–42). Vincent counters that 'the international community cannot be as adept in practice at keeping all the human rights balls in the air at once as Donnelly is in theory. The moral simplicity of the case is its merit'. While not postulating suppression of civil liberties as a pre-condition, he anticipates that 'subsistence might make a more workable international programme, a more neutral undertaking for international society, than liberty' (Vincent 1986: 148).

Despite assertions of 'universality, indivisibility and interdependence' between civil-political and economic-social-cultural rights in official UN pronouncements, re-affirmed in Article 5 of the 1993 Vienna Declaration and Programme of Action (VDPA) by the World Conference on Human Rights,[1] Asian countries claim that unequal status is accorded to each. Historically, both streams of rights are central to the 1948 UDHR and have been woven into all subsequent UN covenants and conventions. They were never intended to be separated. But a false dualism took root as a consequence of the Cold War, de-colonisation processes, and struggles by the Third World for a New International Economic Order (NIEO).

Cranston's distinction between positive and negative rights is used to support western conservatives' refusal to recognise economic and social rights. These are claimed as requiring extensive expenditure and complex policy provision, compared with civil and political rights which only require legislation preventing state interference with the liberties of citizens. In reality, many 'positive' programmes, such as legal education, police training, and establishment of electoral commissions are necessary to ensuring that civil liberties are respected and elections properly conducted. Conversely, state restraint, for example, in not appropriating food producing land for other development purposes may be sufficient to ensure subsistence (Donnelly 1989: 33).

Thus all rights require both positive and negative action for their preservation, with the relative importance of each determined according to context. Even if the distinction is acknowledged, there is no intrinsic reason to favour negative over positive rights, as both serve to counter threats to human dignity. As resources to provide subsistence are almost always available, killing is morally equivalent, whether by positive action or neglect. A liberal conception of human rights thus requires integration between both kinds of rights although, in Donnelly's view, some strands of liberal thought have exaggerated property rights to the extent of distorting overall balance (Donnelly 1989: 33–7). Issues in achieving integration of rights will be taken up in later discussion of links between democracy, development and human rights.

Universalism and relativism

The core issue at stake here, reflected in the Asian values debate explored in the next chapter, is between asserting core values and principles of human behaviour, while allowing some contextual variations, or denying universality by accepting that human rights are determined by culture and associated social identity. While national sovereignty, economic development, the individual's role relative to the state, and rejection of links between democracy and economic neo-liberalism feature strongly, it is culture which provides basic support for the relativist position, fuelling attacks on claims to universality as ethnocentric, and as manifestations of cultural imperialism.

Reference to cultural aspects in relevant treaties is fairly thin. Cultural rights are added to economic and social rights, which are spelt out in far greater detail. Cultural rights are mentioned in this appendage form just once in the UDHR (Article 22). The ICESCR refers only to the right to participate in cultural life (Article 15), conceived primarily in terms of artistic production and intellectual property rights. Rights to enjoy one's culture are set out in Article 27 of the ICCPR, in the context of minority rights, while Article 18 strongly affirms freedom of religion. A UDHR of Indigenous Peoples has been under consideration for several years. But overall failure to integrate notions of culture into mainstream international human rights theory and practice partly explains the sense of distance and lack of ownership which many non-western participants display towards notions of universality claimed for UN instruments.

Prospects for dialogue, leading to either reconciliation between relativist and universalist viewpoints or some more inclusive form of universality, have been widely canvassed. But general consent to the 1993 Vienna Declaration formula of universality with contextual variations did not prevent continuing attacks on the legitimacy of universal human rights. Acceptance, even in principle, to undertake dialogue over their nature and content is proving equally problematic. Liberals urge that communitarian and liberal standpoints are irreconcilably opposed, and attempts at syncretism will result in either a 'lowest common denominator' outcome, or the incorporation of mutually antagonistic values (Donnelly 1989: 58–9).

Others see dialogue as essential to human understanding, even if only to agree to disagree as part of a search for a more peaceful and prosperous world. Camilleri suggests that dialogue may reveal that competing claims of universalism and cultural relativism may prove less contradictory than often assumed. Comparison between distinct religious or ethical traditions can yield universal standards, so long as these are not interpreted as immutable or absolute. To be credible, universalism must be deeply embedded within each culture, requiring a dynamic, ongoing process of interaction, dialogue and re-negotiation (Camilleri 1994: 17, 19–21). Thus it is possible to extract values of respect for the dignity of life, linked to notions of humane and legitimate governance from the four major non-western religions – Islam, Hinduism, Buddhism and Confucianism. Differences with western traditions, it is claimed, are more of form and emphasis (Camilleri 1994: 25–36).

Vincent is more doubtful of finding common ground across cultures, since it is equally possible to identify differences as similarities. The exercise may nevertheless prove useful in encouraging people to articulate their values, thereby providing data bases for identifying potential commonalities. Implicitly, such attempts assume some measure of universalism, in accepting that cross-cultural explorations are not precluded by cultural relativism. Moreover, they can easily end up merely recording variety and allowing groups to pick and choose (Vincent 1986: 48–50).

Third World countries also appeal to universal values, for example, in asserting racial equality, claiming rights to self-determination and development. Nor are they willing to grant the West immunity from criticism entailed by total cultural relativism (Vincent 1986: 52–3, 57). Major world religions all claim universal validity in varying degrees. However, there is no way, in culturally relative terms, to argue against assertions of superiority by one culture or religion over another. Consequently, in the search for at least minimum international standards of justice, surrender to what John Stuart Mill described as the 'despotism of custom' can only be avoided by the procedure of fully testing what is right through debate, and taking necessary action (Vincent 1986: 54–7).

National sovereignty and international human rights law

The notion of universal human rights poses a fundamental challenge to the rationale underlying state sovereignty, by which states are autonomous both in exercising jurisdiction within their territorial boundaries and pursuing their national interest in conducting external affairs. States jealously safeguard, and the international system formally upholds the principle of state sovereignty. Nevertheless, state claims for immunity from external scrutiny are becoming increasingly unsustainable, as are claims for non-intervention against conduct that threatens general stability or outrages the conscience of humanity.

States' capacity to behave autonomously varies greatly according to their relative strength *vis a vis* other states and transnational actors. According to the 'realist' view, states are the sole bearers of rights and responsibilities in international society. Individuals can only access that society through the agency of states and are objects not subjects of international law (Vincent 1986: 113–8). However, international human rights law refers extensively to the rights of individuals. Human rights treaties bind those states which have ratified them, to the extent they have not entered reservations, while membership of the UN entails at least formal acceptance of the UDHR.

Human rights discourse in international relations contexts has tended to assume polarity between realism and idealism. At one extreme are those who assert that the world community consists only of states. At the other are those who see a cosmopolitan community of individuals, which alone can shape political groupings or systems. A third group dismisses entirely talk of a world community and associated human rights as a misnomer concealing vested interests (Vincent 1986: 113–8). Within western traditions, realist challenges to ideas of rights have been mounted by conservatives such as Edmund Burke, espousing the virtues of tradition, hierarchy, mutual affection, duty and obligation; utilitarians such as Jeremy Bentham, who described pursuit of abstract rights, as distinct from real rights deriving from government and society, as 'nonsense on stilts'; organic state theorists, such as Hegel who contends that the individual's ethical existence only finds expression in national community, from which all laws, rights and duties derive; and Marx, who characterises liberal notions of rights as based solely on class interest (Vincent 1986: 19–36).

Parallels are apparent between organic state theory and the communitarian cum corporatist ideology and political practice of several Southeast Asian states. Hegel's notion that the nation-state has its own personality, with positive rights to assert its existence, fits well with assertions of individual subordination to the collectivity. However, according to Vincent (1986: 33–6), ideas of rights based on a universal moral order are proving resilient in the face of these challenges, with contemporary philosophers ranging from Nozik to Rawls returning to pre-eighteenth century natural law concepts. In practice, the 'individual versus community' puzzle can be worked out via standard democratic 'rule of law' formulations. At the same time, one powerful consequence from Marx's challenge has been to spawn a host of new economic and social rights.

De Vries (1994: 232–43) cites three major strands to realist attacks on the role of moral norms in international politics. First, there is no agreed international code of morality. This is ascribed by Hans Morgenthau to the absence of any integrated international society capable of defining the concrete meaning of justice or equality, as in national societies. Secondly, this reality reflects the truth in Thomas Hobbes' extreme dictum that there is neither morality nor law outside the state, so that international anarchy, competition and lack of trust between states necessitates a primary emphasis on survival. While states are not as weak as individuals, and the 'golden rule' of behaving to others as you would wish them to behave to yourself is very relevant to survival, conflict cannot always be avoided. Finally, the ethic of responsibility which this situation imposes on power holders is concerned primarily with outcomes rather than moral qualities or intentions.

K.W. Thompson (1994) argues that the equation of realism with amorality is unfair, evidenced by the concern with issues of morality by distinguished scholars of this school, such as Morgenthau and Niebuhr. Thompson sees the core of realist thinking as a rejection of absolutist views of right and wrong, in which demands for rights are often not linked to acknowledgement of responsibilities for the consequences of actions demanded. Utopians, Thompson claims, assume unilinear progress, a mould-ing of the 'new man' in which self-interest and power balances become obsolete. In that context, moral self-righteousness sees no need for external rules or constraints. A more balanced approach is to gradually build up a sense of international community through networks of overlapping programmes as a basis for evolving international law and government. Traditional diplomacy has a vital role to play here.

Donnelly agrees that realists do not reject notions of morality in world affairs, but considers they are unable to see any way to integrate it with the reality of the states system. Given their view that international politics is a struggle between power-maximising states in an environment of anarchy, those failing to maximise power leave themselves open to attack. According to this equation, it is a danger-ous mistake to use human rights for any purpose other than furthering national interest. But even if this is conceded as the cardinal principle of foreign policy, there is no reason why human rights should be excluded more than other aspects with potential for conflict, such as trade, investment, resources or the environ-ment. States pursue a full range of policy instruments in such matters, including persuasion, incentives, diplomatic signals and, in extreme cases, sanctions or the use of force. *Prima facie*, these are as legitimate for human rights as for other policy goals. Therefore, while sovereignty is the starting point, it is not necessar-ily the end point of international law (Donnelly 1989: 231–4).

Vincent (1986: 150–2) argues that there is no reason why human rights should lead to the destruction of the states system of international relations. Indeed, human rights can add to states' legitimacy, while their absence over time has the reverse effect. In practice, states have a history of co-opting and translating human rights into citizens' rights, gradually integrating them into daily dealings between states. To the extent that this is true, it fulfils Donnelly's paradox by which adopting the content of human rights will cause their universal aspects to become obscured. Such a process might even calm the soul of Edmund Burke, who was fond of contrasting the concrete and 'ancient liberties of England' with the abstract 'rights of man'.

Less reassuring to conservatives, as well as neo-liberals, is Vincent's claim (1986: 151) that state power and authority have expanded rapidly with the growth in human rights ideology. While concentrations of state power have occurred for many other reasons, human rights agendas certainly require extensive legislation and expenditure by governments. Fears of a more active state, and by extension UN-linked international institutions, may well be at the heart of conservative opposition to universal human rights, with dismissals of them as utopian more in the nature of a pretext.

UN human rights regimes and the states system

International human rights law, embedded in UN covenants and conventions, co-exists in constant tension with principles of national sovereignty. At base, UN structures and processes reflect the states' system, operating as a permanent forum and clearing house for transactions between them. Membership consists exclusively of sovereign states, which collectively exercise voting rights and decision-making powers. But as most states are unwilling to accept adverse decisions, negotiation and application of agreements is mainly conducted outside the institutional framework of the UN.

Implementation of human rights regimes is coordinated by the UNCHR,[2] which was established as a Functional Commission of the UN Economic and Social Council (ECOSOC), to which it continues to report. Specialised treaty committees have developed as sub-commissions of the UNCHR to monitor covenants and conventions. Special rapporteurs may be appointed to investigate persistent violations either in particular countries, or thematically, in areas such as torture across countries.

All states are deemed, by virtue of UN membership, to be bound by the UDHR – a situation prompting some, particularly Asian states to call for its review. But the UDHR is not strictly speaking a treaty, and is, therefore, not binding under international law, despite its great moral force. Although some jurists argue that the UDHR enjoys the status of international customary law, this essentially western concept is looked on with suspicion by many developing countries (DFAT 1993: 30–1).

Covenants and conventions, which have the force of treaties, become open for signature and ratification by states following adoption by a majority of the General Assembly. Signature indicates in principle intention to participate. The decisive step of ratification requires states to bring their domestic legal, political and administrative practices into conformity with the relevant treaty. This comes into force once ratified by the requisite number of states specified in the text. Other states may subsequently accede under the same conditions. Ratification or accession entails agreement both to report regularly and submit to Commission investigations.

Several means are open for states to legally limit their responsibility within the treaty process (DFAT 1993: 27–30). Limitations to enjoyment of rights may be indicated as part of treaty texts. Thus Article 19(3) of the ICCPR places limits on rights to freedom of expression asserted in Article 19(2) in terms of protecting the rights or reputations of others, national security, public order, public health or morals. Such provisos potentially legitimise sweeping restrictions on civil rights.

Ratifying states may indicate reservations to their acceptance or declare their own interpretations or understandings of particular clauses. Other states may choose whether to accept these, but silence is assumed to signify consent. Under provisions for derogation, Article 4 of the ICCPR allows states, when declaring states of national emergency, to suspend certain human rights provisions, except for rights to life, freedom from torture and slavery, freedom of thought, conscience and religion. Such restrictions must be non-discriminatory and proportional to the situation, which must genuinely threaten the life of the nation. To limit scope for abuse, special rapporteurs are appointed to monitor derogations.

Although the UNCHR lacks powers of its own to enforce treaties, its comprehensive monitoring and reporting process provides a framework for both international and domestic opinion to exert pressures, which may ultimately alter the practice of offending countries. The open and public nature of this process is much feared and resented by some governments, which commonly defend themselves by invoking principles of sovereignty and non-intervention.

States' monopoly over UNCHR processes is limited by three important provisions. Firstly, Resolution 1503 procedure enables individuals or groups to report evidence of a consistent pattern of serious violations within a given state. Secondly, inter-governmental or non-government organisations with permanent observer status at the General Assembly, registered with ECOSOC or invited to attend by the Commission may submit agenda items, speak and tender written submissions at its meetings, but without voting rights. However, a two-thirds majority of members present and voting is required for an item to be included on the agenda. Finally, the First Optional Protocol to the ICCPR, adopted in December 1966, allows individuals to appeal against alleged violations of that Covenant, providing they have exhausted all domestic remedies. This procedure has been extended to CEDAW and is under active consideration for other instruments.

States' submission to these regimes is voluntary. Ratification is the essential first step, indicating states' willingness to open their processes to outside scrutiny, subjecting themselves to international law on an equal footing with others. To be effective, UN human rights regimes require near universal ratification of core instruments, a minimum of reservations, full compliance with reporting and monitoring requirements and willingness to abide by umpires' decisions. While these goals are a long way from achievement, participation in UNCHR reporting and monitoring networks increased significantly during the 1990s, partly boosted by increased UN membership. The range of new instruments in the process of development is also expanding. Significant institutionalisation and deepening of the UN process has potential to change the overall diplomatic environment and ultimately domestic processes in ways favourable to human rights. This prospect is strengthened by the establishment of national human rights institutions and the spread of human rights education through UN affiliated and other informal non-government organisation (NGO) networks. However, excessive bureaucratisation can threaten slowdown and even reversal of such gains.

Humanitarian intervention

The question of humanitarian intervention against non-complying states, whatever their treaty participation status, is never far from the surface in human rights debates. Unfortunately, advocates of intervention tend to look outside UN processes, due to the perceived impossibility of gaining consensus from member states, and veto powers held by the five permanent Security Council members. The practicality and legitimacy of external intervention mostly flounders on the rock of states' sovereignty. This principle is upheld within the UN Charter and vigorously defended by member states wherever their own interests are involved. It is espoused with particular strength by post-colonial states in Asia, Africa and Latin America.

Military intervention is rarely agreed under UN auspices. Even mass killings bordering on genocide, with conflict posing a threat to regional security, as in Cambodia and East Timor, will not prompt intervention without agreement from all parties. Alternatively, as in Bosnia and Kosovo, western military action may subsequently be legitimised through the UN. In the case of Iraq's invasion of Kuwait, where major powers' interests were at stake, some random human rights protection of minorities may have occurred as a by-product of UN approved intervention. However, subsequent sanctions against Iraq have substantially destroyed the economic rights of its people.

Economic sanctions have never been universally supported, even in the extreme case of South Africa under apartheid. Western attempts to combine economic and diplomatic pressures on Myanmar's military junta rulers have been opposed by China and ASEAN. Policies of linking economic aid to human rights performance command some support in donor countries, but are also resisted on grounds of national sovereignty, as unwisely diluting social and economic disbursement criteria, and as downgrading rights to development relative to civil and political rights. Other types of intervention include low levels of diplomatic protest, advocacy or dialogue, information gathering and dissemination by human rights NGOs, and media coverage. Controversy becomes most intense over measures which impinge on the accused country's domestic politics and administration.

Claims to absolute state autonomy are no longer sustainable, and bases for coexistence and cooperation between states must be continually re-negotiated in an increasingly interdependent world. Difficulties in devising modes of intervention which are legitimate, proportional and not counter-productive to stated objectives rule out any general licence to intervene, with a presumption against all but its least coercive forms under most circumstances (Parekh 1997: 53–9). Primary initiative for change must, therefore, continue to rest with states' domestic institutions and processes. But UN human rights regimes can play a legitimate and significant role in exposing states' regimes to scrutiny by their peers (Vincent 1986: 152). They also provide supporting frameworks for cooperation between domestic and outside groups in achieving change.

Globalisation and human rights

Globalisation has a mixed impact on human rights. Its discourse contains many conflicting accounts and ideology-based agendas for global management. David Held (1995) emphasises pervasive interconnectedness, evidenced in ever more prolific flows of information, ideas, pollutants, drugs, goods, capital, weapons and knowledge across national boundaries. These increase disjunctions between national identity and the globalisation of culture, with potential to develop a sense of global belonging, challenging or transcending national loyalties. Such trends challenge doctrines that international law is exclusively a matter between states, and generate alternative proposals for organising world order (Held 1995: 107, 121–7).

The UN Charter, reflecting a desire to outlaw extreme forms of violence against humanity following World War II, fundamentally challenged doctrines of absolute state sovereignty assumed in the 'Westphalian' model of international relations and law (Held 1995: 83–8). The Charter model includes a rival source of international law, in which (i) people as well as states are subjects of international law; (ii) majority voting in principle overrides consent of individual states. However, constraints such as the Security Council veto and lack of funding have prevented any fundamental break with the logic of the Westphalian system. The UN system, therefore, remains vulnerable to individual state agendas. Even so, it is useful as a forum for seeking solutions to international problems, in which states are at least formally equal. It also has potential as a 'supra-national presence in world affairs championing human rights' (Held 1995: 88–9). According to Bull (1977: 152–3), international human rights law potentially subverts state sovereignty insofar as the rights and duties of a person can be proclaimed irrespective of membership of a state. But although profoundly challenged by globalisation, the nation-state 'continues to command loyalty, both as an idea and as an institution' (Held 1995: 98).

According to Falk (1995: 11–12), states are being by-passed and their legitimacy eroded both by globalising trends beyond their grasp, and by pressures leading to internal fragmentation. This situation is characterised by numerous quasi-government and non-government associations, interests and affiliations crossing national boundaries and jurisdictions, with ethnicity and religion as potent forces in both domestic and international contexts. However, it is premature to expect that the role of states and potency of national sovereignty as an ideological force and focus of popular loyalty will be significantly downgraded in the near future.

Marc Williams (1996) claims that theories stressing global interdependence confuse sovereignty with autonomy. States have never been able to exercise absolute control or implement all rights claimed, exercise of which has always been subject to negotiation and relative strength. Interdependence theories tend to concentrate on economic trends, where governments appear to act as spectators to international transactions over which they have little direct control. But states' legal and administrative powers necessitate their cooperation in consolidating property transfers and overall market operations. Consensus or majority decision-making processes, essential to the operation of regional and international bodies, still require the exercise of sovereignty. It is ultimately unclear whether globalisation will be based on continuing national sovereignty, or whether new global structures will transcend the state. While the old internal–external distinctions are becoming less salient, states remain active participants in forging new arrangements. In a word, the exercise of sovereignty is flexible, and has withstood many challenges (Williams 1996: 114–20).

More disorderly outcomes are possible. Rather than replacing the state with a homogeneous global order, globalisation may result in splintering the existing political order (Cerny 1996: 130). This will have negative outcomes for democratic processes as people's aspirations still focus on their own states' institutions, while the real sites of decision-making are diffused. Systems of control and accountability will become more remote as multilateral regimes accumulate legal powers.

Universal human rights protagonists face major strategic and tactical challenges relating to the future of the states system. It is necessary both to improve ways of integrating human rights within the existing system of sovereign states, and anticipate and adapt to changes resulting from globalisation processes. The human rights implications of any too rapid erosion of state sovereignty, whether legally or *de facto*, are also uncertain and will depend crucially on which global governance models ultimately prevail.

Falk identifies two general paradigms, which he labels as geo- and humane governance (Falk 1995: 47–78). By 'geo-governance' is meant reliance on traditional power politics approaches, elite arrangements between leading players, by-passing or neutralising national governments and such democratic processes as they variously possess. While asserting principles of national sovereignty, the national interests of dominant states, particularly the United States of America (USA), determine overall strategies. Systems of 'inhumane governance' pursued under conventional paths to globalisation stand accused under a 'triple indictment' of causing global apartheid, through divisions within a partly race-based system divided into rich and poor worlds, avoidable harm through militarisation and eco-imperialism processes, causing massive destruction to both the natural environment and people's subsistence systems.

By contrast, 'humane governance' focuses on people-centred goals such as peace, food and a clean environment (Falk 1995: 9–46). In human rights terms this requires comprehensive approaches embracing the full spectrum of civil, political, economic, social and cultural rights, linked to systems of democratic order and security capable of supporting them, including major reforms of the UN (Camilleri *et al.* 2000: 26–32).

Humane governance paradigms commonly oppose notions of democracy based on unqualified systems of majoritarianism, which may marginalise rights of women and minorities or aggravate racial, ethnic and religious tensions. Globalisation, by creating new forms of civil society, opens up possibilities for extending democratisation movements beyond state–society relations to all arenas of power and authority – corporations, banks, workplaces, and even to personal relationships, as home and society are often the source of non-humane cultural values.

Humane governance models are ambivalent towards national sovereignty (Falk 1995: 89–96). On the one hand, self-determination rights are espoused both by recently independent states and by national minorities seeking sovereignty.[3] The interests of these two groupings frequently conflict in the Asian region and elsewhere. Conversely, strong nationalist assertions, especially those based on ethnic or racial identity, frequently undermine both minority rights and democratic processes. Sovereignty is also routinely invoked to resist external criticism of militarisation and environmental destruction within territorial boundaries. Yet it remains important in resisting intervention by powerful states. Even some north European states, as adherents of welfare capitalism, continue to be effective agents for realising economic and social rights, though increasingly challenged by global market forces.

In most developing countries, claims on citizens, based on territorial community, override individual rights. But globalisation is breaking down monopolies of political loyalty and authority, with new trans-territorial forms of association and identity competing, in turn provoking various backlashes aimed at coercing conformity to states' cultural norms. The continuing reality of sovereignty and mixed consequences of these conflicting trends must be accepted by those seeking paths to humane governance (Falk 1995: 95).

Democracy, development and human rights

Article 8 of the United Nations VDPA states that 'Democracy, development and respect for human rights and fundamental freedoms are interdependent and mutually reinforcing' and calls on the international community to strengthen and promote all three equally (DFAT 1993: 180). The logic and implications of these principles will be explored in the remainder of this chapter. Subsequent chapters will draw out regional and local understandings of this triangular relationship, which lies at the heart of Southeast Asian human rights debates.

Democracy and human rights

Democracy and human rights are distinct but related concepts. Links between them are both mutually supportive and conflicting. While democratic forms of government can be conceived as a major, indeed essential means for achieving human rights, minority rights can be overridden by majority will. Elected governments can entrench their position by sweeping national security legislation restricting freedom of expression and association.

Developing countries urge that both human rights and democracy are open to localised understandings and applications. Nevertheless, Articles 21 of the UDHR and 25 of the ICCPR assert equal rights of citizens to take part in the conduct of public affairs, directly or through freely chosen representatives; to vote and be elected at 'genuine periodic elections' based on universal and equal suffrage, secret ballot, guaranteeing the free expression and will of the electors. Coupled with other rights to freedom of speech, association and peaceful assembly, and allowing for variation in electoral and constitutional arrangements, little scope remains, on the basis of UN human rights law, for legitimising 'Asian', 'people's', 'guided' or other adjectivally qualified forms of democracy.

Even so, inclusion of democratic ground rules, commonly described as 'liberal', within the overall framework of international human rights law does not equate to the totality of human rights, which embraces economic and social as well as civil and political rights. Both the content of these rights and the means of achieving them are major objects of democratic contestation. This is implicitly acknowledged by some neo-liberals, such as Hayek, who sees liberalism as a doctrine about what law ought to be, whereas democracy is a doctrine about how to determine the law (Held 1995: 241). Individuals require rules constraining governments and majorities, freeing them from fear of coercive power. Otherwise, neo-liberal protagonists must persuade majorities to their viewpoint. Huntington (1991: 6–8) similarly defines democracy in terms of law and process.

Such minimalist conceptions of democracy have potential merit in undercutting tendencies by both radicals and neo-liberals to define democracy in programmatic terms, labelling disfavoured outcomes from political competition as undemocratic. However, limited focus on democratic competition processes and associated legal rights ignores the impact of globalisation in shifting the loci of decision-making away from national governments and legislatures.

In response, new movements and concepts of democratic governance have emerged transcending national boundaries, expressed in terms such as 'international cosmopolitan democracy' (Held 1995) and 'humane governance' (Falk 1995). Neo-liberals have attempted to depict economic and social rights asserted in UN covenants as merely undesirable objects of democratic contestation rather than as fundamental rights. Gill (1998) claims that neo-liberals have sought by various legal and constitutional devices to privilege rights of capital and entrench disciplines of the world market place beyond the control of democratic politics. Thus, a merely legal and procedural view of democracy may be instrumental in denying human rights. Conversely, constitutionally entrenching every kind of right would represent a limitation on democratic processes, as conventionally defined.

In order to develop participatory structures appropriate to emerging sites of contestation, it is necessary to transcend traditional boundaries between domestic and international politics. Held (1995: 176–85) identifies seven such sites, arguing that asymmetrical power balances in any of them diminish people's life chances, autonomy and participatory possibilities. These relate to physical and emotional wellbeing in terms of health, nutrition and shelter; access to goods and services sufficient to avoid 'poverty traps'; opportunities for enjoyment of cultural life, free from constraints imposed by state, religious authorities, or other hegemonic groups within civil society; access to and control of civic associations; economic life and associated structures of production, distribution and exchange, consumption and social class; the domain of security, violence and other forms of coercive relations, embracing both state and para-state forces and insurgent groups; intra-state legal and inter-state regulatory institutions and networks.

Held considers conventional civil and political rights approaches insufficient to ensure application of what he calls democratic public law in all the above spheres.

This requires establishment of clear rights and obligations pertinent to all spheres of power (Held 1995: 190). Evolution in this direction ultimately requires a strong cluster of democratic states and societies. Sustainability of democratic systems within individual states requires deepening and strengthening of 'international cosmopolitan democracy', applying principles of subsidiarity in determining sites of decision-making appropriate to the context and range of interconnectedness entailed (Held 1995: 22–3, 139–40, 235–8).

While such agendas apparently fly in the face of an international system still largely based on state sovereignty, the case for viewing states' international legitimacy as linked to upholding common democratic values is implicit in UDHR Articles 21 and ICCPR Article 25 cited earlier, and explicit in UDHR Article 28, which asserts that 'everyone is entitled to a social and international order in which the rights and freedoms set forth in this Declaration can be fully realized.' The Council of Europe makes commitment to democracy a condition of membership, while the European Convention on Human Rights explicitly links them. The Declaration of the 1992 Helsinki Conference on Security and Cooperation in Europe – also signed by Canada and the USA – views human rights as matters of direct and legitimate concern to all participatory states, and not exclusively within the domain of the state concerned. Promoting human rights and strengthening democratic institutions is integral to building comprehensive security in Europe (Held 1995: 105). Paradoxically, the international order is increasingly structured by agencies over which citizens have minimal control, at the very time when popular democratic demands are becoming more assertive.

The humane governance school is similarly global in its outlook. However, it is 'hawkish' towards liberal notions of democracy and any hint of special privileging of civil and political rights. In a critique which indicates partial incorporation of communitarian ideas into humane governance models, Falk advocates a system of democracy which is concrete and contextualised, emphasising the locus of authority and distribution of benefits in class, gender, and ethnic terms. While conceding some value to traditional democratic forms as protecting citizens against the state and facilitating a measure of popular participation in selecting leaders, they are seen as unable to provide humane governance in face of relentless pressures to assert the primacy of market principles over welfare, social harmony and environmental protection and even minimal democratic rights (Falk 1995: 105–16).

Humane governance advocates, see a strong transnational social movement as essential to changing this situation (Falk 1989: 120). This idea is reflected in a blueprint proposing to institutionalise representation and consultation of NGOs and civil society groups in a reformed UN structure (Camilleri *et al.* 2000: 26–32). Although this idea is intended to complement rather than replace representation by states, it highlights sharply competing principles of representation. NGOs are mostly unelected, tending rather to play intermediary roles in promoting grassroots empowerment (Eldridge 1995: 17–19). Their links with local members or reference groups become increasingly indirect as they scale up their engagement at national and international levels.

State and civil society

Despite the relative weakness of civil society in most Southeast Asian states, a wide range of advocacy groups and associations have emerged among women, peasants, workers, landless, ethnic minorities, environmental and human rights groups, supported by sympathetic journalists, lawyers and other professionals. They have mostly shown greater capacity to bring their case to wider audiences and gain attention from policy-makers compared with weak, divided and often semi-legal opposition parties. But their future relations with political parties in more fully developed systems of electoral democracy will be more complex than currently acknowledged in their public rhetoric.

The examples of India (Eldridge 1985) and the Philippines (Macuja 1992) indicate sharp and often bitter rivalry with politicians. NGOs and advocacy groups maintain popular legitimacy to the extent that they do not seek power for themselves. When politicians point to such groups' lack of electoral legitimacy, they commonly respond by denouncing money politics and 'the system' in general. As yet there is little consensus concerning division of labour among those seeking democratic change, and reconciling electoral-style representation with more direct, popular forms of participation.

The beneficial impact on many disadvantaged groups need not entail undifferentiated support for strengthening civil society as uniquely representing the forces of good against oppressive governments, as in some radical cum populist rhetoric. Religious and ethnic sentiment can be easily incited and manipulated in times of crisis, indicating a need for cooperative action between state and nonstate groups in developing a civic culture supportive of democratic values and practices.

Fine and Rai (1997) urge moving away from polarised perspectives on civil society, and the need to include those who can currently find no place in its associational life (Fine and Rai 1997: 2–3). In terms of humane governance objectives, governments may at times serve as vehicles of moderation in relation to regressive populism (Falk 1995: 119). Cultural rights are also not unlimited and must be linked to a culture of democratic toleration (Held 1995: 196).

Despite these qualifications, normative and practical convergences between democratic movements and efforts to strengthen civil society relative to the state remain strong. Trends towards incorporating community groups into state structures have placed a premium on forming independent associations with some real measure of autonomy. This entails challenging communitarian ideology designed to suppress individual rights. But equally, non-state groups need not necessarily accept standard liberal pluralist models which construct them as mere interest groups or intermediaries, and may choose to play more broad-ranging community building and identity forming roles.

Relations between governments and NGOs are subject to many strains and contradictions. Elements within governments, particularly those concerned with delivering economic and social development programmes, appreciate the need for some measure of popular participation, and seek cooperation with NGOs for this purpose. Foreign aid donors also impose conditionalities favouring community input. Although governments fear that popular mobilisation will challenge its authority, heavy-handed control will undermine NGOs' popular legitimacy and effectiveness. For their part, NGOs recognise that scattered localised successes will not make any large-scale impact without engagement with macro-political processes. Cooperation with government agencies helps them gain access to resources and opportunities to influence policy and planning in more participatory directions. But these gains must be weighed against ever present dangers of losing autonomy.

Development and human rights

The UN Declaration on the Right to Development (RTD) adopted by the General Assembly on 4 December 1986[4] brought together developing country aspirations for national development in a sharper, more focused way compared with the ICESCR. The language of rights is sustained throughout the document in terms of the full range of human rights set out in UN covenants and conventions. Article 2(1) asserts the human person as the central subject of development, as both active participant and beneficiary.

While the Declaration gives states important rights and responsibilities, nothing in its content supports interpretations of development in purely economic terms or related insistence by some governments that its achievement must precede adoption of civil and political rights. Indeed, Article 6(3) sees their absence as an obstacle to development which states are urged to eliminate. The Preamble asserts that 'the promotion of, respect for and enjoyment of certain human rights and fundamental freedoms cannot justify the denial of other human rights and fundamental freedoms.' Article 9(2) provides that nothing in the Declaration justifies violation of rights set out in the UDHR or associated covenants and conventions.

The RTD Declaration nevertheless accommodates developing country government concerns in important ways. States are acknowledged as having both a right and a duty to formulate national development plans designed to enhance the welfare of all their people. Article 2(2) asserts individuals' rights to participate in planning processes and enjoy a fair distribution of resulting benefits. But they must also accept responsibility for development and their duties to the community as corollaries to enjoying respect for their human rights. Articles 3 and 4 require protection of these rights to be matched by international cooperation to establish a 'new international economic order', and promote more rapid development in poorer countries.

Article 5 calls for resolute steps to eliminate the 'massive and flagrant violations' of human rights resulting from apartheid, racial discrimination, colonialism, foreign domination and occupation, aggression, threats against national sovereignty, unity and territorial integrity, threats of war and refusal to recognise fundamental rights to self-determination. Later articles deal with peace and security, access to basic resources in terms of education, health services, food, housing, employment and the fair distribution of income, including effective measures to ensure that women participate equally in both the processes and benefits of development.

While it is easy to dismiss the Declaration as a pious wish list, offering something to all main protagonists in north–south conflicts, it represents a potentially important step in linking human rights and development agendas, re-affirming principles of indivisibility. But the opportunity which the RTD Declaration offered was not taken up. This was partly due to unfavourable timing, with neo-liberal ideology dominating the thinking of key western countries, and international institutions such as the International Monetary Fund (IMF) and the World Bank. Proposals for a New International Economic Order (NIEO),[5] which would have changed the ground rules for conducting aid, trade, commodity pricing technology transfer, investment and other areas of vital economic concern to developing countries, were similarly rejected. The NIEO's residual Keynesian outlook, favouring mixed economies and government initiative, was similarly unacceptable to international decision makers, who insisted on their own structural adjustment agendas.

Despite some softening in this outlook in the latter part of the 1990s, particularly in light of the Asian economic crisis, there is still underlying reluctance by richer countries to accord either development, or economic and social rights generally, full status as human *rights*, as distinct from desirable objectives. The roots of such reluctance are both legal and political, based on fears that poorer countries will gain open-ended claims on rich country resources. Goals, means and indicators of development are in any case hotly disputed. Consequently, neither definitions nor principles for enforcement can be agreed. India's Constitution implicitly recognises the problem, distinguishing between 'fundamental rights', broadly corresponding to civil and political rights, and economic and social objectives, accorded priority as 'directive principles'. Only the former are justiciable.

While neo-liberals find little support in either the RTD or ICESCR document, parts of the RTD find resonance with developing countries pursuing conventional growth policies but frustrated by external pressures for privatisation, de-regulation and conditionalities imposed on aid, trade and investment, in what they see as an unequally structured global order. Some governments assert developmental rights in international contexts, while repressing them at home, fearing their use by civil society groups to promote participatory and basic needs oriented approaches.

Attempts to entrench indivisibility principles in economic and social planning and overall systems of governance, under the general rubric of a 'right to development', are gaining some momentum. Preambles to the UDHR, ICCPR and ICESCR requiring state parties to respect, protect and promote human rights, justify shifting the onus on governments from moral and humanitarian to legal obligation.

The Human Rights Council of Australia (HRCA 1998), as part of a likeminded international network, has sought to systematise these requirements by developing a 'Rights Way to Development' Manual. Though focusing primarily on external aid policy and practice, its approach links UN treaties and reporting networks, national human rights plans and relevant domestic institutions. The model entails spelling out the implications of each right for corresponding areas of national policy, together with specific sectoral targets.

Many NGOs, including those advocating popular empowerment, are ambivalent about rights-based approaches. While welcoming the shift towards equity-based claims, they sense that one-dimensional legal approaches will prove inadequate and even counter-productive without social, cultural and institutional change. They also fear that externally imposed formulae may weaken participatory objectives, central to their ethos and legitimacy.

Attempts to develop operational models and checklists aimed at integrating UN covenant rights within a framework of overall strategic plans nevertheless provide bases for performance monitoring and application of pressure where appropriate. They further help to concretise human rights discourse and legitimise a praxis of mutual accountability and peer pressure, while the focus on development assistance obligations in RTD blueprints helps redress perceived imbalances in global protection and promotion of human rights.

Post-colonial countries have commonly promoted states as prime agents of development. While earlier notions of public sector dominated planning have been modified or abandoned, with dynamic private sectors emerging in East and Southeast Asia, the legitimacy and need for governments to play pro-active roles represents a strong point of convergence between otherwise diverse states. Active partnership between government and business, culturally underpinned by values of cooperation and harmony, is also extolled. This outlook is challenged by both neo-liberals and advocates of strengthened civil society roles, who see it as promoting patronage, corruption and inefficiency. Asian values rhetoric thus partly represents a form of covert resistance to anti-statist economic ideology, in which it is more politic to denounce liberal democratic understandings of human rights than to openly attack powerful 'sacred cows' of free markets, de-regulation and privatisation.

As Falk (1995: 109–12) has pointed out, there is no necessary correlation between economic efficiency and democracy, with hegemonic powers swinging from support for authoritarian regimes pursuing market-oriented policies to post-Cold War demands for democratisation as necessary to good governance. The paradox is apparently explained by the legitimacy and 'rule of law' which democracy is expected to bring, despite potential for social disorder in the shorter term.

Clarifying the future role of governments is vital to determining strategies for promoting economic and social rights. If life is to be governed overwhelmingly by the interplay of market forces, such rights could become very marginalised, although there will always be a residual role for both state and civil society in regulating rules of engagement and balancing outcomes to disadvantaged groups. According to Cerny (1996: 130–3), while a core role remains for the state, its holistic and overarching character is giving way to a plurality of structures and processes providing public goods. Pressures for states to be competitive push them increasingly in the enterprise association direction, while abandoning or downgrading traditional roles.

Linda Weiss (1998: 187–93) argues that this trend is not inevitable, with neo-liberal policies as much the outcome of ideological choice as of dominance of international capital. States' alleged powerlessness in face of globalising trends serves as a convenient tool for marketing unpopular policies. In reality, states play wide-ranging initiating, capacity-building and adaptive roles in many domestic, regional and international contexts. Some operate as major vehicles of capital accumulation, as in the case of Singapore, which Weiss claims as maintaining active control over its savings and investment levels.

The government-business partnership, Weiss claims, goes to the heart of state capacity. By contrast, Anglo–American economies, including Australia, with their traditional 'arms length' approach to the corporate sector, lack the strategic capacities of their East Asian counterparts, so that the fundamentals of these coordinated economies remain strong despite the post-1997 currency crisis (Weiss 1998: 202–11). Though the crisis generated increased scepticism towards East Asian development models, the inadequacies of neo-liberal alternatives were also exposed. Weiss' analysis goes far in explaining both the core rationale underlying regional resistance to western neo-liberal pressures and the lack of convergence between regional approaches and the major thrust of UN Right to Development and related economic human rights agendas.

Conclusion

Global interconnectedness is gradually limiting autonomous national decision-making, even by the world's most powerful states. National sovereignty nevertheless retains primary legitimacy. While UN treaty processes offer significant scope for interpretation and harmonisation with domestic norms and practices, monitoring and reporting processes place an onus on participating states to explain and justify their position, thereby instituting formal frameworks for mutual accountability.

While the right to enter reservations preserves national sovereignty, other countries retain rights to criticise and even reject arguments framed in terms of domestic law and practice, where these contravene UN treaty objectives. Such arrangements formally refute doctrines that states' internal affairs are beyond external comment. However, treaty accountability requirements, and the opportunities they offer to critics at home and abroad to highlight deficiencies continue to discourage states' participation. As China and the USA still refuse to ratify major covenants and conventions, many issues bearing on human rights are sidelined or resolved outside UN frameworks.

This chapter has highlighted links between debates concerning the relative or universal nature of human rights, reconciling principles of national sovereignty and international human rights law, and practical and philosophical problems of integrating the two major streams of human rights. While UN doctrine strongly asserts the interdependence of all human rights, definitions and causal links between democracy, development and human rights are complex and strongly contested. Resolution of this triangular equation lies at the heart of human rights struggles and discourse, both globally and in Southeast Asia.

2 Human rights, democracy and development in Southeast Asia

The chapter begins by identifying key variants of 'Asian values' and 'Asian democracy' discourse, together with critical responses. This lays the ground for exploring complex links between democracy, development and human rights across ASEAN countries, linked to analysis of the post-1997 regional economic crisis, with country case studies covering Singapore, Philippines and Thailand. The chapter concludes by reviewing prospects for democratic consolidation in Southeast Asia. While conflict between Asian values and neo-liberalism tends to dominate official discourse, trends on the ground indicate that the indivisibility principle, which assumes democracy as integral to both major streams of human rights, enjoys a potential reservoir of popular support.

Asian values

Historically, western governments have tended to accept local conditions as a basis for policy-making, subject to economic and strategic interests and despite intermittent enthusiasm for imposing 'enlightenment'. This outlook persisted into the post-colonial era, according with requirements of diplomatic protocol and pragmatism. Imperatives of political stability during the Cold War period consolidated this approach, which was intellectually reinforced by realist schools of thought in the fields of international relations (Morgenthau 1973; Spegele 1996) and Third World development politics (Huntington 1968). But the balance of forces favouring this approach has been upset both within western democracies and Southeast Asia since the end of the Cold War, encouraging stronger impulses towards democratisation and placing human rights issues firmly on global and regional agendas.

The sudden outpouring of Asian values polemic in the early 1990s was in part a defensive reaction against mounting pressures for political liberalisation and conformity with international human rights standards. Widespread acknowledgement of their economic success added to regional governments' sense of vindication and grievance towards changing trends. But Asian values discourse also represented a conscious attempt to draw together common elements from diverse cultural strands into a coherent alternative concept of politics and society. While legitimising regime dominance, appeals to national and cultural pride also enjoy a measure of popular resonance. Such themes have antecedents in earlier decolonisation struggles and Third World demands for an NIEO.

Singapore and Malaysia have led the way in articulating contemporary Asian values concepts. The best known version emerged from the response by Kishore Mahbubani (1993), an influential member of Singapore's policy-making elite, to Samuel Huntington's 'Clash of Civilisations' thesis (Huntington 1993). Mahbubani expressed both his country's concerns over US regional policies and latent frustrations of regional neighbours (Thong-Bee Koh 1993). Malaysia, angered by US opposition to its East Asian Economic Caucus (EAEC) plan, asserted Third World grievances against western international economic dominance, and perceived ideological and cultural hegemony by the 'west' over the 'rest'.

Key Asian values principles assert the primacy of community over individual rights, respect for family, authority, cooperation and social harmony over interest-based competition. Such values are claimed as a key cause for regional economic success. In institutional terms they support corporatist and state-capitalist rather than liberal pluralist models of political economy. However, Singapore's strict rule of law principles in commercial and criminal law, and meritocracy in the workplace, is nearer to the western outlook than patronage systems common elsewhere in Southeast Asia.

Asian values ideology reflects Singapore's 'core values', which have formed the basis for official ideology during the past two decades. Both tend to be legitimised in terms of Confucius' teachings. However, others have urged that Confucius nowhere advocates total individual subordination to state or community. Knowledge should be pursued for personal self-development as well as public service (Ibrahim 1996: 28–9; Tu Weiming 1989). Similar principles of personal growth pervade Hinduism and Buddhism, while individual responsibility and accountability are key principles within Islam.

A softer variant to the hard-line approach of the 'Singapore school' was initiated in a report prepared for the Commission for a New Asia (1994) by a diversity of Asian intellectuals brought together under the auspices of the Institute for Strategic and International Studies, Kuala Lumpur. The report offers a hybrid of communitarian and liberal perspectives. Asian countries are urged to be discriminating in absorbing external values, but to avoid blanket rejection and relativist extremes, which often serve to cover up internal deficiencies. Democratisation is affirmed, but with an emphasis on family values and social harmony, and 'constructive' as against litigious, interest group forms of politics and government. Distinctive features of Asian cultures, notably tolerance and appreciation for pluralism, should be preserved in the face of globalising trends.

Emphasis on the dignity of the human person is balanced by warnings that citizens possess both rights and duties. The idea that the state is everything and the individual nothing is rejected. But the individual cannot be placed above the community. Government 'of the people, by the people, for the people' requires guaranteed universal suffrage and public accountability of governments. Nevertheless, strong and responsible government is a virtue, not a vice. Stability is vital, but overcoming poverty equally so, to which end it is vital to root out corruption. The 'law of the jungle' in the form of unrestrained market economics is unacceptable and society must ensure that capitalism has a human face. (Commission for a New Asia 1994: 5–9).

Notions of 'inter-civilisational dialogue' were promoted by a group close to former Malaysian Deputy Prime Minister Anwar Ibrahim. A leading role was played by Dr. Chandra Muzaffar, appointed as Director of the newly established Centre for Civilizational Dialogue at the University of Malaya in 1997. Non-renewal of Muzaffar's contract in April 1999 was widely seen as resulting from his outspoken support for Anwar Ibrahim following his downfall and imprisonment.

Ibrahim asserted that

> it is altogether shameful ... to cite Asian values as an excuse for autocratic practices and denial of basic rights and civil liberties. To say that freedom is Western or un-Asian is to offend our own traditions as well as our forefathers who gave their lives in the struggle against tyranny and injustice
>
> (Ibrahim 1996: 28)

Regarding individual rights

> it is true that Asians lay great emphasis on order and societal stability. But it is certainly wrong to regard society as a kind of deity upon whose altar the individual must constantly be sacrificed. No Asian tradition can be cited to support the proposition that ... the individual must melt into a faceless community.

On the cultural front, Ibrahim (1996: 30) urged that

> for Asia to be truly global, its societies must be prepared to transform themselves and discard the harmful residue from the past – tribalism, feudalism, narrow-mindedness and fanaticism ... Asia must not lose its identity, but it must renew commitment to core values such as justice, virtue and compassion, that are in themselves universal.

Ibrahim further insisted on moral and intellectual equality. Former colonial rulers are urged to engage with Asians 'as equal partners in actualizing a new moral vision for the world.' Continued hectoring on human rights, conditionalities on trade and patronising cultural outlooks create suspicion of a hidden agenda, aimed at replacing old with new forms of domination (Ibrahim 1996: 30–1).

Ibrahim's outlook is by no means secular or libertarian, as indicated by his emphasis on integrating religious and moral dimensions as a basis for strengthening community bonds (Ibrahim 1996: 47–60). Rather he reflects the view of many Asian religious leaders and scholars that western hostility to religion derives from the secular rationalist and materialist values of the Enlightenment (Ibrahim 1995; Tu Weiming 1997).

Inter-civilisational dialogue is not necessarily supportive of human rights. The idea arose partly in response to Huntington's clash of civilisations thesis, as did the original Asian values debate itself. Primary goals of tolerance, mutual understanding and peaceful resolution of disputes underlying the dialogue idea may result in new syncretisms which could undermine universal human rights. The idea's democratic intent is also uncertain. Mahbubani (1998: 13) has expressed a conviction that the future lies in a fusion of civilisations, in a world in which the Asia-Pacific region will play a very substantial role. In that context, he argues that dialogue requires an intellectual 'level playing field' based on mutual respect for each others choices, and avoiding smug knee-jerk responses. For example, Singapore favours public safety and health relative to civil liberties of real and potential criminals compared with the USA. While legitimate arguments can be advanced on either side, each society must live with the consequences of its choices. Such principles have not discouraged Singapore from mocking at the Philippines' perceived combination of democratic politics and economic failure (Ghai 1995: 60).

Some of the most telling criticism of Asian values has come from within Southeast Asia. Thus, Yash Ghai rejects claims by some government leaders to speak for the whole region in portraying universal human rights as western concepts without regional relevance. Other Asian voices, he asserts, whose culture has been destroyed by state imposed models of development, such as middle classes seeking more democracy, tribals and minorities, are now speaking out. Elites counter-attack, using developmentalist ideologies to justify domestic repression, while simultaneously demanding economic assistance from western countries, who may not question progress on civil and political rights (Ghai 1995: 58–9).

Communitarian ideology supporting Asian values suffers from weaknesses of overstating the individualism of western societies and philosophies, and false equation of states with communities. Drastic state powers are employed to control and shape communities, and often to destroy them. Ghai claims that community organisation is more vital and lively in the 'individualist' west. Despite western countries' poor historical records, the concept of universal human rights contains potentially dynamic, transformative power in the Asian context, where people suffer major violations at the hands of both state and civil society (Ghai 1995: 61–5).

The Asian Forum of NGOs held a parallel forum in Bangkok from 29 March to 2 April 1993 alongside the official UN regional consultation (United Nations 1993a), and issued their own alternative declaration of principles. These affirmed human rights as both universal and indivisible, according both major streams of rights full equality. Their statement provided the foundation for the Vienna Declaration and Programme of Action (VDPA) agreed two months later. The NGOs' position contrasts sharply with their governments, who formally accepted the VDPA but remained aloof from its action implications. The VDPA conflicts sharply with global neo-liberal outlooks, which are negative or indifferent to economic, social and cultural rights.

While there are many other dissenting non-state voices, such as students, intellectuals, journalists, trade unions and opposition political parties, NGOs appear most organisationally well adapted to networking, mobilisation, advocacy, information sharing and exploiting limited social space under restricted conditions. While the 'associational revolution' they are claimed to have effected (Yamamoto 1995: 4) may be overstated, their role in strengthening civil society and partially balancing state and business power is widely recognised (Ghai 1995: 62–3). Diverse links with disadvantaged groups render most NGOs pluralist and inclusive in outlook, and therefore less inclined to see human rights advocacy as encroaching on national sovereignty. While Southeast Asian NGOs share common ground with their governments in attributing the poor state of human rights to an unjust international economic order, they link economic rights to a less statist view of development, more focused on equity and sustainability (Ghai 1995: 63).

Some western commentary rejects Asian values discourse entirely, as based on selective interpretation of both western and Asian cultures, designed to legitimate power holders (Lawson 1996). Rodan and Hewison (1996) claim that Asian corpo-ratist models of state and society reflect organic state theory originating in Europe. Neo-liberals and business interests are also attracted to East Asian states' capacity to discipline their work forces, thereby limiting welfare demands and related tax burdens characteristic of western social democracies. However, they find its interventionist and patrimonial aspects less acceptable. Robison (1996) argues that societal and structural change arising from East Asian industrialisation will soon necessitate sharp choices between introducing some form of welfare support or abandoning large masses to their market fate – anathema to Asian values-style com-munitarian rhetoric. Simultaneously, predatory and rent-seeking behaviour generate both local and international demands for rule of law and good governance which are hard to institutionalise outside a democratic framework.

Other scholars, both critical and supportive, accept the existence of Asian values as factually based. An example of the former is the illiberal democracy critique (Bell 1995), whose contributors find both cultural substance and tools for state legitimation in Asian values claims. Conversely, Vatikiotis (1996) portrays Asian leaders as making skilful and pragmatic use of cultural tools in forging institutions appropriate to their countries' economic and social developmental needs. Others calling for dialogue (Falk 1995; Camilleri 1997) accept that Asian values polemic reflects genuine cultural concerns.

Asianist scholars increasingly cooperate in comparative studies (Milner 1996), seeking to avoid imposing external interpretations on societies with very different histories, institutions, economy and ecology, yet recognising wide diversity across the region.

Democracy and Asian values

Notions of 'Asian democracy' are interwoven with Asian values discourse. While the details of proposed models differ between countries, common features include Confucian-style values, patron–client relations, personalised authority, dominant political party, and strong state (Neher and Marlay 1995: 13–28). It is unclear whether Asian variants are intended to permanently replace western-style liberal democracy, or provide a transition towards it (Hara 1999). Though almost universally accepted as the currency of political legitimacy, 'democracy' has never been tied down, as in the west, to particular institutions and processes, and operates within an environment of free-floating meanings and associations (Milner 1996: 132–64).

Asian values protagonists claim that their concerns centre on contextualised application rather than principle. But they urge emphasis on good governance and performance over process, and decry western countries' unwillingness to accept responsibility for instability when imperfect governments are overthrown as a result of pressures for democratisation and human rights (Mahbubani 1998: 37–56).

In ideal-type terms, Asian democracy paradigms propose an antithesis between values of state, authority, national unity, community, stability, development and harmony as against individualism, egoism, hedonism, legalism and anarchy. This can be restated from a liberal-democratic perspective in terms of conflict between liberty, pluralism, rule of law, equality, accountability and participation against autocracy, repression, militarism, corruption and exploitation.

In practice, Asian political systems mix many combinations of democratic and non-democratic elements. New terms such as 'illiberal' (Bell 1995) and 'semi' democracy (Neher 1995; Crouch 1996a: 3–12; Case 2001) attempt to grapple with this reality. Such hybrids are proving more resilient than paradigms which either polarise opposites or predict a natural evolution towards liberal democracy (Huntington 1991) in line with an 'end of history' thesis (Fukuyama 1992).

Both western and Asian democracies confront the reality of plural societies with competing moral, social, and political outlooks. Accommodating minorities poses a challenge to principles of democratic majoritarianism in both. While liberal-democracies tend to favour constitutional or legislative safeguards for minority rights, East Asian states tend to manipulate their societies' diversity to impose their own models of harmony and national integration (Bell 1995: 7–9).

In terms of mechanisms, liberal-democrats place their faith, based on scepticism towards fallible rulers, in separation of powers, rules and processes, checks and balances. By contrast, there is strong East Asian cultural resistance to such notions, reflecting the Chinese proverb that there is 'only one sun in the sky'. Cultural preference for concentrating authority similarly de-legitimises boundaries between state and civil society and supports integralist and corporatist political systems. Federalism and other kinds of regional and local devolution of powers are similarly suspect, as are notions of 'rule of law' which limit political leaders' operational discretion. Consequently, while preserving democratic forms, political elites devise means to control or limit the powers and composition of parliaments, and ensure that ruling parties or coalitions remain dominant.

Asian democracy practitioners deny that political opposition is necessarily beneficial, stressing potential divisions and factionalism. Consequently, much dissent takes the form of proposing alternative solutions within the framework of official ideology and institutions. A multi-party structure may be tolerated, as in Malaysia, as a means of articulating communal interests within a pluralist society, without threatening dominant power structures. For liberals, genuine electoral competition and the real prospect of opposition parties gaining government represents a basic test of whether a system is democratic.

Malaysia's system has now been established in much its present form for three decades, reflecting entrenched features of its society and politics (Crouch 1996a: 3–13). However, there can be no certainty whether it will shift over time in a democratic or authoritarian direction. Despite gradual consolidation of democratic rule, the convolutions of the Thai situation were captured in Donald Emmerson's description of its regime as a 'military-influenced multi-party parliamentary-democratic constitutional monarchy' (Emmerson 1994).[1] The case for regarding the Philippines as less than fully democratic, despite extensive constitutional and other reforms since 1986, rests on the continuing dominance of oligarchic elites over processes of law and politics in the regions, criminalisation and corruption in public life and disregard for human rights in many areas.

Notions of transition imply ultimate adoption of a western liberal model. Realistically, many combinations of democratic and authoritarian rule are possible. Ironically, the two countries which started out with Westminster-style democracy, Singapore and Malaysia, are in a stronger position to maintain ruling party dominance than those which have moved to democratic rule after a long period of military dominance, such as Thailand and Indonesia. Singapore's government, from a seemingly impregnable position, is seeking ways of mobilising greater participation for purposes of problem-solving, yet without adopting liberal democratic processes.

Writing before the Asian economic crisis, Jayasuriya (1995) saw democratic transition as based on re-negotiation of intra-state relations, driven by changing needs of capitalist development. Although such re-negotiation may include new elements of the emerging middle class and previously excluded fractions of capital, Jayasuriya insists that the wider civil society will be excluded. This view discounts massive popular upheavals in Indonesia, and earlier mobilisation which contributed to overthrowing authoritarian rule in the Philippines in 1986 and Thailand in 1992.

Earlier optimism that the 'middle class' would represent a driving force for democratic change has become more qualified. Many professionals and business groups depend on their governments for survival. They also fear potential disorder and multiplication of demands from mass democratic empowerment. David Jones (1995; 92–100) considers that many planners and administrators have internalised Confucian-style values of obedience and conformity in an anxious search for certainty and continuity in fast changing times. Nevertheless, middle and lower-middle class elements with some level of educational achievement frequently assist popular mobilisation among workers, peasants and other disadvantaged groups.

Both advocates and critics of Asian democracy approaches agree on the pivotal roles played by states in shaping economic development and political culture and processes. This picture is confirmed, irrespective of constitutional forms, when individual ASEAN countries are compared in subsequent sections.

Democracy and development in Southeast Asia

Most ASEAN governments rated development more highly than human rights and democracy goals in the early 1990s. They showed correspondingly little awareness of contradictions entailed in demanding equality between different streams of rights, while insisting on development as a pre-condition for civil and political rights (Acharya 1995: 170–2). At the 1993 UN regional consultation, only the Philippines refused to accept that economic development must entail sacrifice of individual and political rights, asserting that the nation's recent experience had demonstrated that this was a false choice (Hitchcock 1995: 10).

Outdoing Huntington (1991), and even Marx, Mahbubani (1998: 76) sees economic development as probably the most subversive force in history in promoting political and social change. 'By comparison, the Aquino revolution in the Philippines and award of the Nobel Peace Prize to Aung San Suu Kyi are mere symbols, which barely make a dent in the lives of the teeming billions suffering poverty in developing countries.' As yet, however, Singapore's outstanding economic success has not resulted in political liberalisation.

Attempts to link economic aid with human rights performance are sternly rebuked. Donor criteria should focus on promoting good government, applying key tests of political stability, sound administration, meritocracy, economic growth with equity, fiscal prudence and relative lack of corruption. Change occurs slowly, in most cases requiring cooperation with existing governments. Only states which have allowed their people to stagnate for decades, such as Myanmar and North Korea, deserve condemnation (Mahbubani 1998: 48–9, 76–7).

The relative weakness of the domestic private sector at independence, especially among indigenous groups, has required governments to play leading roles in late industrialising, post-colonial Southeast Asia. Complex networks have subsequently developed between governments, foreign and domestic capital, with favoured groups developing a local capitalist base, although often of the rent-seeking rather than entrepreneurial kind. While abrupt withdrawal of the state from economic involvement could prove destructive, transparent, efficient and equitable management of scarce resources is essential to fulfilling basic economic and social rights on a mass scale.

Popular expectations of governments are ambivalent. A traditional Burmese prayer asking deliverance from fire, famine, disease, flood and government can be set alongside popular quests for a just ruler. While common experience of corruption and exploitation drives the prayer, the mark of the just ruler is to provide security, discipline corrupt officials and ensure peoples' subsistence. This latter is seen as a primary task of economic development. But Southeast Asians, while less concerned about censorship of interference in their personal lives, tend to see welfare as the responsibility of families or religious charity. With the exception of Singapore, they appear less interested in health and safety issues, over which western governments are expected to exercise stringent controls (Milner 1996: 258).

The role of the state in development and the appropriateness of democratic relative to authoritarian systems of government in its achievement are closely inter-linked issues. Unfortunately they have been conflated to produce a falsely polarised choice between a democratic state progressively withdrawing itself from economic involvement and an interventionist state based on authoritarian rule.

One side argues that liberal-style democracy, as a key element in good governance, brings virtues of accountability, transparency and legal regularisation essential to economic management and planning. Personal freedom is claimed as encouraging entrepreneurship, thereby enhancing wealth and prosperity, widening education, skills and sense of competence. Democratic processes build capacity for negotiation and compromise, as the basis of good citizenship. Exposure to western ideas as part of globalisation provides further reinforcement.

Counter-arguments depict sterile competition between groups unable to perceive wider national interests and objectives, as paralysing or seriously slowing down national development. Electoral competition requires their appeasement by means of short term fixes and benefits. Only strong governments are capable of taking difficult, often unpopular decisions necessary to bring longer term benefits (Neher 1995: 191–2). An inversion of this argument is that high rates of growth widen the wealth gap, necessitating authoritarian rule in order to suppress discontent (O'Donnell 1973: 21). Both Prime Minister Mahathir of Malaysia and former Philippines President Ferdinand Marcos have argued for democratic freedoms to be rationed out sparingly, for fear of hampering economic growth (Neher 1995: 192).

Lee Kuan Yew, in one of his periodic forays into Filipino politics, commented that development requires discipline. This can be undermined by too 'exuberant' forms of democracy, resulting in corruption and stagnation, particularly where 'gridlock' of the American variety occurs. President Ramos responded that democracy is intrinsic to development and warned against throwing away hard won political gains for a 'quick fix'. Some Filipinos, reported as agreeing with Lee, see American emphasis on individualism as undermining Filipino community values (Neher 1995: 25).

Human rights-based concepts of development emphasise basic physical wellbeing, human dignity and opportunities for self-development, with rights to participate in shaping relevant public policy and institutions. The Human Development Index (HDI), devised by the United Nations Development Programme (UNDP), provides a general measure of welfare, combining life expectancy at birth; education based on adult literacy and mean years of schooling and income. UNDP's annual Human Development Reports are developing a progressively more comprehensive picture, supplementing HDI with disaggregated data relating to regions, ethnic, gender and other socio-economic groups, linked to macro and micro income and expenditure data.

Table 2.1 indicates the HDI and world ranking for ASEAN countries in 1997, together with their real Gross Domestic Product (GDP) per capita in US dollar purchasing power parity terms for that year (UNDP 1999*a*: 134–7).

HDI ranking gives no clear correlation with democratic orientation. Neher and Marlay (1995) categorised Southeast Asian countries as democratic, semi-democratic, semi-authoritarian and authoritarian on the basis of citizen participation, electoral competition and civil liberties. The Philippines, Thailand and Malaysia were classed, in descending order, as semi-democratic; Singapore and Indonesia as semi-authoritarian. The four poorest states – Myanmar, Laos, Cambodia and Vietnam – plus the richest in per capita terms, Brunei, are categorised as authoritarian (Neher 1995: 195–8). Brunei's HDI ranks second among ASEAN states, only slightly below Singapore.[2] Their successes in delivering economic and social human rights offer *prima facie* support for Asian democracy claims favouring strong government, although their special features as city-state and oil rich kingdom with relatively small populations must be taken into account.

The Philippines experienced economic decline under both Marcos and his immediate democratic successor. Judgements that most Filipinos were too preoccupied

Table 2.1 ASEAN Human Development Index and Gross
Domestic Product ($ US) 1997

	Real GDP per capita	*HDI value*	*HDI ranking*
Singapore	28,460	0.888	22
Brunei	29,773	0.878	25
Malaysia	8,140	0.768	56
Thailand	6,690	0.753	67
Philippines	3,520	0.740	77
Indonesia	3,490	0.681	105
Vietnam	1,630	0.664	110
Myanmar	1,199	0.580	128
Cambodia	1,290	0.514	137
Laos	1,300	0.491	140

with subsistence, preventing them from participating in the political life of the nation (Neher 1995: 196) raise issues of comparison – for example, with the USA where deep pockets of poverty still exist and where electoral turnout even for Presidential elections barely exceeds 50 per cent. Malaysia, the most authoritarian of the three countries classified as 'semi-democratic', ranks third in terms of both GDP and HDI indicators. But the deeply authoritarian nature of the lowest income ASEAN countries can be seen as negatively reinforcing pro-democracy arguments.

World Bank analysis currently posits strong links between democratic participation and economic growth. Changes in mental outlook central to development, it is argued, will not reach deep into the society if changes are introduced without open and extensive discussion. Inclusive processes are more likely to generate a wider sense of ownership towards new policies and practices. External imposition of 'best practice' by means of conditionalities or other pressures may fail to produce lasting change, undermining incentives to develop peoples' own capacities. For these reasons, often 'maddeningly slow' processes of democracy may yield more sustainable results than authoritarian quick fixes (Stiglitz 1999). Also, the knowledge and communications revolution is transforming economic and production structures in ways which require cooperative modes of problem-solving rather than vertical industrial structures employed in coordinating masses of workers for purposes of assembly line production.

The economic costs of weak financial regulatory frameworks, linked to lack of transparency and accountability, became starkly apparent during the recent regional crisis. A democratically empowered citizenry, it is claimed, would have demanded swifter and stronger action against fraud and mismanagement, while threats of civil action will in future provide a sharper spur to legal enforcement. Weak governance discourages investment, and dissipates the effectiveness of aid programs. Asian democracy advocates claim that their models are designed with precisely these problems in view. Liberals retort that if individuals have a voice in shaping changes, they are more likely to be internalised and accepted over the longer term (Stiglitz 1999).

Regional economic crisis

The economic crisis, beginning in mid-1997, and its aftermath have posed fundamental threats to the economic and social rights of Southeast Asians. However, the experience has brought issues of democracy and human rights to the fore, revitalising debates over economic development strategy. While there was evidence of recovery by mid-1999, the original causes of the crisis remain in dispute.

All East Asian countries were seriously affected, with Indonesia, Thailand and South Korea suffering the worst effects. For around three decades, GDP per capita had grown by at least five per cent annually in these countries and Malaysia, with still higher average growth rates in Singapore. Growth had brought increased educational opportunity and dramatic reduction in poverty rates. Indonesian poverty declined from 64 per cent in 1975 to 11 per cent in 1995. Secondary school enrolment rates doubled in East Asia over twenty-five years. The countries cited above saved over one-third of their GDP prior to the crisis, compared with the US national savings rate of 17 per cent (Stiglitz 1998).

Currency devaluations, beginning with the Thai baht, were most severe in the case of the Indonesian rupiah, which fell from 2,500 to 17,000 to the US dollar at one stage, fluctuating throughout 1998 between 7,500 and 15,000. Devaluation, as both cause and consequence of rising indebtedness, resulted in an abrupt credit squeeze and rising interest rates, with a chain reaction of business closures and worker layoffs. The World Bank warned of fifty million people returning to poverty in Indonesia, with twenty million set to lose their jobs. 1.5 million were laid off in South Korea, while unemployment rose from 1.8 at the end of 1997 to 2.7 million jobless in Thailand six months later (Richardson 1998). Governments compensated for revenue losses with severe cuts in health, education, other public and social services. Prices for fuel, food and other necessities rose sharply. Longer term damage will have been caused by loss of schooling and malnutrition suffered by millions of children.

According to the World Bank (1999*d*), household strategies to cope with falling family incomes included cutting back on food spending, thus increasing vulnerability to illness; withdrawing children from school to supplement household income or undertake household chores; cutting back on medical expenditures. Women suffered worst, losing their jobs first and providing for their families before themselves. Violence against women also increased as a result of heightened social conflict.

There was significant social unrest among workers laid off in Thailand and South Korea. However, apart from Indonesia where protest extended more widely as part of a more general political crisis, violence was substantially contained. In Malaysia, public protest was very moderate, and did not become violent until the dismissal and arrest of Deputy Prime Minister, Ibrahim. While the crisis helped influence popular sentiment in favour of change, major focus was on daily survival. Policy debate was similarly reactive.

Asian values polemic became muted, and a source of some embarrassment in the light of the crisis, generating a quiet sense of relief, even complacency among westerners that the subject could now be quietly dropped. Much neo-liberal commentary has been triumphalist, pointing out the dire consequences of intervention and crony-ism by authoritarian governments as evidence of the illusory, or at least contingent nature of Asian values, with virtues now seemingly turned into vices.

Such attitudes have fuelled resentment among some Asian leaders. Dr. Mahathir, bitterly attacked the destructive behaviour of international currency speculators. Far from being merely an expression of market forces, the crisis had been deliberately engineered, he alleged, by forces in the west alarmed by Asian economic success and determined to defeat challenges to their domination (Woollacott 1998). If Asian countries were forced to submit to globalisation on western terms, with westerners using the opportunity to buy up local companies at bargain prices, resentment would persist, possibly leading to some form of revenge via guerilla warfare.[3]

Most attempts at explanation begin with a long list of perceived problems, leading to the assumption that any problem that existed prior to the crisis is auto-matically part of its cause. Thus the supposedly special Asian mixture of govern-ment intervention and market capitalism was widely acclaimed as contributing strongly to the supposed economic miracle. Yet an excess of one or both was freely blamed for the subsequent crisis. Authoritarianism was also identified as a prime cause. Yet Singapore, adapting earlier prescriptions, weathered the storm better than all others in East Asia. Recently democratising South Korea and Thailand, which had been regarded as model pupils of International Monetary Fund (IMF) neo-liberal orthodoxy, were the worst sufferers after Indonesia, while the region's most closed economies, the socialist countries and Myanmar, remained relatively untouched, albeit at very low levels of development.

Fierce controversy has surrounded the role of the IMF, seen by its detractors as more cause than cure of East Asia's economic woes. Its standard prescriptions call for balanced budgets, credit restrictions and higher interest rates, liberalisation of the financial sector, public spending cuts, dismantling of price controls, import barriers and restrictions on capital movements, and privatisation of public enter-prises. However, in East Asia the problem was one of private sector debt rather than budgetary imbalance. Removal of subsidies on fuel and food in May 1998 provided an immediate trigger for riots in Indonesia. Delays in disbursement of IMF funds, due to resistance to its terms by recipient governments and conditionalities imposed by the US Congress, further aggravated the crisis.[4]

Criticism of the IMF has been by no means confined to radical ideologues or Asian nationalists. World Bank President, James Wolfensohn, complained that emphasis on billion dollar rescue packages was obscuring the crisis' human and social dimensions. To place such differences in context, the World Bank's focus is more broadly developmental, while the IMF's brief mainly covers currency and financial management. IMF 'structural adjustment' programmes nevertheless entail deep incursions into countries' macro economic policy-making. During the 1980s, the World Bank had adopted a broadly neo-liberal outlook supporting privatisation, de-regulation and export-oriented industrialisation. This contrasted with its earlier, Keynesian-style mixed economy approach, influenced by redistri-bution-with-growth and 'basic needs' strategies (Chenery 1974; Streeten 1981). By the early 1990s, revived concerns over poverty and social impact, brought renewed emphasis on equity, and some re-casting of neo-liberal policies in terms of 'adjustment with a human face' (Cornia *et al.* 1988).

A comprehensive effort to address the crisis was mounted at a regional meeting in Bangkok on 21–22 January 1999, initiated jointly by the IMF and the World Bank (1999*a*). Two hundred and thirty delegates, representing ninety-six countries, donor, and civil society delegations concluded that official policy and rhetoric of decentralisation and empowerment was not matched by adequate listening required to accurately gauge the needs, objectives and capacities of poor families and communities. There was also an incomplete understanding of social and family breakdown among the poor. Governments should adopt facilitating and cooperative rather than command roles, in turn requiring major changes in political culture among politicians and administrators, unwilling to devolve either resources or authority. This also implies changes in people's expectations of governments – seen in most societies as providers, enforcers and problem-solvers of both first and last resort.

Within this general framework, the World Bank (1999*d*) announced plans to nearly triple its new lending commitments to social sectors over a three-year period, including $6 billion channelled directly to governments through Structural Adjustment Loans (SALs). The Korean $2 billion loans contained guidelines for labour market reforms and strengthening social safety nets. The Indonesian $1 billion SAL focused on maintaining availability of key goods with only modest price increases, initiatives to maintain access to quality basic education and health, and labour-intensive public works programmes.

The UNDP continued to promote balancing human with economic development, if need be accepting lower growth rates in the interests of equity. Policies designed to minimise disproportionately negative impact on the poor and maximise opportunities for them from globalisation included managing trade and capital flows more carefully, investing in poor people, particularly among farmers and the informal sector, stimulating exports from small enterprises, managing new technology, setting safety nets for the poor, and improving governance. While the financial cost of such policies was proportionately modest, the political will and administrative skills required are considerable. Their effectiveness also depends considerably on empowerment of relevant communities (UNDP 1999*b*).

The UNDP's mandate requires it to deal officially only with governments, preventing it from confronting IMF policies directly, although oblique criticism was indicated by Phillips Young, Resident Representative of UNDP in Malaysia, Singapore and Brunei, who warned of the management and social consequences arising from too rapid growth, and urged that financial recovery measures that exacerbate emerging social problems should be 'avoided like the plague' (Padman 1998).

Can a workable consensus for change emerge from such debates, or will a 'dialogue of the deaf' ensure continuation of 'business as usual'? Ideological polarisation persists between Asian and neo-liberal cum globalising versions of democracy and governance. Both detract from any systematic focus on universal human rights, all forms of which have been damaged by the economic crisis, despite important democratic openings. The East versus West polemic flowing from both streams of discourse is similarly unhelpful to developing cooperation necessary to addressing both global and local dimensions of the crisis and its aftermath.

Singapore

Singapore achieved independence initially as part of Malaysia in 1963, from which it separated in 1965. As a small island state, imperatives of survival have always dominated Singapore's strategic outlook, with strong emphasis on social discipline, political authority and stability as the foundation for economic prosperity. Maintaining harmony between the three major ethnic and religious groups[5] is a fundamental priority. Economic development has been impressive in both growth and distributional terms, with real GDP surpassing that of most western countries. Excellent standards of health, housing and education have been achieved for the vast majority of Singaporeans, funded by compulsory payments to the Central Provident Fund (CPF).[6]

Singapore's political system has remained firmly under civilian control from the outset, with regular elections every five years. The People's Action Party (PAP) has dominated the political scene since it swept to power in 1959. Long-serving Prime Minister, Lee Kuan Yew stepped down in 1991, but retains strong influence as Senior Minister. International observers accept the electoral process itself as honestly conducted, though some Singaporeans are uncertain as to the secrecy of the ballot, in a context of pervasive government scrutiny of citizens.

The PAP held all Parliamentary seats from 1965 until 1981, when the Workers' Party candidate S. Jeyaratnam won a by-election. Opposition parties gained ground very slowly thereafter, winning only four out of eighty-one seats by 1992, reduced to two in 1997. While opposition parties regularly receive between 30 and 40 per cent of the popular vote, this is fragmented in a 'first past the post' electoral system. Gaining representation was made more difficult for poorly resourced parties by the introduction of enlarged multi-member electorates. This change has also strengthened minority ethnic representation among PAP parliamentarians. Provision has been made for a few candidates who come closest to gaining election to serve as Nominated Members of Parliament, though with reduced powers.

During the 1960s and 1970s, opposition centred on the Barisan Socialist party, labelled left-wing by the PAP and reflecting earlier socio-cultural divisions between English and Chinese educated among the majority community. These became less relevant following elimination of non-English medium schools. During the 1980s and 1990s, the opposition flag was carried by the Workers' Party and Singapore Democratic party. Both proposed very moderate reform platforms, which assumed their continuance in opposition (Rodan 1996: 114–20). Recognising continuing popular support for the PAP and its entrenched powers, appeals to voters were couched in terms of electing a few opposition members in order to provide some balance and critical voice. In 1992 and 1997, nominations were put forward for less than half the electorates, thus ensuring a PAP victory before polling day.

Despite such efforts at reassurance, notions of opposition as necessarily beneficial have been attacked as contrary to Singaporean notions of good government.

After the 1997 election, Prime Minister Goh Chock Tong labelled 'opposition for its own sake' as an unwanted feature of western liberal democracy, and called on opposition parties to propose comprehensive alternative programmes. In principle, this would legitimise genuine electoral competition, which the government has never explicitly opposed. However, alternatives are hard to develop, given the PAP's proclivity to take out libel suits against criticism deemed unfair or inaccurate. The more fundamental problem lies with opposition parties' lack of ideological, policy and organisational coherence. Consequently, opposition has mostly been articulated by a series of courageous individuals, notably S. Jeyaratnam, Francis Seow (1994) and Chee Soon Juan (1994).

Civil and political rights in Singapore's outwardly Westminster-style political system are constrained by a range of powerful legal and structural obstacles. These include sweeping internal security legislation, controls over media, rights to organise and public protest. Student activity on campus is tightly regulated, while labour relations are controlled within a tripartite framework comprising union, employer and government representatives. High wages and benefits, such as fair price shops and recreation facilities in return for constantly improved productivity have helped to make such arrangements acceptable to workers. Foreign publications selling over 300 copies locally must be licensed and funds deposited against any legal suits. If declared to be engaging in domestic politics, they can be banned or their sales restricted. However, such restrictions are increasingly by-passed via cyberspace information channels, despite efforts to introduce controls in these areas also.

Scope for growth of autonomous social movements or any but strictly recreational, cultural or welfare-oriented associations is similarly circumscribed. Religious bodies are constrained from involvement in public issues by laws which forbid any mingling of religion and politics. State assumption of a right to define the nature of religion implied here sets limits to freedom of religion itself. State domination over civil society has been enhanced by establishment of residents' associations, through which all policy suggestions and requests for services must be directed (Chan 1976). While genuine community leaders can play active consultative roles, Members of Parliament, who chair such bodies, act as the only effective channel for representing local needs at higher levels. Since 1988, MPs also head town councils. Local councils are responsible for administering housing estates, giving them significant control over the lives of residents in public housing, which accommodates around 80 per cent of the population, including an increasing proportion of private owners. Disadvantages of electing an opposition representative in this situation are obvious.

Asian values paradigms underlie Singapore's own core values, declared in 1989 (Vasil 1995: 78–80). These include familiar principles of community over self, upholding the family as the basic building-block of society, consensus rather than conflict and maintaining racial and religious harmony. Community support for the individual was added by Goh Chock Tong, soon after his appointment as Prime Minister, to harsher earlier formulations stressing subordination of individuals to authority. Goh also called for the building of a nation of character and grace based on dignity and mutual support.

Vasil (1995) argues that re-emphasis on Chinese culture, including the campaign to learn the Mandarin language, was aimed both at consolidating the Chinese community and as a corrective to earlier policies which had constrained its expression in order to reassure ethnic minorities. Indian and Malay sense of disadvantage has been partially addressed via special training and enterprise promotion bodies, designed to equalise opportunities without infringing principles of meritocracy zealously pursued by the government. But expressions of ethnic and religious identity which might emphasise difference from other groups or identify with overseas conflicts are strictly excluded.

Partial re-construction of Singapore identity around consolidation of ethno-religious communities has created uncertainty regarding principles of secularism. Emphasis on family authority holds potentially negative consequences for women by reinforcing patriarchy, while devolution of authority to community leaders constrains freedom of religious and cultural choice. Partly in order to shore up the Malay vote and maintain social harmony, and partly out of concern to avoid conflict with powerful neighbours, religious conversions and inter-religious marriages, particularly in cases involving Moslems, are quietly discouraged.

Support for the PAP is likely to continue at a high level, given its capacity to maintain prosperity amidst surrounding instability, with most Singaporeans accepting government arguments that strong political authority, social order, economic and technological progress are closely integrated. Initiative for change may ultimately emerge from within the state system itself, with some government leaders recognising an underlying problem of participation. Rapid change linked to globalisation require cooperative problem-solving at many social levels. Passivity and conformity in the political sphere by an increasingly well-educated population can only be maintained by ever more convoluted forms of managerialism.

Prospects for opening up new participatory channels within existing corporatist frameworks, as alternatives to western-style political liberalisation, were signalled by Deputy Prime Minister, Lee Hsien Loong, who has urged the need to coopt people and ideas at all levels and to adopt more open approaches to governance and administration. Apparently qualifying earlier doctrines about the need for strong authority, Lee observed that

> outside observers, perhaps not understanding how consensus building works in Singapore, sometimes attribute our ability to make fast and drastic changes to our lack of freedom and dictatorial methods. If coercion and regimentation were the secrets of success, the highest growth rate in Asia would be North Korea.

Active citizenship must, therefore, move beyond consultation to partnership in both private and public sectors, which will in turn require a major reorientation of outlook within the civil service (A. Lim 1999).

Lee Hsien Loong's concept will presumably also require re-evaluation of Confucian notions of governance by wise leaders. These are likely to be retained in some form in order to focus on problem-solving rather than encourage populist demands (Jones 1995: 66–74). Rule of law, which operates impeccably in the criminal, civil and business spheres, will remain limited by executive discretion in areas deemed too sensitive for public debate – though criteria for identifying 'out of bounds' markers is itself emerging as a subject of public discourse.[7] Effective participatory processes cannot be developed without clearly defined rights, linked to regularised systems of law and representation. Contradictions here are reflected in the replacement of executive intervention via internal security provisions by more legalistic resort to libel actions and tax audits against opposition figures. Artificial separation between political, civil and commercial spheres will become increasingly difficult in the face of increasing market liberalisation, wider consumer choices and information flows.

Singapore's experience has so far refuted the idea that liberal democracy must automatically flow from economic prosperity. Its corporatist structures have proved resilient, retaining a high measure of popular legitimacy. Political opponents have proved unable to aggregate issues, let alone offer coherent alternatives. Pervasive state penetration of civil society, plus a cautious and materialist outlook among the middle class, discourages open debate necessary to building a democratic culture. Yet it would be surprising if increasingly high levels of excellence achieved in the economic, technological and scientific spheres did not ultimately result in calls for wider political participation.

The Philippines

The Philippines gradually faded from the international human rights spotlight following the overthrow of President Marcos in April 1986. During Marcos' fourteen year rule, basic civil and political rights were suspended, and detentions without trial, torture and 'salvaging' of labour, peasant, women, students and social activists by military, para-military, thugs and vigilantes became rife. Marcos was eventually forced to step down by a coalition between a broad-based 'people's power' movement and a military reform faction, with some assistance from the USA. These events followed a Presidential election contest between Marcos and Mrs. Corazaon Aquino. Monitoring by the National Movement for Free Elections (NAMFREL) and international observers revealed widespread ballot fraud, confirmed by a walkout of electoral officials.

With expiry of his second Presidential term imminent, Marcos' justified seizing power in 1972 on grounds of instability from communist and other insurgencies, corruption and the need to focus on economic development. Politics was recast around the government-controlled New Society Movement (KBL), structured along similar lines to Indonesia's Golkar organisation. Marcos' position was legitimised by constitutional changes which replaced the Philippines' US-style Presidential system with one reflecting that prevailing in France, where a Prime Minister and Cabinet are responsible to Parliament but the President retains substantial executive powers to overrule and dismiss Parliament. Marcos held both top positions until 1984 under various interim arrangements (Rosenberg 1979).

During the early years of martial law, Marcos' attacks on patronage, corruption, money politics and violence (popularly known as 'guns, goons and gold'), prevalent in pre-1972 politics struck a popular chord, as did his emphasis on economic development. Early opposition focused on concentrations of power and wealth associated with dominant development models. Protests focused on land and labour issues, particularly exploitation of women in export processing zones. Mass-based social movements emerged, which generated demands for political change. The Catholic Church, despite its historical conservatism, lent significant support at many levels. The murder of Marcos' main political opponent, Senator 'Ninoy' Aquino, in 1983 galvanised the middle class into demanding a return to constitutional democracy.

There was nevertheless widespread scepticism about returning to narrowly-based intra-elite conflict characterising pre-1972 electoral politics, if this entailed leaving structural imbalances in power and wealth untouched. Divisions sharpened between those whose first priority was restoring electoral democracy and basic civil and political rights, and groups seeking more basic social and economic transformation linked to broader understandings of democratic participation. Calls for boycott of the 1986 Presidential elections by leftist coalitions were ignored by most voters, but similar ideological and tactical differences persisted into the post-Marcos era. Ultimately a measure of convergence has been achieved. While restoration of an essentially liberal democratic system reflected long established Philippines' political culture, mobilisation of civil society against Marcos substantially broadened political awareness, organising capacity and participation to include a wide range of new groups and agendas.

Following President Corazaon Aquino's accession, a new constitution was approved by popular referendum in February 1987.[8] This restored the main features of the US-style 1935 constitution, but with important variations. These include a Bill of Rights (Article III), covering freedom of speech, assembly, access to bail and legal assistance, public information and official documents, freedom from detention without due process of law, torture, loss of property without compensation and prohibition of religious tests for public office. Extensive provisions in Article XIII for 'Social Justice and human rights' cover social and economic rights across all major groups and sectors. Article XII on 'National Economy and Patrimony' requires an active state role in promoting economic development and use of resources for national benefit. Sections 17–19 of Article XIII provide for institution of a national Commission on Human Rights.

In an effort to limit concentrations of power, the President is limited to one six-year term. The Chair of both the Civil Service and Electoral Commissions may serve only one term, and may not have contested immediately preceding elections. Key public officers may be removed by impeachment initiated by the House of Representatives, to be tried by the Senate. House members may serve a maximum of three three-year terms and senators two six-year terms. The independence of the Supreme Court was entrenched, together with full rights of judicial review.

In order to broaden representation in the 250 member House of Representatives, 80 per cent are elected on a proportional representation cum electoral district basis, with 20 per cent appointed from party lists on a nation-wide basis. As well as giving smaller parties some representation, it was provided that for three terms after ratification, half the party list seats would be allocated to labour, peasant, urban poor, cultural minorities, women, youth and other sectors provided by law. Congress was instructed to provide for referendums to be initiated by 10 per cent of voters, with at least 3 per cent from each legislative district (Article VI, Section 32). Requirements for autonomy of provincial and local government (Article X), linked to democratic reforms and allocation of revenues on an automatic basis, were substantially implemented via the 1991 Local Government Code, which also requires the transfer of many national officials to local government service (Rood 1998).

The transition from military to civilian rule under President Aquino was disturbed by several coup attempts. These were defeated through the loyalty and vigilance of Defence Secretary General Fidel Ramos, who had held a top military position under Marcos, but had led the Reform of the Armed Forces Movement (RAM) together with Juan Ponce Enrile, who later turned against Aquino's administration. Her dependence on Ramos for political survival necessitated giving the military considerable freedom of action in combating the still active New People's Army (NPA) and Moslem secession movements in Mindanao. Such powers were often used indiscriminately against labour, peasant and other cause-oriented groups, with 'low intensity' counter-insurgency strategies promoting campaigns of propaganda and disinformation against both local and overseas supporters. These used local vigilante groups operating as a form of civil guard, trained and equipped by the military but largely beyond legal controls (van der Kroef 1988). Reports of human rights abuses, and killings of activists consequently equalled or even exceeded those of the Marcos period, with investigations of earlier crimes scaled down.

President Ramos, elected in 1992 from a field of seven candidates with a primary vote of slightly under 25 per cent, was able to construct a workable coalition, enabling him to focus major attention on economic development. Annual growth had averaged 0.9 per cent between 1980 and 1992, with real per capita income down by 7.2 per cent over the same period (Hutchcroft 1998: 23–4). Thus, the Philippines' performance did not match that of other ASEAN neighbours who, prior to the 1997 currency crisis, could credibly claim a link between authoritarian rule and high economic growth rates. Economic stagnation during Marcos' rule and the transitional period under Aquino was widely attributed to dominance of monopolies and cartels linked to state-based patronage networks. Ramos promoted policies of liberalisation and privatised infrastructure development. Annual growth rates reached 6.8 per cent in 1996. World Bank assistance to continue structural reform and anti-poverty programmes in the face of the regional economic crisis was stepped up with a loan of US $3 billion in December 1997 and approximately US $4.5 billion pledged in March 1999 (World Bank 1999*f*).

The Ramos administration introduced a Social Reform Agenda programme. Its 'Minimum Needs' approach embracing thirty-three indicators and targeting twenty poorest provinces, supposedly identified after extensive national consultations. But only marginal reduction of chronically unequal income distribution was achieved, with the share of the lowest 20 per cent of the population rising from 5 to 5.9 per cent from 1970–75 to 1990–96. During the same period the share of the highest 20 per cent declined from 56 to 49.6 per cent (World Bank 1999*e*). The Marcos administration did not record poverty data, but official poverty incidence declined between 1985 and 1994 from 49.2 to 40.2 per cent based on income measurement and from 32.7 to 23.4 per cent on expenditure measurement. Average annual population growth rate declined only gradually between 1970–75 and 1990–96 from 2.8 to 2.3 per cent,[9] with opposition from the Catholic Church inhibiting the impact of official programmes.

Encouraged by the restoration of democracy, the presence of NGOs and other advocacy groups post-Marcos became pervasive across all fields of policy and social action.[10] Competition for influence became intense (Macuja 1992), not least with political parties who commonly see themselves as prime agents for popular representation, and may resent potential challenges to their capacity to dispense patronage and protection (Kothari 1984; Eldridge 1985). Both Presidents Aquino and Ramos made strong efforts to involve NGOs in decision-making processes, institutionalising their role within the Local Government Code. Assessments of their performance in terms of capacity, outlook and autonomy from the state and other powerful interests has varied widely (Rood 1998: 129–30; Hutchcroft 1998: 40–1).

President Estrada was elected in 1998 with strong support from poorer groups. Rapprochement with Marcos family and associates, and proposals for constitutional change which would allow Presidents a second term soon built up strong opposition among both the urban middle class and social activist groups. Confidence in the autonomy of Filipino media was called into question by Estrada's threats of libel action against the *Manila Times*, causing it to apologise unreservedly for allegations of corruption against presidential palace staff. The apology caused divisions among senior staff, evoking a strong statement by journalists, intellectuals and others claiming that the affair undermined press freedom.[11]

By 2000, accusations of gross corruption and misappropriation of funds led to calls for Estrada's impeachment from Catholic Church leaders, business groups and a broad spectrum of popular advocacy groups. Under procedures laid down in Article XI, Section 3 of the Constitution, one-third of the House of Representatives may vote for impeachment, which requires a two-thirds majority in the Senate to succeed. In that event, the Vice-President assumes the President's powers.

Motions for impeachment on charges of 'economic plunder', which carry the death penalty under Filipino law, passed the House of Representatives on 13 September 2000. As the President sought the necessary eight Senators to reject the charges, Vice-President Arroyo was threatened with sedition charges by Estrada supporters for calling for the President's resignation. Expectations of acquittal were confirmed on 16 January 2001, when the Senate, by an 11–10 majority, rejected calls to compel disclosure of crucial information concerning bank accounts. Prosecutors walked out, compelling Presiding Officer Chief Justice Hilario Davide to adjourn proceedings pending action by the House of Representatives. Popular anger spilled on to the streets, with several violent clashes between pro and anti-Estrada demonstrators. On 19 January, Estrada left the Presidential Palace and was declared as unable to govern. Arroyo was sworn in as President. Estrada asserted his continuing status as President. The Supreme Court subsequently ruled against him, clearing the way for criminal and fraud charges.

Serious questions continue to be raised over the constitutionality of Estrada's ouster by commentators as diverse as Lee Kuan Yew[12] and leftist veterans from the 'people's power' movement which overthrew Ferdinand Marcos (Alford 2001b). Estrada had neither formally resigned nor been dismissed. Withdrawal of military support for the President in face of popular outrage could set dangerous precedents. Notwithstanding the actions of President Estrada and eleven supporting senators in undermining confidence in democratic processes and the 'rule of law', in this case 'people's power' seems to have dangerously stretched the democratically endorsed 1987 Constitution.

More positively, Estrada's overthrow can be seen as evidence of Filipino democracy's resilience, despite some lack of constitutional punctiliousness in its manner of achievement. Overall, the Philippines appears to be progressing on both civil-political and socio-economic rights fronts. But doubts remain whether state institutions and ideology are strong enough to deal decisively with powerful oligarchic interest groups, and more recently Peronista style mass violence by Estrada supporters.

Previous emphasis on a 'strong state' as necessary to development has given way to a more confused neo-liberal outlook, in which privatisation has become the main weapon. Hutchcroft (1995: 26–9) questions whether Filipino state institutions are capable of providing minimum political foundations for economic transformation, in supplying electricity and other vital infrastructure, protection from illegal logging, arbitrating business disputes, or even-handed regulation of the financial system. Liberal perspectives are also challenged by analyses emphasising democratic change of a kind which goes beyond institutions and processes to effectively confront structural links between class interests and state power (Hutchison 1993: 209).

Since President Ramos' election in 1992, the military has ceased to pose serious threats to civilian rule, although low level violence remains endemic across society. Crime and kidnapping, often involving the military have proved pervasive threats to human rights (Robles 1997a). Killing and kidnapping of journalists has further inflamed an environment of conflict and lawlessness. Truth here is confused by claims and counter-claims about the practice of journalists carrying arms either for self-protection or, in the view of critical colleagues, to act as self-appointed enforcers of justice or make money by obtaining additional gun licences (Robles 1997b).

Armed opposition, together with the state's response, still poses considerable threats to social stability and democratic order. The New People's Army (NPA), though weakened and divided, retains capacity to strike at the security forces in outlying regions, while urban guerilla groups are able to cause occasional disruption. The long-running Islamic insurgency appeared to have been settled in September 1996 when the Moro National Liberation Front (MNLF), signed a formal peace agreement. MNLF leader Misauri was subsequently elected Governor of the Autonomous Region of Moslem Mindanao (ARMM), covering four out of fourteen provinces which had given majority support. He also chairs the Southern Philippines Council for Peace and Development, which oversees the development of all (mostly Christian) provinces and cities.[13] However, the MNLF's factional rival, the Moro Islamic Liberation Front (MILF) and other militant Islamic factions have continued the insurgency. Some have embarrassed the government with a series of kidnappings. Land issues, together with rising food shortages and population growth remain a central focus of conflict (Canuday 1999).

Residual violence in civil society and illegal use of state power and resources has created widespread popular disaffection, which threatens democratic consolidation and establishment of a political culture based on respect for universal human rights.

Thailand

Thailand avoided colonisation, unlike other Southeast Asian countries, enabling it to adapt to a changing external environment while maintaining continuity in its core institutions, centred on the monarchy and Buddhist religion. Thai monarchs were historically revered as absolute rulers, carrying a divine mandate. During the nineteenth century, a succession of reforming kings embarked on modernisation programmes, thereby creating a technocrat cum bureaucrat class and an increasingly powerful military. A military coup in 1932 replaced absolute with constitutional monarchy. But prior to the 1990s, political participation was confined to a limited elite. Thailand experienced thirteen constitutions, variously classified as democratic, non-democratic and semi-democratic, between 1932 and 1987, with thirteen general elections, sixteen coups, forty-three cabinets, sixteen prime ministers, of which six were military and ten civilian (Samudavanija 1994). While parliamentary institutions were invariably re-established, indicating their underlying legitimacy, constitutions were designed to serve the interests of their creators, usually by arranging for bureaucrats and military to join cabinets or exercise veto powers and influence via a Senate elected on a restricted franchise.

In a major push for democratic change in 1973, student demonstrations triggered the downfall of the military-led government. A new constitution and elections followed in 1975, but reform parties failed to win a clear majority. Extensive peasant and labour mobilisation alarmed conservative forces, leading to street clashes in Bangkok. Martial law was declared in October 1976, followed by a severe 'anti-communist' crackdown. This was relaxed one year later, following another coup by younger military moderates. Amnesty was offered to dissidents and a relatively liberal constitution promulgated in 1979, followed by elections. Military cooperation with democratic forces grew during the 1980s, under the leadership of General Prem Tinsulanond, though there were unsuccessful coups attempts in 1981 and 1985.

In 1988, Chatichai Choonhavan was elected as Prime Minister with a parliamentary majority, and Thailand finally seemed set on a firm course towards electoral democracy. But Chatichai was overthrown by a military coup led by General Suchinda Khraprayun in 1991, on the pretext of eliminating corruption. Following military dominated elections in March 1992, plans to install Suchinda as Prime Minister set off mass demonstrations, culminating in a violent crackdown by security forces in Bangkok in May 1992, in which over fifty people were killed. Following the King's intervention, Suchinda stood down and an interim government under the widely respected Anand Panyarachun pushed through constitutional changes. These required the Prime Minister to be an elected Member of Parliament (MP), and significantly reduced the powers of the Senate.

Thailand's 1997 constitution[14] sets out principles of transparency, accountability and checks and balances between all arms of government, based on specification of their respective powers. The ninety-nine member Constitution Drafting Assembly (CDA), comprising one member from each of Thailand's seventy-six provinces plus legal and other experts, undertook extensive popular consultation. Its autonomy from political pressures and consequent legitimacy were enhanced by arrangements whereby Parliament could only approve or reject but not amend the draft, which was then put to popular referendum (Amnesty International 1997*a*).

Chapter VIII establishes a network of Courts of Justice, Constitutional and Administrative courts with substantial powers to check unaccountable or unlawful executive action, but with courts themselves bound by clear constitutional guidelines. Structures of accountability are strengthened by provision for Parliamentary Ombudsmen (Sections 196–198), a Counter Corruption Commission (Sections 297–311), a State Audit Commission (Section 312) and an Election Commission (Sections 136–148). Persons assuming political office must declare assets and debts, lists of which must be publicly reviewed, checked and certified, both at the time of appointment and departure. Those giving false reports face five year bans and other penalties (Sections 291–5). One-fourth of members of the National Assembly can ask the Commission to investigate any of their number suspected of corruption, or may request the Supreme Court to launch a similar investigation against any Commission member (Sections 299–300).

The House of Representatives consists of 500 members, with 400 representing individual constituencies and 100 chosen under a party-list system on a proportional representation basis. In an attempt to reduce notorious party-switching, candidates on party lists must be party members. Senators are elected for six years and may not be re-elected to the next Senate term (Section 126, para 3). The Senate's powers to delay either money or other bills have been effectively reduced to six months (Sections 175–180), though it has powers to seek information, express no confidence, and request investigations by judicial and other bodies. The King can delay Bills for up to ninety days. A two-thirds majority of the National Assembly is required to override his veto (Sections 93–94). Senators may not hold public office or be members of political parties. But indirect election as provincial representatives may enhance their influence.

Several elections between 1992 and 1998 were characterised by entrenched vote-buying, patronage and money politics. Elections in January 2001 also saw significant violence including widespread intimidation of canvassers (Buriram 2001; East 2001). One apparent reason was increased pressure exercised by the National Counter Corruption Commission,[15] using its new powers to deeply probe members from all parties. The Interior Minister under Chuan Leepkai was banned from politics for five years. One week prior to the 2001 elections, Thaksin Shinawatra, leader of the Thai Rak-Thai (Thai Love Thai) Party, was convicted of false assets declaration in 1997. His party subsequently retained an outright majority, following re-staged elections after the Election Commission had disqualified over fifty originally elected candidates. Thaksin has continued as Prime Minister pending appeal to the Constitutional Court.

Reflecting a widening economic gap, sharp differences in political culture and outlook have emerged during the 1990s between Bangkok, where democratic-oriented parties dominate, and much of rural and regional Thailand, particularly the impoverished north east, where traditional patron–client styles of politics persist, including direct vote-buying. The first stream, led by the Democratic Party under Chuan Leepkai, were broadly successful at elections in 1992 and 1998. This stream is viewed favourably in international business circles and has proved responsive to calls for economic and governance reforms. The second stream dominated under Prime Ministers Banharn and Chavalit following the 1995 election.

Thaksin's campaign in 2001 combined traditional patronage politics with new styles of populism. Widespread poverty, linked to slow economic recovery, generated impatience with the Leepkai government's 'dull' reform agenda, in sharp contrast with Thaksin's charisma, economic and cultural nationalist appeal. Many were pre-pared to regard his false assets declaration as a 'technical' error, hoping that as a multi-millionaire he would prove less vulnerable to corruption. Thaksin's over-whelming victory avoided the need to form a multi-party coalition – a long-standing cause of instability and corruption (Alford 2001a). Thus the popular legitimacy of Thai democracy and 'rule of law' imperatives may prove at odds, at least in the short term, as the Constitutional Court's pending ruling on Thaksin's case takes effect.

The Buddhist religion, while retaining its organisational and spiritual autonomy, has traditionally supported the social order, both directly through the Buddhist Sangha and by emphasising personal spiritual pilgrimage within a context of outward conformity to social customs and hierarchy, linked to values of harmony and non-competitiveness. Respect for authority is to be balanced by the powerful exhibiting moral virtue. While this traditional outlook tends towards pragmatic acceptance of the status quo, many monks preach against corruption, environmental destruction and materialist trends. There is also an individualist strand to Buddhist spirituality, which influences, for example, the formation of meditation and prayer sects among professional and business groups, which have in varying ways influ-enced the anti-corruption movement in Bangkok at the base of the democracy struggle in 1991–2.

The monarchy as an institution, particularly the present King Bhumipol, is deeply respected, even revered throughout Thai society, and disrespect to him is regarded as a near treasonable offence. The monarch has played crucial mediat-ing roles in crises, supporting pro-democracy forces in 1973 and 1992, more moderate democratising versus right-wing military in 1981, though endorsing a military takeover in 1976. The continuing thread to his exercise of monarchical powers is the preservation of national unity. King Bhumipol is also pro-active in specific policy areas, notably rural development, local administration and envi-ronment, thereby forging closer rapport between the royal family and hill tribes.

The military's power appears to be finally waning after some sixty years of dominance. Military leaders have long assumed a 'guardian' role in upholding national identity and institutions, employing sweeping definitions of 'national enemies', commonly labelling pro-democracy activists as communists. While originally the major agent in limiting the king's powers, the military invariably claims to act in his name, though ultimately obliged to obey him. As in Indonesia, the military has played multiple modernising and developmental roles, including extensive involvement in economic enterprises. Its control over media is threatened by recent legislation (Nanuam 1999). But internal disunity, linked to factionalism and shifting alliances with bureaucrats and parliamentarians, has limited scope for military dictatorship.

Concentration of administrative and economic power in Bangkok has resulted in dependence and lack of regional and local initiative. Chapter IX of the 1997 Constitution indicates a broad plan to devolve powers to directly elected local administrative councils, which are to enjoy 'autonomy ... in accordance with the principle of self-government according to the will of the people in the locality' (Section 282). Effective transfer of resources will be crucial to successful outcomes.

Economic growth rates averaged above 8 per cent annually between 1980 and 1992. Gross National Product (GNP) per capita increased from US $810 to US $2110 over a decade from the mid 1980s, with life expectancy at birth reaching sixty-eight. Literacy rose from 50 to 90 per cent between the early 1960s and 1990s, with a rise in Thailand's HDI index from 0.465 to 0.798 between 1970 and 1992 (Neher 1995: 44, 190). Although 76 per cent were reported to have access to safe drinking water, more rapid investment in industrial relative to agricultural development, together with other 'urban-biased' public spending policies, continues to widen the urban–rural gap.

In recovering from the economic crisis, Thailand gained international confidence by supporting orthodox principles of economic management and good governance. At the same time, democratisation strengthened mobilisation by non-governmental groups. The Forum of the Poor organised many thousands of members to camp in front of government offices in Bangkok from late January until early May 1997 protesting government inaction on disputes involving land rights, problems of the urban poor, construction of dams and other projects resulting in loss of livelihood for farmers and fishermen. Proposed community forestry legislation generated further protest (Jesdapipat 1997).

While evolution of democratic politics may ultimately lead to greater diffusion of citizen participation, party structures as yet lack popular roots and internally democratic organisation, with electoral competition based more on personalities than policy and ideology. Successful mobilisation by NGOs and other groups in support of the 1997 Constitution have caused some to regard them as the 'real opposition'. But others are sceptical towards NGOs acting as self-appointed representatives of the people without having to account for their actions. Independence from the political machinery enables them to undertake campaigns and initiatives impossible to others.

Labour groups have intensified pressures on both political and enterprise fronts. But despite a comprehensive new labour law enacted in August 1998 (Human Rights Watch 1999*a*), labour remains in a relatively weak position, worsened by the 1997 economic downturn. High levels of rural poverty cause a continuing influx of labour into Bangkok, swelled by migrant workers from more impoverished neighbouring countries such as Bangladesh, Cambodia, Laos and Myanmar. Around 600,000 are estimated to be working illegally, while the government wages running battles with 'people smuggling' syndicates (Charoensuthipan 1999; Bai-ngern 1999).

Hewison (1996) has argued that business, and the middle class generally, remain ambivalent towards democracy, questioning its compatibility with political order and economic stability, with militant labour posing a special threat. However, regularised laws and mechanisms for arbitrating disputes are seen as essential to conducting globally-oriented business. Transition to democracy may thus be a convenient arrangement for ruling elites, without indicating ideological change. Though plausible, this thesis fails to account for the continuing upsurge of mobilisation outside the control of elites, whose divisions open up space for new groups to participate in the formal political sphere.

Has Thailand finally broken through to sustainable democratisation or will the present period prove to be yet one more phase in a cycle of semi-democratic cum authoritarian rule? Pessimists see corruption, electoral violence and money politics intensified during the January 2001 campaign, as aggravating the rich–poor gap, undermining Thailand's fragile democratic institutions, and reversing improvements in human rights. Optimists draw confidence from the survival and evident strengthening of democratic institutions during the post-1997 economic crisis, broadly-based social mobilisation and constitutional entrenchment of independent anti-corruption and electoral commissions. While the independence and integrity of these institutions has yet to be fully tested, the 1997 Constitution provides clear remedies for wrongdoing.

Thailand's long period of semi-authoritarian rule can be partly credited with sustained economic growth, but it also promoted uneven development and associated inequalities. Democratic consolidation requires broadening of support beyond the urban middle class, by addressing the needs of farmers, landless peasants, urban labour and minorities, and overcoming pervasive exploitation of women and children.

Democratic consolidation in Southeast Asia

A comparative global study by Larry Diamond (1999) explores conditions under which democracy is likely to take root, with a primary focus on consolidating recently established democratic systems rather than their initiation. Over and above specific institutions, processes, and other supports, democratic systems need legitimacy. However great a constitution's philosophical appeal; citizens must be willing to defend it (Weingast 1997: 251). This will depend greatly on perceived benefits, citizens' sense of ownership and potential alternatives.

To test the depth of democratic consolidation, Diamond (1999: 68–70) proposes normative and behavioural indicators at the level of elites, organisations and the mass public. At the elite level, most significant opinion-formers, cultural, business and political leaders should uphold democracy as the best form of government, supporting constitutionally based laws and processes in their public comments and practice. In organisational terms, the right to pursue power by peaceful means should be mutually respected and illegal methods and incitement to violence and intolerance outlawed. At the popular level, a majority of at least 70 per cent should support democracy as the best system of government, with no more than 15 per cent actively preferring authoritarian models. No anti-democratic movement, party or organisation should enjoy a significant mass following, with little or no public tolerance of violent or illegal means of political expression.

Not a few western democracies would find difficulty in passing all these tests, although only fringe groups may transgress the behavioural requirements. In some western countries, the required 70 per cent positive belief in democracy could probably be achieved only in a negative sense, in terms of the late Sir Winston Churchill's adage – that democracy is the worst system of government in the world, except for all the others! The USA struggles to attain a 50 per cent turnout at Presidential and Congressional elections, while scepticism towards politicians is pervasive in established democracies. Though partly due to conscious rejection of low standards, money politics and the like, much apathy is due either to lack of perceived relevance to personal interest, or to a more basic sense of alienation.

Consolidation in recently democratising countries is by no means an automatic process. Some may retain an empty institutional shell, with democratic norms and processes regularly violated, but with minimally free and fair elections held frequently enough to ward off external sanctions. Without systematic democratic deepening, embracing the whole gamut of regime performance, such states will sooner or later regress (Diamond 1999: 73–116). The behaviour of state officials may enhance or weaken respect for democratic institutions, legal and constitutional processes, setting off correspondingly positive or negative cycles in the wider society. Economic performance is also salient in bringing credit or discredit on governments in areas of vital personal concern to citizens, even though its causal relationship with particular forms of government is problematic.

Diamond's model is salient in the currently volatile Southeast Asian context. Several countries are in highly uncertain states of transition. Among ASEAN's ten countries, the model appears most relevant to Thailand, the Philippines and Indonesia, which have recently gained or regained constitutional democratic institutions. There are apparently high levels of elite consensus favouring democracy in Thailand and the Philippines. Popular mobilisation supporting democratic values is strong in both countries, though institutions and processes remain threatened. Politicians are only partly responsive to demands from groups outside formalised political structures. With limited internal democracy, parties are based more on personalities than policy or ideology. The impact of corruption, violence and criminality on public life, particularly in the Philippines, remains the most serious systemic weakness in both countries.

Indonesia is difficult to categorise, having recently experienced its first broadly 'free and fair' election since 1955, but with the direction of constitutional and institutional reforms still uncertain and the future role of the military unresolved. Nevertheless, Indonesia has a long history of social and political mobilisation, based on widespread popular awareness, which proved major factors in overthrowing President Suharto. These participatory traditions will provide strong in-principle support for democratic institutions. But Indonesia's weak democratic culture, together with endemic corruption and poverty, is likely to sustain instability over many years.

Malaysia and Singapore articulate and practice their own unique brands of illiberal cum Asian democracy. Dissent and advocacy of alternative systems are marginalised in Malaysia, and virtually outlawed in Singapore. However, high electoral support for ruling parties is in large measure uncoerced. Malaysia has historically enjoyed high levels of party membership, particularly among Malays in both ruling and opposition parties. Sustained economic growth and relatively broad distribution of benefits has been impressive in Singapore and, until the 1997 downturn, in Malaysia also. There is no certainty that either country will move in the near future towards forms of democracy based on international standards of civil and political rights.

Cambodia appears most to resemble Diamond's empty shell example. Two national elections have been conducted under UN scrutiny during the 1990s, in a situation of extreme dependence on international economic assistance. Cambodia's institutions and processes threaten principles of democracy and human rights at every turn. But the traumas of the past three decades must always be borne in mind. Against that background, the limited extent of democratisation so far achieved could be considered encouraging.

Vietnam and Laos, as Communist one-party states, and Brunei under the benign but authoritarian rule of its Sultan, are at this stage obviously irrelevant to any assessment of democratic consolidation. Each are in their own way gradually opening to regional and international influences. Brunei is the second most economically prosperous country in ASEAN, but tolerates no kind of political dissent or even debate. Laos has tentatively begun the process of opening up its economy, with the Friendship Bridge across the Mekong river providing a direct road link with Thailand. Both Laos and Vietnam are cautiously following the Chinese road in seeking to combine capitalist development with continuing political monopoly by the Communist Party. Vietnam has an embryo democratic movement, though at this stage overshadowed by the strength of expatriate lobby groups. Although serious restrictions on civil and political rights continue (Human Rights Watch 1999*b*), notably in relation to freedom of religion, Vietnam seems largely free from mass brutality against its population. The opposite applies in Myanmar, which evidences no plans for even minimal democratisation. But the strength of its democracy movement, and quality of leadership under Aung San Suu Kyi, will provide a strong popular support base when democratic systems are eventually established.

Diamond's model, by bringing civil society and associated modes of popular mobilisation into the picture, goes beyond Huntington's limited, process view of democracy. However, it falls short of the more globalised and multi-contextual concepts of Held, Falk and others canvassed in Chapter 1. It also tends to view economic and social aspects as instrumental to democratising objectives. Asian democracy paradigms pursue a reverse approach, adapting selected democratic elements to social, economic and state-building objectives.

3 ASEAN and international human rights

The chapter begins with an overview of regional perspectives on UN human rights regimes, drawing out links with Asian values and opposition thereto identified in Chapter 2. Brief comparison of the five UN Security Council permanent members' stance provides a benchmark for assessing individual ASEAN countries' participation in major covenants and conventions. Cambodia, which has accepted extensive UN compliance monitoring as part of its international rehabilitation and Myanmar,[1] which has outraged international opinion by extreme human rights abuses, are the focus of special study. ASEAN's stance towards these two countries illustrates deep contradictions in its human rights outlook. The chapter concludes by assessing the emerging roles of national human rights institutions and associated regional networks, particularly their capacity to link ASEAN states with UN human rights regimes.

Regional outlook towards UN human rights regimes

The consensus principle, which lies at the core of ASEAN's ethos and practice, requires countries to avoid interference in each others' internal affairs and to cooperate in resisting outside intervention. However, finding consensus at either pragmatic or normative levels is proving elusive, as ASEAN states find it easier to engage in polemical debates with the west than to come up with practical alternative approaches (Acharya 1995: 173, 179). Asian values rhetoric only thinly disguises the lack of agreed core values and the pervasiveness of inter-ethnic and religious rivalry across Southeast Asia.

The need to formulate a regional response to a UN sponsored global human rights consultation in 1993 significantly sharpened Asian values advocacy. Reluctance to engage in direct confrontation with the UN as an institution was managed by stressing national sovereignty, protesting against western, particularly US dominance, and demanding reforms of the UN, including broader Security Council representation and reducing or eliminating the veto powers of the five permanent members (Camilleri *et al.* 2000: 27).

Several ASEAN governments have criticised the 1948 UDHR on the grounds that many states were not yet independent and had no part in its formulation. Assertions of universalism are portrayed as deriving from western philosophical and cultural assumptions. But the two major covenants based on the UDHR, the ICCPR and ICESCR, were adopted by the UN General Assembly in 1966, after most Southeast Asian countries had gained independence.

The issue of relativism versus universalism featured prominently in the 1993 UN consultation process. The Bangkok Declaration by Asian governments affirmed that while human rights are universal in nature, they are set in the context of '... a dynamic and evolving process of international norm-setting, bearing in mind the significance of national and regional particularities and various historical, cultural and religious background' (Tang 1995: 25). In Thai Prime Minister, Chuan Leepkai's words, '... although there is only one set of fundamental human rights for whatever part of the world... implementation ... (must) vary because of differences in socio-economic, historical and cultural backgrounds' (Hitchcock 1995: 9).

Practical choices centre on whether such particularities will mildly vary or drastically strip the idea of universal human rights of substantive content. The 1993 VDPA guarded against the latter danger by asserting that states have a duty to protect all human rights and fundamental freedoms, irrespective of their political, economic or cultural systems. The issue, therefore, hinges on the 'margin of appreciation' allowed for local differences in interpretation and implementation (Tang 1995: 25–38).

Scope for variation can be read into the text of some human rights instruments. Thus, Article 29(2) of the UDHR allows for legally determined limitations of rights and freedoms to secure recognition and respect for those of others, meeting the just requirements of morality, public order and general welfare in a democratic society.[2] Tang argues that the intention of this clause requires that rights be read broadly and limitations narrowly. Nevertheless, a 'margin of appreciation' can be allowed with regard to public interest or morals, as these vary even between democratic societies, and between liberals and conservatives within them. Differences regarding political morality justify variation, given the value placed by Asian societies on social harmony and respect for elders, and lesser support for rights to publish pornography, advocate homosexuality or make statements considered offensive or blasphemous to religions. Similarly, China's one child policy and Singapore's compulsory urine test for drug addiction are seen as unacceptable invasions of privacy in the west, but as legitimate trade-offs for public health and welfare by many Asians (Tang 1995: 33–6).

In an effort to meet the universalist position half way, Mahbubani acknowledged the need for minimum civilised codes of behaviour which would outlaw torture, arbitrary killings, slavery and disappearances, which no one would claim as part of their cultural heritage. But limited recognition of universality should not be used to deny or mask the reality of diversity (Mahbubani 1998: 78). Tang sees basic rights to life, liberty, justice, freedom from violence in a universalist light, along with contingent rights derived from modern ideas and circumstances, such as universal and equal suffrage, freedom of marriage choice, social security benefits and minimum legal protections from the state and other powerful institutions. However, civil and political rights grounded in ideas of personal autonomy are more relative (Tang 1995: 27–31).

The Commission for a New Asia's proposals on human rights (1994: 21–30) seek to integrate the broad principles of the ICCPR and ICESCR, and the UN Declaration on the RTD with a moderate version of Asian values. These affirm rights to economic, social, cultural and religious self-determination, including national economic sovereignty in disposing national wealth and resources; freedom from hunger and absolute poverty; health and education; employment with just wages, working conditions, occupational health and safety; protection and nurturing of families and children, with social security where necessary; marriage only by free consent; freedom of thought, conscience, religion, cultural practices and preferences; personal privacy and honour; freedom of movement and residence; intellectual and cultural freedom; full participation in economic life; equal social dignity and respect, eliminating caste and class discrimination.

Regarding civil and political rights, the Commission (1994: 25–30) affirms a basic right not to be arbitrarily deprived of one's life, with a phasing out of the death penalty. Accused persons are to be considered innocent until proved guilty, enjoy access to legal assistance and not be subject to retrospective punishment. Equality under the law is to be guaranteed, with universal access to a fair, transparent and independent legal and judicial process. Freedom of expression, association and peaceful assembly are to be assured, subject only to restrictions in Article 18(3) of the ICCPR regarding respect for rights and reputations of others; protection of national security of public order, public health or morals. All expressions of national, racial or religious hatred are to be prohibited. Rights to democracy and representative government are nevertheless to be balanced by a right to order and freedom from anarchy and chaos. ICCPR, Article 4(1), allowing suspension of democratic rights in time of public emergency threatening the life of a nation, is cited in support, subject to carefully defined limitations laid down elsewhere in Article 4.

Overall, the Commission's report conveys mixed messages. Despite close informal links between many Commission members and their respective governments, parallels with the two major UN human rights covenants go well beyond the official, indifferent, even hostile stance of several ASEAN states. But neither the possibility nor desirability of ratifying major UN human rights instruments were canvassed, which could have proved premature and even counter-productive, in light of prevailing consensus norms in East Asian diplomacy.

The need for responsibilities to balance rights has been a familiar theme in Asian values discourse. This principle is acknowledged in Article 19(3) of the ICCPR. Demands nevertheless mounted for a UN declaration on this score, though it is unclear whether this was intended as complementary or as a substitute for the UDHR. In March 1999, the UN General Assembly effectively turned regional demands on their head by adopting the Declaration on the Right and Responsibility of Individuals, Groups and Organs of Society to Promote and Protect Universally Recognized Human Rights and Fundamental Freedoms.[3]

The Declaration asserts responsibilities of individuals, societal groups and governments to promote and not impede human rights, and for necessary information and facilities to be provided. The UDHR and associated UN treaties remain the standard frame of reference, and nothing in the new declaration is to be interpreted as contravening them. NGOs' role in promoting and protecting human rights is affirmed in the preamble, as are rights of individuals and groups to associate for this purpose (Article 12), the right to call governments to account for human rights violations (Article 8) and to seek redress for abuses (Article 9). Article 10 forbids participation in violating human rights 'by act or by failure to act where required', while no one is to be punished for refusing such participation. Rejection of regional doctrines of relativism and national autonomy could scarcely be more complete.

UNCHR interpretations of the indivisibility principle have been more favourable to Asian concerns. Under the leadership of High Commissioner Mary Robinson, the Declaration on the RTD was established as a key element in its strategy for implementing the VDPA's goal of a holistic and integrated approach to human rights by the entire United Nations system (UNCHR 1998*d*: Para 23). The issue of balancing statist or state-capitalist and participatory models of development nevertheless remains a bone of contention between Southeast Asian governments and civil society groups.

Compliance with UN human rights treaties

Participation in UN human rights instruments can most realistically be seen as a necessary but not sufficient condition in assessing states' commitment to universal human rights. While countries' ratification record may not fully represent their performance, it represents at least *prima facie* acceptance of international accountability. Together with reservations and declarations against various treaties, it can shed useful light on states' underlying outlook, idiosyncrasies and understandings of national interest in dealing with international human rights obligations. Participation also influences domestic awareness of human rights outcomes from foreign policy actions.

A recent shift can be noted among East Asian states in the politics of engagement with UN human rights regimes. Governments were formerly more sanguine in allowing adoption of new human rights instruments, as participation remains within the control of individual states. But combined pressures to accede to UN treaties from the international community and domestic civil society has induced greater wariness in accepting new human rights instruments, and stronger efforts to shape UNCHR processes in recent years. Amnesty International (1998) charges that consensus principles weaken reporting and compliance, allow obstruction by a minority of governments to bring pressures for acceptance of lowest common denominator standards. Drafting of the ICCPR provides historical precedent for majority voting. This should be employed to finalise the Declaration on the Rights of Human Rights Defenders after twelve years without agreement, overcome delays in drafting optional protocols to the conventions on torture and children's rights, and reject draft rules designed to weaken powers of thematic special rapporteurs.

A UN sponsored workshop in Teheran in February/March 1998 adopted a Framework for Regional Technical Cooperation in the Asia Pacific to develop national human rights action plans, education and national institutions (UNCHR 1998*b*). The Framework's aim is to strengthen national capacities as a basis for regional links with the UN system. But provisions for choice by member states of priority areas according with national conditions opens the door for a selective approach to human rights.

Security Council permanent members

In the light of international pressure experienced by ASEAN states, it is useful to compare stances adopted by the five permanent members of the UN Security Council, whose compliance with key treaties is set out in Table 3.1.

This table indicates that France and Russia participate in all listed treaties other than the Second Protocol to the ICCPR outlawing the death penalty. The United Kingdom (UK) participates in all except the First ICCPR Optional Protocol, enabling groups and individuals to access the UNCHR. China and the USA are only party to six and four treaties respectively.

Despite its history of extensive human rights violations, the former Union of Soviet Socialist Republics (USSR) ratified most of the above treaties within a few years of their adoption, acceding to the Refugees Convention in 1993 and the First Optional Protocol to the ICCPR in 1991. The only reservation consistently entered by the USSR, and not revoked by the Russian Federation, was against articles confining access to treaties to UN member states. Such reservations were directed against dependent territories of western countries, as part of an anti-colonialist propaganda campaign. Apart from one fierce protest in 1983 against 'Democratic Kampuchea' under Pol Pot signing international conventions, USSR and Russian reservations have been limited and technical in scope.

The People's Republic of China has yet to ratify either the ICESCR or ICCPR, although it has signed both. However, it ratified more specialist conventions – CERD, CEDAW, CAT, the Genocide and Refugees Conventions during the 1980s

Table 3.1 Ratification of UN Human Rights Treaties by Security Council permanent members (Entry into force date as at 28 March 2001)

UN treaty	China	France	Russian Federation	United Kingdom	USA
ICCPR	—	4/2/81	23/3/76	20/8/76	8/9/92
ICESCR	—	4/2/81	3/1/76	20/8/76	—
CAT	3/11/88	26/6/87	26/6/87	7/1/89	20/11/94
CROC	1/4/92	6/9/90	15/9/90	15/1/92	—
CEDAW	3/9/81	13/1/84	3/9/81	7/5/86	—
CERD	28/1/82	27/8/71	6/3/69	6/4/69	20/11/94
Refugees	24/9/82	23/6/54	2/2/93	11/3/54	—
Genocide	18/4/83	14/10/50	3/5/54	30/1/70	25/11/88
1st ICCPR Protocol	—	17/5/84	1/1/92	—	—
2nd ICCPR Protocol	—	—	—	10/12/99	—

Details regarding states' ratification of treaties and associated reservations Online. Available. http://www.unhchr.ch/tbs/doc.nsf and http://www.unhchr.ch/html/intlinst.htm

and CROC in 1992. China does not recognise the competence of the Committee against Torture in Article 20, which is crucial to the operation of that Convention. Detailed procedures requiring cooperation with states, confidentiality during the inquiry process and only summary publication of findings have proved insufficient to satisfy China's sensitivities. Certainly, many states regard naming in annual reports to the General Assembly under Article 24 as a powerful sanction. China takes a consistently strong line in defence of national sovereignty in this as in other fields.

The US Department of State reports on every country's human rights performance other than its own. The USA has steadfastly refused to ratify the ICE-SCR, which it signed in 1977, but eventually ratified the ICCPR in 1992 with substantial reservations. It acceded to the Genocide Convention in 1988 and CERD and CAT in 1994, but not yet CEDAW, CROC, the Refugees Convention or either optional protocol to the ICCPR. Treaty ratification is subject to the 'advice and consent' of the Senate, which routinely insists on reservations affirming that UN covenants and conventions are not self-executing and that no provisions may override US laws and Constitution. Many, especially European states, protest that invoking national law to claim general exemptions breaches Article 27 of the Vienna Convention on the Law of Treaties,[4] and creates doubt as to the extent of commitment to a treaty's objectives, thereby undermining the basis of international law.

The USA asserts discretion to discriminate on grounds of race, colour, sex, language, religion, political or other opinion, national or social origin, property, birth or any other status, forbidden in Articles 2(1) and 26 of the ICCPR, where this is 'rationally related to a legitimate governmental objective.' Rights are retained against separating accused from convicted prisoners, as required in Articles 10(2a and 3), while goals of punishment, deterrence, and incapacitation are affirmed as legitimate purposes for a penitentiary system, not diminished by requirements in Article 10(3) that reformation and rehabilitation should be the essential aim.

Citing Article 5(2) in support, the US asserts, in relation to Article 19(3) of the ICCPR which permits some restrictions on freedom of expression, that it will not accept lesser freedoms than in its own Constitution. It also refuses to authorise legislation or other action prohibiting war propaganda, incitement to national, racial and religious hatred required in Article 20, where these would restrict rights of free speech and association protected by US laws and Constitution. A similar reservation was entered in relation to the racial discrimination convention. US interpretations of several aspects of CERD assert distinctions between public and private life, in order to protect individual privacy against governmental interference.

The US stance towards the Convention against Torture is confusing, requiring that 'in order to constitute torture, an act must be specifically intended to inflict severe physical or mental pain or suffering'. Acquiescence by public officials requires them to have prior awareness of such activity and thereafter breach their legal responsibility to intervene. Non-compliance with applicable procedural standards is not, of itself to be regarded as constituting torture. These reservations are seen by several countries as potentially diminishing responsibility of public officials for behaviour of their subordinates. The US has itself been recently subject to a UN Special Rapporteur's report relating to procedures during arrest and interrogation of criminal suspects (Human Rights Watch 1999*c*).

A similarly obtuse approach to the Genocide Convention evoked outraged responses from a more than usually large number of countries. Even Britain protested against the US exempting itself from all dispute settling procedures under Article 9, to the extent of omitting the customary statement that its objection did not constitute a barrier to the treaty coming into force between the two countries. US participation in any international penal tribunal, as provided in Article 6, depends on a treaty being entered into on each occasion with Senate approval.

While both the UK and France have entered significant reservations in favour of their respective laws and constitution, they are more precise in specifying reasons. Where wider interpretative discretion is claimed, this is based on potential conflict with other covenant clauses or in terms of superior obligations over all other international agreements laid down in Article 103 of the UN Charter. Articles 1 and 2, specifying basic UN objectives are cited by both countries. In fact, Article 1(3) of the Charter includes 'promoting and encouraging respect for human rights and ... fundamental freedoms for all' among basic objectives, thereby invalidating claims of conflicting mandates.

France's reservations focus mainly on autonomy of its armed forces, and supremacy of French nationality and immigration laws determining residence of aliens. It resists potentially illiberal interpretations of 'family education' in Article 5(b) of CEDAW, insisting that no convention provision should be interpreted as prevailing over French laws more favourable to women. Both France and Britain protect their right to practice abortion by interpreting reference in Article 6(1) of CROC to children's 'inherent right to life' as applying only to live births. References in CEDAW's preamble to objectives of peace and nuclear disarmament are considered 'out of place' in this text. France's overall stance nevertheless appears supportive of the wider aims of UN human rights law, with strong attacks on reservations by states, including the USA, seeking open-ended exemptions from key treaty requirements.

France adopts a similar stance as the USA towards racist propaganda and organisations, but employs Article 5 of the ICCPR to claim superiority of fundamental rights and freedoms over requirements in Articles 4 of CERD and 20 of ICCPR for strict controls. Britain employs Article 19 of the ICCPR for this purpose, which focuses more precisely on freedom of speech and association. These more diplomatically subtle and legally precise approaches, manifesting more formal respect for UN processes, invite considerably fewer objections than those directed against the USA.

UK reservations, and special declarations are extensive. Apart from exemptions claimed earlier on behalf of dependent territories, on grounds of cultural and material conditions cited in Article 73 of the UN Charter, extensive reservations apply to Britain itself. Thus UK law concerning discipline within prisons is deemed to prevail over ICCPR requirements. The right to mix adult and juvenile offenders is maintained where this is deemed to be 'mutually beneficial'. UK nationality and immigration law is to prevail over provisions open to more liberal interpretations of entry–exit rights. Long-standing reservations and understandings in relation to ICESCR and CEDAW requirements for non-discrimination in employment, pay and conditions, social security, pensions, taxation, property and care of children were mostly revoked in 1995 and 1996. But bland declarations asserting conformity of UK affirmative action legislation to the requirements of Articles 1 and 4(1) of CEDAW have been retained, while the Throne and the entire system of peerages, titles of honour, armorial bearings, the affairs of religious denominations, and procedures for admission into the Armed Forces are declared as outside the scope of the Convention.

This brief survey indicates an overt diplomatic stance by Security Council permanent members, according clear precedence to their national interests and sovereignty. China and the USA are particularly uncompromising in exempting themselves from UN human rights obligations. Additionally, the US Congress refused for many years to pay overdue UN subscriptions. Britain and France, though more diplomatic, are versatile in avoiding inconvenient obligations and scrutiny. Selectivity and imbalance in rights covered, open-ended self-exemptions based on domestic practice and inadequate self-monitoring (Howard 1990) thus mirror the behaviour of most ASEAN states, freely labelled by the west as backsliding in human rights matters.

Finally, failure by the USA and China to ratify the ICESCR undercuts core UN principles of indivisibility and interdependence between major streams of rights. This undermines potential bases for dialogue between western and developing countries, and diminishes prospects for coherent responses to attacks on civil and political rights by non-western states. It also serves to weaken human rights consciousness and pressures on power holders in western countries, where full acceptance as *rights* of economic and social provisions in UN treaties would facilitate claims against governments and business in an environment where unemployment, declining labour rights, social security and services are keenly felt as domestic issues.

ASEAN ratification

ASEAN states' participation in the same ten major human rights treaties at the end of 1999 is indicated in Table 3.2.[5] Their overall record remains weak, but with some marked improvement during the latter part of the 1990s. As several countries have experienced major regime changes, timing and context are important in explaining apparently random patterns. Some states, notably Singapore, are more meticulous than others in only ratifying treaties they are prepared to support with domestic laws and policies.

At either end of the spectrum, the Philippines participates in nine treaties and Brunei only one. All ten countries are parties to the children's rights convention (CROC) and nine in the convention to eliminate discrimination against women (CEDAW). Indonesia, Malaysia, Singapore and Thailand have entered extensive and widely challenged reservations and interpretations of both conventions, as has Brunei to CROC. Conversely, no ASEAN country is willing to abandon capital punishment, the focus of the ICCPR's Second Optional Protocol. Only the Philippines allows individuals or groups to directly approach the UNCHR as per

Table 3.2 Ratification of UN Human Rights Treaties by ASEAN states (Date Entered into Force)

	Brunei	Cambodia	Indonesia	Laos	Malaysia	Myanmar	Philippines	Singapore	Thailand	Vietnam
ICCPR	—	26/8/92	—	—	—	—	23/1/87	—	29/1/97	24/12/82
ICESCR	—	26/8/92	—	—	—	—	3/1/76	—	5/12/99	24/12/82
CAT	—	14/11/92	27/11/98	—	—	—	26/6/87	—	—	—
CROC	26/1/96	14/11/92	5/10/90	7/6/91	19/3/95	14/8/91	20/9/90	4/11/95	26/4/92	2/9/90
CEDAW	—	14/11/92	13/10/84	13/9/81	4/8/95	21/8/97	4/9/81	5/11/95	8/9/85	19/3/82
CERD	—	28/12/86	25/7/99	24/3/74	—	—	4/1/69	—	—	9/7/82
Refugees	—	15/10/92[a]	—	—	—	—	22/7/81[a]	—	—	—
Genocide	—	14/10/50[a]	—	8/10/50[a]	20/12/94[a]	14/3/56[a]	7/7/50	18/8/95[a]	—	9/6/81[a]
1st ICCPR Protocol	—	—	—	—	—	—	22/11/89	—	—	—
2nd ICCPR Protocol	—	—	—	—	—	—	—	—	—	—

a   date of accession.

the First Optional Protocol. Only Cambodia and the Philippines have ratified the Convention on the Status of Refugees. Cambodia, Philippines, Thailand and Vietnam have ratified both the ICCPR and the ICESCR. Indonesia, Philippines and Cambodia participate in the CAT, while seven of the ten ASEAN countries support the anti-Genocide Convention, excluding Brunei, Indonesia and Thailand. Cambodia, Indonesia, Laos, Philippines and Vietnam support the anti-racial discrimination treaty (CERD).

Of founding ASEAN countries, only Thailand and the Philippines are parties to the International Covenant on Social, Cultural and Economic Rights. Thus, despite vehement rhetoric about the priority of economic over political development, most ASEAN states recognise significant democratic and participatory substance in both the ICESCR and the UN Declaration on the RTD.

Since President Suharto's fall in May 1998, Indonesia has been undergoing a painful democratic transition. While accession to UN treaties has been formally placed on the political agenda, the timetable for required legal and administrative reform is uncertain. By the end of 1999, Indonesia had only ratified conventions relating to women, rights of the child, torture and racial discrimination. CAT was signed in 1985, but not ratified until October 1998, immediately following President Suharto's fall. Accession to CERD in July 1999 could represent a sign of Indonesia's intention to reverse anti-Chinese discrimination following major riots in May 1998 and in face of other ethnic upheavals.

Malaysia and Singapore have pursued parallel paths. Each has ratified only CEDAW, CROC and the anti-genocide convention. Neither had previously participated in any human rights treaty. However, Malaysia acceded to all three between December 1994 and August 1995, with Singapore following suit between August and December 1995. Each entered extensive reservations asserting the supremacy of domestic laws and subordinating participation in international tribunals to government consent. Other countries predictably objected that such reservations breach basic principles of international law. Participation in these treaties could represent a token response to international pressures or, more positively, a cautious beginning by the two countries most outspoken in championing Asian values.

These three conventions represent the less overtly political end of the human rights spectrum, and could be seen as a 'soft option'. Neither country is likely to breach the genocide convention and both have defensible records regarding welfare of children and legal status and opportunities for women. Even so, participation opens windows of opportunity to challenge patriarchal outlooks towards women in both countries, while Article 14 of CROC requires respect for children's rights to freedom of thought, conscience and religion. Islamic law is a significant factor in determining Malaysian policy, especially regarding women, and also determines Brunei's refusal to accede to CEDAW. Singapore's reservations were stated in terms of its situation as a multi-ethnic and multi-religious society. Construction of Malay rights by Malaysia and policies of maintaining ethnic identity within a framework of inter-ethnic harmony in both countries have been key reasons why neither Malaysia nor Singapore have participated in CERD. The gap between Singapore's policies and practice and the convention's requirements appears a good deal narrower, but would still be potentially open to challenge.

Singapore and Malaysia both strongly advocate reform of UN structures, highlighting the need to expand the number of permanent Security Council members, and for greater input from developing countries. States should at least have the right to be consulted when questions affecting them are considered. In Singapore's view, rapid change towards a global economy and expansion of UN membership place the UN's credibility at risk if it continues to postpone critical examination of fundamental issues (Jayakumar 1996).

The Philippines leads ASEAN in ratifying nine of the ten treaties, while only in that country is the death penalty the subject of serious domestic opposition. It ratified the ICESCR as early as 1974, reflecting President Marcos' emphasis on economic, social and cultural development, in contrast with then widely perceived negative aspects of democratic politics experienced before 1972. The philosophy and direction of development was a prime focus of contestation between the state and societal groups throughout the long period of authoritarian rule in the Philippines, persisting into the post-Marcos era since 1986.

Immediately following Marcos' overthrow, the Philippines acceded to the CAT in June 1986 and the ICCPR in October of that year. The Philippines ratification of the First Protocol to this Covenant in 1989 recognised the internationally acknowledged strength of its NGOs, advocacy groups and other 'cause-oriented' popular associations. The women's and refugees conventions were ratified in 1981, the anti-racial discrimination and anti-genocide conventions in 1969 and 1950. CROC was ratified immediately after its adoption in 1990.

Thailand represents several points of intersection within ASEAN, as a country in transition to democratic politics, though retaining deep traditional roots centred on the monarchy and Buddhist religion; as historically friendly to western countries, but deeply integrated within ASEAN culture and practice; as the country geographically, historically and strategically closest to the four newest members. Perhaps due to its avoidance of direct western colonisation and historical continuity of institutions, Thailand has remained relatively aloof from Asian values polemic, despite obviously strong pride in its cultural identity and determined defence of national sovereignty and institutions.

As the place where the Asian currency crisis first struck in June 1997, Thailand assumed a highly visible presence at the eye of the storm, with its efforts at political and economic reform acting as a weather vane for prospects of regional recovery. As with other ASEAN countries Thailand's post-crisis capacity to meet human rights obligations regarding employment, education, working conditions, nutrition and health to all citizens will be sorely tested, but its accession to the ICESCR in December 1999 indicated willingness to take up the challenge.

Thailand currently participates in four of the ten listed UN treaties – the two major covenants, CEDAW and CROC. Accession to the ICCPR and ICESCR reflects objectives in the 1997 Constitution, although Thailand does not yet participate in conventions relating to torture, racial discrimination, genocide and refugees. Accession to the ICCPR in October 1996 was hailed as a major breakthrough by international human rights groups. But reports of police and military violations, including torture, continue. Prison conditions were reported to be 'cruel and inhuman', with shackling and solitary confinement in regular use. Police are perceived as operating with impunity, intimidating and harassing those who investigate abuses (Amnesty International 1997a).

The death penalty is a source of contention between Amnesty International and many countries, although it is not included in the CAT Convention. Since 1996, after a nine year gap, at least four people have been executed, most recently in October 1998 (Amnesty International 1999a). Death sentences are mandatory for some crimes and discretionary for others. The King usually commutes death sentences, but in January 1996, a man convicted of murdering a policeman, was executed by firing squad under conditions of secrecy without prior public notification. Denial of appeal rights to people sentenced to death by military courts violates Article 14(5) of the ICCPR, requiring states to ensure that everyone convicted of a crime has the right to have their conviction and sentence reviewed by a higher tribunal, according to law.

In an effort to bring its laws in line with international standards, a new labour law enacted in August 1998 outlawed sexual harassment and discrimination, raised the minimum working age from thirteen to fifteen, and otherwise regulated working hours, overtime, and benefits (Human Rights Watch 1999a; US Department of State 1999a). As an important centre for regional non-governmental work on HIV/AIDS, cross-border trafficking in women and children, child prostitution and child labour, Thailand can expect to remain in the international spotlight on these issues.

There is considerable documented evidence of both forcible repatriation of Myanmar's tribal minorities, and failure to protect those in border camps from incursions and harassment by that country's military (Amnesty International 1997a,b). Burmese nationals in Bangkok, most of whom participated in the 1988 pro democracy movement, are at continuing risk of arrest and deportation. Military ties with Myanmar and earlier ties with the Khmer Rouge in Cambodia may have inhibited participation in the anti-genocide convention.

Unwillingness to accede to UN treaties relating to racial discrimination and refugees can be partly explained in terms of sensitivity in ethnic relations with its several neighbours and internally. Thailand contains several tribal minorities located in border regions. Compared with Indonesia and Malaysia, the Chinese minority is more closely integrated with the majority ethnic Thai population, both culturally and politically. But other minorities are mostly marginalised from mainstream politics. Despite separation across political borders, their ethnic links with neighbouring counterparts still render their national commitment and integration suspect to many Thais. Issues relating to land, forest and environmental degradation, aggravated by rising population, cause further tensions.

While earlier border conflicts with China, Laos and Cambodia are largely dormant, repression of tribal minorities by the Burmese military has caused a significant refugee spillover into Thailand. Periodically violent insurgency by the Pattani Liberation Front in the predominantly Moslem south has been largely moderated into negotiations for religious and cultural autonomy within a context of regional devolution. The issue was formerly a source of tension in relations with Malaysia.

Despite resisting pressures to accede to the International Convention on the Status of Refugees (Amnesty International 1997c), Thailand has cooperated closely with the Office of the United Nations High Commissioner for Refugees (UNHCR) in hosting many hundreds of thousands of refugees. Prior to the exodus from Myanmar, Thailand acted as staging post and country of first refuge for successive waves of refugees from Vietnam, Laos and Cambodia, following the end of the war in Vietnam in 1975. In 1998, Thailand reached in-principle agreement with Myanmar for return of 500,000 Karen refugees, claiming approval by the UNHCR. Human Rights Watch (1999a) claims that asylum-seekers are categorised as 'illegal immigrants', with an apparent lack of care in ensuring that repatriations do not occur without independent assessment and UNHCR monitoring.

Vietnam acceded to the ICCPR, ICESCR and the conventions relating to women, children, genocide and racial discrimination in 1981–82. However, its engagement with the UN human rights system is at best 'arm's length'. Constitutional guarantees of political and religious freedom appear more formal than real. National security laws define offences in ways which include peaceful expression of political and religious views. The December 1998 report of the UN Rapporteur on Religious Intolerance, sees relevant legal provisions as 'vague and imprecise', conceding excessive discretionary powers to authorities with regard to religious activities which fully conform with international law (Human Rights Watch 1999b). There is no consensus on the number of political or religious prisoners in Vietnam. Estimates vary from 30 to 150 people. Regular activities, held at places of religious worship are registered annually, but specific permission must be obtained for all other activities such as conferences, fund raising and opening of new training institutions – also promotions of senior clergy. These rules weigh most heavily on smaller Protestant and Buddhist groups (DFAT 2000e).

Extensive treaty accession was driven by Vietnam's desire to legitimise its position with the UN, in face of isolation following its participation in overthrowing the Khmer Rouge government in Cambodia in 1979. The 'Democratic Government of Kampuchea' (GDK) nevertheless retained Cambodia's seat at the UN until 1992, at the insistence of China, ASEAN and the USA. The farcical nature of this situation was illustrated by ferocious accusations of genocide by the GDK towards Vietnam following its accession to that treaty in 1981. This convention had been ratified by the French colonial government of Cambodia in 1950. Vietnam responded by denouncing the GDK's credentials when acceding to CEDAW.

Laos, relatively isolated from regional affairs until quite recently, has been cautious in joining UN human rights treaties, becoming a party to CERD in 1974, CEDAW in 1981 and CROC in 1991. The former French-sponsored government acceded to the anti-genocide convention in 1950. The Lao Peoples' Democratic Republic government was widely accused of using chemical weapons between 1975–80, resulting in killing of up to 100,000 out of 400,000 Hmong people. Allegations of genocide followed, supported by evidence from escaping refugees. The Lao Human Rights Council (1999), based in the USA, claims that killings and chemical warfare are still continuing, but the US government and UNCHR have persistently declined to accept evidence on this score, including from former

Hmong refugees who had returned to Laos under either voluntary or involuntary repatriation programmes.

Myanmar

Political and economic background

Military power is rooted in the troubled history of civil war following the withdrawal of British colonial rule in 1947. This was caused by ethnic divisions between the majority Burmans and minority groups in the border regions. Following the long period of rule by the Burma Socialist Programme Party (BSPP), led by General Ne Win who seized power in 1962, there appeared to be some prospects for political opening during a brief period from 1988–90. Following nationwide protests, in September 1988 the BSPP agreed to hold elections and to transfer government to the strongest party in the Parliament, but the military immediately resumed power, establishing the State Law and Order Restoration Council (SLORC). Despite many restrictions, including imprisonment of its General-Secretary, Daw Aung San Suu Kyi, the National League for Democracy (NLD) won 392 out of 485 seats when elections were finally held in May 1990.

The Parliament has never been summoned. Reinterpreting both its own and the BSPP's undertakings, the SLORC has insisted that the election was intended only as a step towards drafting a new constitution (JSCFADT 1995: 67–8). However, that process lacks minimum democratic legitimacy. Only 99 out of 700 representatives elected at the May 1990 elections were appointed as delegates to the National Convention Committee established in 1992. The SLORC controls the Convention's agenda, access to documentation, consultation and communication processes (JSCFADT 1995: 70–3). The military has demanded 25 per cent of seats in any future parliament. However, consensus deemed necessary to legitimise constitutional change has so far not been forthcoming.

In a largely cosmetic exercise the SLORC was replaced by the State Peace and Development Council (SPDC) in November 1997. The change represented a partial response to deteriorating economic conditions. Fourteen ministers were sacked and anti-corruption investigations launched against several of them. But military and ex-military overwhelmingly dominate the new body.

Daw Aung San Suu Kyi was isolated under house arrest from July 1989. Though supposedly released unconditionally in 1995, her movements have been tightly controlled and efforts to travel outside Rangoon thwarted on several occasions (Amnesty International 2000*d,e*). She has continued to seek dialogue and cooperation between the NLD and military. However the regime insists that discussions about the country's future can only take place within the framework of the National Convention. Although the NLD was permitted to hold a party meeting at Suu Kyi's house in May 1998, some two hundred party supporters and elected parliamentarians were detained. Those present passed a resolution demanding that a parliament be convened by 21 August. In a further wave of arrests, over 700 NLD members were detained, with a total of 194 elected parliamentarians in detention, together with students, dissident junior army officers and Buddhist monks (Human Rights Watch 1999*e*). SLORC/SPDC has fostered a strong mood of xenophobia by likening international criticism with post-1945 intervention by foreign powers.

Economic factors may prove decisive in determining Myanmar's political future. The BSPP's fall was triggered by economic breakdown and currency collapse. The re-vamped government sought to reverse earlier closed economy strategies and entice capital through liberalised foreign investment laws. Official data, albeit grossly distorted by official currency overvaluation,[6] show modest increases in foreign direct investment between 1990 and 96, with significant interest from Britain, France, Singapore and Thailand (Mason 1998: 212). However, in March 1997 the European Union suspended Myanmar's access to its generalised system of preferences. The Burma Freedom and Democracy Act of 1995 led to bans on most direct US investment, prohibiting US Export–Import Bank assistance to American firms operating in Myanmar, limiting its imports and placing bans on lending from the IMF and World Bank (Mason 1998: 220).

While the political environment surrounding these suspensions has discouraged many US and European companies, Asian investors, notably from China, Singapore, Thailand and Malaysia, moved to take their place, with interest also from Japan and India. China has expanded investment in telecommunications, mining, automotive, aviation and oil industries. Opening of Burma's borders with Yunnan province in 1988 boosted trade (Jannuzi 1998: 199–200; Steinberg 1998: 281–2). China has also delivered arms on a large scale – a major factor in defeating ethnic rebel groups (Jannuzi 1998: 200–5). Asia's economic stake in Myanmar thus limits potential for western leverage via sanctions and other pressures (Mason 1998: 224–5). Attempts to overthrow SLORC rule will also encounter strong Chinese resistance (Steinberg 1998: 277–8).

Myanmar's economy nevertheless manifests basic weaknesses which SLORC/SPDC rule only serves to exacerbate. Rising military expenditures, reaching as high as 46 per cent according to a 1995 World Bank Report, have caused a sharp decline in basic social and economic spending (Brandon 1998: 234, fn. 4). Despite abundant rice supply, there are significant levels of malnutrition, with infant mortality rates at 105 per 1000 and the under five mortality rate at 150 (Chandler 1998: 248–50). Historically high literacy rates are declining. Although Myanmar has passed laws to provide free primary education, as required by its ratification of the Convention on the Rights of the Child in 1991, extra-curricular charges render such education beyond the means of many families. Only around 25 per cent of children complete primary education, despite introduction of UNICEF programmes. Closures of schools and universities as sources of political dissidence continue to undermine educational standards at higher levels (Brandon 1998: 235–41).

There is virtually no autonomous civil society. Instead, the SLORC has set up the Union Solidarity and Development Association (USDA) under its own direct control. Some limited scope may exist for local initiative in less overtly political areas such as health, where it appears that international agencies and NGOs are trying to facilitate cooperation between the government and 'indigenous NGOs' (Chandler 1998: 248).

The large state sector, alongside a weak and dependent private sector, discourages foreign investors. Monopolistic powers of supply and distribution in many sectors force them to deal with inefficient state firms, while licensing and currency controls generate extensive corruption (Mason 1998: 221–2). The military dominates trade, investment, production and economic decision-making, and is likely to retain residual control, even if the SLORC is eventually replaced (Steinberg 1998: 279–80). Subordination of minority ethnic groups has led to cease-fire agreements allowing regional drug lords to continue operations under mutually profitable arrangements with the SLORC, linked to Chinese involvement (Lintner 1998). The growing power of drug-trafficking cum military mafias, associated with mass impoverishment could ultimately push Myanmar towards a Colombia-type situation, while failure to control heroin exports increases tensions in relations with the USA and regional neighbours (Gelbard 1998: 186–95).

UN treaty compliance

Myanmar acceded to CROC in 1991 and CEDAW in 1997, responding like other ASEAN countries to external pressures by ratifying the two human rights treaties perceived as least controversial. Even so, allegations persist against the military of widespread murder, beating and rape of women and children, particularly among minorities subjected to forced labour (UNCHR 1998c; Amnesty International 1997b). Major counter-insurgency campaigns after 1996 led to forcible relocation of tens of thousands of women belonging to ethnic minorities from their ancestral lands without compensation, forcing them to migrate to neighbouring countries or hide in the jungle (Amnesty International 2000a).

Myanmar joined the anti-genocide convention in 1956, during its democratic period. Though not yet named under this convention, Myanmar was warned in a UN General Assembly resolution on 12 December 1998, following a special rapporteur's report (UNCHR 1998c), to fully respect obligations under international humanitarian law, particularly the Geneva conventions of 12 August 1949, to halt the use of weapons against the civilian population and protect all civilians, including children, women and persons belonging to ethnic or religious minorities from violations.

Myanmar ratified the Forced Labour Convention in 1955, but continues to flout its provisions. The International Confederation of Free Trade Unions (ICFTU) filed a complaint with the International Labour Organisation (ILO) about widespread use of forced labour in Myanmar. The resulting report in August 1998 found the government '… guilty of an international crime that is also, if committed in a widespread or systematic manner, a crime against humanity' (Amnesty International 1999b). In the context of massive forcible relocations, hundreds of Shan civilians were killed when they attempted to return to their farms, with thousands seized by the army to work without pay on roads and other projects (Amnesty International 2000c).

In summary, Myanmar's record remains uniformly deplorable on all human rights fronts, irrespective of accession to particular UN instruments.

Cambodia

Prior to the 1991 Comprehensive Settlement, known as the Paris Peace Accords, Cambodia had suffered over twenty years of civil war, with massive internal and external disruption. Prince Sihanouk, who had led Cambodia since the departure of the French in 1955, was ousted by Lon Nol in a coup in 1970, assisted by the USA which sought to shift Cambodia from a neutral to pro-western stance in the Vietnam war. Sihanouk, who retained the loyalty of the rural and Buddhist majority, threw his weight behind the Khmer Rouge, enabling them to eventually take power in 1975. Saturation bombing by the USA, which killed up to one million people, intensified Khmer Rouge hatred of westerners and Cambodia's urban middle class, perceived as their allies. Nevertheless, the brutality and policies of enforced urban exodus, isolationism and economic autarchy imposed by Pol Pot surprised many, both foreigners and Cambodians.

Despite their long-standing affiliation with the Indo-China Communist Party, the Khmer Rouge broke ties with the Vietnamese communists after 1975 and laid claim to the 'Khmer Krom' region of the Mekong delta in southern Vietnam. Many Vietnamese were killed in cross-border raids. Khmer Rouge aggression was acknowledged by Prince Sihanouk who spent much time in exile in China. Internal Khmer Rouge faction fights erupted into full scale rebellion in the eastern region in 1977–78. The uprising was crushed with heavy reprisals, and many defeated cadres fled to Vietnam. Finally, the Vietnamese military joined with these dissidents in 1979 to overthrow the Khmer Rouge.

Despite widespread relief at Pol Pot's demise, and near universal support within Cambodia, international circumstances combined to sustain civil war until well into the 1990s. Vietnam's diplomatic rift with China after 1975 had forced it into economic and military dependence on the USSR. The new Cambodian government was obliged to follow suit, inviting hostility by China which regarded Cambodia as a client state. The USA, whose Cold War strategy then favoured China against the USSR, adopted a similar position. ASEAN countries, with many vital interests at stake with China, also feared to legitimise external invasion to overthrow a sovereign government, however tyrannical. As a result, Cambodia suffered over a decade of diplomatic isolation and economic boycott. 'Democratic Kampuchea', consisting of an unequal coalition between the Khmer Rouge, elements close to Prince Sihanouk and the pro-western Sonn Sann group retained the country's seat at the UN. Some humanitarian assistance, including from governments, was channelled indirectly via NGOs but aid in restoring infrastructure was severely held back (Mysliwiec 1988).

Despite Cambodian participation in overthrowing the Khmer Rouge, the new government was dependent for its security on Vietnamese military and other support during the 1980s. External demands for Vietnamese withdrawal failed to address fears that the Khmer Rouge, with support from China and Thailand, would return. By the late 1980s, the Cambodian army had been somewhat strengthened. The end of the Cold War terminated Russian assistance to Vietnam, opening the door to peace. Cambodia received guarantees of assistance and security, linked to withdrawal of foreign forces, disarmament of internal factions, national reconciliation and a government of national unity based on externally supervised elections. Sihanouk was installed as a constitutional monarch. Despite many irregularities and violent incidents, elections in 1993 finally gave Cambodia an internationally legitimate government.

The Khmer Rouge, though a party to the Peace Accords, created many difficulties over their interpretation and implementation, and continued fighting for several years. Despite residual ties with China and elements in the Thai military, external support gradually weakened, leading to its ultimate demise. But extreme hostility towards ethnic Vietnamese, expressed in numerous human rights violations, has become more firmly embedded within governmental and military structures through incorporation of deserting Khmer Rouge personnel.

The will of the Cambodian people expressed at the 1993 elections was effectively thwarted by marginalisation and eventual ousting of the National United Front for an Independent, Neutral, Peaceful and Cooperative Cambodia (FUNCINPEC), which had received a majority of votes, from its coalition with the Cambodian People's Party (CPP). Major fighting erupted between the government and FUNCINPEC in July 1997, fuelled by competition between them to attract Khmer Rouge defectors (Downie 2000). Prince Ranaridh and many supporters were forced into exile in face of likely arrest, based on charges of collaboration with the Khmer Rouge. They were allowed to return a few weeks before elections held in July 1998, following massive international pressure. Thus, although the formal voting and counting process itself was adjudged free and fair by official international observers, the overall context seriously disadvantaged opposition groups (Downie 2000).

FUNCINPEC was persuaded by the international community to continue participating as reluctant minority partner in a coalition effectively dominated by the CPP. However, reports persisted into late 1999 of intimidation and violence against both FUNCINPEC and opposition parties, particularly the Sam Rainsy Party. The military frequently exercises illegal powers of arrest against persons variously accused of sabotage and collusion with the Khmer Rouge (UNCHR 2000a: paras 23–5).

Elements within Cambodia's political leadership, notably FUNCINPEC and King Sihanouk, have strongly favoured policies of national harmony and reconciliation. These are also constant themes in international pronouncements on Cambodia, sitting oddly with demands for Khmer Rouge leaders to be tried for crimes against humanity as part of a regime of strict adherence to international human rights law. By contrast, Prime Minister Hun Sen and the CPP see themselves as national saviours who overthrew the Khmer Rouge and are frustrated at the international community's slowness to recognise them as the continuing legitimate government. The UN has thus taken on the daunting task of imposing universal human rights regimes in a situation of extreme division and conflict, bordering on covert civil war.

UN treaty compliance

Following the peace agreement, Cambodia acceded in 1992 without reservations to the ICCPR, ICESCR, CAT, CROC, CEDAW and the refugees convention. It became a party to CERD in 1986. The former French dominated state had ratified the anti-genocide convention in 1950. Cambodia is unique among the ten ASEAN states in the extent to which it has accepted and encouraged a UN human rights monitoring presence on its territory. But its subsequent record of non-compliance, detailed in UNCHR and other international reports, indicates the extent to which embracing international human rights law was a necessary price for Cambodia's international rehabilitation. The Cambodian Office of the High Commissioner for Human Rights (COHCHR), which derives its authority from Part III, Article 17 of the Paris Peace Accords, was established by UNCHR Resolution 1993/6, accepted by the Royal Government of Cambodia in a letter dated 6 November 1993. A Memorandum of Understanding, signed in 1996, has been twice re-negotiated and extended at the Cambodian government's request, most recently until 2001.

The COHCHR's main functions cover educational and technical assistance; assisting the government in meeting its human rights treaty obligations; preparing reports to relevant monitoring committees; supporting local human rights groups; developing and strengthening national institutions to promote and protect human rights; drafting and implementing relevant legislation; training of persons responsible for the administration of justice. Active contact with Cambodian people and civil society for these purposes also forms part of COHCHR's mandate. The Special Representative reports annually to the General Assembly and the UNCHR, which sent sixteen official missions to Cambodia between 1996 and 1999.

Major focuses of criticism in Special Representative's reports (UNCHR 1998*a*; 2000*a*) include lack of judicial independence, torture, jail conditions, child prostitution and trafficking. Weaknesses in the rule of law are widespread, highlighted by the perceived impunity of civil servants and military. A more general struggle continues for the free functioning of multi-party democracy in an atmosphere free from intimidation and violence. The issue of prosecuting former Khmer Rouge leaders remains unresolved.

Judges and prosecutors complain of provincial governors, military commanders and high-ranking Ministry of Justice officials directing them on the handling of individual court cases. Police failure to carry out court judgements and orders further undermines respect for and independence of the judiciary (UNCHR 2000*a*: para 54). In December 1999 the Prime Minister ordered the rearrest of persons arrested earlier for robbery, kidnapping or drug-trafficking, who had been released either on bail, or because charges against them were dropped, or prior to serving the complete sentence. The Prime Minister expressed respect for courts' independence but considered that improper acts by bad people inside the court system could not be allowed (UNCHR 2000*a*: para 55).

In May 1999, the Interior Ministry responded to often fatal mob attacks on suspected thieves by forming a 'People's Protection Movement', whose units are permitted to carry clubs, sticks and knives. The Special Representative observed that joint mobilisation of citizens, police, the armed forces and civil servants to perform internal security functions contradicts the letter and the spirit of the Cambodian Constitution and several Cambodian laws (UNCHR 2000*a*: paras 44–5).

Prison numbers are swollen by excessive pre-trial detention. Delays in food disbursement threaten prisoners' health and nutrition, prompting the Special Representative to observe that 'a government which cannot feed its prisoners has no right to keep them locked up'. Inadequate budgets, bureaucratic confusion and neglect are key causes (UNCHR 1998*a*: para 96). New procedures seeking to apply international standards have recently brought some improvement. Special problems of women and minors in detention are nevertheless inadequately addressed (UNCHR 2000*a*: paras 62–3). Access to prisons by NGOs and international organisations is considered essential to effective monitoring of conditions. However, confidential interviews with pre-trial detainees were prohibited by the Minister of Justice on 7 October 1999. The COHCHR considers such interviews important in preventing possible torture (UNCHR 2000*a*: para 65).

Use of torture to extract confessions has been acknowledged by the Interior and Justice Ministries. Prosecutors and judges have been advised to reject such testimony, though with limited effect (UNCHR 2000*a*: para 56). Following COHCHR representations, the Director-General of National Police undertook to investigate thirty-two cases of alleged torture of persons in police custody in Battambang, to prohibit abuse of police power and take firm disciplinary measures against violators. The National Police response stressed the need for training in investigation, interrogation and evidence-gathering techniques, inviting technical and material assistance from national and international human rights organisations. However, it found only a few cases of 'beatings and harsh words' not amounting to torture, and recommended against any disciplinary or legal action against the police interrogators.

The issue of impunity concerns the capacity of those exercising authority to violate legal processes and accepted human rights standards at will. Impunity undermines faith in the administration of justice and the moral authority of the courts (UNCHR 1998*a*: para 68). Strong advocacy by the UN Special Representative finally persuaded the National Assembly to approve amendments to Article 51 of the 1994 Law on Civil Servants, removing requirements for government permission to prosecute civil servants (UNCHR 2000*a*: para 80). Impunity also widens scope for political violence associated with electoral processes and freedom of expression in general.

Prior to the July 1998 elections, Cambodia's National Assembly enacted UN approved electoral laws and establishing a Constitutional Council and National Electoral Committee (NEC). However, the law on political parties contained clauses requiring 4,000 signed-up members, together with additional personal and professional data, in order to be registered. This apparent violation of the constitutional right to form a party was moderated by provisions allowing public campaigning in order to recruit members (UNCHR 1998*a*: paras 33–4). Clear procedures were also lacking to resolve who had rights to use a party's name in the event of factional splits (UNCHR 1998*a*: paras 35).

The National Electoral Committee combined parliamentary cum party, government, citizen and NGO representation. Consensus decision-making was not applied in the election of the NGO representative and for party representatives of FUNCINPEC and the Buddhist Liberal Democratic Party (BDLP). The National Assembly approved the composition of the NEC without any discussion of complaints by the two main NGO election monitoring coalitions, a student group, the Secretary-General of FUNCINPEC and a parliamentary member of the Son Sann faction of the BDLP. In the longer term, the NEC's establishment as a permanent body should enhance its independent status. But in order to avoid unbalanced and politically biased committees, its structures need to be strengthened at provincial and communal electoral level by specifying relative rights to participate by citizens, civil servants and local authorities (UNCHR 1998*a*: paras 36–7).

Many incidents of intimidation and pressure from CPP officials, aimed at FUNCINPEC and other parties, were reported prior to the July 1998 elections, particularly from Kampong Cham and Siem Reap provinces. The electronic media was especially dominated by the CPP, with little visible indication, such as party signboards, in the provinces of the existence of other parties. At one stage, police in several provinces declared the Khmer Nation Party (KNP), led by Sam Rainsy, as illegal, forcing its offices to remain closed. FUNCINPEC-affiliated student organisations were unable to operate (UNCHR 1998*a*: paras 28, 45–50). After July 1997, parties other than the CPP were largely denied radio and television access. Newspaper editors experienced threats, suspensions and requests for apologies. Newspapers opposed to the CPP also declined after mid-1997, with circulation largely confined to Pnom Penh.

Drafting of the 1995 press law contained potential for executive intrusions into media freedom. In December 1997, the Ministry of Information issued instructions that two government sources be cited when reporting on issues relating to national security and political stability. Definition of these concepts in a new sub-decree potentially further restricts freedom, contravening the Constitution and international standards. Killing and intimidation of media workers have continued throughout the whole period since 1993 (UNCHR 2000*a*: paras 56, 58–60).

Prosecution of former Khmer Rouge leaders became an increasingly sharp bone of contention between Cambodia and the international community following the death of Pol Pot. In December 1998, the Prime Minister warmly accepted, in the name of national reconciliation, requests by Khieu Samphan and Nuon Chea, to return to Cambodia as 'ordinary citizens'.[7] On 6 March 1999, Chhit Choeun, more commonly known as Ta Mok, the most senior Khmer Rouge leader still at large, was captured and placed in military detention. UNCHR Resolution 1999/76 appealed to the Cambodian government to take all necessary measures to ensure that those most responsible for very serious human rights violations were tried in accordance with international standards of justice, fairness and due process of law.

Faced with this dilemma, Hun Sen sought a compromise whereby Ta Mok, and possibly others, would be tried in a Cambodian court, with foreign judges and prosecutors invited to participate fully in ensuring that the trial met required international standards. A draft law would be submitted to the National Assembly to facilitate these arrangements. These proposals evoked a blunt response that any

UN involvement would depend on full guarantees of respect for international standards.

Expert advisers indicated that significant legislative changes would be required in both substantive law and procedures, to ensure protection against undue pressure, satisfactory arrangements for the arrest of persons indicted, assessment of evidence, appeal processes, mechanisms for appointing judges, prosecutors and other professional staff; organisation and funding of the tribunal. The Prime Minister responded by requesting international expertise in drafting the necessary legislation. However, the Special Representative indicated that this would be conditional on agreement to include legislative guarantees that appropriate international standards would be respected.

Amnesty International (1999c) declared that

> It would be a tragedy for Cambodia and its people if the arrest of Ta Mok, instead of being the catalyst in the establishment of an international court which can deliver justice, serves simply to bury the truth and further institutionalise the impunity which lies at the heart of Cambodia's human rights problems.

Though rejecting proposals for the UN to appoint the majority of judges, Hun Sen indicated willingness to accept a 'super-majority' arrangement, whereby most judges would be Cambodians, but a broad majority would be needed for any decision. After refusing several times, the UN eventually accepted a proposal along these lines, which was unanimously approved by Cambodia's National Assembly on 2 January 2001.[8] Both the time frame, which may well be protracted, and selection of persons to be tried will be determined by the government, which will certainly take potential security risks into account.[9]

Resistance by Cambodia to imposition of detailed processes on its legal system illustrates the extent to which states are willing to defend their national sovereignty even when seriously disadvantaged. However, Cambodia's weak position internationally and within ASEAN have precluded any too intransigent stance. Instead, assurances of willingness to cooperate with the UN are linked to requests for further assistance and advice. But agreements constantly break down at the point where change is required beyond the political will of Cambodia's leaders, culture and habits of administrators and judges, and capacity of its still fragile institutions and societal structures. Close integration between governmental and CPP party structures (Downie 2000) in any case set limits to the extent to which the judiciary, parties or civil society will be allowed to operate independently.

Ultimately, the government seeks to retain flexibility to either punish or accommodate former Khmer Rouge leaders according to its own priorities. An international tribunal would limit their room for manoeuvre. The UN has similarly limited scope for flexibility in its human rights processes. Cambodia's experience is reflected, albeit in less dramatic fashion, in many other ASEAN contexts where domestic priorities and imperatives of national sovereignty collide with international human rights law.

ASEAN's role in Myanmar and Cambodia

Myanmar and Cambodia illustrate problems faced by ASEAN in developing a collective stance on human rights issues. Sharp differences have arisen between ASEAN and western countries in responding to human rights abuses and repression of the democracy movement by Myanmar's military government. While this has resulted in suspension of most western and some Japanese aid, ASEAN prefers a 'constructive engagement' approach towards Myanmar.

The idea of constructive engagement was originally developed by the USA and Britain as a means of persuading the former South African apartheid regime to accept political change without the need for economic sanctions. ASEAN countries saw potential parallels whereby a pariah state can become socialised towards acceptable behaviour through a combination of diplomacy and economic development. Confronting Myanmar would have conflicted with ASEAN principles of non-interference and seeking cooperative solutions. ASEAN fears both Myanmar's potential as a source for regional instability and its growing dependence on Chinese military support (Ott 1998). Economic interests forged between Thai and Burmese military together with common security concerns relating to tribal minorities in their border regions, were key considerations shaping ASEAN policy. ASEAN states have also felt obliged to look benignly on Myanmar's calls for a redefinition of human rights in a local cum Asian context, anticipating that to do otherwise might provide precedent and justification for external scrutiny of some of their own repressive activities (Steinberg 1998: 271).

While human rights abuses in Myanmar have been more extensive and blatant than in other ASEAN states, with the possible exception of Indonesia, most also wish to uphold their rights to deal with secessionist or dissident minorities with equal ruthlessness. But the increasingly supportive international and domestic political environment towards human rights has precluded any too aggressive ideological counter-attack against western pressures on Myanmar, which can scarcely be presented as a flag ship for Asian values. Instead, it is argued that cooperation will facilitate economic development, giving Myanmar a stake in regional prosperity and security, leading eventually to improved systems of governance. Softening the regime's approach could also reduce spillover of refugees into neighbouring countries. In any case, ASEAN disagrees with imposing specific models of democracy.

No attempt has been made to define constructive engagement or strategies to realise its goals beyond a general belief in a 'Southeast Asian way' of gentle persuasion, avoiding embarrassment or isolation of the junta. This approach has so far produced little by way of economic or political results, with no attempt at high level dialogue between ASEAN and Burmese leaders (Acharya 1995: 173–9). The latter's presence in ASEAN delegations has several times threatened to disrupt the conduct of business in forums between ASEAN and the European Union. In December 1998, the UN General Assembly strongly condemned the SLORC's conduct and called for dialogue with the NLD (Human Rights Watch 1999*e*). ASEAN countries have declined to support such calls.

Concerns to safeguard national sovereignty had also motivated ASEAN in opposing Vietnamese intervention in Cambodia throughout the 1980s, despite evidence of widespread massacres under Pol Pot. Access to timber and precious metals was a factor for elements in the Thai military and business community. The issue of internal stability during the breakdown of relations between Hun Sen and Prince Ranaridh factions within Cambodia's governing coalition delayed Cambodia's entry into full membership for over a year. However, ASEAN saw an overriding imperative to finalise and consolidate the enlarged membership of ten countries, despite apparent unwieldiness in terms of cultural, political and economic differences. It also placed greater weight on internal stability and reconciliation than on human rights legalities. On the other hand, Cambodia lacked sufficient standing and close leadership rapport with key ASEAN states to galvanise any strong protest against UN human rights tutelage.

Myanmar's admission to ASEAN was a source of tension for the Philippines and Thailand, which had both experienced relatively recent transitions from military to democratic rule, and are more responsive to western human rights concerns. NGOs are also strong and well organised in both countries. While Thailand's strategic and economic interests proved too entrenched, the Philippines at one stage appeared on the verge of voting against Myanmar's entry, and so breaking ASEAN's consensus principle.

Major instability in Cambodia provided an opportunity to delay the entry of both countries. However, it appears that the Philippines was persuaded by Indonesia into reversing its position in return for its casting vote for the vacant position of Secretary General (Bello 1997). Subsequently, Thailand and Philippines attempted to regain initiative by proposing some variation to ASEAN's non-intervention principle. This would have allowed states to express concerns and encourage solutions where human rights violations in one member country were of sufficient magnitude to cause spillover effects among neighbours. The proposal was vigorously rejected by several ASEAN countries, led by Malaysia.

Recent trends suggest possible emergence of a more favourable climate, with the possibility of SPDC negotiations with NLD leaders.[10] Under strong pressure from the ILO, the SPDC agreed to a European Union team conducting unrestricted political consultations in Rangoon, to lift house arrest restrictions and engage in reconciliation talks with opposition groups.[11] ASEAN countries are evidently encouraging this trend, with a senior Malaysian diplomat appointed as the UN Secretary-General's special envoy to Myanmar.[12] Both Malaysian and Thailand's Foreign Ministers have visited Daw Aung San Suu Kyi. Reduced capacity and willingness of ASEAN countries to invest in Myanmar following the regional economic crisis have lent greater weight to her calls to foreign investors to stay away.

National human rights institutions

The idea for national networks which could effectively link the UN, governments and people in promoting human rights dates back to the UN's earliest years. Establishment of national human rights institutions (NHRI) in their current form developed in piecemeal fashion during the 1980s, as states sought to align their domestic laws and processes with ratification of UN instruments.

The trend was given coherence at a UNCHR-sponsored meeting of NHRI representatives in Paris in 1991, at which the 'Paris Principles' were approved (APFNHRI 1998*c*). These were subsequently endorsed by the UNCHR and General Assembly (United Nations 1993*c*). The Vienna Declaration and Action Programme designated a key role for national institutions in monitoring standards, and liaising with governments in developing national human rights plans (United Nations 1993*b*: Part II, Sections 83–87). The UNCHR's Centre for Human Rights was empowered to offer technical, training and documentation assistance to governments and NHRIs as requested, acknowledging their right to choose institutional frameworks best suited to their needs.

The Paris Principles set minimum standards for NHRIs, including independence from governments, secured by statutory or constitutional guarantees; a broad mandate based on universal human rights standards; adequate resources and powers of investigation. Pluralism in outlook and membership is to be ensured by representing human rights NGOs, trade unions, social and professional organisations, trends in philosophical or religious thought, academic and other qualified experts and Parliament. Government departments should only be represented in advisory capacities (APFNHRI 1998*c*).

NHRIs are to receive, report and act upon complaints of human rights violations, submit opinions, recommendations and reports to competent legislative and executive bodies; encourage ratification, monitor compliance and contribute to preparation of reports to UN treaty committees, conduct research, public discussion and campaigns relevant to promoting awareness of human rights. Operating procedures should ensure direct action on complaints without reference to higher authority; access to all relevant documents and information; effective access to media; regular meetings; active working groups, local and regional sections; consultation with jurisdictional and other bodies responsible for promoting and protecting human rights, particularly Ombudsman offices; close liaison with both general and specialist human rights NGOs and advocacy groups, regional and country NHRIs and UN bodies.

The pervasiveness of human rights considerations in almost every sphere of governmental activity, public and even private life has multiplied new institutions and processes, generating multiple and diffuse expectations of NHRIs. However, they are not intended to replace the role of courts, legislative bodies, government agencies, political parties or civil society organisations, but to play a distinct, complementary role as independent authorities established by law to protect human rights in their country (APFNHRI 1998*a*).

NHRIs' status is established by constitutional, legislative or other statutory authority. These define commissions' precise functions and powers, determining their effective levels of independence. The definition of human rights may embrace the full range of UN instruments or be confined, as in the case of Malaysia, to rights specified in the national constitution.[13] The powers and range of discretion allowed to commissions in investigating alleged violations also varies. Indonesia's National Human Rights Commission was established by Presidential decree in 1992 and its position has been strengthened by subsequent legislation.[14] Constitutional entrenchment of NHRIs' role and status gives greater protection against potentially limiting legislative or administrative changes. Funding depends on annual budgetary allocations, supplemented by international assistance.

Comprehensive definitions of human rights provide a strong frame of reference for the Philippines Commission on Human Rights. Article III of the 1987 Constitution sets out a comprehensive Bill of Rights, concerned centrally with civil rights and legal due process. The Commission has power to cite for contempt in accordance with Rules of Court for violations of its procedures, visitorial powers over all detention facilities and grants of immunity to persons required to testify. However, its complaints mechanism is geared towards mediation and conciliation as well as legal approaches. The Commission's powers to monitor compliance reinforces extensive ratification of international instruments.

The 'Declaration of Principles and State Policies' in Article II sets out a broad range of social, economic, educational and environmental objectives. However, more specific protections accorded to legal and civil rights of individuals illustrate problems of entrenching economic and social objectives as rights. In practice, the Commission appears to have given equal weight to both major streams of rights. Significantly, its legal framework is set out in Article XIII on Social Justice and Human Rights (Sections 17–19). This Article focuses on labour, agrarian and natural resources, urban land reform, housing, health, women and people's organisations. In opposition to neo-liberal concepts of rights, Section 1 requires the State to regulate acquisition, use and disposal of property in pursuing goals of social equity and human dignity.

The Commission has adopted a consciously participatory approach in developing its work. Government, non-government and people's organisations are brought together to develop the Philippines Human Rights Plan. Grass roots consultation links fifteen social sectors in a master plan embracing women, children, youth, the elderly, people with disabilities, prisoners/detainees, urban poor, indigenous people, Moslems, internally displaced persons, migrant and other workers in both formal and informal sectors. Personnel and budgetary constraints evidently limit realisation of the Commission's extensive objectives, diminishing its effective autonomy and authority. Regional outreach is similarly constrained (Navarete-Recina 2000).

Efforts to coordinate human rights protection in Thailand can be traced back to the Union for Civil Liberties in 1973 and the Co-ordinating Committee for Human Rights Organisations in Thailand in 1983. The drafting process for the 1997 Constitution, involving widespread civil society participation, opened the way for establishing the National Human Rights Commission (Tamthai 2000). Its legal basis and functions are set out in Sections 199–200 of Thailand's 1997 Constitution. These entrench the objectives and structures of the National Human Rights Commission as an autonomous institution. Section 200(1) defines human rights in terms of acts which by commission or omission 'violate human rights or which do not comply with obligations under international treaties to which Thailand is a party'. Advice on further accession is not specified as part of the Commission's duties, although this is included as an objective in subsequent legislation.

Commission members are to be appointed by the King, with the advice of the Senate, for a term of six years. Qualifications are to be set out in law, but regard is to be given to participation by representatives of 'private organisations in the field of human rights.' (Section 199) Broad responsibilities are assigned, with powers of investigation including powers to summon witnesses and demand relevant documents. Where recommendations are not acted on, the Commission must report to the National Assembly. However, Section 200 also includes an ambiguous requirement for the Commission to 'have regard to the interests of the country and the public' in performing its duties.

Sections 26–65 detail the 'Rights and Liberties of the Thai People', balanced by a short list of responsibilities to uphold Thailand's democratic law, constitution and national institutions (Sections 66–70). Sections 58–9 open up access to both personal and policy information held by state authorities. Section 30 prohibits discrimination on grounds of sex, race, language and religion. Sections 52–7 assert rights to basic personal and public health services, protection of children and youth, rights of aged and disabled persons, environmental and consumer rights. Cultural and environmental rights of traditional communities are affirmed in Section 46. However, most economic and social rights are covered under 'Directive Principles of Fundamental State Policies' (Chapter V), which are not justiciable. Sections 233–54 spell out the rights of accused persons and procedures to be followed by police and courts.

Some critics see NHRIs as detracting from the capacity of independent judiciaries and democratically elected parliaments to protect against human rights abuses. Supporters argue that a more distinctly separated body can take a leading role in promoting and protecting human rights. NHRIs' powers to systematically review government human rights policies and laws and compliance with international standards give them significant public standing. Though unable to impose legally binding outcomes on parties to a complaint, they have powers to establish tribunals, whose findings carry weight. Unresolved cases can be transferred to the courts for final determination.

NHRI networks are becoming increasingly significant in developing regional processes for promoting and protecting human rights, particularly in Asia, where formal regional links with the UN system are historically weak. Several national institutions cooperated with the UN to establish the Asia-Pacific Forum of National Human Rights Institutions (APFNHRI), which held its first meeting in 1991. In May 2000, Forum members included Australia, Fiji, India, Indonesia, New Zealand, the Philippines and Sri Lanka. Bangladesh, Mongolia, Nepal, Papua-New Guinea (PNG) and Thailand are considering or in process of setting up national institutions (APFNHRI 1998*b*). Malaysia established a Human Rights Commission in 1999, but is not a member of APFNHRI.

Cooperation with NGOs, as part of NHRIs' mandate, has increasingly taken the form of critical collaboration. Local and regional NGOs attend Forum meetings, while dialogue and cooperation were assisted by establishment of the Asia Pacific Human Rights NGOs Facilitating Team (APHR-FT). Both parties recognised common interest and complementary roles, given the importance of civil society in promoting and protecting human rights. For example, finalisation and adoption of the UN Draft Declaration on the Rights of Human Rights Defenders is a matter of extreme urgency to both NHRIs and NGOs throughout the region.

However, NGOs press NHRIs to be more proactive and widely involved. NGO delegates at a Jakarta Forum in September 1998 urged NHRIs to press governments, bilateral donors, international financial institutions and investors to recognise the human rights implications of the regional economic crisis (APFNHRI 1998*d*). Responses should focus on the needs of the most vulnerable groups, emphasising popular participation and ensuring that development is seen in the context of realising human rights as universal and indivisible. Calls for states to ratify both international covenants served to remind the APFNHRI not to neglect economic, social and cultural rights, and governments to incorporate civil and political rights.

Regional NGOs criticise wide variation in NHRIs' legal basis, ranging from constitutional or legislative mandate to executive ordinance; dubious procedures for appointing members; lack of powers to investigate abuses by the armed forces; limited definition of human rights by some governments. Lack of enforcement capacity should at least be modified by assigning powers to award compensation and interim relief to victims of human rights abuses (APFNHRI 1998*d*).

The Forum's proposals for enhancing human rights jurisprudence in the Asia-Pacific region via establishment of a Judicial Advisory Council concerned NGOs, which called for dissemination of model statutes and case law to support rigorous and principled human rights jurisprudence. Materials should not be regionally limited, but also include the best international examples of human rights commentaries that best articulate principles set forth in international human rights law. Acceptance of confidentiality provisions in draft terms of reference raised concerns that lack of transparency would defeat the proposal's basic objectives. Development of law in a democratic society, as an ongoing, open-ended process, requires public understanding and input. NHRIs' recommendations to governments, and the principles underlying them, must therefore be openly known and subject to public scrutiny. NGOs also sought opportunity to recommend names of suitable Council appointees (APFNHRI 1998*d*).

Practices of national institutions in receiving, investigating and resolving complaints are crucial to their reputation. NHRIs should be accountable to complainants, who should be informed of procedures, outcomes and reasons for decisions, and avenues for obtaining enforceable decisions. Regional and local outreach is essential, supported by adequate training and resources. Human rights commissions should not passively wait for complaints, but seek to empower victims by all possible means, where necessary assuming powers to litigate on their behalf.

Although solving individual cases has educational and other benefits, systemic abuses remain little touched if deeply embedded in institutional structures. These could be addressed through public inquiries into broad themes of human rights violation such as torture, economic exploitation, rights of indigenous peoples, racial and gender discrimination. Trans-border issues such as the trafficking of women and children and the plight of refugees require both regional inquiries and strong advocacy. National security laws prevailing throughout the region under various guises should be rigorously monitored (APFNHRI 1998*d*).

Wider consultation and involvement is a constant theme underlying NGO representations. Acceptance of this principle in the Paris Principles is reinforced by claims of research expertise, political neutrality, ethnic and geographical diversity, field experience and capacity for representation at all levels. Such capacities and advocacy skills in getting recommendations adopted would complement NHRIs' investigatory role. NGOs also seek a role in shaping future NHRIs in countries where they are yet to be established, with greater two-way flow of personnel and training (APFNHRI 1998*d*).

The Office of the High Commissioner for Human Rights (OHCHR), formerly the Centre for Human Rights of the UNCHR, announced its intention to develop direct cooperative links with the Asian Pacific NGOs Facilitating Team (UNCHR 1998*b*). Fears nevertheless persist that Asian governments seek to limit NGOs' access to the UNCHR, as part of wider attempts to weaken UN human rights processes. Asian Group's UNCHR representative nevertheless insisted that they aim to improve efficiency and communications between governments and NGOs.

It is not clear whether the wider interests of either people or NGOs will be served by the close integration with NHRIs proposed. While there is often a fine line between investigative cum advisory and advocacy roles, the distinction is important to the effective performance of each function. NHRIs' mandate requires that international human rights law remains their central focus rather than promoting particular groups and causes. Confusion of roles could undermine NHRIs' credibility with governments and people, possibly to the extent of threatening their independence. NGOs' capacity to critically monitor NHRIs could also be at risk.

Diversity could prove a weakness as well as a strength, if consultation with NGOs were to be built into every level of OHCHR and Forum decision-making. Modalities of representation will always prove difficult, although that problem was partly addressed by establishing the APHR-FT. Friction between small local and large national and international NGOs and networks does not assist their cause. Government-sponsored NGOs also divert energies and resources.

Conclusion

Both regional and national responses by ASEAN countries to UN human rights regimes evidence conflicting tendencies. Civil society groups have become stronger and better organised in the past decade. International pressures, strengthened by the economic crisis, have pushed governments towards greater formal and rhetorical accommodation with international standards, while resisting or obscuring their operational requirements.

Accession by ASEAN states to UN human rights instruments, though improving during the 1990s, remains weak and uneven. Governments are often slow in following up policy declarations with necessary legal and administrative action. Regional interests identified in this chapter have provided networks of mutual support and tolerance for very serious human rights violations, particularly in Myanmar and Cambodia. Principles of mutual non-intervention have held fast, to the extent of resisting legitimate international scrutiny via UN processes. A similar language of resistance to international standards pervades bureaucratic and diplomatic discourse.

Irrespective of treaty participation, only Thailand, Philippines and Cambodia have seriously engaged with the UNCHR, the latter semi-reluctantly. Indonesia may be slowly moving towards accommodation.[15] There are also signs that combined international and strong civil society pressures on a resistant Malaysian government will finally bring change, though probably not until after Prime Minister Mahathir's retirement. The UNCHR features very little in the policies of the remaining five ASEAN states. To the extent it has become harder to ignore the UN human rights system, conflict has focused on shaping its modalities.

The UNCHR has made strong efforts to engage both nationally and regionally with Southeast Asia. However, the only formal regional outcome following the June 1993 Vienna Declaration and Programme of Action was a re-assertion of key themes by the Kuala Lumpur Declaration on Human Rights adopted by the ASEAN Inter-Parliamentary Association the following September (Sajoo 1994: 91–5).

ASEAN's unwillingness to establish a regional counterpart to the UNCHR has brought national human rights institutions to prominence. However, the Asian Pacific Forum of National Human Rights Institutions extends beyond Southeast Asia. Also, only Indonesia and the Philippines of ASEAN countries have well established NHRIs. Thailand's comprehensive legislation has only recently been completed. While serious doubts have been raised about the autonomy or likely effectiveness of Malaysia's National Human Rights Commission,[16] it may be recalled that scepticism when Indonesia's national commission was inaugurated in 1992 has proved largely unfounded.

Despite limitations identified in this survey, experience to date suggests that once established, NHRIs open up many areas of human rights violation for scrutiny and bring new pressures on governments. They have so far not proved amenable to control by governments, though the orientation of individuals can influence the extent to which they are proactive in each area. Officially sanctioned establishment of NHRIs greatly enhances the legitimacy of universal human rights, undercutting Asian values rhetoric seeking to label them as western. As such attacks ignore the west's ambivalent outlook and uneven compliance revealed earlier in the chapter, they can perhaps be seen as a form of diversion from engagement with the UN human rights system.

4   Malaysia

'Illiberal democracy' and human rights

Despite rapid economic growth, Malaysian politics are not following classical patterns of evolution towards western-style democracy. Jesudason (1993) describes Malaysia as a 'statist' democracy, linking interventionist forms of government, based on the state's pivotal role in national and economic development, with a structurally weak civil society. Another paradigm portrays its system of government as a 'semi-democracy' (Crouch 1996a: 3–12; Case 2001), neither fully dictatorial nor democratic, partially responsive to public opinion but uncompromising in suppressing challenges to its authority. Strong institutionalisation of 'semi-democratic' structures and processes over time are cited as evidence of their appropriateness to Malaysia's situation. But currently unrelenting repression of opponents renders claims of even fifty per cent democracy far too sanguine.

Malaysia's patchy performance, ambivalent and often hostile approach to human rights are contextualised within this framework. Earlier discussion in Chapter 2 indicated that state-initiated Asian values cum democracy polemic has dominated Malaysian human rights discourse, unequally opposed by partially liberalising civil society advocacy. Entrenched security and other repressive legislation remain totally at odds with major UN human rights treaties (Amnesty International 1999d), most of which Malaysia shows little inclination to ratify.

Overthrow and detention of former Deputy-Prime Minister, Anwar Ibrahim, has upset the overall balance of Malaysian society and politics. The short term outcome has been a deeper lapse into illiberal democracy (Bell 1995), with only the outward forms of electoral democracy observed, and concentration of power in the Prime Minister's hands. This trend is dysfunctional to Malaysia's changing needs, and is unlikely to survive his foreshadowed departure from politics. Democratic change is also held back by conservative religious and populist authoritarian outlooks permeating civil society and some opposition groups. Contrary to official wisdom, incorporation of universal and indivisible human rights principles could greatly improve Malaysia's public life and national development.

Overall context

The Federation of Malaya was established as an independent state in 1957. In 1963, this was incorporated into the Federation of Malaysia, together with Sabah,

Sarawak and Singapore, which separated in 1965. Ethnic composition is approximately 55 per cent Malay, 30 per cent Chinese, 8–9 per cent Indian, plus various other indigenous groups, mostly concentrated in East Malaysia. Islam is the national religion, but other groups enjoy religious freedom within prescribed limits. Malaysian politics are dominated by issues of race and religion, with protection and advancement of Malays a cornerstone of state policy. Organisation of political parties along racial lines was well established before 1957, and interracial accommodation achieved prior to independence determined subsequent political directions.

Malaysia considers that its historical situation is insufficiently understood by western human rights critics, who expect religious and racial equality to be accorded in unqualified form. Thus Malaysia could never ratify the CERD and anti-racial clauses in other human rights instruments on the basis of its current arrangements. The government nevertheless insists that these are directed towards overall equality and harmony, particularly by breaking the nexus between race and occupation. Opponents retort that affirmative action policies should support a determined attack on poverty regardless of race.

Malaysia's political system conforms outwardly with the Westminster model. But its democratic functioning is heavily circumscribed. Security legislation inherited from British colonial rule gives the government sweeping powers, buttressed by many new laws restricting civil and political rights. Malaysia's Constitution affirms basic political and personal freedoms, with due legal process. However, these can be overridden via emergency powers in Article 149. Governments have routinely used their parliamentary dominance to amend the Constitution. Electoral boundaries are set by Parliament rather than the Electoral Commission. Despite relative freedom to form political parties, political competition is constrained by this overall legal environment.

Communally based politics stifles and distorts political and policy debate, also tending to reinforce intra-community hierarchies. Attempts to build cross-community coalitions outside this framework continually fail. The ruling coalition National Front (BN) is founded on dominance by the United Malays National Organisation (UMNO). Although the Malay vote is strongly contested by the Islamic Party (PAS) which remains outside the ruling coalition, both regard the pre-eminence of the Malay race, as the original 'sons of the soil' (*bumiputera*), as a non-negotiable fundamental of Malaysian politics. Although UMNO until quite recently enjoyed a mass membership and vigorous internal competition, it plays a hegemonic role towards other BN components. UMNO holds key Cabinet positions and determines party representation at elections. Considerable bargaining scope remains in practice so long as UMNO dominance is not challenged. Non-Malays accept Malay constitutional privileges and seek concessions within that framework. Intra-party battles are fought out across the BN to ensure that not too much is conceded to other groups.

The two major opposition parties, PAS and the Democratic Action Party (DAP) appeal respectively to Malay and non-Malay voters, but their diametrically opposed views on religious and racial issues enable the government to generate fears of extremism, and so retain the political middle ground. Prior to 1999, parties attempting to construct opposition alliances transcending communal affiliations were not supported by Malays, and therefore shifted their focus towards Chinese and Indian concerns (Vasil 1971). A swing to PAS among Malay voters in 1999 was offset by a pro-government swing among non-Malays in reaction to PAS' plans for an Islamic state.

Inter-communal accommodation initially conceded freedom to Chinese economic interests in return for Malay dominance over politics and administration.[1] Opposition gains in May 1969 elections sparked racial disturbances, resulting in suspension of Parliament and a major political re-structuring. The New Economic Policy (NEP) was initiated to fast track Malays' advancement in business and education, reasoning that national unity necessitated breaking the nexus between ethnic, urban-rural and occupational divisions inherited from British rule, linked to comprehensive cultural change by Malays. These views were strongly promoted by then dissident backbench UMNO MP, Mahathir Mohamad, in his book *The Malay Dilemma* (Mahathir 1970).

A key NEP goal was to increase Malay capital from 2 to 30 per cent by 1990. Achieving this goal without expropriation depended on rapid and sustained economic growth. Apart from a slowdown in the mid-1980s, growth commonly averaged 7–9 per cent between 1970s and the economic crisis beginning in 1997. Malay-based companies were set up with infusions of state capital or as semi-public corporations with favourable access to credit and contracts, in fields such as transport, construction, property and tourism. Training programmes aimed at producing a Malay technical and managerial class.

By 1990, bumiputera capital ownership had reached only 20.3 per cent, with non-Malay ownership increasing to 46.2 per cent and foreigners' share declining to 25.1 per cent.[2] While significant reductions in overall poverty were achieved, it was considered too politically sensitive to disclose further data on ethnic comparisons, thus abruptly cutting short public evaluation of the NEP. Subsequent evidence indicated that Malaysia had reduced overall poverty from 29 to 13 per cent and its Gini coefficient from 0.49 to 0.45 between 1980 and 1993 (UNDP 1999a: 88).

The NEP was replaced in 1991 by the 'New Development Policy' (NDP), also known as 'Vision 2020'. This emphasised efficiency and productivity, avoiding specific Malay ownership targets. Racial inclusiveness in overcoming hard core poverty was also affirmed, recognising the plight of Indian plantation workers and indigenous people.[3] The blueprint essentially envisages an advanced, industrialised society, applying East Asian models combining modern technology and management, harmony, cooperation and discipline. Company unions and tripartite wage bargaining systems are favoured over western-style trade unions, which are seen as inefficient and divisive.

The NDP was conceived against the background of severe internal UMNO divisions after 1986 which had opened up opportunities for opposition groups. Although Mahathir re-emerged from the 1990 election in a seemingly unchallengeable position, intra-Malay conflict encouraged the government to reach out to non-Malays. Vision 2020 opened up a new concept of Malaysian as against Malay nationality and a partially liberalised political environment. Greater inclusion of non-Malays was offset by a sense of insecurity among some Malays, providing the government with a rationale for maintaining the Internal Security Act.

The Prime Minister and his Deputy emphasised inter-racial and religious toleration. Asian values and civilisations discourse reinforced these goals, supported by diplomatic efforts to strengthen ties with China, India and the Moslem world. But conflicting approaches between Mahathir and Ibrahim became increasingly evident in approaches to balancing economic growth and equity, security legislation and issues of civil and political rights. Wider public debate on policy issues became possible, as business competition between rival supporters over ownership of media outlets led to more vigorous coverage of controversial issues. But apparent evolution towards political openness was reversed after 1997 by the regional economic crisis, the impact of political turmoil in Indonesia, and the downfall of Anwar Ibrahim.

Legal context

Security legislation

Executive dominance over the legislature and judiciary is a key characteristic of Malaysian governance, reinforced by an extensive body of security legislation. The Internal Security Act (ISA) allows arrest without warrant for up to sixty days of persons considered as present or potential threats to national security. Thereafter the Minister for Home Affairs can renew detention for an indefinite number of times every six months. Judicial review of the ISA's application in individual cases has been removed by a series of legislative and constitutional amendments. Exclusion of *habeas corpus* opens up serious dangers of torture, particularly during the initial sixty-day period (Amnesty International 1999*d*: 13–32, 82–4). While relatively small numbers are usually detained under the ISA, its sweeping and arbitrary nature generates pervasive fear and uncertainty, inhibiting serious political debate. Abolition, or major modification of the ISA is consequently a prime goal of opposition groups, human rights and social activists.

The 1971 Sedition Amendment Act removes four major areas from public discussion. These relate to Malay rights, citizenship rights of non-Malays, the status of the national language and the Islamic religion, and the rights and privileges of the King (Yang-di-Pertuan-Agong) and Sultans, who act as state rulers. The sweeping and uncertain nature of these restrictions obstructs debate on key issues of public policy. Thus bans on discussing the status of national language distorts discussion of its application to education policy, for example, in relation to ethnic quotas at tertiary institutions. Scrutiny of recruitment and employment practices in the civil service is entangled with the Malays' special position. Issues of domestic violence, the rights of women and family law are claimed as subject to

Islamic law. However, immunity under the Act against criticising King and Sultans was set aside in 1983, when the government sought powers to prosecute alleged crimes and to restrict rulers' powers to delay legislation and intervene in government affairs (Crouch 1996a: 142–7).

Prohibition of unauthorised publication under the Official Secrets Act 1972 extends to 'any information in the hands of the government, no matter how insignificant or widely known' (Crouch 1996a: 84). In 1986, the scope of the Act was reduced to cover only Cabinet and Executive Council documents and those relating to security, defence and international relations. But the scope of remaining provisions, together with mandatory jail sentences ranging from one to fourteen years, deters critical commentary.

Judiciary

The extent of judicial independence has been placed in serious doubt since the dismissal of the Chief Justice and five other Supreme Court judges in 1987–8 (Crouch 1996a: 140–2). While the judiciary can reasonably claim to operate in strict accordance with Malaysian law, this law has been increasingly framed to restrict courts' freedom to determine their own procedures, interpret laws or exercise review of legislation (Amnesty International 1999d: 10–111). Dr. Mahathir has several times criticised the notion of judicial review, as giving judges open-ended powers to oppose government policies and throw out laws they dislike (Crouch 1996a: 140–1. Khoo 1995: 289). In practice, Supreme Court judges have always interpreted their review powers in far more restricted fashion than their Indian counterparts (Aliran Kesadaran Negara 1987: 54–113). Ultimately, Parliament's will and capacity to use its continuing two-thirds majority to amend the constitution is decisive in restricting courts' powers.

Edwards (1996: 35–6) claims that Malaysia's judicial system allows wide scope for executive intrusion. For example, the impartiality of magistrates is placed in doubt by oversight powers granted to the Judicial and Legal Services Commission, chaired by the Attorney-General. Executive power to move cases between courts and appellate divisions also weakens judicial independence.[4] The Criminal Procedure Code (CPC) fails to guarantee defendants information concerning charges against them until they arrive in court. Most damaging to defendants are prosecutors' and courts' powers under Article 158 of the CPC to amend charges at any time up to the conclusion of a trial. New witnesses may be introduced, their identity and nature of their testimony similarly withheld, thus confusing defence preparations (Edwards 1996). Such procedures contravene principles of equality of defence and prosecution in ICCPR Article 14.

Malaysian Bar Council

The Malaysian Bar Council has maintained relative independence from the government. It contains prominent human rights activists, such as Param

Curumaswamy, a member of the UN Human Rights Commission, Cecil Rajendra, whose passport was withdrawn for several months for criticising Malaysia's environmental and tourism policies, and Sivarasa Rasiah, President of Voice of Malaysia (SUARAM), a leading human rights NGO. The Bar Council has its own self-governing structure (International Law Book Services 1992), and is self-funded from members' subscriptions. All practising barristers and solicitors must join the Council, with state associations integrated into one national body. Government efforts to weaken and possibly replace it by promoting the Association of Moslem Lawyers were successfully withstood, not least because senior Moslem Council members stood firm in its defence. Strained relations with the government have resulted in lack of consultation over key appointments, in which practising lawyers are frequently by-passed.

Freedom of expression and association

Media controls operate both overtly and covertly. The Printing Presses and Publications Act 1984 requires licensing of all journals and newspapers subject to annual review. Licenses may be revoked where publications aggravate sensitivities or fail to serve national development goals. The Home Affairs Minister enjoys absolute discretion, not subject to court challenge, to ban or restrict publications considered prejudicial to public order or morality or likely to alarm public opinion. 'Malicious' publication of 'false' news renders printers, publishers, editors and writers who fail to take 'reasonable measures' to verify an item's truth liable to prosecution (Amnesty International 1999*d*: 39–40). Uncertainty over application of these sweeping rules serves to maintain a compliant media environment.

Newspapers and television are mostly under the control of factions within UMNO or other BN parties. The range of news and viewpoints offered is thus a function of rivalry within the National Front, particularly within UMNO. But censorship of books is inconsistent, with not a few critical, mostly English language writings appearing on book stands. NGO periodicals and newsletters not destined for mass circulation are subject to less stringent censorship than mass circulation Malay language publications.

The 1975 University Colleges Act requires the Vice-Chancellor's written permission for any student to join or demonstrate support for political parties, trade unions, other organisations and groups. Similar restrictions are placed on academic staff, although they may join such bodies without holding office. The Vice-Chancellor's permission is even required for comment on political parties in academic books and articles and in seminars, though this provision is widely ignored in practice (Crouch 1996*a*: 93).

The 1966 Societies Act requires all non-profit organisations to register with the Registrar of Societies, an official of the Ministry for Home Affairs. In 1981, the government proposed amendments distinguishing political from other societies. Early drafts proposed sweeping definitions of advocacy on policy issues as political. This would have excluded academic and professionals from membership, and reduced access to foreign funds. Although these provisions were withdrawn, extensive controls remain, including requirements for annual registration.

Labour legislation

The Malaysian trade union movement was characterised by high levels of militancy on both political and industrial fronts after World War II and during early post-Independence years (Jomo 1994). This was reversed by comprehensive industrial legislation – notably the 1959 Trade Unions Act (International Law Book Services 1995) and the 1967 Industrial Relations Act (International Law Book Services 1994). Ignoring basic International Labour Organisation (ILO) conventions, registration requirements give the government effective powers over unions' coverage and names, and dispute settlement. Strikes are subject to severe restrictions. Civil servants are prevented from joining trade unions, although privatisation may allow unionisation of statutory authority employees. Replacement of industrial by enterprise-based unions and agreements with enterprises granted pioneer status, notably in the electronics, garments and textiles industries have reduced unions' bargaining power. While some belong to the Malaysian Trade Union Congress, enterprise-based unions commonly lack resources for effective negotiation, and are discouraged from linking up through federations.

One of the few areas in which the government cooperates with the ILO relates to improving occupational health and safety, including training and assistance in drafting new legislation. But trade union resources for monitoring and follow-up measures are limited, as is awareness of these issues among workers and employers.

Labour organisations have become more active in mobilising migrant labour. The Trade Union Act allows for legally resident migrant workers to be trade union members, but not hold office. This right is commonly excluded by workers' contracts. Migrant workers' plight was brought to light by Tenaganita, an NGO promoting women's rights led by Irene Fernandez. Interviews with 340 foreign workers from several detention camps revealed deficiencies in health, sanitation and living conditions, which violated international human rights and labour standards (Toha-An Nee 1995). A common reason for detention was lack of necessary documents, kept by employers.

A Human Resources Ministry Task Force reached similar conclusions,[5] also noting frequent contracting out by employers to foreign workers to avoid paying insurance and benefits; unauthorised pay deductions to repay levies; violation of registration laws; failure to provide employee compensation insurance coverage or written employment contracts, and collection of illegal deductions on behalf of agents (Singh 1995).

A complaint of criminal defamation was lodged against Irene Fernandez over Tenaganita's report. SUARAM and the Bar Council protested against the threat to democratic rights, and potential for abuse by authorities. The police claimed an equal democratic right against misrepresentation. In March 1996 Fernandez was charged with malicious publication under Section 8 of the Printing Presses and Publications Act (Amnesty International 1999*d*: 41–2), in a case yet to be decided.

Popular mobilisation

Compared with Indonesia, Thailand and the Philippines, Malaysia's entrenched security legislation and wide outreach of political parties provide less space for civil society groups to play representative and advocacy roles. Active NGOs have nevertheless emerged in the fields of women's rights, environment, consumer affairs, civil and political rights, plus networks promoting inter-cultural and religious dialogue. Despite their small size, many groups have good informal media links, enabling them to place issues on the public agenda. Malaysia also hosts several Asian regional NGO networks, contributing to the high profile adopted by some local NGOs on Third World issues.

While most NGOs' share a common focus on dismantling the ISA and other restrictive legislation, they have experienced serious differences over ideology, strategic direction and relations with the government. While one stream has supported opposition parties in struggling against such legislation, and in, so far, vain efforts to deny the government the two-thirds majority necessary to change the Constitution at will, others are closer to the government on Third World issues, cultural outlook towards the West, protection of the Malay language, and the domestic and international role of Islam.

Prominent among the first stream are the Voice of Malaysia (SUARAM), Aliran Kesadaran Negara, the National Association for Human Rights (HAKAM), student, trade unions, women's groups, and the Malaysian Bar Council. The second stream networks via the Malaysian Action Front (MAF). Key organisations include the Movement in Defence of Malaysian Islam (ABIM), the Centre for Peace (CENPEACE), and Penang-based organisations Friends of the Earth (SAM), the Consumers' Association of Penang (CAP), Third World Network and Just World Trust.

Although both streams are predominantly urban and middle class, the MAF network's stronger Malay and Islamic links enable it to take up more local action campaigns. The latter stream combines critiques of inequities in the international order with Asian values style attacks on liberal and secular interpretations of human rights and western culture. Attacks on western 'hypocrisy' (Muzaffar 1995*a*) and double standards (Rajamoorthy 1995) converge with the Prime Minister's views, generating tensions among NGOs. Pro-Islamic sentiment mobilised by wars in the Persian Gulf and Bosnia fuelled such attacks. The legitimacy of the UN is also questioned, with demands to end domination by major powers and reform of the Security Council. Internationalisation of protest has thus tended to deflect criticism from Malaysia's repression of basic civil rights. In practice, the activities of many NGOs reflect a combination of both aspects. Thus ABIM and CENPEACE strongly advocate abolition of the ISA. CAP and SAM frequently clashed with the government over local issues, notably the construction of the Bakun dam in Sarawak.[6] SUARAM and the Bar Council assisted in these campaigns.

SUARAM was established in 1987 to coordinate responses to the government's arrest of over one hundred social and political activists under Operation Lalang (Crouch 1996*a*: 106–12). It provides legal support and engages in public advocacy against Malaysia's security and other repressive legislation, working closely with the Malaysian Bar Council on issues relating to land and women's rights. For example, the 1993 Land Acquisition Act provides that land resumed for development with government approval cannot be subject to reversal claims. Only the compensation amount is justiciable.

Aliran Kesadaran Negara, based in Penang, has sustained a strong critique of Malaysia's legal and political processes since its formation in the early 1980s.[7] Despite informal alliances with opposition parties, its primary aim is to promote inter-communal and religious understanding. Malaysia's growth-oriented development paradigm is seen as distorting and marginalising these concerns. By the early 1990s, anti-western critiques increasingly dominated Aliran's publications, leading to a split which resulted in director and co-founder, Chandra Muzaffar, leaving to found Just World Trust.

Just World Trust links a broad-ranging critique of inequities in the global order with issues of western cultural and intellectual domination, based on secular and individualist outlooks derived from the 'Enlightenment' (Muzaffar 1993; 1995*a*). Severe rifts among Malaysian activists over the nature of human rights came to a head when Dr. Mahathir was invited to open a conference on human rights in December 1994 convened by Just World Trust, generating debate over dangers of legitimising government discourse on Asian values (Ichyo 1995; Muzaffar 1995*b*). In practice, Just World favours the softer Asian civilisations outlook. Muzaffar maintains that his position is consistent in terms of commitment to democracy, equality and justice on both domestic and international fronts.[8]

CENPEACE, initiated by Fan Yew Teng, a former DAP Secretary-General, has taken up a wide range of domestic and international causes, stressing peace and disarmament. The 1991 Gulf War led to a hardening anti-West position, based more on opposition to US bombing than support for Saddam Hussein. CENPEACE positions on Bosnia, Libya and Kashmir have been closely aligned with ABIM and other Islamic groups within MAF. Nevertheless, CENPEACE maintains a strong commitment to inter-cultural and religious understanding. Its cooperation with Tenaganita on migrant labour issues indicates commitment to civil and political rights.

ABIM membership covers a broad range of Moslem backgrounds. Anwar Ibrahim played a key role in its founding. Personal ties remained strong while he held ministerial positions. But anger at his arrest and conviction weakened support for UMNO, reflecting general shifts within the Malay community. ABIM nevertheless urges subordination of party affiliation to overall Moslem community interests, both nationally and internationally. Toleration towards non-Moslems in Malaysia is seen as assisting Moslems' well-being elsewhere. ABIM supports these objectives through domestic and foreign policy lobbying, including extensive networking with overseas Islamic groups (Nair 1997: 70–80). An Islamic state in any formal sense is not seen as necessary to achieving goals of social justice, clean and efficient administration.

Environmental NGOs link critiques of dominant development models with local group formation. They also stress themes of democratic accountability, notably the government's unwillingness to release details of environmental impact assessments. Thus failure to release relevant studies of the Bakun dam project made it difficult for critics, indiscriminately labelled as anti-development, to propose alternatives based on accurate estimates of energy demand.

While Mahathir's attacks on western hypocrisy in denying Third World countries the fruits of development, achieved through destruction of their own environment, has resonance among environmental NGOs, government emphasis on global environmental concerns are also perceived as a means of playing down local issues. Demands that western countries prove their sincerity by paying compensation are only partly supported, as effective outcomes depend on identifying and supporting good quality projects. Negative western technical and funding responses have hindered local environmentalists from developing consistent strategies.[9]

Adoption of the Malaysian Charter on Human Rights in December 1994 (SUARAM 1994) represented a significant attempt to reconcile conflicting approaches. This manifesto was signed by approximately eighty persons, representing some fifty Malaysian NGOs, several trade unions plus Semangat 46, the DAP and the Malaysian People's Party (PRM). The Charter, which resulted from extensive consultation, attempted to incorporate both streams of universal human rights embodied in the two key UN covenants, which the Malaysian government was urged to ratify. Just World Trust and CAP declined to support the Charter.

The crackdown on Anwar Ibrahim's supporters following his arrest has brought NGO networks closer together. Ibrahim's informal connections with ABIM and other NGO leaders had previously offered the MAF network a measure of protection. The formation of the Justice (*Keadilan*) Party, under the leadership of Ibrahim's wife, Dr. Wan Azizah Wan Ismail, with Chandra Muzaffar as Secretary, reflects earlier efforts to build a cross-communal coalition capable of challenging the ruling National Front. But despite efforts to include all communities, the Mahathir–Ibrahim conflict appears to many non-Malays as an intra-Malay affair, from which they wish to remain aloof.

Major political parties, particularly UMNO, have active women's wings. Despite achieving some gains, for example, in equalising wages, their main purpose is to maintain electoral support (Manderson 1980). The Office for Women's Affairs in the Prime Minister's Department consults with peak bodies such as the National Council of Women (NCW). While some concessions and gradual changes in official outlook can be achieved through high level access,[10] independent women's groups see such bodies as reinforcing domestically-oriented social constructions of women.

Independent groups all emphasise civil and political rights, particularly as affecting women. The All Women's Action Society (AWAM), registered in 1988, is probably Malaysia's best known group. It undertakes public education and advocacy, particularly on issues of rape, violence and sexual harassment. AWAM and SUARAM cooperate closely. Successes have included amendments to rape laws in 1989, and changes to domestic violence laws in 1994. The Malay language press is seen by women's groups as more hostile than English language counterparts due, in their view, to the influence of Islamic authorities.

Sisters in Islam seeks to empower Moslem women, focusing on practical, legal and theological issues within a purely Islamic framework. This enables them to challenge conservative clerics (*ulama*) whom they accuse of issuing pronouncements (*fatwa*) and interpretations without consulting those affected. The Sisters claim the right to a women's reading of Islamic texts and for these to influence Islamic court procedures. They publish booklets on wife-beating and male–female equality, joining with others in successfully lobbying for amendments to the Domestic Violence Act. This Act's proclamation was obstructed by Pusat Islam, the Islamic advisory group to the Prime Minister, claiming overlap with *Shariah* law. As domestic violence laws derive from the Penal Code, the Sisters argue they should apply universally.

The Prime Minister has strongly supported the Sisters' objections to the Kelantan government's *Hudud* laws (Ismail 1995), as part of a more comprehensive attack on the PAS and obscurantist interpretations of Islam (Mahathir 1995). Anwar Ibrahim also expressed strong, in principle, support for women's equality and rights (Ibrahim 1996: 50, 114), but is perceived by Sisters in Islam as silent on key issues and more concerned for consensus within the Moslem community.

Independent women's groups, along with most NGOs, are criticised as being urban, middle-class and non-Malay in composition. The emergence of Sisters in Islam represents an important breakthrough among Malay women, while the middle-class tag is being gradually countered by the efforts of groups such as Tenaganita which support working class women. In addition to its advocacy for migrant labour, Tenaganita promotes self-organisation among estate, industrial and sex workers.[11] Mobilisation and training of estate workers entails struggles both within the National Union of Plantation Workers (NUPW), and at the domestic level to democratise families. Women have gradually gained executive positions in NUPW state branches through union elections. Informal women's courts have been set up on estates, thus avoiding problems with the police and legal system. Women workers are active in the electronics and textiles industries. Union leaders dismissed in several firms have waged lengthy court battles, with partial successes. Though barred from forming a national union, textile workers set up a federal union via formation of state unions.

While the negative impact of the Societies Act and other restrictive legislation has been considerable, lack of direct grassroots involvement in social development also limits NGOs' direct field experience on which to base policy advocacy. However, combining with elements in the media, professions, universities and individual politicians, they have contributed to broadening public debate, and modest strengthening of civil society relative to the still strongly concentrated power of the Malaysian state.

Asian values, Islam and human rights

Asian values discourse in Malaysia serves both internal and external political goals. The government appears torn between accepting the principle of universal human rights but insisting that time is needed to ensure national unity, development and stability, and asserting a specifically Malaysian culture-based paradigm. A far-reaching project to shape national identity and the outlook of Malaysians overrides such seeming inconsistencies. National development goals, linked to inter-communal harmony, lie at its core. This harmony continues to depend on maintaining a leadership position for the Malay race and Islamic religion, balanced by well-targeted concessions to non-Malays.

Modernisation of Malay culture confronts major problems in balancing ethnic identity, the claims of Islam and diffuse external influences. Articulation of non-Malay identity must equally avoid conflict, particularly with the dominant Malay community. However, during the 1990s there has been greater tolerance, even positive official enthusiasm in celebrating Chinese and Indian festivals. These can be presented as evidence of successful multi-culturalism, and as tourist attractions. While non-Malays are mostly left to organise their own cultural life, subject to general guidelines, reconstruction of Malay culture and associated Islamisation policies have been closely guided and monitored. Though primarily an intra-Malay affair, these policies bear significantly on overall human rights in Malaysia.

The 'Islamic resurgence' during the 1970s was initially attributed to the combined effects of urbanising rural Malays through the NEP (Muzaffar 1986) and as an ultimate assertion of Malay identity (Khoo 1995: 159). But intensification of piety and missionary (*dakwah*) activity, partly spurred by the Islamic Revolution in Iran in 1978, posed growing challenges to the nexus between race and religion on which Malay nationalism and identity depend. Equality and rejection of racial distinctions are core Islamic beliefs. There are also non-Malay, particularly Indian Muslims. Such issues were taken up by more radical Islamists in opposition ranks (Nair 1997: 132–70).

While moderating Malay assertiveness assists inter-communal harmony, potential conflict between ethnic and religious definitions of identity has stirred intra-Malay tensions, already aggravated by uneven socio-economic outcomes from NEP programs. The official solution has been to construct Malaysian Islam in terms of values emphasising rationality, toleration, education and discipline, thereby reinforcing overall goals of both Malay and national development. Mahathir (1986: 56–82) has actively justified accumulation of honestly gained material wealth as according with the spirit of Islam, providing this does not become an end in itself and promotes the Islamic community's overall welfare. These goals were pursued by initiatives such as the International Islamic University and the Malaysian Islamic Bank (Bank Islam Malaysia Berhad). But these became instruments in a more general competition between UMNO and the opposition PAS during the 1980s for Malay support, against the background of escalating claims and counter-claims as to who most truly supported the cause of Islam.

External challenges with potential to upset the delicate balance of this project have come from diffuse sources in both the Islamic world and the west. The government has sought to develop closer links with the international Islamic community, while seeking to obviate dangers of importing militant influences promoting a fully-fledged Islamic state. Conversely, Malaysia has sought to legitimise its model of Islamic polity and national development within the Organisation of Islamic

Countries (OIC). It also undertakes more general advocacy of its claimed model of inter-religious toleration, building a society based on Islamic values but avoiding excessive legalism

Official constructions of Islam and Asian values are mutually supportive within this framework. Both project similar values towards Malays and non-Malays, while potentially sharing a common core across communal contexts. While discipline, educational and work ethic values extracted from Islam aim to legitimise modernisation programs among Malays, Asian values rhetoric performs a similar function for Malaysian society overall. At one stage, these goals were reinforced by the 'Look East' policy whereby Malaysians were encouraged to learn from the economic successes of Japan and South Korea. Construction of a differentiated Asian identity also provides a convenient tool for managing relations with the west, or at least influencing the terms of political and cultural exchange.

Despite sometimes strident anti-western rhetoric, overall priorities appear defensive. While seeking to reform culture and religion on its own terms, the government cannot tolerate external assaults perceived as undermining their foundations. Malaysia's carefully constructed national project may be equally upset by random social and cultural influences as by overt attacks on its political system. Vigorous counter-attacks emphasising very real injustices in the international economic order provide a powerful tool to de-legitimise western-based human rights critiques. These enhance Malaysia's influence in the international Islamic community and among developing countries. Malaysia nevertheless continues to encourage the inflow of foreign, including western capital and technology.

The strident and sweeping nature of much Malaysian anti-western rhetoric lacks the carefully crafted and targeted nature of Singaporean discourse. Much of Mahathir's human rights commentary is apparently driven by a 'domino theory' outlook in which initially moderate and reasonable demands for freedom of expression, workers' and women's rights are replaced by increasingly extreme demands, resulting in sexual anarchy, family breakdown, and ultimate societal disorder (Mahathir 1986: 99–103). Such views must be set against his advocacy of modernist and tolerant interpretations of Islam, including greater equality for women and cross-cultural understanding. One explanation sees Mahathir's rhetoric as that of a 'man in a hurry' to achieve national economic development adopting a form of least time-consuming pre-emptive strike against potential intrusions (Shamsul 1996).

As discussed in Chapter 2,[12] Anwar Ibrahim is highly critical of the tendency to use Asian values as blanket protection for lack of accountability and abuses by power holders. Another former Deputy Prime Minister, later UN Human Rights Commissioner, Musa Hitam holds similar views.[13] Both share Mahathir's perceptions of western double standards in applying human rights principles, while asserting that all Asian societies value family life more highly than individual rights. But this does not diminish obligations to promote core human rights values and democratic practices.

Philosophical and policy differences, now irreconcilable, emerged before Anwar's dismissal. Mahathir and Ibrahim nevertheless worked together over many years towards commonly agreed national objectives. In May 1997, Mahathir claimed that Anwar expressed similar views, but in a more conciliatory and academic fashion. 'He likes to quote, but he says the same thing. I just give my opinion. I don't read very much.[14]

Ibrahim contributed to the overall national project outlined above in three essential ways. First, he shared Mahathir's commitment to capitalist development strategy, but urged more targeted focus on poorer groups, for example, in relation to low cost housing, even if this entailed moderating overall growth rates. He was fiscally conservative in budgetary management, constantly pressing for transparency and an end to cronyism.

Second, Ibrahim's promotion of Asian civilisations discourse reinforced goals of inter-community tolerance and understanding, encouraging a search for common values supportive of human rights. Emphasis on dialogue helped reassure western interests, maintaining identity difference, yet softening the harsh edge of Mahathir's rhetoric. The institutional support base for 'Asian renaissance' discourse has been considerably weakened since Ibrahim's arrest. While this movement may have found new expression via the Justice Party, like similar earlier efforts, it is driven largely by intellectuals. Some opponents argue that notions of civilisation tend to elitism, with the practical effect of downgrading Malay culture relative to the globally civilising influence of Islam.[15]

Finally, Ibrahim played a pivotal, possibly irreplaceable role among Moslems in communicating and mobilising support for the government's Islamic modernisation policies. As leader of ABIM, then an activist Islamic youth movement, he was detained under the ISA. His surprise recruitment to UMNO by Mahathir in 1982 caused a split in ABIM, with the majority shifting support to the government. In return, ABIM enjoyed increased scope for its educational, social and other missionary activities. It contributed to developing the idea of an International Islamic University, designed to promote high standards of Islamic learning and international exchange of ideas. Ibrahim advocated cultural tolerance both among Moslems and in relations with other races and religions as a historically strong tradition within Islam. In this way Southeast Asian Islam could provide a model for the wider Moslem world, presenting a moderate face to the west, challenging an image of fanaticism harmful to all Moslems (Nazri 1995).

Prophet Mohammed's injunction to seek knowledge from all sources has provided strong support for cultural, technological and scientific aspects of Malaysia's nation-building project. But neither multicultural Islam nor civilisational dialogue necessarily lead to universal human rights. Anwar Ibrahim's declared inability to accept the UDHR, as partly assuming western values,[16] qualifies his claims that universal human rights are the common heritage of humankind. Chandra Muzaffar (1995*a*: 102–5) was still more explicit in opposing the UDHR and other UN instruments, as implicitly based on the concept of 'the "individual human being" as the only true bearer of human rights.' Muzaffar argues that rights, responsibilities, relationships and roles must be integrated in line with the core Islamic concept of man's 'vice-regency' derived from God.

The relationship between Islam and universal human rights in Malaysia is the subject of complex political and theological debate. Economic and social rights appear to fit with Islamic principles of mutual obligation, social justice and relieving poverty (Kamali 1994*a*: 55–6). While there are strong Qu'ranic injunctions defending property, the principle of trusteeship over the earth's resources sets limits to wealth accumulation. In practice, a wide combination of state, market and cooperative approaches are possible, excluding extremes in any one direction. Injunctions against charging interest have been resolved, at least in a formal sense, by establishing the Malaysian Islamic Bank, which adopts a 'joint venture' approach to lending.

Key civil and political rights issues are bound up with ongoing debates about relationships between Islam, state and society. In recent years, the parameters of this debate seem to have shifted strongly, if not yet decisively towards the concept of an Islamic society as an alternative to earlier demands for an Islamic state based on Shariah law. Not a few Moslems claim that there are no specific Qu'ranic injunctions requiring an Islamic state, and its nature is not specified.[17] However, Moslem rulers are still expected to uphold Islamic values of social justice, integrity, clean and efficient administration. Historically this has resulted in systems of government combining consultation and religious authority (Kamali 1994*a*: 45–6). In that context, the notion of the *ummah*, referring to the whole Islamic community as well as local groupings, is central to Moslem identity and social organisation.

Both authoritarian and democratic political interpretations of Islam appear possible. The former would regard God's commands, as set out in the Qu'ran, *hadith* (sayings attributed to the Prophet) and subsequent body of *Shariah* law as absolute. The popular will can have no legitimate right to override the manifest will of God. The liberal riposte is more complex. While acknowledging the supreme authority of the Qu'ran and *sunnah* (authoritative sayings of the Prophet), practical application to contemporary problems is seen as open to a range of approaches. Reformers seek to re-assert freedom of interpretation (*ijtihad*), suspended by religious leaders and scholars (*ulama*) in the tenth century CE, in order to challenge the cumulative legal interpretations which make up *Shariah* law. Mahathir (1995) has supported such calls, pointing out the dilemma for Moslems in having an infallible divine revelation without infallible interpreters.

While conservatives define an Islamic state as one which applies the full letter of *Shariah* law, reformers assert the primacy of the Qu'ran and the freedom which they see it giving each generation of Moslems to apply basic principles of social justice, equality and mutual welfare in their various situations. *Shariah* law was never intended to cover every detailed contingency. A 'broad, comprehensive and correct understanding of the *Shariah* should always favour justice, compassion, and a sound and robust commitment to truth, to equality, to tolerance and to the realisation of the legitimate interests of the people' (Kamali 1994*a*: 49–50, 62). So far as models of government are concerned, Kamali asserts that *Shariah* rules out all forms of absolutism and Islam advocates only limited forms of government. Representative government principles are thus natural and legitimate within an Islamic framework. At least, principles of popular consultation must be observed.

While consensus (*ijma*) is highly desirable, majority-based decision-making also has many precedents (Kamali: 1994*a*: 57–60).

Despite intellectual and theological trends away from legalistic concepts of an Islamic state, institutional realities are less favourable. *Shariah* is entrenched at state level, taking precedence over civil law in many areas of family law and public morality. The *ulama* jealously guard their powers of interpretation, although they must share administration with state rulers. They also bitterly resent the Prime Minister's assertion of *ijtihad*. He in turn has sought to counter their assertions of authority by strengthening his control of the national religious bureaucracy, via the Islamic Centre (Pusat Islam) under the Prime Minister's Office, and by establishing an Institute for Islamic Knowledge to propagate modernist interpretations. Pusat Islam also monitors 'deviant' versions of Islam, identifying forty-seven such groups in 1997.[18] These tend to favour authoritarian over liberal versions of Islam, but are in any case considered to represent a threat to stability and harmony.

The most serious threat to the government's position comes from PAS, which rarely commands less than 40 per cent of the Malay vote. In 1999, PAS increased its parliamentary seats from eight to twenty-seven and gained control of Terengganu in addition to Kelantan. Both states have introduced *Hudud* laws prescribing strict segregation between men and women and cutting off thieves' hands. Rape laws, requiring four male witnesses, have been ridiculed by women's groups and the Prime Minister, especially as failure to provide the necessary proof renders women alleging rape subject to indictment for adultery (Ahmed 1995; Mahathir 1995: 66–7). However, enforcement of such laws requires federal consent, which has so far been withheld. Extension of *Shariah* law restrictions on personal behaviour in other states has raised concerns as to the extent of their application to non-Moslems.

The government, with assistance from the Law Faculty of the International Islamic University, has sought to develop civil law in ways which both conform with general Islamic principles underlying *Shariah* law yet also commands general appeal. Each community's customs are to provide reference points for common law where such universality is lacking. *Shariah* courts' performance is to be improved by introducing a case law system. Such processes are necessarily slow and difficult, illustrating a more general difficulty in reconciling fears of non-Moslems with impatience of Moslems to realise Islamic ideals. Moreover, this model excludes non-Moslems from interpreting Islamic principles on which common law is to be based. Classical models of Islamic citizenship have proved unable to accommodate non-Moslem participation on equal terms, though some liberal thinkers are willing to consider more pluralist and inclusive concepts of what constitutes the *ummah* (Othman 1994).

According to Hussin Mutalib (1993: 49) the supremacy of the popular will and exclusion of the state from control over religion and individual conscience advocated by western philosophers such as Locke and Rousseau are antithetical to Islam, in which the state is to be an instrument of God's will, according to the Prophet's teachings. By contrast, Kamali, drawing widely on Qu'ranic and *Shariah* sources, seeks to correct the widely held view of both western and conservative Moslem commentators that Islam is a religion of duties, to which concepts of rights, including fundamental rights are alien (Kamali 1994*b*: 3, 13).

The problem arises, he argues from one-sided emphasis placed by religious scholarly commentary and the *Shariah* itself on divine revelation and sense of mission conveyed via the Prophet, in which God's law (*hukum*) is supreme.

The question of rights, as understood in terms of western legal philosophy is not addressed in Islamic source documents. But the content of *hukum*, rightly understood, bestows many kinds of rights relevant to both personal life and citizenship (Kamali 1994b: 18–19). Notions of right and duty are subsumed by the idea of truth (*al-haqq*) as representing the supreme value to which both ruler and ruled must submit (Kamali 1994b: 9–13). The absolute right of Moslems to defend their life, liberty, honour and property was consistently asserted by the Prophet.

Kamali (1994b: 29–57) draws affirmative evidence from five core Qu'ranic principles regarding rights of citizens – the right and duty of commanding good and forbidding evil (*hisbah*), offering 'sincere advice' to rulers (*nasibah*); consultation between rulers and people (*shura*), personal reasoning (*ijtihad*) and the right to constructive criticism (*haqq al-muraddah*). Such processes could not occur without freedom to express opinions and protection for those exercising such rights, which in turn requires freedom of association and assembly for lawful purposes. There is nevertheless a presumption that individual expression of opinion will be exercised for the public good within a community context (Kamali 1994b: 61–85). Further dispute centres on who can express opinions, with a consensus that *ulama* cannot claim exclusive rights. Mahathir (1986: 103) asserts that expressions of opinion on matters of both religion and policy should be confined to the educated and well-informed.

Limitations to freedom of speech relate essentially to its misuse for purposes of slander, libel, insult, sedition and blasphemy (Kamali 1994b: 161–228). But overall, the *Shariah* is primarily concerned with moral aspects and protecting the belief structure of Islam, to the extent of being intrusive in areas deemed as personal under western law. However, Kamali (1994b: 9) argues that, by comparison with some 'over-regulated areas of modern law in relationship to such matters as sedition and criticism of government authorities, *Shariah* rules encourage flexibility and tolerance.'

Regarding freedom of religion, Malaysia, like other Islamic countries, forbids proselytising towards Muslims, although conversion to Islam is both allowed and encouraged. Qu'ranic injunctions against compulsion in religion commands general assent. But there has been reluctance to accept its logic by allowing Moslems to leave their religion without penalty. The PAS supports traditional *Shariah* law prescriptions of death for apostasy. UMNO has felt obliged to respond to PAS' recent election gains with legislative proposals for 'rehabilitation centres' for apostates (Stewart 2000a). Only Sisters in Islam has firmly rejected legislation on issues of faith. Some Moslem scholars question whether those who leave Islam should suffer penalties where no treason or hostility towards the Islamic religion or community is involved (Kamali 1994b: 85–102).

The clear right to leave one's religion set out in article 18 of the UDHR can only be weakly inferred from Article 18(2) of the ICCPR, following pressure by

Moslem countries. The obligation on non-Moslems marrying Moslems to convert is far less disputed by Moslems, although it represents another form of religious coercion and conflicts with the absolute right to choice in marriage in UDHR Article 16. Article 23 of the ICCPR fails to specify the right to marry the person of one's choice, only offering protection against forced or under-age marriage. Finally, two of the three UN human rights treaties ratified by Malaysia relate to the rights of women and children. Blanket reservations upholding the primacy of Islamic law have been declared in both cases.[19]

Post-1997 economic crisis, fall of Anwar Ibrahim and the politics of illiberal democracy

Politics of economic crisis

Until 1990 both overall and inter-ethnic equity had been improved alongside sustained growth, with a subsequent mild reversal thereafter.[20] Abandonment of the NEP and accelerating privatisation provided a context for Malay discontent prior to the crisis. The crisis itself caused remarkably little inter-ethnic strife, probably due to the multi-ethnic nature of Malaysia's growing middle class (Shari 2000).

Though constrained in expressing his views as heir apparent for an indefinite period, the prospect of Anwar Ibrahim's eventual accession as Prime Minister had become a source of hope in both international and domestic human rights communities. He was also able to gather support from even relatively conservative Muslim opinion for democratic reform, while his calls for greater equity in economic planning, transparency and an end to corruption struck responsive chords in many quarters. Ibrahim's capacity for economic management, fiscal prudence and support for market disciplines attracted confidence in international business circles. Despite official denials, these qualities became an important cause of his undoing.

From the outset, Mahathir and Ibrahim adopted different approaches to the economic crisis, which caused rapidly falling currency values and share values. At its lowest point the Malaysian ringgit fell from its pre-crisis value of around 2.50 to 4.60 to the US dollar (Daly and Logan 1998: 27), while the Kuala Lumpur Stock Exchange (KLSE) index plunged from 1200 to 260 points (Mahathir 1999). Mahathir immediately blamed western (but not Asian) currency speculators, at one stage linking a vicious personal attack on George Soros with his Jewish identity. Soros, who had himself expressed reservations about the consequences of unbridled laissez-faire economics, responded by describing Mahathir as a menace to his own country. By contrast, Anwar cut government spending by around 20 per cent, cancelling or pruning several major projects. A system of restructuring bank debt was set in place, but failed to prevent a major diversion of funds to bail out powerful interests (Daly and Logan 1998: 22–8).

Although Malaysia avoided approaching the IMF, it faced problems of rising indebtedness and bankruptcies by previously sound companies caused by rising interest rates and overall economic contraction. Increasingly vocal regional and international reaction against IMF prescriptions by the second half of 1998 gradually turned the tide in favour of the Prime Minister, who had been effectively sidelined from economic policy-making for almost a year. Anwar Ibrahim, as Finance Minister and moderate advocate of IMF prescriptions, bore the brunt of this reaction.

Former Finance Minister, Daim Zainuddin, appointed as Economic Adviser to shadow Anwar, advocated an alternative strategy of rebuilding the economy by assisting small and medium-size enterprises, ignoring ethnic ownership, via the Small Scale Industries Fund. Interest rates should be reduced and funds directed away from excessive property investment. Domestic savings were to be mobilised through repatriation of Malaysian capital (Zainuddin 1998). Ibrahim attributed his downfall to the influence of Zainuddin, a close long term associate of the Prime Minister, who became Finance Minister following Ibrahim's dismissal (Reform Movement 1998).

Regulations which came into force on 1 September, 1998 set a limit of one month to repatriate Malaysian ringgits held overseas, after which their import would be banned and so rendered worthless. Trading outside Malaysia duly ceased, and the ringgit exchange value was fixed at 3.80 to the US dollar – probably a conservative undervaluation by that stage. Rights of nominee companies to hold clients' shares were terminated, preventing trading of unregistered shares in Singapore and elsewhere (Mahathir 1999). Repatriated funds increased available investment capital, relieving pressure on interest rates. Speculative capital movements were discouraged by a modest exit tax on funds leaving Malaysia in less than twelve months.

To sceptics who argue that its economy would have recovered in any case, Malaysia claims that its recovery was earlier and stronger than other East Asian countries, and even that its example helped create a regional climate discouraging to speculators. The Prime Minister claimed widespread support from business, with even the IMF and World Bank willing to concede merit in his approach.[21] He thanked China for not devaluing its currency, Japan for a loan of $US 300 million and Malaysian Chinese for their support during the crisis.[22] Predicting boom days ahead for the region, Mahathir said Asians would remember friends who had shown compassion and shared their misery, but find it hard to forget those 'who have laughed in our face, were insensitive to our anguish, hit us over the head with the sacred tablets on which are inscribed the holy mantras of market opening.'[23] Loans totalling US $400 million focusing on health, education and other social sector programs, with a three year strategic loan of US $1 billion – US $1.5 billion pledged over three years to strengthen human development (World Bank 1999*b*) were ignored.

Anwar Ibrahim's dismissal and imprisonment

The Prime Minister was at pains to point out that the then Deputy-PM had been present at the Cabinet meeting which approved the new controls, without objecting in any way. This enabled him to claim that economic reasons were not involved in Ibrahim's dismissal. Malaysia was about to defy the world with a strategy that it could not be certain would work, and no one in his right mind would want to add political instability to an already difficult economic situation, he argued. If his Deputy's removal had been planned, a more propitious time would have been found (Mahathir 1999).

The dismissal occurred on 2 September, 1998, one day after the new regulations came into force. The element of surprise ensured that Ibrahim could not cite economic policy differences as the cause. Dismissal or resignation on such grounds could have further weakened international market confidence, and left Anwar free to challenge the government from within both UMNO and Parliament. Only the most damaging personal charges would suffice to politically destroy him.

On the day of his arrest, Ibrahim had led around 35,000 demonstrators in calling on the Prime Minister to resign and demanding reform. Twenty-seven supporters from across the Malay community, including senior persons from UMNO, ABIM and the International Islamic University, were held under the ISA. None were held beyond sixty days, but some were charged under other laws. Ibrahim's wife was served an ISA restriction order prohibiting meetings at her home and other public appearances (Amnesty International 1999*d*: 24–5). During subsequent months over 1000 demonstrators were arrested under Police Act or Penal Code provisions, both of which grant sweeping discretion to police to control political gatherings. Many allegations of police violence and other abuses were reported (Amnesty International 1999*d*: 53–65). Violent aspects of mass demonstrations were eventually seen as counter-productive to emerging political strategies of building support for reform through the ballot box, supported by discussions at seminars, religious and other informal gatherings. Modest opposition gains in 1999 indicated the long-term nature of such strategies.

After nearly three weeks of addressing mass rallies across Malaysia, Ibrahim was arrested on 20 September under the Internal Security Act. He was denied access to lawyers until his ISA status was withdrawn on 14 October. Bail was denied as sodomy and conspiracy charges were prepared. Major deficiencies were identified in relation to the conduct of two consecutive trials.

On 22 September, the Prime Minister publicly asserted Anwar Ibrahim's guilt in an interview with national and foreign journalists, claiming that his sodomising and womanising rendered him unfit for public office. Mahathir's statement cited two witnesses who later alleged that their testimony had been coerced. Ibrahim's subsequent suit for defamation was unsuccessful, although Mahathir was never obliged to appear in court. Following fierce exchanges between counsels, the presiding judge ordered a ban on media comment as to the guilt or innocence of the accused (Amnesty International 1999*d*: 77–8). The Prime Minister's intervention was nevertheless hugely damaging to prospects for a fair trial.

On 29 September, Anwar appeared in court with a visible black eye, resulting from a severe beating when blindfolded soon after his arrest. The Prime Minister suggested that the injuries could have been self-inflicted in order to gain sympathy, but Rahim Noor, Inspector-General of Police, confessed that he had personally inflicted the beating, having 'lost his cool' under alleged provocation from Anwar.[24] Noor subsequently retired with only token punishment. Ibrahim's wife called on Mahathir, as Minister for Home Affairs, to accept responsibility.

Justice Paul, the sole presiding judge, persistently disallowed all testimony and cross-examination claiming political conspiracy. At one stage he issued contempt orders against one of the defence team for seeking to use an affidavit from another case in which the defendant alleged police pressure to testify against Ibrahim. Paul also cited the attorney in that case for contempt, until he apologised for allowing the affidavit to be used in Anwar's case – though not for its substance. Half way through the trial, the judge struck out all charges relating to sexual misconduct. This prevented the defence from disproving the sex charges, central to their strategy for substantiating accusations of political conspiracy and for clearing the good name of the accused (Amnesty International 1999*d*: 79–80).

The corruption charge hinged on whether Anwar directed police to pressure witnesses to withdraw testimony against him alleging sexual misconduct or, as he claimed, to ensure it was withdrawn after being proven false. The prosecution acknowledged that outgoing Police Special Branch chief, Mohamad Said Awang, had reported to Mahathir on August 20, 1997, that sexual misconduct allegations against Anwar were baseless. Awang further reported the possibility of a group, including government ministers, with an interest in encouraging testimony to discredit him. He also asserted that it was legitimate for his officers to obtain retractions from witnesses. Under questioning from both defence lawyer and judge, Awang was unable to state under what circumstances he might lie in court if instructed to do so by someone higher than the Deputy PM (Pereira 1998).

Amnesty International (1999*d*: 28–30, 67–70, 82–3) documents testimony of despicable police behaviour in forcing confessions, under conditions of ISA detention, by key witnesses against Ibrahim, notably Sukma Darmawan, Munawar Anees and Mior Abdul Razak. All subsequently retracted their evidence, but this was nevertheless allowed by the trial judge in the second trial on sodomy charges. That judge twice allowed amendments to the date in one alleged sodomising case, when it emerged that the apartments in question had not yet been built on the initially alleged date.

Amnesty's confusion of the above cases with justified concern over bias in Malaysian laws against same sex relationships is unhelpful to the victims and their families, as all assert that police allegations are pure fabrication. Indeed, portrayal of the former Deputy Prime Minister and Finance Minister as simultaneously prolific sodomiser and womaniser in the midst of his highly visible and demanding public life both strain credibility and render Malaysia's public image ridiculous. On the other hand, Malaysian arguments about different social standards have some merit in international law, as no UN human rights treaty yet recognises a right to either homosexual or extra-marital sexual relationships. Rather, such rights can be inferred from the right to privacy stated in Article 12 of the UDHR and Article 17 of the ICCPR.[25]

Post-trial responses

Trial and appeal processes were protracted, leading to eventual sentences of six years on conspiracy and corruption and nine on sodomy charges. The initial verdict generated large street demonstrations and other protests, and the electoral swing against the government could have been greater among Malay voters had the second trial been completed before November 1999. But although perceived injustice and harsh treatment towards Anwar will have long-term consequences for Malaysian politics, the government had substantially contained both international and domestic reaction. Cynicism has become deep-rooted, with the realisation that Anwar has been excluded from political life for up to twenty years, even if he is eventually released on compassionate grounds.

Chandra Muzaffar observed that most Malaysians expected a guilty verdict, although they were convinced of Anwar's innocence – in itself a 'damning indictment' of Malaysia's justice system. Mainstream media had spread 'poison pen' and ludicrous sexual allegations, finding him guilty in advance (Muzaffar 1999a). The power of the Prime Minister to shape the vital institutions of society to his will had been re-emphasised by this affair (Muzaffar 1999b). Param Curumaswamy, a Malaysian UNCHR special rapporteur for the independence of judges and lawyers, stated that the trial was flawed, did not appear to meet standards for fairness laid down in international law and had brought no credibility to Malaysia.[26]

Human Rights Watch declared the trial and sentence unfair. Both raised profound questions about the independence of the Malaysian judiciary, with further fears that the Malaysian government would crack down on rights to freedom of expression, assembly and association (P. Lim 1999). Amnesty International (1999d: 80) declared Anwar a prisoner of conscience. However, western official reaction was relatively restrained. International media interest could not long be sustained, in the absence of any immediate political threat to the Prime Minister. Protracted appeal processes rendered the case *sub judice*. Repeated warnings against external commentary on Malaysia's judicial processes induced further caution.

The government skilfully used an outburst by US Vice-President Gore supporting 'brave fighters' for reform, to rally nationalist sentiment, also charging that Gore's use of the Indonesian term 'reformasi' (reform) endorsed Jakarta-style street rioting aimed at the government's overthrow.[27] US Secretary of State Albright's meeting with Ibrahim's wife was ridiculed by sarcastic and inaccurate comparisons with the Monica Lewinsky affair by Minister for Trade, Rafidah Aziz (Richburg 1998).

Ibrahim's cause evoked sympathy in the regional and international Moslem community, in which he enjoys significant esteem. The Philippines President Estrada's reception of Wan Azizah at a private audience and comment that he was 'saddened' by Ibrahim's conviction[28] angered Malaysia's leaders. The Prime Minister also accused her of seeking the Philippines' support to achieve political change in Malaysia.[29]

Overall, the international community has not chosen to see Malaysia's abridgement of human rights as comparable with more extreme cases in Southeast Asia. Nevertheless, the International Court of Justice, based in The Hague, sent three representatives to probe the independence of Malaysia's justice system. This prompted the new Deputy Prime Minister, Abdullah Ahmad Badawi to ask what business foreigners had to question the fairness of Malaysia's courts and laws.[30]

Wholesale purging of Anwar supporters has weakened UMNO and affiliated organisations although, as with earlier splits, it retains a powerful position through continuing control over patronage and business opportunities. But a sense of alienation and a desire for reform has emerged in the hitherto relatively unpoliticised middle ground of Malay–Muslim opinion. With the halo of martyrdom surrounding him, Anwar's speeches and letters smuggled from jail (Reform Movement 1998) allege massive conspiracy aimed at maintaining corruption and cronyism by those whom he claimed to be pursuing prior to his dismissal.[31] Mahathir has responded by alleging large scale cronyism by Anwar supporters,[32] strengthening attacks on intervention by foreigners, whom he claims see Anwar as more compliant with their wishes.

Mahathir's strongest card has been the recovery of the Malaysian economy. GDP growth was estimated at 5.8 per cent in 2000, compared with 8.5 per cent in 1997 and negative growth of 7.5 per cent in 1998 (Thillainathan 2000). Unemployment of around 3 per cent must be set against the human cost borne by large numbers of repatriated migrant workers (Shari 2000). The Prime Minister gained considerable credit for defying conventional international economic wisdom, which he claims Ibrahim supports. Anwar claims he accepts only some of the IMF's prescriptions and has called for new global financial arrangements. However, he strongly supports the IMF on issues of corruption, bailouts of cronies, transparency and megaproject extravagance. Mahathir's anti-western attacks are a smokescreen to avoid addressing these deficiencies, as is his labelling of all dissent as anti-national (Reform Movement 1998).

Opposition coalition

An Alternative Front (BA) was established to fight the 1999 elections, with the DAP, PAS, the Justice Party (Keadilan) led by Dr. Wan Azizah, and the Malaysian People's Party (Partai Rakyat Malaysia – PRM) as principal components. Agreements to avoid competition ensured a straight fight with National Front parties. The government retained its two-thirds Parliamentary majority. The BA won forty-two seats, with the independent United Sabah Party (PBS) winning a further three out of a total of 193 Parliamentary seats. PAS won twenty-seven, DAP ten and Keadilan five seats (compared with eight, nine and zero in 1995). Wan Azizah, an eye specialist with no previous political experience, easily won the Penang seat formerly held for UMNO by her husband.

The results signalled problems for both government and opposition alliances, as well as the future balance of Malaysian politics. BN's majority was sharply reduced in many seats which it held, with twenty-six seats with majorities between 0 and 5 per cent and another twenty-four between 5 and 9 per cent.[33] Losses to PAS and Keadilan pose serious challenges to UMNO's long-term dominance among Malays. Ironically, earlier gerrymandering of constituencies in favour of Malays will soon represent a threat to UMNO's position. For the first time, UMNO, with seventy-one out of 148 BN seats, holds less than half the total representation of government coalition MPs.

The loss of Malay votes was partly offset by increased support from non-Malays. This was reflected in weak performance by the DAP, which had also lost heavily in 1995. Despite a net gain of one seat, its veteran leaders and high profile human rights champions, Lim Kit Siang and Karpal Singh both lost narrowly.[34] Agonising continues as to how far DAP's disappointing performance was due to fears of an Islamic state if PAS were to win, or whether relative success by some younger candidates indicates non-Malay voters' desire for a more conciliatory style of leadership, accepting realities of Malay political leadership.[35]

The continuing viability of the opposition coalition in its current form is doubtful. Malay electoral support gives PAS little incentive to soften its hard line promotion of an Islamic state, although its practical implementation would probably be open to negotiation in the unlikely event of an opposition victory. Assurances that its rigidly legalistic understanding of Islam's social and political role will not apply to non-Moslems are not widely trusted. Many moderate Moslems, particularly women, also view PAS' advance with alarm. Both PAS and DAP nevertheless strongly support abolishing the ISA and other restrictive security legislation. They also reflect popular anger against corruption, cronyism and lack of accountability.

An important difference in the present situation may be that, whereas previous constructions of opposition coalitions along non-communal lines have mostly appealed to non-Malays, Malays dominate the current coalition. The 1999 elections again illustrated the extent to which Malaysian politics reflects parallel intra-communal conflicts, with race-based politics intruding into both government and opposition coalitions.

Militant demands to restore the New Economic Policy have been advanced by a recently formed Malay Action Front, reasserting Malay overlordship in response to Chinese groups demanding abolition of special rights (Stewart 2001). There have also been some communally-based neighbourhood disturbances. The government, while striving to maintain inter-communal balance, also aggravates tensions by divisive commentary and heavy-handed use of the Sedition Act against opposition groups which dispute official interpretations.[36] Several Keadilan leaders have been held under the ISA during 2001 for allegedly promoting violence.[37]

The DAP felt obliged to withdraw an Indian nominee as Alternative Front candidate at a Kedah state by-election in November 2000 in favour of a Keadilan Malay candidate. This resulted in a large swing to defeat the Malaysian Indian Congress (MIC) candidate representing the BN who had easily won the seat in 1999 (Stewart 2000*b*). Nevertheless, both Keadilan and PAS rejected notions of Malay dominance implied in talks proposed by the government to restore Malay unity (Hamid 2001). Cooperation in practical struggles by NGOs, labour, environmental and women's groups over several decades have improved trust between communities. Jailing of Lim Guan Eng, a DAP Member of Parliament for taking up the case of a fifteen year old Malay girl charged by the authorities, and protesting against the acquittal of a Cabinet Minister, whom she alleged had sexual intercourse with her, attracted strong cross-community protest.[38]

National Human Rights Commission

On 25 April, 1999, the Foreign Affairs Minister announced the government's intention to establish the Human Rights Commission of Malaysia (SUHAKAM). Based on his statement and press reports, thirty-eight NGOs submitted a Memorandum in May, to which the government partially responded on 15 June (Rachagan 2000: 263–74). Legislation was tabled in July and the Act gazetted on 9 September 1999.[39] This rapid timetable caused widespread complaints of lack of consultation (Just World Trust 1999; Amnesty International 1999*d*: 74–5). NGO concerns, reiterated in a meeting with SUHAKAM on 15 May 2000,[40] ranged broadly across issues relating to the transparency, independence, powers, mandate and resources of the Commission.

The Memorandum expressed concern with the statutory authority model, based on experience with other bodies. Thus, the King, advised by the Prime Minister, is to appoint and re-appoint both Chairman and members for two year periods. A broader-based selection committee was proposed to ensure balance. Longer periods of tenure would strengthen independence and continuity. Location in the Foreign Affairs Ministry building could weaken public confidence in SUHAKAM's autonomy.

The Commission's mandate is limited by the Act in several significant ways. Human rights are defined with reference to those specified in Part II of Malaysia's Constitution rather than UN covenants and conventions. But such constitutional rights have been rigidly constrained by extensive security legislation. The Commission's task of advising the government on ratifying UN human rights treaties may nevertheless accelerate bureaucratic processes necessary to fulfilling promises made over many years (Rachagan 2000: 267).

The Commission is precluded from involvement in cases either in process or already determined by the courts. Powers to visit prisons are subject to compliance with procedures governing the relevant places of detention. Since the ISA and other security legislation give the authorities sweeping discretion, not subject to judicial review, SUHAKAM visits are likely to be on a correspondingly discretionary basis. Finally, funding will depend on annual allocations from the national budget, which will in turn determine the extent of its outreach beyond Kuala Lumpur.

The Commission's mandate, structure and powers thus fall short of minimum requirements of the Paris Principles. SUHAKAM has not applied to join the Asia-Pacific Forum of National Human Rights Institutions, though the government has indicated support for any decision to seek membership (Rachagan 2000: 274). This could well be refused in the Commission's present form. Constitutional entrenchment, and broadening of its powers and mandate to more fully reflect international human rights law are essential to establishing SUHAKAM's effectiveness and legitimacy.

Given its obvious inadequacies, the initiative has been widely regarded as a tokenistic attempt to improve Malaysia's tarnished image. However, much the same was said initially about Indonesia's National Human Rights Commission.[41] Although both the appropriateness of selecting a former cabinet minister and his liberal credentials have been questioned (Fan Yew Teng 2000), appointment of former UNCHR Commissioner Musa Hitam as Chairman, could open the door to wider change. Ultimately, the Commission's effectiveness will depend on the quality of its members, creative advocacy, pressures for accountability and use of its services by civil society groups.

Conclusion

Structures of illiberal democracy appear entrenched for the immediate future. Malaysia's example illustrates that formally democratic countries based on the rule of law and a written constitution can, if their leadership so determines, develop political structures and processes profoundly hostile to popular enjoyment of civil and political rights.

Removal of Anwar Ibrahim has left a vacuum in Malaysia's political life. Centralisation of power in the Prime Minister's hands have virtually reduced elections to personal plebiscites. UMNO's internal processes are similarly paralysed. Potential successors are neither obvious nor impressive. While hinting at possible retirement, Dr. Mahathir retains a strong sense of mission to defend Malaysia against forces on all sides seeking to undermine his vision. His ubiquitous presence stifles discussion of humane and democratic forms of governance.

Yet Malaysia's problems are at base structural rather than personal. The quest for national unity, based on permanent dominance of one ethnic group can be seen after some forty years to have increased divisions both within and between communities. The accommodation which seemed to be emerging by the mid-1990s was in retrospect too elite-centred to survive a major economic downturn and associated political upheavals. Despite impressive economic advances, the country still appears stuck between competing visions of a Malay and Malaysian nation, constraining initiative at all levels. Both government and opposition models of inter-community coalition have so far reproduced the same stalemate.

In this environment, models seeking to transcend racial and religious blocs appear utopian. Yet Malaysia remains an essentially pluralist society. The range and volume of dissent has grown in proportion to state power, as has the search for alternative directions. Winds of change in neighbouring countries are influencing the dynamics of Malaysian public life in a reformist direction, despite the government's siege mentality.

An increasing range of Malaysian groups incorporate universal and indivisible human rights values into their discourse and goals. The urgency of links with UN human rights regimes was evident in NGOs' strong joint submissions to Malaysia's newly established National Human Rights Commission. Despite its current low recognition, international human rights law can assist change in Malaysia by affirming each group's cultural and religious identity, while strengthening mutual respect; validating economic development goals while integrating them with civil and political rights; reducing both intra and inter communal conflict by focusing on poverty eradication; transcending east versus west dualisms by practical application of universal rights in local contexts. The non-threatening and inclusive nature of universal human rights frameworks may thus even yet enable Malaysia to finally 'break the mould'.

5 Indonesia

Democratic transition and human rights

President Suharto's resignation on 21 May 1998, under conditions of widespread disorder, launched Indonesia into uncharted political waters. Despite initiating major political reforms, his immediate successor, President Habibie, lacked adequate legitimacy to survive. Abdurrachman Wahid became Indonesia's first democratically elected President in October 1999. Despite achieving important democratic changes, his presidency has operated under severe strains from the outset (ICG 2001c) and currently appears unsustainable. Wahid's commitment to religious and cultural pluralism and tolerance has not spared Indonesia from extensive inter-ethnic and religious violence, social and political disorder.

Underlying causes of continuing crisis reach beyond personalities to fundamental problems of democratic transition. While Thailand and the Philippines are undergoing similar transitions, Indonesia historically lacks both the continuity of Thailand's core institutions and the Philippines' democratic legal and constitutional infrastructure. Contemporary struggles display both continuity and discontinuity, rooted in Indonesia's unique history, political and cultural configurations. Human rights issues must be understood within a similar frame of reference.

The first part of the chapter identifies relevant ideological and institutional inheritances from Suharto's 'New Order', featuring both government and civil society, including NGO, labour and Islamic discourses surrounding human rights and democracy issues. These reflect conflict between communitarian and liberal-democratic outlooks familiar from earlier chapters. The account traces the beginnings of change under Suharto into the post-1998 period, including constitutional reform, military–civilian relations, the economic crisis and regional devolution, particularly the strained situation in Aceh and Irian Jaya. The final section reviews current trends in human rights policy, particularly the role of Indonesia's National Human Rights Commission (Komnas HAM) and politics surrounding recent human rights legislation.

History and institutions

Indonesia declared independence on 17 August 1945, although Holland did not finally surrender sovereignty until November 1949. Conflicts fought out during these four years (Kahin 1952; Reid 1974) vitally influenced subsequent political development. The Indonesian military (ABRI) invoked its struggle against Dutch rule to legitimate claims for a powerful role in national decision-making. Assertion of national unity and stability as overriding priorities have thwarted democratic aspirations, reinforced by culture-based definitions of Indonesian identity favouring authority and hierarchy.

During the 1950s, Indonesia pursued a system of parliamentary democracy. But the Constituent Assembly of delegates appointed to a national consultative body in 1946 was unable to agree on a permanent constitution. Elections in 1955, supported by a 90 per cent popular turnout, proved inconclusive. Seven cabinets coalitions were attempted between 1950 and 1959 (Feith 1962). Regional rebellions in West Sumatra and South Sulawesi led to strong military demands, supported by President Sukarno, for a return to the 1945 Constitution. This was decreed by the President in 1959 after the Assembly had twice failed to deliver the necessary two-thirds majority.

This period of 'liberal democracy' was portrayed by both Presidents Sukarno and Suharto as one of chaos and instability, based on competition between self-serving personal interests mobilising regional, religious and ethnic conflicts. Such judgements ignore destabilising roles played by both Sukarno and ABRI, and substantial progress towards drafting a democratic constitution guaranteeing civil and political rights by the Constituent Assembly before its overthrow (Nasution 1994).

From 1959 to 1965, Indonesia experienced a triangular power struggle between ABRI and the Indonesian Communist Party (PKI), balanced by President Sukarno. Between 500,000 and one million people were killed in upheavals following an alleged coup attempt on 30 September 1965. General Suharto assumed full powers as President in March 1967. Communist and left-wing elements were ruthlessly killed and imprisoned. Up to 100,000 were detained without trial for suspected involvement in the 'coup',[1] many for over ten years. Post-release harassment and discrimination continued to the end of Suharto's rule.

The new government, though military dominated, appointed civilian professionals to key technical and economic planning positions. But Suharto soon dashed hopes of democratic restoration, instead extracting key concepts from Sukarno's 'Guided Democracy' system as building blocks for his 'New Order'. This monolithic, territorially based system has retained residual strength through the upheavals of reform, particularly in outlying provinces where the military retains considerable operational autonomy.

The 1945 Constitution formally vested supreme powers in the People's Deliberative Council (MPR). This body met every five years to appoint the President and Vice-President and determine state policy guidelines. It can approve constitutional amendments by a two-thirds majority. Though sharing law-making powers with the House of Representatives (DPR), the President could effectively legislate by decree, using administrative regulations. Ministers were appointed by and answerable to the President rather than the DPR, which also lacked clear powers to amend budgets. Courts' independence was undermined by the Ministry of Justice's control over appointment and tenure of judges.

The Ministry of Internal Affairs extended territorial control across the country, liaising closely with parallel military command structures (Crouch 1988), into which functional ministries were integrated at local and regional levels. Military-controlled intelligence agencies, now officially dismantled, monitored civilian groups, assessed socio-political trends and gave 'guidance' to civilian authorities and representative bodies at each level.

Military–civilian integration was originally legitimised in terms of unity between army and people in a common national struggle, based on a strategic doctrine of 'territorial' warfare in resisting invasion (Lowry 1996: 25–9). This was developed into the 'middle way' concept under Sukarno, designed to avoid either total civilian domination or outright military rule. Suharto substituted the 'dual function' principle, appointing many ABRI personnel to non-military administrative and technical posts.

After 1959, over eighty political parties were reduced to ten. The modernist Moslem party, Masjumi, which had gained over 20 per cent of the popular vote and the smaller, pro-western Indonesian Socialist Party (PSI) were excluded. Political party MPs were joined by representatives of 'functional groups' in a restructured Parliament. Suharto outlawed the PKI, replaced Masjumi with the less assertive Indonesian Islamic Party (PARMUSI), and intervened heavily in the remaining parties' management and choice of candidates to ensure conformity with official ideology and policies.

Under Suharto, the functional groups (golkar) concept was developed into a quasi-party structure, which all civil servants, military, police and other government employees were obliged to join. Labour, business, farmers, women, youth, lawyers, journalists and other professional and special interest groups were grouped in affiliated associations, which monopolised representation in each field (Reeve 1985). Golkar communicated official policies within a framework of 'mono-loyalty'. Although Golkar was not a party according to its official theory, its vote in elections between 1971 and 1997 never fell below 60 per cent, twice exceeding 70 per cent. Voting targets, set for each area, were often exceeded by enthusiastic officials.

Nine parties plus Golkar contested the 1971 elections. Immediately afterwards, these were rationalised into two broadly Moslem and non-Moslem cum secular nationalist groupings. Parties were thus defined as representing different socio-cultural streams (*aliran*), based on common commitment to goals of national unity and development. Though theoretically enabling citizens to contribute towards shaping national goals and policies, such arrangements abridge principles of freedom of association enshrined in the ICCPR. Parties' vitality was further emasculated by regulations barring them from operating below district level outside prescribed election periods, so as not to 'distract' people from developmental tasks.

Democracy and human rights discourse under Suharto

The five principles of *Pancasila* provided the normative and ideological base for both Sukarnoist and New Order institutions. These affirm belief in one God, national unity, civilised humanitarianism (or internationalism), representative government and social justice (Kahin 1952: 122–7). Decisions are to be made and disputes resolved on the basis of deliberation (*musyawarah*) and consensus (*mufakat*), avoiding competitive voting and associated conflict between majorities and minorities. Cooperative principles are to extend to all economic and social spheres. The language and spirit of Pancasila thus parallels much of the discourse of 'Asian' values and democracy. The functional groups system of representation which it supports has no clear principle for determining which groups are represented, in what proportions and by whom. Such decisions depend on centralised selection by the President and close associates.

Integralist doctrines, first propounded in 1945 during the process of preparing a constitution for the new Republic, assume unity between government and people, thereby denying notions of individual or group rights towards the state, which is conceived as a large family. Parallels with European and Japanese fascist concepts of the organic state were acknowledged by key protagonists. Integralist interpretations of Pancasila, rejected in 1945, were nevertheless incorporated into New Order ideology and practice (Bourchier 1996). Thus the 1985 Law on Social Organisations required organisations to define their objectives in terms of Pancasila as 'sole foundation'. Compulsory Pancasila education courses were conducted in educational institutions and workplaces. Christians and Moslems perceived threats to core tenets of their religious faith, but the government denied any such intent.

Mohammed Hatta, Indonesia's first Vice-President, urged the need to limit state power. His ideas were enshrined in Article 28 of the 1945 Constitution, guaranteeing freedom of expression, assembly and organisation. The Article's practical effect was weakened by the qualifying words 'according to law'. The New Order asserted superiority of integralist interpretations over legal and constitutional forms. Opponents replied that derivative laws must accord with the Article's plain words and underlying intent, supported by independent judicial review.

New Order discourse revived interest in Hatta's ideas (Simunjuntak 1994). Hatta was commonly seen as a western-style democrat, due to his championing of basic freedoms and staunch defence of government accountability via an elected Parliament. But other aspects of his thought suggest a Pancasila frame of reference (Wahjono 1991). His comment that the French Revolution upheld liberty but forgot equality and fraternity indicated rejection of individualist assumptions underlying western liberal democracy. Basing 'fraternity' on the compassion of Allah (Wahjono 1991: 235–6), some Moslem commentators subordinate Hatta's democratic outlook to his Islamic faith (Noer 1991). Emphasis on social justice and popular participation in decision-making fits better with Pancasila's rejection of interest group politics associated with liberal democracy. However, Hatta's rejection of the functional groups concept indicates his belief that participation is to be achieved via elected representatives (Haris 1994: 110–22).

The late Suharto years saw diffuse attempts to reconcile Pancasila with principles of democratic openness and religious tolerance (Ramage 1996). Abdurrachman Wahid shares a similar philosophy with Hatta, despite differences in religious and cultural origins. Wahid founded Forum for Democracy in 1991 primarily to counter threats to national unity from rising religious sectarianism.[2] Yet liberal-pluralist democracy naturally articulates conflict between contending viewpoints and interests, including religious and ethnic groups, in ways which are not always benign. Wahjono (1991) argues that liberal democracy does not exclude consensus based on dialogue and bargaining, while Pancasila, as expressed in the 1945 Constitution, can embrace majority voting. The first proposition has been sorely tested by the post-Suharto proliferation of political parties. Exclusion of left-wing groups by branding ideology based on class conflict as subversive similarly undermines claims that Pancasila accommodates all major streams of society.

Integralism follows communitarian principles in linking rights to citizens' responsibilities. Media reporting, for example, is to be 'free but responsible'. Despite some temporary and partial liberalisation during the early 1990s, regulatory frameworks allowed the government to set guidelines requiring media to encourage implementation of national development, using Pancasila democracy as a tool (Massakh 1995).

Pancasila-style democracy was defended as widening participatory opportunities. Former Chairman of the National Human Rights Commission, Baharuddin Lopa, observed that democracy requires 'openness' to avoid conflicting interests 'narrowing' the political process (Massakh 1995). Former Armed Forces Commander, General Benny Murdani saw openness as entailing harmony and responsibility – not contempt, hostility and verbal abuse. General Rudini asserted that openness was only possible under Pancasila as distinct from rougher (*kasar*) forms of democracy. Former Security chief, Admiral Sudomo saw a need to reconcile order and creativity, with dangers of stagnation if security prevented all popular initiative (Sinjal 1991).

A similar logic was employed to coopt values of free speech and expression, whereby opinions may be expressed openly, but '... without prejudice against any person or organisation (as) the essential principle of democracy' (Sudradjat 1995). Chairman of the DPR and MPR, Wahono, stated that (Pancasila) democracy requires differences of opinion to be clearly stated as a pre-condition for agreement to be reached.[3] By contrast, liberal democracy limits neither the content of opinions nor their manner of expression, nor assumes agreement as an objective.

Pancasila democracy affirms 'the people' as the ultimate source of sovereignty. Even Abraham Lincoln's famous slogan of 'government of the people, by the people, for the people' was cited as endorsing Pancasila principles.[4] In practice, notions of popular sovereignty served to legitimise state dominance. The New Order monopolised representation processes by denying rights to organise independently (Nusantara 1995). Even selected groups represented in the DPR were hamstrung by its operational rules, whereby the constitutional right of members to speak freely was interpreted to mean the right of the whole DPR to express its view. DPR factions were similarly obliged to await emergence of a common position on any given issue.[5] Reserved seats for the military further detracted from popular sovereignty.

Echoing earlier nationalist debates, reformers include both optimists, who see indigenous cultures as supporting democratic values, and pessimists who see feudal and hierarchical traditions as buttressing authoritarianism (Haris 1994: 158–60). The activist poet, W. Rendra, portrays the political class as steeped in bureaucratic attitudes inherited from Majpahit and Mataram,[6] without any concept of either popular sovereignty or individual citizenship rights.[7] But Ignas Kleden denies that democracy is rooted in or excluded from any particular location, as all people can adapt culture to their situation and needs.[8]

The issue of voting remains a core of contention. Pancasila seeks to avoid outcomes based on winners or losers by ensuring that all groups gain some representation. Differences are to be further resolved by the majority showing respect and as far as possible accommodating the concerns of the minority, which in turn must adapt itself to majority wishes. Such logic can, as in the initial reaction to the 1999 East Timor referendum, result in the aspirations of even a large majority being placed on an equal footing with those of a deeply unpopular minority.

President Habibie's abolition of Pancasila's ideological monopoly and associated indoctrination courses has left its status uncertain. During the current uncertain transition period, norms of social harmony can nevertheless be useful in balancing individualist, competitive and secular values associated with liberal democracy as well as dangerous trends towards religious sectarianism and authoritarianism.

Social and political mobilisation

Popular mobilisation around democracy and human rights issues has included NGOs, students, journalists, lawyers and other professionals, intellectuals, educational and religious movements. By the end of the 1980s the strength and diversity of civil society groups was making a significant public impact, reaching out to farmers, landless, industrial labour, women, minorities and other marginalised groups. Civil and political rights concerns conventionally associated with the middle class were popularised by linking them with issues impacting on people's daily lives relating to land, wages and working conditions, environment, violence and harassment against women and corruption at all levels.

In 1980 the government was challenged by a group of well known former military, including General Nasution, politicians and intellectuals in the so-called 'Petition of Fifty' (Jenkins 1984; Bourchier 1987). This group objected to the government's assumed right to monopolise Pancasila's interpretation. Though later overtaken by more radical groups which perceived it as pro-establishment, the group played a strategic role in legitimating dissenting versions of official ideology in face of New Order repression.

Three broad approaches to democracy, deriving from earlier traditions (Eldridge 1995: 20–2) were evident among civil society groups during the late Suharto years, favouring respectively open and pluralist versions of Pancasila, liberal cum social democracy and direct mass action (Eldridge 1996). While the first two focus on legal and political reform, 'popular democracy' radicals emphasise transformation of basic power structures in order to gain social and economic justice for Indonesia's masses. Influenced by Gramscian ideas of ruling class hegemony, radicals see distinctions between state and civil society, fundamental to liberal thinking, as contingent and instrumental. But labelling them as 'communists' by the Indonesian government, because they emphasise class conflict, is misleading. Emphasis on direct action and people's sovereignty (*kedaulatan rakyat*) place them more in line with radical mass movements which erupted in the early post-independence years (Anderson 1972).

Liberal and radicals join forces in viewing 'Pancasila democracy' as a tool of state hegemony. Forum for Democracy, founded by Abdurrachman Wahid in 1991, and the 'Petition of Fifty' group sought to reconcile Pancasila values and practice with the institutions and processes of liberal democracy. This approach also suited many mainstream NGOs struggling to reconcile Pancasila as their 'sole foundation', as legally required, with their ideals of democratic participation (Eldridge 1995: 47–9).

These accommodationist approaches were sharply rejected by younger activists, who also felt alienated from dominant philosophies of developmentalism. Fachry Ali (1992) saw Wahid's model of democracy as built on false assumptions of openness between ruler and ruled, failing to appreciate that democracy is based on conflict between different viewpoints and interests. In reality, New Order politics was built on non-public negotiations and accommodations with selected groups.

The Information Centre and Action for Democratic Reform (PIJAR), a loose network established in 1989 by student groups in major cities, sought to link civil and political rights with public interest issues, in order to demand openness and accountability from government officials. PIJAR achieved prominence during protest action against the banning in mid-1994 of three popular oppositionist weekly magazines – *Tempo, Editor* and *Detik* – which criticised Technology Minister Habibie's programmes. This was followed by formation of the Independent Journalists' Alliance (AJI) and publication of a new periodical, *Suara Independen* (Independent Voice). These actions directly challenged official controls and the monopoly held by the Golkar-front Indonesian Journalists' Association (PWI). AJI's Chairman, Ahmad Taufik, and three other journalists received 6–7 year jail sentences for publishing material hostile and insulting to the President and Vice-President (Article 19 1995: 9–20). Publication of *Suara Independen* nevertheless continued via the internet.

In 1993, PIJAR and AJI joined with legal, policy research, church, student, and other human rights groups to form the Indonesian People for a Humanitarian Community (MIUK) with a broad goal of reforming the Indonesian Constitution. From a core focus on gaining release of political prisoners (*tapol*) and 'political criminals' (*napol*), and removal of discrimination against those released,[9] MIUK's efforts extended to campaigns for abolishing security legislation, and advocacy on behalf of the least politically acceptable, often unpopular prisoners, including 'socialist' activists and campaigners for secession in East Timor, Irian Jaya and Aceh. A general amnesty for all *tapol* and *napol* was achieved soon after President Wahid's accession, accompanied by dismantling of military dominated internal security bodies.

The Centre for People's Democracy (PDR) is a network of labour, student and peasant solidarity groups striving for a just society, in opposition to 'capitalist and imperialist domination', and describing itself as the Indonesian Pro-Democracy Movement. Though it joined with PIJAR and MIUK to support self-determination for East Timor and oppose closure of the three journals banned in 1994, PDR is critical of what it terms 'elite opposition groups'. It further claimed that only it could supply the necessary mass action in defence of the three journals banned in mid-1994, although these reflected 'elite' groups' own liberal ideology (SPRIM 1995). Such claims ignore severe jail sentences passed on 'liberal' activists and associated journalists in defence of press freedom. It also represents a continuing tendency to claim credit for actions undertaken jointly – a less attractive feature of many activist networks.

The International Forum for Indonesian Development (INFID) represents the major forum for networking between NGOs and other social advocacy groups, consulting with overseas counterparts on the basis of prior consensus among Indonesian groups. INFID evolved from the International Non-Government Group for Indonesia (INGI), established to monitor Indonesia's aid negotiations with international donors along with its overseas collaboration and funding, INGI's lobbying against major development programmes relating to forestry, transmigration and large dams angered the Indonesian government (Eldridge 1995: 195–201).

INFID extended INGI's focus on aid to trade and investment, causing Indonesia's National Planning Board (BAPPENAS) to request its exclusion from World Bank consultative meetings, including a study on NGOs' role and effectiveness. The economic crisis proved such exclusion untenable, with the Bank and other donors demanding evidence of community participation in official programmes. NGOs responded by demanding proper evaluation of projects' environmental and social impact in return for their cooperation.

There was a parallel resurgence within the student movement from the late 1980s (Aspinall 1993). Tight controls had shifted students to off-campus activities in the early 1980s. Younger activists resolved not to be trapped by what they saw as developmentalist outlooks of larger NGOs initiated by their predecessors. Lacking organisation, they engaged in various forms of conflict and dialogue with NGOs, in efforts to shift them towards a more political outlook (Eldridge 1995: 38–43). This often painful conflict achieved a measure of consensus, as some larger NGOs took up grassroots issues and struggles. INFID membership and policies came to reflect a broader constituency, embracing small and rural-based groups.[10] Ultimately, a division of labour emerged, recognising a need to link popular mobilisation to survival strategies accepted as feasible by poor people. These require careful balance between struggle and cooperation with relevant authorities and power holders.

Labour issues provided a growing focus of mobilisation during the late Suharto years, as greater proportions of the work force became industrialised (YLBHI 1995: 102; Harris 1995: 36–7). Major grievances related to wages, which failed to meet minimum living costs, unfulfilled obligations by employers, enforced payments to officials, harassment of women workers, and military involvement in labour negotiations, despite withdrawal of their legal rights to intervene.[11]

The legal monopoly held by the government-controlled All Indonesian Workers' Union (SPSI) represented a fundamental breach of ILO conventions. Emerging independent labour organisations included the reformist Indonesian Labour Welfare Association (SBSI) and the socialist Centre for Indonesian Labour Struggles (PPBI) advocating comprehensive structural reform. Both groups cooperated with major legal aid organisations in opposing restrictions on workers' rights to organise. Though not banned, both were refused registration on the grounds that they were NGOs rather than labour unions. SBSI General Secretary, Mochtar Pakpahan, was detained for two years following major labour unrest in Medan in March 1993, while PPBI leader Dita Sari was jailed from 1996 until early 1999.

SBSI coordinates campaigns for ratifying ILO conventions and reforming Indonesian labour laws with the International Confederation of Free Trade Unions (ICFTU 1995: 83–9). Joint complaints over labour rights violations (ILO 1995) and calls for economic sanctions brought both organisations into conflict with the Indonesian government. But the ICFTU remains uncertain about NGOs' role in SBSI, believing they have little organisational capacity or understanding of trade union principles. PBBI's approach of linking industrial organisation with political education via the People's Democratic Party (PRD), formed in 1996, also dilutes specifically labour oriented struggles.

Independent women's groups have played active roles in labour organisation. The Jakarta network within Women's Solidarity (SP), which networks directly with working class women, supports migrant women workers (Harris 1995: 71–80). SP sees government policy as superficial and motivated by concern to avoid diplomatic conflict, for example, by forbidding women to talk publicly about their experiences. SP informs migrant workers' families about their rights, using contacts thus gained to gather further information. Mobilising returned workers as local cadres for new support groups, provides a basis for publicity and campaigns. Kalyanamitra, a Jakarta women's NGO, undertakes research and publications, providing forums for discussing a wide range of women's issues, particularly domestic and workplace violence. It cooperates with the Women's Section of SPSI and the labour section of the Foundation of Indonesian Legal Aid Institutions (YLBHI) in such campaigns and in programmes for educating and empowering domestic servants (Kalyanamitra 1986; Eldridge 1995: 161–5).

While partly reflecting ideological tensions between activist groups discussed earlier, independent women's groups have shared a common struggle for autonomy from official bodies associated with Golkar, notably Dharma Wanita and the Family Welfare Association (PKK), which replicate their husbands' position in official hierarchies. Although they have now lost their official monopoly, these organisations continue to signify forms of patriarchy embedded in Indonesia's ideology and institutions – for example, in state doctrines about the 'family basis' of state and consultative structures at sub-village level, based on 'heads of households' as the building blocks of village government.

During the constitutional democracy period, women gained important civil rights and theoretical equality in several areas of work. However, they only achieved the longstanding goal of a uniform marriage law, which set limits to one-sided divorce and polygamy rights by Moslem men, in 1974. The New Order also brought significant improvements in the health and nutrition of women and children, as well as personal freedoms deriving from birth control programmes. But such gains were offset by stifling controls and stereotyped construction of female roles (Blackburn 1994).

Post-Suharto democratic change led to a proliferation of women's organisations, reflected in new government institutions established to oppose violence and enhance women's empowerment. However, heady freedoms have been accompanied by extensive disorder and violence from which women have suffered disproportionately (Blackburn 2001). The strategic gender interests of women, as in the past, thus remain in danger of being submerged by larger political conflicts and agendas, unless articulated by strong coalitions at every level of government and society.

Overall, the resilience of civil society groups in popular advocacy, mobilisation and direct initiation of programmes, including capacity for internal renewal, has added to the momentum for political change, and sustaining pressure for its continuation. But civil society groups' future social mobilisation roles in relation to elected politicians have yet to be adequately defined or understood.

Human rights and democracy discourse in Indonesian Islam

Diffuse outlooks of Indonesian Moslems' on democracy and human rights reflect long-standing struggles and debates over Islam's political role and relations with the state, the impact of modernisation, and rights of majorities, minorities and individuals in a pluralist society. Dutch colonial policy encouraged Islamic piety and freedom of worship, but banned political expressions of religion. This represented a fundamental misreading of Islam, which rejects distinctions between public and private spheres of faith. Many Moslems see post-independence governments as similarly seeking to de-politicise Islam.

The status of *Shariah* law has been central to Islamic discourse since June 1945, when the 'Jakarta Charter' declared it obligatory for all citizens professing Islam. The far vaguer commitment to 'One God who is Great and Almighty' in the final version of Pancasila declared two months later was designed to reassure both Christians and many Moslems who wish to follow Javanese and other local customs free from binding religious rules.[12] Demands to enforce Islamic law dominated debate during the 1950s 'constitutional democracy' period. More recently, compromise has been sought via notions of an 'Islamic society', in which Islam is to be pursued as a purely ethical and social ideal, not enforced by legislation. This could logically render Islamic parties redundant. Equally, denial of Moslems' rights to form parties would negate democracy.

Islamic parties depend on support from base-level organisations with pre-independence origins, which play extensive social, economic, cultural, educational as well as religious roles. While parties are created and dissolved according to changing needs, these networks have proved resilient in face of massive upheavals. The two largest and best known are Muhammadijah and the Religious Scholars' Association (Nahdlatul Ulama – NU), whose respective orientation has been described as modernist and conservative.

Like fundamentalist, liberal, radical, traditional, secularist and similar epithets, these terms quite inadequately describe the infinite subtleties and cross-currents within Indonesian Islam.[13] 'Modernists' have always demanded explicit identification between Islam and the state. Their movement emerged in the early twentieth century, seeking a stricter, more rational approach to Islam, purifying it of local cultural accretions perceived as irrelevant or superstitious. Modernists advocate using contemporary knowledge and technology to strengthen Islam and its people's welfare, if necessary using the west's own weapons against it. Modernism's slogan is Prophet Mohammed's injunction to seek knowledge from all sources 'from the cradle to the grave'. But too often the outcome has been one of sterile and legalistic attempts to impose idealised historical blueprints on quite different contemporary societies.

During the 1950s, the Masjumi Party, based on Muhammadijah, demanded imposition of *Shariah* law on all Moslems. But it also vigorously advocated western-style democratic institutions, resisting to the end President Sukarno's enforced dissolution of the Parliament and return to the 1945 Constitution. Although Muhammadijah survived, Masjumi was banned in 1960 and never re-established itself in any comparable form. While alleged support for secessionist demands in Sumatra and Sulawesi provided the pretext, its Islamist agendas and strongly pro-democratic outlook were the underlying causes for the party's banishment.

By contrast, the traditionalist NU was viewed more benignly by both Presidents Sukarno and Suharto. A major reason is NU's concentration of strength in Java, which has historically shaped Indonesian political culture and institutions. NU is more open to the semi-mystical Sufi stream of Islam than its modernist counterpart. Consequently, despite serious tensions between NU *santri* and the majority, custom-oriented *abangan* population, which escalated into violence in 1965–66 (Cribb 1990), shared cultural values have facilitated NU's assimilation into the mainstream of national politics.

NU continued as a political party until 1971, when it won an almost identical 18 per cent vote as in 1955. It was then merged into the newly created Development Unity Party (PPP). This enforced association was dissolved in 1984, when NU withdrew from political activity to re-focus on social and educational activities. NU's willingness to accommodate Pancasila ideology was a major cause of tension within the PPP. Its withdrawal provided a catalyst for opening up Indonesia's political system, by implicitly abandoning demands for an Islamic state. Along with possible communist resurgence, the military perceived such demands as the greatest threat to national stability, justifying their continuing political control.

Bitterness grew among remaining groups within PPP, whose vote dropped by nearly 50 per cent between 1982 and 1987. Thereafter, modernist groups recovered to achieve a position of considerable influence by the mid-1990s. Both NU and modernists promoted extensive social and economic development programmes (Eldridge 1995: 74–98, 177–83) as part of the general Islamic resurgence from the late 1970s. In NU's case modernisation of the often feudal environment of *pesantren* was also a key objective.[14] Despite NU support for Pancasila, high levels of legitimacy accorded to modernisation and developmental values under Suharto favoured Muhammadijah. Other political shifts finally opened the way for incorporation of modernist Islam into state structures.

Weakening ties with the military caused President Suharto to seek wider support. After several years of economic liberalisation, Suharto sought to curb the influence of technocrats, whose reforms threatened his family's interests. Even General Benny Murdani, effectively Suharto's closest aide for many years, was marginalised for criticising their economic privileges. B. J. Habibie, modernist and moderate Moslem, Minister of Research and Technology, and Suharto's protege, provided a convenient instrument. His enthusiastic advocacy of high technology and a proactive state role in national development, served to re-legitimise bureaucratic intervention, on which continuation of patronage depended.

Establishment of the Institute of Indonesian Muslim Intellectuals (ICMI) in 1990 represented a decisive breakthrough for Islamic modernists. While ICMI contains several factions, based on competing views of its role (Schwarz 1999: 162–93; Ali-Fauzi 1995), it was well represented in both Suharto and Habibie governments. Although some NU intellectuals became ICMI members, NU Chairman Abdurrachman Wahid refused to join, describing the notion of an institute for intellectuals as exclusivist, and indeed redundant if Moslem intellectuals courageously pursued the public good in all areas (Wahid 1995). Wahid's stance reflected his concern to avoid formalising an Islamic role in politics and government.

Assumptions promoted by important elements within ICMI (Ali 1995; Sasono 1994) of an Islamic majority which will naturally bring about a society closely modelled on Islam, are questionable. As in 1955, the 1999 election results[15] challenged claims that, since Moslems constitute 85–90 per cent of Indonesia's population, appointments to public office and state policy should reflect these proportions. By contrast, Nurcholish Madjid (1995) has urged Moslem parties to compete in promoting Islamic notions of justice and social order within a pluralist democratic culture. As no single group is likely to prevail alone, there is a need to identify common values shared by Muslim and non-Muslim groups. Universal human rights principles could provide a key frame of reference.

This last scenario offers old-style Islamic modernists a sharp choice between revising their aims along more inclusive lines, or abandoning democratic approaches in favour of capturing state power by other means. Some appear to favour the latter approach, after being 'brought in from the cold' during the final Suharto years (Schwarz 1999: 162–93). Violence by some Habibie supporters during his transitional presidency, equating opposition to him with enmity towards Islam, conveyed a similar outlook.

While ICMI is commonly seen as having been coopted by Suharto, it has also become a vehicle for penetrating the state, unwilling to surrender newly won power and influence lightly. The right of Moslems, as the majority, to be at the centre of government, including the military, is defended as a natural state of affairs. One apologist applied integralist principles to the role of Islam in binding state and society together, asserting that only elements antagonistic to Islam would seek to create a dichotomy between them (Husaini 1996).

Economic grievance linked to religion and race is a major weapon in current power struggles. The economic wealth and political connections of Indonesian Chinese caused resentment throughout the whole colonial period. The Suharto government added accusations of involvement in communist subversion to this stigma, but prominent Chinese businessmen soon came to play a key role in financing New Order joint ventures. Capital was commonly contributed by foreign investors and Chinese Indonesians, with military, bureaucrats and others closely connected to the first family gaining shares at subsidised or nominal rates. Opponents found it safer and more convenient to attack the Chinese, as the politically weak link in this triangle. This generated indiscriminate hostility towards Chinese, many of whom are professionals, petty traders, market gardeners, shop, hotel or factory workers.

Protests against corruption and conglomerates in the 1970s led to introduction of various, largely ineffective credit and training programmes designed to benefit indigenous (*pribumi*) 'weak economic' groups. All non-Chinese Indonesians, constituting 96–7 per cent of the population, were defined as *pribumi*, making the racial aspect explicit, incidentally undermining any potential benefit from UN declarations on the rights of indigenous people in Irian Jaya and across the archipelago.

The issue of promoting small and medium enterprises among non-Chinese Indonesians has gained greater prominence since the fall of Suharto. The rhetoric underlying these campaigns has become increasingly anti-Christian, with simplistic equations between rich, Chinese Christians and poor, indigenous Moslems. In reality, most Christians are not Chinese, while by no means all Chinese are Christians. There is a high concentration of Christians in Indonesia's eastern provinces, where incomes, health and nutrition are among the lowest. Conversely, Moslem business interests formed part of Suharto's and Habibie's corporate networks.

Anti-Chinese outlooks are easily exploitable for political purposes. Riots in Jakarta and Medan during May 1998 were probably contrived by military elements loyal to Suharto's son-in-law, Major-General Prabowo (Schwarz 1999: 345–58), in alliance with the Indonesian Committee for Solidarity with the Islamic World (KISDI). Abdurrachman Wahid blamed ICMI-linked militants and groups linked to former President Suharto for creating a conducive environment for ethnic and religious conflict in West Java (Schwarz 1999: 331–2) and more recently Ambon and Lombok.

Exclusive attribution of church and mosque burnings and violence against minorities to economic and political rather than sectarian motivations is questionable, failing to confront the deep-rooted nature of ethnic and religious conflict in Indonesia. Thus the incursion of the Islamic Holy War militia (*Laskar Jihad*) from West Java into Ambon, 'turned intermittent fighting between two communities into a campaign of "religious cleansing"' (ICG 2000c). Labelling of

Maluku Christians as belligerent infidels, asserted a powerful religious licence to kill'. Laskar Jihad's theology poses a basic antithesis between God's law, expressed in *Shariah* law, and peoples' will, expressed via electoral democracy. Women are to be similarly subordinated and banned from leadership positions (Fealy 2001). Government inaction is linked to support by military elements and unwillingness to openly confront a pro-Moslem force. This episode illustrates a dangerous convergence between nationalist and radical Islamist populism,[16] likely to provoke violent indigenous responses in several outlying regions.

Pancasila implicitly supports freedom of religion, which is also guaranteed by Article 29 of the 1945 Constitution. At the same time, atheism or agnosticism was deemed to indicate opposition to Pancasila, and evidence of marxist sympathies. The Suharto government therefore required citizens to choose between five officially sanctioned religions – Islam, Catholic or Protestant Christianity, Buddhism and Hinduism. Confucianism has been added by President Wahid, with freedom for Chinese to openly display their language and culture.

Religious interpretation and practice is monitored by the Ministry of Religion. Its allocation of financial and other resources provides religious leaders with a framework for imposing their versions of orthodoxy. In the case of Islam, sharp differences exist between *santri* and non-*santri* groups. Even President Suharto, an *abangan* Javanese, was unable to gain recognition of syncretic and customary belief systems. In approving new places of worship, the government mostly maintains the status quo in face of local or externally induced opposition.

Though bans on conversions of Moslems to other faiths are less absolute than in Malaysia, serious bureaucratic obstacles are common, while social pressures effectively negate such choices in many regions. Shariah courts were granted greater powers over marriage and family matters during the 1980s. Rights of inter-marriage between Moslems and non-Moslems were consequently lost, unless the latter convert to Islam. Denying Moslems access to secular courts abridges their civil rights. Advantages and disadvantages to women from such courts are disputed, though modernisation programmes are being put in place.

President Wahid has been a strong champion of religious tolerance, both between religions and in advocating a pluralistic approach to Islam.[17] But the nature of the coalition which achieved his election obliges him to move cautiously. While secular definitions of religious freedom along western lines are probably unhelpful, the willingness of a democratically elected Parliament to lift requirements for Indonesians to register their religious affiliations, or at least to widen available choices, provides a basic test. Registration precludes interpretations and combinations disapproved by religious authorities, who commonly respond to perceived challenges to their authority with accusations of blasphemy or apostasy. The issue has yet to be politically articulated.

Seeds of change under Suharto

Seeds of democratic change were sown by initiatives during the last decade of the New Order, which generated trends and movements beyond the government's control. They were also nurtured during over two decades of democratic discourse and social mobilisation in both secular and religious contexts.

A sharp decline in world prices in 1986 pointed the need for drastic reduction in oil dependence for export and budget revenues, then both around 60 per cent. The search for new export opportunities required extensive de-regulation of external trade, finance and capital investment. The rapid success of this policy created a buoyant economic environment, expanding Indonesia's middle class and its potential as an agent of reform (Tanter 1990). Economic liberalisation generated corresponding demands for political liberalisation. The government responded by allowing greater media freedom, while official slogans advocating 'openness' legitimised public discussion of political and constitutional reform alternatives. Establishment in 1992 of the Indonesian National Human Rights Commission[18] was probably the most enduring institutional initiative. Modest initiatives were also undertaken in relation to labour organisation, regional and local government reform.

Processes of independent party formation began after 1994, with several new parties emerging in breach of official controls. The two legally established parties also became increasingly politicised. Advocacy of democratic reforms by the Indonesian Democratic Party (PDI), led by ex-President Sukarno's daughter, Megawati Sukarnoputri, raised prospects of an increased vote in 1997, particularly among younger people. Despite her having little chance of winning, the precedent of a presidential challenge in 1998 was viewed with alarm. The government intervened to oust her at a specially convened Congress at Medan in July 1996.

Megawati's dismissal led to sustained demonstrations, culminating in the storming of the PDI's Jakarta headquarters, occupied by her supporters, on 27 July 1996. This led to serious rioting, which Komnas HAM blamed on the pro-government Suryadi faction, supported by groups closely linked to the military.[19] Association with 'communist' and 'extreme radical' elements was nevertheless invoked to justify exclusion of Megawati's faction from the list of PDI candidates for the 1997 elections.

Prominent parliamentarian and former senior PPP member, Bintang Pamungkas, formed the Indonesian United Democratic Party (PUDI) in May 1996, claiming that Golkar, PPP and PDI were incapable of championing popular aspirations. He was later gaoled for urging his supporters to organise a boycott, if the new party was banned from participating in elections.[20]

The Democratic People's Party (PRD) was formed in 1996, based on the radical PDR network. PRD's aims and strategy are not primarily electoral. Its leader, Budiman Sudjatmiko, declared a prime focus on poverty, injustice and inequality, caused by corrupt and repressive state structures. Imprisoned labour leader, Dita Sari, sought to give 'democratisation' a class meaning, over and above opposition to Suharto and the military. But alliances are necessary with reformist elements whose aims are limited to legal democratisation (ASIET 1996: 14–16). Parallel 'solidarity from below' strategies operate in all arenas of joint mobilisation in which the PRD/PDR network participates.

The Independent Committee to Monitor Elections (KIPP), initiated by a cross-section of democracy and human rights advocates, was formed in early 1996.[21]

Both established parties welcomed KIPP's advent, but Golkar questioned its necessity and constitutional validity, later establishing its own election watch team, under the auspices of the pro-government Pancasila Youth organisation.[22] The Suharto government granted KIPP no status or guaranteed rights to monitor or observe election administration. However, it was accorded a key role in the 1999 election monitoring and counting process.

Labour

Labour reform became a high priority following a damning report on the SPSI by the high-level National Defence Institute (LEMHAMNAS), which recommended military withdrawal from labour relations.[23] The report attributed strikes and demonstrations to non-payment of minimum wages and non-fulfilment of basic conditions. But Suharto's instruction to restore the former industry-based All-Indonesia Workers' Federation (FSBI) encountered continuing resistance from military and Golkar interests.[24]

The ILO subsequently assisted Indonesia in an extensive reform programme aimed at equipping labour leaders to effectively represent workers' interests, improve efficiency and adapt to changing global labour market conditions.[25] Support for employment creation and self-employment via small informal sector enterprises was included, strengthening efforts initiated by the Women's Section of SPSI, in cooperation with non-government women and labour activists (Eldridge 1995: 163–65). Indonesia undertook to continue participation in the ILO's International Programme for the Elimination of Child Labour, adopting a graduated strategy of prohibiting labour by the youngest, most at risk children, and supporting older children through educational and training programs.[26]

The ILOs' priority has been to strengthen labour organising capacity by drawing Indonesian unions into international industry and sectoral networks. The government believed that Pancasila principles of consensus could be made compatible with ILO requirements for free association and bargaining by workers, but encountered strong opposition from independent labour organisations and their overseas supporters, despite offers to include independent unions. It is argued that western trade unions took many years to build adequate industrial capability before becoming politically involved. Unions formed as appendages to parties in developing countries commonly lack the will and capacity to meet workers' economic needs. Even so, the adequacy of purely industrial, non-political approaches is doubtful in Indonesia's emerging democratic climate.

Post-Suharto democratic transition

During President Habibie's seventeen-month tenure, Indonesia was locked into a dangerous cycle in which solution of political and economic crises became inter-dependent. Political reform could only be effected through New Order institutions. Their lack of legitimacy suggested a need for Habibie to declare himself an interim

President. This both conflicted with his personal inclinations and carried potential for a dangerous loss of authority.

Weaknesses in Habibie's position nevertheless concealed several strengths. He had strong incentives to achieve rapid reforms to gain either re-election or an honourable place in history. The crisis environment obliged major power-brokers to acknowledge the necessity for change, legitimated under the all-purpose ideological umbrella of 'reformasi' (reform). Habibie's technological background and instincts for problem-solving rather than politics and mass communication motivated him to focus on legislative and constitutional reforms. Habibie also enjoyed solid support from modernist Moslem groups with whom his successor has been mostly at odds. Finally, as a non-Javanese, he attracted support outside Java and Bali.

President Wahid's accession brought strong hopes for consolidating change on all fronts, given his long established support for democratic reform and religious tolerance, linked to an eclectic view of Islam. Yet these characteristics have also generated confusion and resistance, particularly from military elements loyal to ex-President Suharto. Wahid felt obliged to accommodate opposed party groups in his ministry, to maximise unity. This resulted in loss of policy coherence necessary to consolidating reforms, particularly in relation to economic management.[27] Wahid's operational style is also widely perceived as erratic.

Though critical of its feudal aspects, Wahid is steeped in Javanese culture, and seen as such by many non-Javanese. His *pesantren* background encourages personal charisma rather than careful accountability and problem-solving. Reflecting the Javanese proverb of 'looking north and hitting south', Wahid's strategy appears calculated to neutralise both allies and opponents. Thus cooperation with Golkar under Suharto served to check ICMI militants while protecting his NU base. Nationalist rhetoric and partial collaboration with the military may have been aimed at allowing a peaceful transition for East Timor and space for domestic reforms, while using human rights investigations to remove recalcitrant generals. Alliance with the 'central axis' of Moslem parties to gain the Presidency may later assist purging of militant sectarian elements. However, this prospect has been negated by the periodically violent mobilisation of Wahid's NU socio-religious base in his current battle to survive as President against opposition from long-standing Islamic modernist opponents and secular-nationalist groups.

As with President Sukarno, balancing political forces and preserving a veneer of national unity may become an end in itself if Indonesia's accumulating problems prove too intractable. Wahid's efforts at dialogue and compromise with regional dissidents have been opposed by the military and other militantly nationalist forces, notably Vice-President Megawati Sukarnoputri's Democratic Party of Struggle (PDI-P). President Wahid has nevertheless shown capacity for decisive action, as with his abrupt axing of the Ministry of Information, representing a major blow for media freedom, and abolition of military-dominated security bodies.

Media

In the media field, the 1984 decree allowing the Minister of Information to cancel press publication licenses was revoked, together with requirements to obtain business licences. But the Government retained its right to suspend publishing licenses for unspecified periods, provoking objections from the PWI and the Association of Indonesian Publishers. Regulation of the quantum of advertising and number of pages allowed also remained (US Department of State 1999*b*).

Media freedom was reinforced by Law No. 9 of 1998 on the Freedom to Express One's Views before the Public. Habibie's gloss on this law shows how the principles of John Stuart Mill and Pancasila can be made to converge in Indonesian discourse. Thus guarantees of freedom of expression are to be balanced with 'ways and procedures' designed to ensure that this is exercised in an orderly fashion, without harming other people's rights and freedoms. An excessive spirit of freedom would gradually be balanced by a combination of legal instruments and a maturing 'culture of democracy' (Habibie 1999). Nevertheless, Habibie terminated the ideological monopoly of Pancasila and dissolved its administrative infrastructure. People would now be free to develop their understanding of Pancasila, as the basic state ideology '… in a more open, dynamic, contextual fashion congruent with the growing process of democracy' (Habibie 1999). However, President Wahid's proposal to legalise Marxist thought has encountered uncompormising opposition, particularly from Moslem groups.

Labour

Indonesia quickly ratified ILO conventions relating to rights to organise, gender-based wage discrimination, elimination of forced labour and minimum age of workers. A new labour law, enacted by ministerial decree on 28 May 1998,[28] declared workers free to organise associations from enterprise level upward on a voluntary, democratic and self-reliant basis. But organisations at each level must register with the Department of Labour, supplying details of membership, component organisations, objectives, statutes and by-laws. Pancasila and the 1945 Constitution were retained as organisations' legal base.

Electoral and constitutional reform

The only legal vehicle for constitutional reform is the MPR, which consisted of 1000 representatives under Suharto. Lack of confidence in its capacity to enact meaningful change generated calls for a transitional government led by prominent reformist personalities Amien Rais, Megawati Sukarnoputri and Abdurrachman Wahid. These were all unwilling to accept such a constitutionally questionable arrangement. Violent conflict erupted between students, police and military during the special MPR session summoned to introduce political changes in November 1998.

The immediate priority was to democratise electoral laws, call fresh elections and re-structure the MPR. Military representation, cut from 100 to seventy-five by Suharto, was further reduced to thirty-eight, and from 20 to 10 per cent in regional parliaments. The size of the new MPR to sit after elections was reduced to 695. In addition to 500 DPR members, 130 delegates were to be appointed by regional parliaments and sixty-five from a cross-section of interest groups.

Chapter VII of the Constitution was amended to end military representation in the DPR in 2004, though some representation may be retained in the MPR until 2009.

Elections for both national and provincial parliaments were finally called for 7 June 1999. The only restriction on new parties was that they should have executive boards in nine provinces, and in half the towns and districts in those provinces. Forty-eight parties successfully registered under these rules. Despite serious consideration of single-member electorates, the system of proportional representation by provinces was retained. Twenty-nine parties failed to gain representation. The Election Commission was consequently unable to obtain the necessary two-thirds majority to endorse the election results, which were instead confirmed by Presidential decree. A new electoral administration law is foreshadowed to eliminate parties' role in the Commission.

Four parties secured 80.05 per cent of votes (Budiman 1999: 13) – the PDI-P (33.98 per cent); Golkar (22.6 per cent); the National Awakening Party (PKB) (12.69 per cent), representing Wahid's personal support base and PPP (10.78 per cent) representing a rump of the major Muslim-based party established under Suharto. The combined vote of Islamic parties at the 1999 elections was 35.06 per cent compared with 43.9 per cent in 1955 (Budiman 1999: 14). Votes for Christian parties also declined drastically from 4.6 per cent to 0.55 per cent.

The results have been variously interpreted (Blackburn 1999) as consolidating demarcation lines between Islamic and secular nationalist parties, allied to Christians; as rejecting 'hard-line' in favour of moderate versions of Islam; as re-affirming the *aliran* basis of party support, evidenced by lower than expected support for both the more inclusive Moslem-based PKB and National Mandate (PAN) parties, led by Muhammadijah Chairman, Amien Rais, which had tried to reach out beyond their core socio-religious communities; as a defeat for New Order elites, represented by Golkar; and as illustrating the salience of regional factors, evidenced by Golkar's strong showing outside Java and Bali.

Despite violence in many regions and in Jakarta itself in earlier months, campaigning and voting were mostly peaceful, with rallies well attended, mutual assistance between parties other than Golkar, and a high turnout across 320,000 polling booths. Irregularities were acknowledged by the Election Commission, but international observers agreed that these did not affect the overall result. Vote counting was a very public affair, with counting and tallying at each level taking several weeks to complete. After initial fears, the slow counting process reinforced confidence in the election's transparency and fairness.

The experience of competitive voting both for Parliamentary elections and later appointment of President and Vice-President produced mixed signals as to its acceptance. Nine parties with over 90 per cent of votes accepted the results. But many of the remaining thirty-nine did not, and demanded representation. Wahid's defeat of Megawati in the MPR by 373 votes to 313 triggered riots across the country, but the feelings of her supporters were substantially assuaged by her appointment as Vice-President one day later. Megawati's party emerged as the largest, with nearly 35 per cent of votes, but failed to understand the need for other groups' support. Moslem objections to appointing a woman as President were also influential.

The MPR's rejection of President Habibie's accountability speech by thirty votes outraged his supporters in South Sulawesi, who set off violent demonstrations calling for regional secession. Students entered the MPR building demanding that Golkar representatives who had voted against him be tried for treachery.[29] Such examples lend support to characterisation of elite attitudes as undemocratic, with routine allegations of cheating by those who lose (Santoso 1996). Alternatively, they illustrate the continuing strength of 'primordial' loyalties of religion, culture and region as bases for political mobilisation.

The re-structured MPR, summoned in October 1999, elected Amien Rais as Chairman. The Council heard and voted on President Habibie's accountability speech, finalised East Timor's separation from Indonesia, approved fresh Guidelines of State Policy (GBHN), elected a new President and Vice-President and considered a series of amendments to the 1945 Constitution. The Parliament planned a process of ongoing constitutional review.

Relations between President and Parliament have become central to constitutional deliberations, following a series of measures aimed at limiting presidential powers. Article 7 now allows presidents only two five-year terms. The President is obliged to consult with the DPR over appointments of cabinet ministers and ambassadors, reducing prison sentences, granting amnesties and honours (Articles 13–15). Articles 19–22 clarify and strengthen the DPR's rights to exercise legislative, budgeting and oversight functions, including rights to initiate legislation and investigations and question the President through 'interpellation'. Presidential powers to legislate via administrative regulations in lieu of laws were limited by requirements to obtain DPR approval at its next session. However, legislation still requires both DPR and presidential agreement.

Demands have been raised, supported by President Wahid, for popular election of the President to replace indirect election via the MPR. This partly reflects discontent over Megawati's rejection by the MPR, despite winning a plurality of votes. However, the PDI-P helped the MPR defeat this proposal in August 2000 (NDI 2000). Direct election would allow Presidents to select their own ministers, without needing to balance party representation in Parliament, where no group is obviously connected to either government or opposition. Presidents would also be more likely to complete a full term. However, either preferential or a second round of voting between the two leading contenders would be necessary to prevent minority candidates being elected from a large field in 'first-past-the-post' voting, as in the Philippines. Parliamentary selection over several rounds avoids this danger.

The task of reform is far from complete, due both to ongoing instability and resistance to constitutional change evident in the August–October 2000 session of the MPR (NDI 2000) particularly by Golkar and PDI-P representatives. These, together with modernist Moslem groups provide the driving force behind moves to impeach President Wahid. Open-endedness of constitutional provisions for impeachment, whereby the MPR must judge the President to have 'truly violated' the broad guidelines of the national will and constitution (ICG 2001c) render the process hostage to political fortune. Overthrow of President Wahid by such means could endanger the legitimacy of Indonesia's nascent democratic institutions. But Wahid's request to the military to support the declaration of a state of emergency and suspension of the DPR is both politically and constitutionally unsustainable and undermines his own democratic legitimacy. The military's refusal to cooperate illustrates their continuing pivotal role as arbiters of future constitutional development.

Economic crisis

Despite economic liberalisation in the mid-1980s, Indonesia cannot be described as pursuing capitalism in any complete sense. While economic development goals were central to the New Order's modernisation agenda, it sought to minimise resulting social tensions by retaining a strong state planning role, encouraging foreign capital in designated areas, but maintaining a national stake via joint ventures. The redistributionist ethic implicit in Pancasila's social justice principle also represents an ideological barrier to unqualified adoption of economic liberalism.

Indonesia's pre-crisis economy had combined sustained growth rates with widespread distribution of benefits. Official poverty estimates reached as low as 11.3 per cent in 1996, though such figures are sensitive to where the poverty index line is drawn (Hill 1999: 5). Onset of the regional currency crisis caused rapid contraction. The rupiah fell by up to 80 per cent, with inflation exceeding 50 per cent. Indonesia's Central Bureau of Statistics estimated that by the end of 1998 numbers living in absolute poverty had risen by 120 per cent over three years to reach almost a quarter of the population.[30] Health, nutrition and education suffered extensively (Buchori 2000). But regional and occupational impact were more mixed. The urban manufacturing and construction sectors were worst hit, with 'new middle class' families in outer Jakarta suffering sharp reversals of fortune (Jellinek 1999). Declines in real wages varied between 30 and 50 per cent for rural labour in Java (Hill 1999: 38–40), but employment opportunities in agriculture and export cash crops sectors outside Java improved as a result of currency devaluation. There was also a shift in favour of urban informal sector employment (Buchori 2000).

Hill (1999) concludes that no single cause can be exclusively identified, with Indonesia experiencing simultaneous crises via political, ethnic and religious upheavals, drought and fires, falling oil prices and regional financial turmoil. Diffuse explanations based on hindsight appear more pertinent to current agendas. Explanations emphasising corruption, collusion and nepotism ignore President Suharto's overwhelming importance in determining investors' perceptions of Indonesia's stability, even into early 1998. Nevertheless, a cumulative change in risk perception occurred in face of intricate webs of vested interests frustrating decisive action (Hill 1999: 51). Kwik Kian Gie (1996), Economics and Finance Minister in Wahid's government, and close associate of Megawati, had earlier claimed that her forcible displacement as PDI leader was seen as evidence of political instability by foreign, particularly regional-based Chinese investors.

Trade liberalisation measures undertaken in 1986 were not matched by transparent banking, financial and other reforms necessary to sustain Indonesia's competitiveness. Loss of influence by the economic technocrats who initiated reforms (Hill 1999: 77–9) rendered faith in them seriously misplaced. Internal paralysis during the Suharto administration's final months led to public rifts with the IMF, as the government signed up to packages which it was neither willing nor able to fulfil. International confidence was further weakened by Habibie's nomination as Vice-President. Appointment of family members and prominent business associates to Cabinet positions in March 1998 was seen as additional proof of economic nationalist and 'crony' ascendancy over liberalising economists and technocrats – a perception which Habibie worked hard to reverse after becoming President.

The IMF was widely blamed for financial chaos caused by closure of sixteen banks in November 1997, and for demanding fiscal tightening, despite the national budget being broadly in balance. Rather than concentrating on immediate recovery, it adopted a 'scatter gun' approach, causing the reform agenda to become overloaded relative to the country's bureaucratic capacity (Hill 1999: 51–2, 70). The World Bank, by contrast, urged that food, medicines and other essentials remain available at affordable prices, if necessary by subsidising key commodities. A focus on education, employment and income generation programmes was essential in order to avoid long-term impact from malnutrition and school dropouts. Transport, communications and energy infrastructure should not be allowed to fall into disrepair, with the urban poor especially vulnerable to system failures in water supply, sanitation and solid waste management. Environmental quality should also be central in shaping future adjustment programmes. Foreign assistance required for these goals was estimated at $US 8 billion for fiscal year 1998–99 (Severino 1998).

Funding was stalled for much of 1998 by disputes in the US Congress concerning overall IMF policies and management, and while various delegations verified the direction and capacities of Habibie's administration. Disbursement of $43 billion was postponed pending resolution of IMF demands for disclosure of an independent audit report on alleged misuse of Bank Bali funds for Habibie's Presidential re-election campaign.[31]

The main elements of an assistance package eventually agreed between the IMF and World Bank in May 1999 covered loans for policy reform, including bank re-structuring and social safety net adjustment (World Bank 1999c). Bank recapitalisation was assigned to the Indonesian Bank Restructuring Agency. Estimates of non-performing loans at 75 per cent illustrate the immensity of the problem. Implementation of the Bankruptcy Law passed in late 1998 favoured debtors over creditors. Recapitalisation will entail massive, as yet poorly estimated costs to both government and banks.[32]

Abrupt economic decline and renewed dependence on international agencies dominated by western, particularly US interests and opinion, have created a sense of resentment and humiliation. Imposed prescriptions have been followed in formalistic rather than whole-hearted fashion. While support for democratic reforms has deep domestic roots, opponents of change have been adept in manipulating nationalist sentiment to portray them as promoted by outsiders, taking advantage of Indonesian weakness. INFID and human rights activists have countered by demanding that external funds be closely tied to democratic reforms. They also demand relief from debts incurred through New Order mismanagement and corruption (Buchori 2000).

Overall, international agencies have been reluctant to impose tight condition-alities, whether on human rights, governance or economic efficiency grounds, which they fear might cause total social and economic collapse in Indonesia.

The military and democratic reform

Indonesia's democratic future depends on civilian governments' capacity to effectively control the military.

President Habibie was quick to dismiss Lt.-Gen. Prabowo, Suharto's son-in-law, who mounted an immediate threat to his incumbency. Commander-in-Chief, General Wiranto remained loyal, necessitating a cautious approach towards the military. Apart from reduced parliamentary representation, Habibie's other potentially important reform was separating the police from the re-named Indonesian National Army (TNI). Establishing an autonomous and effective police force which enjoys popular legitimacy will pose legal, conceptual and organisa-tional problems for many years (ICG 2001*b*). Police subordination to the TNI remains evident in battles with students and regional dissidents, while its capacity for crime prevention and detection has yet to be established. Neighbourhood security systems have historically been under military control.

In October 1999, plans by the Suharto-appointed MPR to endorse new security legislation giving the TNI wide-ranging powers sparked demonstrations and threats of civil disobedience.[33] The proposal highlighted potential to interpret Article 7(1) of the Constitution to mean that the President can act without parliamentary approval.[34] It was feared that the military would use the wave of nationalist senti-ment generated by the East Timor independence ballot to revive its political fortunes, cooperating with a weakened Habibie administration desperate to secure re-election. Fears were heightened by interrogation of student and NGO leaders labelled as provocateurs (Kraince 1999). The legislation was subsequently shelved.

President Wahid appointed a civilian minister, Yuwono Sudarsono, as Minister of Defence, on the recommendation of General Wiranto. Wiranto was appointed as Minister for Security Coordination, but was first forced to resign from military command and later from the ministry, after being named in relation to human rights abuses in East Timor. A major reshuffle of top military appointments followed, favouring officers considered loyal to the President and supportive of democratic reforms.

The military was obliged to maintain a neutral position during the June 1999 elections. Golkar's diminishing support and uncertain future direction render continuing ties potentially counter-productive to TNI interests. Formal ending of its role in ideological monitoring of individuals and groups also weakens TNI's direct role in domestic politics. However, it is unlikely to abandon its self-appointed mission as ultimate guarantor of national identity and security. This is evidenced by military veto of a referendum with an independence option in Aceh, continuing ruthless suppression of dissent in that province and in Irian Jaya, and 'scorched earth' policies before its departure from East Timor.

An entrenched presence and *de facto* parallel administrative status give the military continuing strength at regional and local level (ICG 2000*b*). On the other hand, internal divisions and lack of popular legitimacy have rendered it ineffective in controlling inter-religious and communal conflict. Accusations persist that military elements close to ex-President Suharto are promoting violence, or at least not intervening to prevent it, in order to de-stabilise Indonesia's struggling democratic system.

Regional government, democracy and human rights

Regional devolution, cautiously initiated under Suharto, has been pursued with greater urgency under Habibie and Wahid. Secessionist demands in some provinces have lent urgency to issues of regional reform. While conventional wisdom currently prescribes democracy and devolution as solutions, threats to national unity and stability can also be invoked as justifying return to authoritarian rule.

Centralisation of governmental structures is historically deep rooted, with financial and other resources heavily concentrated in Jakarta. This has been variously ascribed to inherited colonial structures, Javanese norms whereby power radiates outward from centre to periphery (Anderson 1972), and survival pressures on the new Republic post-1945. Federalism, though an obvious option for such a dispersed archipelagic country, was discredited by Dutch attempts to 'divide and rule' after 1945 through puppet federal structures. Village governments, which enjoyed significant autonomy under Sukarno, have been increasingly subordinated to higher level control (Warren 1990).

The Indonesian republic has consolidated itself as a unitary state since the Dutch transferred power in November 1949 to the 'Republic of the United States of Indonesia'. This consisted of the Republic of Indonesia, which had declared its independence in August 1945, and a Dutch created federation. All elements of this federation acceded to the Republic within one year. This background, plus later experience of regional rebellion and attempted economic autarchy by resource-rich provinces fuels continuing suspicion of federalism.

It is necessary to distinguish Irian Jaya, Aceh and the newly independent former province of East Timor, where demands for independence have dominated relations with Jakarta, from other Indonesian provinces, where secession is less at issue. The military's outlook is strongly coloured by perceived threats to national unity from any source, but it has responded with exceptional brutality in these three regions, where the role of NGOs and the Indonesian human rights community has also been curtailed.

While some regions, notably Maluku, South Sulawesi and West Sumatra have earlier histories of rebellion, with disparate voices again calling for secession since Suharto's fall, these do not yet reflect significant local support or any coherent independence movement. For most provinces, the issue is one of devolution of powers from Jakarta, and equitable sharing of economic resources. More radical demands may nevertheless be raised if acceptable reforms cannot be negotiated.

Reform options are confused by free-wheeling use of the imprecise and potentially open-ended term 'autonomy'. Federalism, by contrast, requires clear legal division of powers, with inbuilt provisions for amendment and dispute resolution. While retention of security and major taxation powers are important centralising characteristics of federal systems, these can be constructed to give greater or lesser measure of devolution, as the contrasting examples of Australia and Malaysia show.

The difficulty of rational debate on this issue is illustrated by PDI-P demonstrations against MPR Speaker, Amien Rais' support for federalism as a means of defending national unity.[35] Party representatives claimed that by merely expressing a personal view on the matter, Rais was violating his oath of office of loyalty to Pancasila and the unitary state prescribed in the 1945 Constitution. Such critics ignore constitutional provisions for amendment. The PDI-P, invoking New Order principles, asserted that the unitary system is not open to negotiation and can only be raised in Parliament after collective agreement between MPR factions. Golkar Chairman and DPR Speaker, Akbar Tanjung also believed the Assembly can only discuss federalism if the idea gains general popular assent.[36]

Divisions between Java and resource rich provinces emerged at a seminar between 135 provincial representatives on unitary versus federal systems of government in December 1999.[37] While Aceh and Irian Jaya sought outright independence, Riau and East Kalimantan linked demands for federalism with greater shares of oil and gas revenues.[38] Opponents of federalism argued that it would be better to correct deficiencies in the unitary system, fearing a rash of demands for new provinces based on ethnicity and religion.

Law No. 25 of 1999 on Regional Autonomy and Fiscal Balance Between the Central and Local Governments devolved powers to districts rather than provinces, transferring responsibility for public works, health, education, agriculture, communications, industry and trade, environment, land, cooperatives and labour. Provinces' role will be limited to regional administration of central government affairs, cross-district matters and functions that district administrations are not yet ready to handle. Districts will be permitted to keep 80 per cent of revenues from forestry, fisheries, and general mining, 30 per cent from natural gas and 15 per cent from oil. Under Law 22 of 1999, both provincial and district heads will be directly elected (Habibie 1999; ICG 2000*a*).

These changes were subsequently incorporated in amendments to Chapter VI of the Constitution (NDI 2000). State Minister of Regional Autonomy Affairs, Ryaas Rasyid, therefore, urged that the new law be given a chance to work before looking at alternative systems. Rasyid nevertheless resigned in January 2001, frustrated by the Wahid government's tardy and inconsistent implementation of reforms, notably transfer of some 1.9 civil servants from central to district government payrolls.[39]

Aceh and Irian Jaya

Indonesia originally asserted sovereignty over the whole former territory of the Netherlands East Indies. Annexation of East Timor turned out to be a temporary departure from this original definition. The impossible and divisive nature of alternative ethnically or religious-based definitions of statehood was recognised during debates in the Independence Preparatory Commission in 1945. Regional claims for independence on such grounds thus strike at the heart of Indonesian national identity. This goes far to explain, though not justify the harshness of state responses in Aceh and Irian Jaya, where reports of detention without trial, subversion charges, killings and other abuses by the military against civilians continue unabated.

Despite similarities in the two provinces' relations with the Indonesian state, there are also significant differences. Aceh is staunchly Moslem, while Irian Jaya's indigenous population is predominantly Christian and animist. Aceh fought for nearly a century against Dutch rule, while the former West Irian's ties with the Netherlands were relatively close. The Acehnese are historically and culturally homogeneous, resulting in cohesive and articulate expression of popular aspirations. Aceh is geographically placed within a wider, Islamic majority culture region, with links further afield in Southeast Asia and the Middle East. Irian Jaya, by comparison, is relatively isolated.

Unlike East Timor, Aceh and Irian Jaya are both firmly recognised by the international community as part of Indonesia. Third World countries have obdurately insisted that self-determination rights set out in the UDHR and ICCPR do not extend to re-drawing boundaries of formerly colonised, now independent states. While neither province can, therefore, expect anywhere near the same level of outside support as East Timor, their causes have gained considerable, if discontinuous exposure over many years. Acehnese consider that, as Moslems, they are relatively neglected by international human rights advocates and receive less sympathy from western public opinion – a claim not borne out by the volume of material in international agency reports.

Irian Jaya has a somewhat better case in international law. Holland retained control of 'West Irian' until 1962, when agreement was reached that an 'Act of Free Choice' would be conducted after seven years under UN administration. Indonesia immediately occupied and administered the territory, with only a minimal UN presence. Extensive eye-witness reports claim that the Indonesian military ignored local people's rights to a free and fair vote. In place of a universal ballot, some 4000 representatives selected from among local leaders were grouped in regional assemblies. Voting was conducted openly in front of Indonesian authorities, with military coercion of representatives into voting unanimously to join Indonesia. Sufficient documented evidence could probably be assembled to mount a credible case that the UN's original intentions had been flouted and that a fresh consultation should be conducted under independent UN auspices (Blay 2000).

Aceh has no such obvious line of appeal to the UN, but is better placed to exercise political leverage via strong links with Indonesian Moslems. They are currently pressing for devolution of powers plus serious engagement over human rights, but oppose secession. Experience over East Timor has hardened military and political resistance to separatist demands, with greater wariness towards suggestions that Indonesia could win referendums at the ballot box with reform packages. It is also unclear what can be offered to Aceh beyond current autonomy proposals for all provinces, apart from rights to fully implement Islamic law – a response which ignores the historical, cultural and economic nature of Acehnese claims.

In August 1998, General Wiranto apologised for past military behaviour and declared Aceh's 'military operations region' status revoked. But popular anger boiled over against departing troops (Human Rights Watch 1999*d*) providing a pretext for their continuing presence. Troop levels were increased in December 1998 after major clashes in North and East Aceh and Pidie.

Following a preliminary report by Komnas HAM, the provincial government set up broad-based teams to intensively investigate the three worst affected districts. Their findings indicated extensive killing, including women, children and disabled, destruction of property and credible allegations that hundreds of women had been raped during the nine-year military operation (US Department of State 1999*b*). Full naming and prosecution of those responsible appears to be a minimum requirement for any prospect of reconciliation. However, military impunity continues to escalate (Amnesty International 1999*e*). Mounting future trials will encounter problems of retrospective prosecution (Johanson 1999: 44; ICG 2001*a*).

These trends caused Acehnese NGOs, students and human rights activists to re-consider relations with Jakarta. Discussion of autonomy and federalism escalated into demands that independence be included as a third option in a UN supervised referendum. While President Habibie responded ambivalently, the military branded these calls as subversive. Escalating disturbances and military counter-action resulted in low voter registration and turnout at the June 1999 elections. Accusations of intimidation by the guerilla Free Aceh Movement (GAM) were denied and turned back against the TNI (Aspinall 1999: 30–3). The GAM responded coolly to the referendum campaign (Johanson 1999: 45), fearing confusion and loss of authority if options other than outright independence were considered.

Referendum demands in Aceh, supported by one million strong demonstrations during November 1999, generated alarm among national elites. Initially, President Wahid appeared to support open-ended dialogue, but denied there would be an independence option in face of strong political and military reaction. While international support can be largely neutralised, and anti-referendum sentiment remains strong in the rest of Indonesia, capacity to maintain order against overwhelming local unpopularity is more questionable. The military appears to face a stark choice between withdrawal, with full legal acknowledgement of past abuses, or re-imposing martial law.

Independence mobilisation in Irian Jaya lack comparable strength and cohesion. Nevertheless, factions loosely linked under the Free Papua Organisation (OPM) umbrella have maintained sporadic guerilla warfare for over three decades. Acts of defiance have become more open and widespread since Suharto's demise, while the government's response has been uncertain and confusing. This can be illustrated with reference to two essentially symbolic issues – the name of the province, and the status of the 'Morning Star', the would-be independent nation's flag.[40]

The term 'Irian Jaya' was intended to signal both victory and reassurance to regional neighbours that Indonesia had no plans for further expansion. But for local freedom fighters, ethnic ties with kinfolk in Papua-New Guinea (PNG) remain a basic source of motivation and moral support, reflected in their choice of 'West Papua'. This term asserts the essentially indigenous, Melanesian identity of the freedom movement in face of both official and spontaneous transmigration programmes, which will ultimately lead to minority status for indigenous people.

Papuans complain of lack of cultural respect, with many Indonesian officials conveying a sense of 'civilising mission' similar to that of earlier colonial rulers, and not a few contemporary Australians towards aboriginals, in bringing order and development to 'backward' people. Other major causes of discontent arise from dispossession of land for mining, forestry, plantation and transmigration programmes. Indigenous people are concentrated in increasingly overcrowded districts of the central highlands, where they can maintain subsistence from vegetables, tree crops, and animal husbandry in a relatively cool climate. At one stage, official policies appeared directed towards driving Papuans to coastal areas. Improved delivery of services provided a convenient rationale for pursuing security and control objectives.

The Forum for Reconciliation of Irian Jaya Society (FORERI), a coalition of churches, students, women and NGOs coordinated a delegation to meet President Habibie in Jakarta in February 1999. Its strong declaration in favour of independence surprised him, leading to tightening of military and administrative controls (FitzSimons 2000). President Wahid, in a more determined attempt at reconciliation, announced the province would be re-named as 'Papua'. This acknowledged Papuans' cultural claims. But exclusion of 'West' indicated rejection of both independence and links with PNG. Although 'Papua' gained wide currency, the name change was never legally implemented, with Parliament and the military forcing reversion to 'Irian Jaya'.[41] Wahid also permitted the Morning Star to be flown freely. But similar military and political opposition obliged him to back down. Flags were not to be forcibly removed in the immediate future, in order to avoid unrest (Greenlees 2000c).

The armed struggle road to independence has been substantially blocked by so far successful pressure on PNG from both Indonesia and Australia to deny the OPM bases on its territory and cooperate with Indonesia in border policing. While democratisation has opened more outlets for peaceful advocacy since 1998, strong Indonesian nationalist sentiment following East Timor's separation has obstructed meaningful progress. Papuan groups are unwilling to accept 'autonomy' packages, with more militant elements attacking non-indigenous settlers. A weakened TNI, has responded by mobilising pro-integration militia, along similar lines to East Timor.

Representation of Papuans' plight is variously undertaken through the Indonesian Communion of Churches (PGI), local affiliates of national environmental and human rights networks (Philpott 1999: 65–8). Komnas HAM also undertakes periodic investigations. All have strong international support and communication networks. The PGI and the International Commission of the Red Cross provide basic medical assistance, supported by a small foreign missionary presence. NGOs such as the Javanese-linked Institute for Rural Development (YPMD) pursue programmes of cross-ethnic understanding and popular empowerment. However, the nature of these networks points towards reconciliation and improved welfare as part of Indonesia rather than offering options for independence.

Indonesia, human rights and the UN system

Formal links between Indonesia and the UN human rights system were limited under Suharto, until in August 1998, the Habibie government agreed a comprehensive cooperation programme with the UN High Commissioner for Human Rights. Ratification of major UN treaties was endorsed as a policy goal by the newly elected Parliament, reinforced by President Wahid's appointment of Marzuki Darusman, formerly Chairman of Komnas HAM and liberal-oriented former Deputy-Chairman of Golkar, as Attorney-General.

The Suharto government sought to incorporate international human rights law within the framework of Pancasila. The Foreign Affairs Ministry claimed many convergences between the 1945 Constitution and major UN human rights instruments, notably in Articles 27–33 (Budiarjo 1994: 177) relating to equality of citizens before the law, rights to work, and quality of life; freedom of speech, association and religion; participation in national defence; rights to education; people's welfare through cooperative national economic development, land, water and natural resources use. These vaguely worded provisions were considered sufficient to obviate the need for constitutional reform guaranteeing universal human rights.

National human rights plan

In January 1998, Foreign Minister Alatas announced a 'National Plan of Action on Human Rights 1998–2003' in which Indonesia acknowledged the universality and indivisibility of human rights.[42] A general statement envisaging future legal action, was simultaneously incorporated into the GBHN.[43] Military practice of torture and disappearances nevertheless continued unabated in controlling mounting student and other protests (Human Rights Watch 1999d).

The Plan aims to incorporate UN human rights instruments into national laws; disseminate information and education; protect basic human rights and report on implementation to UN agencies. However, those advocating 'anti-constitutional action' such as secession from the Republic are excluded from protection. The anti-torture and racial discrimination conventions were subsequently adopted under Laws No. 5 of 1998 and 29 of 1999. Habibie (1999) evoked the Pancasila principle of a 'just and civilised humanity' to legitimate these actions.

A new Chapter XA greatly expanded Article 28 of the Constitution in the form of a Bill of Rights (NDI 2000: 12–4, 24–6). Its language substantially follows the UDHR, with a strong focus on individual rights. However, three areas of uncertainty may be noted.

Firstly, the right of 'every person... to practice the religion of his/her choice' asserted in Article 28E may conflict with Pancasila, which upholds monotheistic religion and remains the primary source of national law.[44] Secondly, 'citizens', who are to enjoy equal opportunities in government (Article 28D(3)), are defined in Article 26(1) as indigenous Indonesians and people of foreign origin who have been legalised as citizens. Such language maintains distinctions between 'indigenous' and Chinese Indonesians. While Articles 28D(4) and 28E assert every person's right to citizenship status, Article 26(3) states that citizenship and residence matters will be regulated by law. Finally, provisions in Article 28I(1) forbidding prosecutions under retrospective law will constrain the operations of future human rights tribunals.[45]

National Human Rights Commission

The National Human Rights Commission (Komnas HAM) was established against the background of the UN's 1993 global review of human rights. This initiative was influenced by regional strategists urging a pro-active role, recognising that purely defensive postures had become unrealistic in the face of rising popular awareness, while state sovereignty was taking on more relative meaning in international relations (Wanandi 1992: 18). It also complemented official policies of 'openness' and Suharto's objective of weakening some military leaders. But the Commission's establishment by Presidential decree[46] and later by the 1999 Human Rights Act,[47] rather than entrenchment in the Constitution, limits its political autonomy.

The extent of Komnas HAM's independence is unclear despite its high profile critical stance on many issues. Suspicion surrounds secret meetings and the possibility that some reports are cleared with the military in contravention of the Paris Principles (SAHRDC 2000: 9–11). The Commission also appears to act as intermediary for the government in international forums. Its budget is fixed annually by Parliament, with many costs paid by the State Secretariat.

Constraints of operating within the framework of New Order ideology and institutions generated little optimism that Komnas HAM could prove effective. But a flow of strong statements condemning military and police actions[48] dramatically enhanced its credibility, in the international arena.[49] Indonesian human rights activists remain sceptical, as styles and practices necessary to operating under Suharto persist into the democratic era.

The Commission's objectives were defined as spreading human rights awareness; offering suggestions on accessing and ratifying UN human rights instruments; monitoring, investigating and making recommendations on Indonesian human rights practices. Its mandate is guided by Pancasila, the Constitution and UN human rights conventions (Talwar 1997). Contradictions entailed here are reflected in the Commission's composition, outlook, structures and operating styles.

Objectives have become confused by establishment of a Human Rights Ombudsman and a Ministry of State for Human Rights (SAHRDC 2000: 15–18). The ministry currently lacks a clear mandate or procedures for handling complaints. Poor communications and undefined division of labour with Komnas HAM have caused confusion in relation to Irian Jaya and Aceh, and in determining where cases should be directed.

Issues of institutional culture, operating style, transparency and effectiveness are linked. The South Asian Human Rights Documentation Center (SAHRDC), which has special consultative status with the UNCHR, sees Komnas HAM membership as dominated by appointees from the Suharto era, and insufficiently pluralist in terms of gender, background and region. President Suharto appointed the initial commissioners, who replace themselves by internal ballot. The 1999 Human Rights Act empowers the DPR to select new members, endorsed by the President, from a list prepared by the Commission. Komnas HAM thus remains substantially self-selecting (SAHRDC 2000: 3–8).

The Commission's Pancasilaist outlook is evident in its emphasis on dispute settlement (SAHRDC 2000: 19–22). Its high status membership, drawn from universities, the professions, government, judiciary and Parliament, has facilitated the Commission's cooperation with authorities at all levels. But a YLBHI survey of Commissioners' attitudes cited two members, including Professor Muladi, who became Minister of Justice under President Habibie, as favouring an integralist state outlook on ten out of eighteen questions. Both vigorously denied the finding, questioning the report's methodology. Muladi nevertheless claimed scope for local, culture-based interpretations of the UDHR.[50]

NGOs report pressures on complainants to accept conciliation before all facts have been established, particularly in land and labour disputes, to which 41 per cent of letters received in 1999 referred (SAHRDC 2000: 19–22). Commissioners training and competence in these areas, and mediation skills generally, are disputed. Such approaches can misrepresent Islamic practices, reproducing statist notions of consensus. Internal processes also aim at consensus – a near impossible prospect with membership expanding from 25 to 35 in 1999 (SAHRDC 2000: 36–7).

While the Commission considers its informal 'good offices' highly effective, secrecy leaves the Commission vulnerable in the absence of public pressure (SAHRDC: 50–1). Confidentiality guidelines associated with the Paris Principles require that complainants, while free to publicise their cases, are guaranteed confidentiality. The 1999 Human Rights Act contradicts this principle by granting Komnas HAM discretion over confidentiality, also obliging it to take into account dangers to state security, individual or public safety, and cases *sub judice* or under investigation (SAHRDC: 53–4). Although the Commission appears to take individual confidentiality seriously, emphasis on conciliation logically entails sharing information with authorities.

Difficulties in accessing Komnas HAM (SAHRDC 2000: 40–6) impact on both its effectiveness and transparency. Resources and personnel are concentrated in Java, specifically Jakarta. No training or legal analysis sessions are held outside Java or Bali. Lack of regional presence and travel difficulty reduces people's awareness of their rights or the Commission's potential role. Even so, many remote local groups succeed in contacting the Commission through NGOs, other informal networks, and extensive travel by commissioners.

Apart from the former East Timor office, the only Komnas HAM office outside Jakarta is in Aceh. Little responsibility has been devolved and long communication delays are common. Confidence of local complainants was undermined when an extensive report on rape cases by out-of-uniform military was not pursued in Jakarta. Some Commissioners claimed that the Aceh office had no authority to undertake the investigation (SAHRDC 2000: 42–3).

While Komnas HAM has limited powers and resources, its effectiveness could be greatly enhanced by utilisation of both to full effect. Perceptions of powerlessness weaken public credibility and confidence in approaching it. These largely stem from false expectations that Komnas HAM can enforce its own recommendations. These latter can nevertheless prove powerful tools, in terms of the space they open up for further investigation and action, and by raising both domestic and international awareness (SAHRDC 2000: 28–9).

Preference for conciliation may hold back strong reference to courts or other authorities. NGOs charge that the Commission often condemns widely known human rights abuses without naming those responsible or providing supporting legal detail necessary for prosecution. Changes in policy and practice require active monitoring and advocacy, supported by well researched recommendations citing relevant domestic and international human rights laws. The Commission and its critics have sought direct powers to refer cases to prosecutors. But the Human Rights Act also grants Komnas HAM powers to advise courts on the human rights implications, interpretation and application of relevant laws, which have so far not been adequately taken up (SAHRDC 2000: 34–5). Undue secrecy and failure to publish comprehensive catalogues and descriptions of all cases brought to the Commission's attention needed by legal aid lawyers and social activists (SAHRDC 2000: 58) limits effective use of Komnas HAM's services.

Human rights activists urge greater willingness to use *subpoena* powers, via the Head of Court, granted by the 1999 Human Rights Act (SAHRDC 2000: 22–4). Komnas HAM argues that strong reminders of its powers have ensured that no witness has refused to give evidence. However, prosecutions may be held back where there are fears that witnesses will refuse interrogation. Judicial corruption and uncertain political support represent major barriers.

Komnas HAM's limitations partly reflect problems of democratic transition, which strong national human rights institutions can assist in overcoming. The Commission operates in an overwhelmingly difficult context, but has substantially reversed initial negative expectations. Most importantly, its advent has made it no longer possible to dismiss human rights as a western liberal concept, and legitimised it as integral to Indonesian public life (Nasution 1995).

Human Rights Tribunals

Law No. 39/1999 on Human Rights set out a long list of internationally recognised human rights, including 'crimes of omission', whereby those in authority who knew of, but failed to prevent violations committed by subordinates can be prosecuted along with direct perpetrators. It was originally intended that human rights offences would be tried in ordinary courts until new human rights courts were established within four years. But destruction and killing in East Timor, inadequacies in the Criminal Code and poor performance by the courts in a series of investigations relating to the late Suharto years (ICG 2001*a*), caused the Habibie government to fast-track their establishment by issuing a regulation in lieu of a law.

Clauses 4 and 18.2 forbidding prosecution based on laws not in force at the time of the alleged crime attracted strong controversy at the next DPR sitting. But fearing that this provision would frustrate the international community's demand for trial of those responsible for East Timor violations, the government prepared a new bill on human rights courts specifying a wider range of offences and providing for retroactive prosecution. Law No. 26/2000 on Human Rights Courts, adopted in November 2000, extended coverage of internationally recognised violations. However, failure to carefully follow the wording of relevant UN conventions against torture and genocide caused confusion according to Amnesty International (2000*b*: 3–8), which also feared that granting an exclusive inquiry role to Komnas HAM could weaken reform of ordinary legal processes.

Ironically, international law principles opposing retroactive trials were strongly invoked by military and Golkar representatives in the DPR. A compromise provided for special ad hoc human rights courts to try human rights violations occurring before the new law came into force. Such courts must be established in each case by the President on the recommendation of the DPR, thus ensuring politicisation of the process.

Inclusion by the MPR in August 2000 in the new Article 28I of the Constitution of the right not to be prosecuted on the basis of retroactive laws, among human rights 'that cannot be diminished under any circumstances' undermined the validity of such courts. Claims that MPR members were variously pre-occupied with attempts to impeach the President, overwhelmed by the weight of constitutional amendments, and ignorant of the legal implications of such wording carry little weight, in light of numerous assurances to the international community by the Ministry of Foreign Affairs (ICG 2001*a*).

Attempts to find other clauses which might validate ad hoc courts are futile, as the Constitution takes precedence over specific laws. The provision in Clause 7.2 of Law No. 39/1999 on Human Rights for international human rights law accepted by Indonesia to become national law, offers a more promising means of prosecuting past abuses. While Article 15(1) of the ICCPR prohibits application of retroactive law, Article 15(2) allows trial and punishment for acts of omission recognised at the time as crimes against humanity under international human rights law. But as Indonesia is not a party to the ICCPR, its courts are unlikely to uphold this principle. The amended Article 28 of the Constitution also makes no mention of the UN system or international human rights law.

International pressure to bring retrospective prosecution has diminished, as some countries fear upsetting Indonesia's fragile political balance. It is argued that nationalist backlash could reverse democratic gains if the military are pushed too hard. Conversely, failure to end impunity for human rights crimes will further weaken respect for law, not deter continuing violations, and even destroy Indonesia's territorial integrity. A middle view argues for avoiding premature prosecution of the most senior military officers until the effectiveness of the new human rights laws has been established, and new legislation adopted to make military personnel subject to civilian courts in criminal cases.

Recognising that not all past human rights violations can be resolved judicially, establishment of a Truth and Reconciliation Commission (TRC) is being planned (ICG 2001a). Its objectives are defined as 'revealing the truth' about human rights violations under both Presidents Suharto and Sukarno. The twenty-seven members of the TRC will be nominated by Komnas HAM and appointed by the President.

A major goal is for human rights transgressors to express remorse and confess crimes in exchange for amnesty, for which the Commission will determine criteria. A broader view of the TRC concept is based on belief that reconciliation requires full exposure of the truth. Traditional and localised methods may prove more successful in situations where victims and perpetrators must continue living in close proximity. But there are also dangers of replicating statist symbolism of deliberation and consensus.

Criteria for deciding whether a case should be heard by an ad hoc court or by the TRC remain unclear. The TRC is expected to hand over cases for trial which it believes can be proved in court, and to concentrate on major events, such as the Tanjung Priok affair and 1965–66 mass killings, where the passing of time makes successful prosecution unlikely. Primary concerns of many families of victims of the anti-communist massacres are for injustices to be acknowledged and stigmas against them removed. The idea of reconciliation could weaken concern for justice, even serving to extend perpetrators' impunity. Ultimately, the TRC's effectiveness will be greatly influenced by the performance of the new human rights courts. If these fail to provide justice, there will be no need to grant amnesties to offenders as they will be free in any case (ICG 2001a).

Conclusion

Prospects for democracy and universal human rights in Indonesia are closely linked. While both have made important advances during the past decade, they remain vulnerable in cultural, ideological and institutional terms. While levels of popular mobilisation have risen dramatically, such mobilisation is often coercive, driven by a spirit of aggressive nationalism, competitive religious and ethnic sectarianism, inimical to meaningful participation in policy debates or political processes.

Solid constitutional advances have been recorded, assisted by annual MPR sessions. But important issues relating to relations between President and Parliament, the military's role, regional and local devolution remain unresolved. Indonesia appears torn between a presidential and parliamentary system. The Parliament, which acted as a rubber stamp under Suharto, has both gained and asserted new powers. The President retains substantial executive powers and can select ministers from both within and outside parliament. Though sharing budgetary and legislative powers, presidential accountability is only formally required in annual appearances before the MPR. However, the shadow of impeachment will now always hang over any President.

The grand coalition of parties which supported Wahid, and subsequently turned against him, indicates the lack of obvious demarcation between government and opposition supporters in a multi-party Parliament with limited practical responsibilities. This situation discourages parties from focusing on policy development and associated coalition building, as well as mobilising traditional constituencies for elections and demonstrations. Internal democratisation of parties, built on active grassroots units, is equally needed if political participation is to extend beyond intra-elite rivalry and develop an issues-based political culture. Notions of loyal opposition, essential to democratic culture, have yet to emerge.

Although many of their formal powers are being eroded, the military retain continuing influence at regional and local levels, based on the territorial system of internal security on which governmental structures continue to rest. Their presence is heaviest in Aceh and Irian Jaya where secessionist threats are greatest. However, neither police nor military, have proved willing or able to provide protection for citizens against outbreaks of religious or ethnically based disorder in other provinces. The military's performance is variously attributed to incompetence, factionalism, indiscipline or deliberate intent to undermine democratic reforms.

Judicial reform remains an urgent task, both for reasons of overall governance, and as bearing strongly on the implementation of human rights law. While debate has necessarily focused on prosecuting earlier human rights offenders, the future work of human rights courts will centre on enforcing the extensive list of new rights listed in Article 28 of the Constitution, and the Law on Human Rights Courts. However, little progress has been made under Wahid on harmonising Indonesian law with UN human rights instruments since the Habibie government acceded to the anti-torture and racial discrimination conventions.

Social and economic rights were seriously set back by the regional economic crisis. Despite some alleviation, there has been no sustained economic recovery or coherent strategy to overcome mass poverty in Indonesia. Issues of governance and human rights bearing on poverty require sharper definition, with appropriate conditionalities enforced by the international community.

Confusion over core national values underlies all Indonesia's problems, reflecting strains of democratic transition. While removal of Pancasila as the sole ideology was essential to democratic pluralism, it has caused an ideological vacuum dangerous to social, especially religious harmony. Although Pancasila's integrity was weakened by New Order manipulation, its role in promoting values of tolerance was a major support to nation-building. Alternative political ideologies, whether based on Islam, regionalism or popular radicalism are more communitarian than liberal, and in many of their common expressions threaten both humanitarian values and constitutional processes.

6 East Timor, Indonesia and the United Nations

This chapter outlines the process of separating East Timor from Indonesia, and associated political conflict. The account includes the role of the Indonesian military and local militias, UN intervention, mass exodus to West Timor, and post-ballot investigations of human rights abuses. The chapter concludes with brief commentary on nation-building problems facing East Timor, including relations with Indonesia.

Processes of separating East Timor from Indonesia reflected an extreme conflict between principles of national sovereignty and universal human rights. Although its cause attracted support from human rights activists throughout the world, the international community and a reluctant Indonesia ultimately conceded the legitimacy of East Timor's claims for self-determination on the basis of the technicality of its former status as a Portuguese rather than Dutch colony.

Consultation process

Responding to persistent international pressure, and continuing East Timorese resistance, Indonesia began talks with the UN and Portugal in mid-1998, indicating willingness to grant a degree of autonomy. In January 1999, President Habibie rejected the notion of autonomy as an interim arrangement, along lines proposed by East Timorese leaders over several years (Ramos-Horta 1994; Spaeth 1996), instead announcing that if Indonesia's offer proved unacceptable, the government would recommend to the MPR annulment of the original act of integration (Tap VI/MPR/1978). Agreement was reached on 5 May 1999 on modalities for a UN supervised ballot, with Indonesia retaining sovereignty until the process was completed. It also undertook responsibility to ensure an environment free from violence and intimidation (United Nations 1999a).

The TNI expanded training and mobilisation of local militias from early 1999. Unarmed staff from the United Nations Mission for East Timor (UNAMET) experienced sustained harassment, forcing closure of outlying centres. This disrupted voter information and education programmes, conveying a message that UNAMET was unable to offer protection. Television evidence of TNI and police collaboration with militias outraged international opinion, but requests for international peacekeeping forces to operate alongside Indonesian security forces were firmly rebuffed.

Militia violence and intimidation was aimed at discouraging anyone not clearly opposed to the independence cause from registering to vote. The UN twice postponed the ballot due to inadequate security, with a prospect of embarrassing Indonesia by abandoning the whole exercise. Around 90 per cent of eligible voters were eventually registered, and sufficient agreement between protagonists achieved to allow the ballot to proceed peacefully on 30 August 1999. But militias resumed violence the following day, accusing UNAMET personnel and foreign journalists of manipulating the ballot to favour independence.

Complaints included allegations of Muslims being asked for baptismal certificates as evidence of Timorese identity; confusion over voting hours; UNAMET staff allegedly directing voters to pierce the pro-independence symbol; and refusal by UN staff in Yogyakarta to allow photographing of voters.[1] These objections were investigated and rejected by a UN team from several countries (United Nations 1999*b*). Baptismal certificates were one of several possible documents which those registering to vote might produce. Polling hours were widely publicised. Voter education programmes, disrupted by militia violence, would have clarified that those wishing to vote for integration should pierce the Indonesian flag symbol, and pro-independence voters the National Resistance Council for Independent East Timor (CNRT) symbol. Polling officers were asked by voters to clarify the voting method to match voter's intentions, in face of misinformation that those against integration should 'stab' the Indonesian flag. Refusal to photograph voters was considered necessary to protect them from possible intimidation. Unaccredited supporters of either group who demanded to observe the ballot were refused for similar reasons.[2] Militias used these refusals as a pretext to unilaterally end the truce.

Post-ballot violence and transfer of sovereignty

Three weeks of mayhem followed the announcement that 78.5 per cent had voted for independence, with 98.6 per cent of those registered voting (United Nations 1999*b*). Foreign Minister Alatas insisted on Indonesian sovereignty during the interim period, in accordance with the May 1999 agreement. But wholesale violence against East Timorese, intimidation of UN personnel, foreign journalists, and humanitarian workers including the Red Cross, negated such arguments in the eyes of world opinion. Apparent aims of military strategy following failure in the ballot were to remove foreign media and UN personnel, create a refugee flood to reinforce the stereotype of East Timor as a divided society, and provoke the pro-independence guerrilla army, Falintil, to strike back. The first two objectives were substantially achieved, but Falintil discipline in avoiding retaliation held firm (Van Klinken 1999*a*).

Indonesia's request on 12 September 1999 for assistance in maintaining security in East Timor opened the way for Security Council Resolution 1264 three days later. This provided for entry of the International Force for East Timor (INTERFET) acting under Chapter VII of the UN Charter. Major violence and destruction was effected by the military and militias during the interim period between initial deployment of INTERFET and completion of Indonesian military withdrawal by mid-October. Despite suggestions of resistance by several political and military leaders, the MPR revoked East Timor's integration into Indonesia on 25 October 1999, followed by formal administrative transfer to the newly established United Nations Temporary Administration in East Timor (UNTAET).

Exodus to West Timor

Up to 300,000 people were evacuated to the West Timor region of Indonesia's East Nusa Tenggara (NTT) province, with an estimated 167,000 returning by mid-2000 (United Nations 2000*a*: 3). Such mass exodus required coordinated support from military and provincial authorities. Some identified with Indonesia and feared for their future safety. Others fled to avoid violence. But many who later returned reported being rounded up by TNI and militias, and herded on to trucks and boats. Militias noted identities at numerous checkpoints. Trucks returned empty to Dili to collect further people.[3] Militias took control of refugee camps and actively sought out pro-independence groups, many of whom remain unaccounted for. Militia presence has obstructed access by humanitarian agencies and the work of the UN High Commission for Refugees (UNHCR). Refugees are consequently unable to freely choose whether to return home or remain in Indonesia.

An international delegation found that refugee camps in Atambua lacked clean water, cooking utensils and mats, with threats of disease from malaria, diarrhoea and tuberculosis.[4] Responding to mounting international pressures, including from the Association of Medical Doctors of Asia (AMDA)[5] and East Timor's international spokesman Jose Ramos-Horta (Miller 2000), Indonesia sought to close refugee camps by announcing withdrawal of assistance on 31 March 2000, thus forcing a choice to either return home or accept an offer of Indonesian citizenship. This deadline was extended indefinitely in face of both external pressure and domestic criticism.[6]

Indonesia's failure to end militia control of refugee camps is widely perceived as the root cause of the problem. This situation culminated in the murder of three UNHCR personnel in Atambua. The catalyst was supposedly a revenge killing of a militia leader, Olivio Moruk, deemed responsible for the murder of priests at Suai, East Timor, on 16 September 1999. Moruk was due to give evidence to the Indonesian Human Rights Commission investigation team (Fox 2000). Five thousand militia attending his funeral were inflamed by speeches blaming 'white' interference via the UN. Several entered the UN compound, hacked UN workers to death with machetes and set their bodies alight. The military remained inactive despite prior warning (Woodley 2000). Six persons appeared in a North Jakarta court on 11 January 2001.[7]

A UN Security Council Resolution on 8 September 2000[8] referred to an 'outrageous and contemptible act against unarmed international staff' and stressed there would be no return of UN workers without credible security guarantees, including 'real progress' towards disarming militias. Even China and Malaysia, as members of the Council, though supportive of Indonesia, condemned the militias' actions and failure to control them (United Nations 2000*b*).

President Wahid strongly condemned the killings in a letter to the Security Council on 7 September,[9] But Defence Minister Mahfud asserted that a foreign intelligence operation, coordinated by Australia, was behind the Atambua killings (Greenlees 2000*b*). With $5 billion in World Bank sponsored assistance at risk, Indonesia responded by despatching two fresh battalions to West Timor and inviting international observers to check progress in confiscating weapons.[10] These continue to circulate. Eurico Gutteres, named as a key organiser in Komnas HAM's report on atrocities in East Timor, was eventually sentenced to six month's jail for weapons offences.[11] He has joined the PDI-P and organises protection for party leaders visiting West Timor.

East Timor in Indonesian media and domestic politics

President Habibie was accused after the ballot of lack of consultation by many, including TNI leaders, who had expressed little public opposition when Indonesia accepted the East Timor consultation process in May 1999 (Sumarno 1999). More probably it was calculated that Indonesia would win the vote. Megawati Sukarnoputri, who had been similarly silent, criticised Habibie for lack of nationalistic awareness in offering to surrender East Timor. She considered the independence vote represented a rejection of New Order human rights abuses rather than of Indonesia itself.[12]

The ballot crystallised differences between those who saw offering East Timor an independence option as a necessary step in stabilising democracy at home and Indonesia's position internationally, and those who saw its loss as the first step towards national disintegration. Media reporting reflected similar divisions.[13] There were nevertheless many cross currents, reflecting both a sense of bitterness and a need to accept harsh realities.

The 'democratic-internationalist' stream recognised that East Timor's incorporation into Indonesia had never been accepted in international law. Indonesia's good name would continue to suffer if an independence option had not been offered. The ballot process had been more or less fair, and Indonesia would encounter intolerable pressure if it broke its undertaking to abide by the outcome. This would also be out of line with its new democratic aspirations. Loss of East Timor would be compensated by regaining international goodwill, with freedom to redirect resources to other provinces. Indonesia should acknowledge its shortcomings, support goals of normalisation and humanitarian relief, cooperate with UNHCR calls to remove militia influence in West Timor and repatriate all who so wished.

The opposing 'military-nationalist' stream emphasised the dangerous precedent for other provinces of East Timor's separation. The ballot process and outcome was biased and manipulated by unfriendly outsiders. The militia were 'our brothers' who deserved support and understanding. Western countries, particularly the USA and Australia, were driven by racial, religious and geo-political motives, using East Timor to destroy national unity. External pressure, economic dependence and political ineptitude had combined to force Indonesia into a humiliating surrender of national territory.

While competing to become President, Abdurrachman Wahid partially adopted 'military-nationalist' discourse. Indonesia must follow its own rather than others' understanding of East Timor. NGOs were accused of colluding with foreign associates in using East Timor to 'corner' Indonesia. Criticism of military errors was exaggerated. These derived more from individual than institutional causes, and were in process of correction.[14] Wahid continues to view foreign condemnation of Indonesia's human rights record as, in principle, unacceptable.

Often violent demonstrations against the UN, Australian and other embassies in Jakarta were mainly military inspired, as part of a wider attempt to restore TNI's declining fortunes. A 'domino theory' of national collapse tapped strong chords of national sentiment, linked to resentment at Indonesia's economic downturn and renewed dependence on foreign financial assistance. Even pro-democracy activists tended to see East Timor as a security rather than human rights issue (van Klinken 1999*b*). The demonstrations, if not their underlying sentiments, largely dissipated after the Presidential election and completion of formalities for ceding East Timor by the MPR.

Extensive economic interests of the Suharto family, military and other associates, plus networks surrounding former provincial Governor, Jose Abilio Soares, also motivated the military-nationalist lobby. These involved over half a million hectares of land held for coffee, sugarcane, sandalwood, timber and marble extraction, a stake in three oil wells plus numerous construction enterprises. Proposed partition of East Timor aimed to protect oil reserves concentrated in the western region (Aditjondro 1999).

UN and Komnas HAM human rights investigations

Indonesia and the UN launched parallel investigations into human rights violations in East Timor. The Indonesian investigation, conducted by Komnas HAM, represented a bid to pre-empt the UN inquiry and assert national pride and sovereignty. Indonesia initially indicated that the government would not cooperate with the UN investigation,[15] pointing out that the UNCHR resolution establishing it was not binding, as it was not from the Security Council and opposed by East Asian countries represented on the UNCHR. Indonesia nevertheless felt obliged to cooperate as a UN member.[16] The UN team were received in Jakarta from 5–8 December, for purposes of dialogue rather than investigation. Requests to visit camps in West Timor were refused. Though smooth cooperation between the two investigating teams was established, Indonesia refused to accept either the legitimacy or findings of the UN inquiry.

The five-member UN team was drawn from Costa Rica, Nigeria, India, Papua-New Guinea and Germany. The thrust of its findings (UNCHR 2000*b*) was consistent with information flows from UNAMET and UNTAET and other independent observers, in identifying military collusion with militias; systematic intimidation and terror directed primarily at pro-independence groups; rape and sexual assault against women from families of independence fighters or men who had fled to the hills; damage to both public and private property ranging from

60 to 80 per cent across the whole territory; forcible displacement of people to West Timor and continued prevention of their return.[17] These actions all violated Indonesia's responsibilities as a member of the UN and specific undertakings in various agreements.

The team was nevertheless unable to confirm killing of many thousands, as widely alleged in international media. Available forensic and other evidence indicated 165 deaths reported, 180 bodies recovered, 171 remains examined and 77 individuals tentatively. New evidence is constantly coming in, but mass graves similar to Rwanda or Yugoslavia have yet to be found. Capacity for forensic storage was essential for future investigation (UNCHR 2000*b*: Sections 98–100). More recent estimates range between 1000 and 2000, as displaced persons return from West Timor, investigations extend into remoter regions, and allowing for possible dumping of bodies at sea (Timberlake 2000).

Foreign Affairs Minister, Alwi Shoaib, asserted that Indonesia, having opposed the original inquiry, was under no obligation to respond substantively to the report. But he rejected both its methodology and conclusions, on the grounds of failing to cross-check hostile testimonies with pro-integration groups or to give weight to their testimony alleging violations by pro-independence groups.[18] Such objections are unconvincing as the team had no access to West Timor where most such groups are located, and were granted no rights of investigation in Indonesia. Nevertheless, the UN team enjoyed two detailed exchanges with the Komnas HAM investigating team in Jakarta and Darwin.

Initial grounds existed for doubting the national inquiry's autonomy and effectiveness. Leading Indonesian human rights groups considered Komnas HAM lacked credibility among East Timorese.[19] Location of its Dili office opposite military headquarters had discouraged access, with one inside source suggesting collusion by some Commissioners (SAHRDC 2000: 10). Military objections to the team questioning senior generals were eventually overcome, but excluded General Wiranto.[20] Inclusion by Team Chairperson, Albert Hasibuan, of alleged Indonesian flag burning by INTERFET as a breach of human rights[21] indicated a military-nationalist outlook, reflecting poorly on the team's understanding of universal human rights.

However, despite different styles of approach and constraints on both inquiries, the two teams reached broadly similar conclusions. Komnas HAM found evidence of mass murder, torture, false evidence, forced disappearances, sexual slavery and rape, scorched earth, abduction as refugees, destruction and theft of property. The civilian, military and police apparatus had created conditions for these humanitarian crimes in deliberate and systematic fashion.[22]

General Wiranto was named as bearing ultimate responsibility for failure to take effective steps to protect human rights following the 30th August ballot. Several other generals and high ranking officers were cited, plus former provincial governor Abilio Soares and key militia commanders.[23] The report acknowledged killings at Liquica Church on 6 April, in Dili diocese on 5 September and destruction of some eighty per cent of the buildings in the town of Maliana on 4 September 1999. The Subdistrict Military chief was alleged to have participated in looting and arson during an attack on a church complex in Suai, estimated to have killed over fifty people, and in removing twenty-six bodies, later secretly buried in East Nusa Tenggara.[24] The inquiry also recommended full research into human rights violations during Indonesia's twenty-four year occupation for possible prosecution, and purposes of historical documentation. Allegations of abuses by pro-independence Timorese and UN forces were forwarded to INTERFET and UNTAET.[25]

The Komnas HAM team forwarded its evidence, plus recommendations regarding further investigation of those cited with a view to prosecution, to the Attorney-General, who moved to establish an appropriate team. Suggestions that naming TNI officers was libellous were rejected by the DPR Legal Affairs Commission, as they had not been pronounced guilty.[26] After a dangerous two week stand-off, President Wahid, persuaded General Wiranto to step down as Minister for Political and Security Coordination pending investigations. On 1 September 2000, the Attorney-General's office named nineteen suspects, including thirteen military officers and three militia leaders.[27] Generals Wiranto was not named at that stage. Four more militia leaders, including Eurico Gutteres, were named the following month.

As previously discussed, establishment of special human rights courts necessary to prosecution will encounter serious constitutional and political obstacles.[28] The idea behind these courts is to prove to the international community that Indonesia can effectively investigate and prosecute abuses in East Timor. But there is strong cross-party support in the DPR for regarding accused military and militias as patriots rather than war criminals.

Weakened by prospects of impeachment, President Wahid established a special Human Rights Court on East Timor. However, only alleged offences following the ballot on 30 August 1999 will be tried. This decision excludes major violations involving both military and militia preceding this date – a decision condemned by Amnesty International (2001) as an attempt to prevent investigation of the 1999 events in their entirety. By contrast, retrospectivity was not considered a problem in establishing a special court on the 1984 Tanjung Priok incident, in which many Moslems were killed by the military. UNTAET is also proceeding with investigations. Indonesia's inadequate response will strengthen pressures to establish an international tribunal. However, the Security Council currently appears reluctant to intervene (ICG 2001*a*).

Transition to nationhood

Direct involvement in establishing an independent state represents a new departure for the UN. While human rights have remained at the centre of this mission, its ultimate task is to assist East Timorese to assume national sovereignty. Issues relating to security, institution-building, social and economic reconstruction, developing a democratic culture and relations with Indonesia are integrally linked.

UNTAET treads a fine line between over-control which alienates East Timorese and premature withdrawal before adequate stability, infrastructure and capacity for self-government are in place. In light of physical destruction and trauma experienced by East Timorese, this is necessarily a long-term process. But political realities will necessitate formal transfer of sovereignty around 2002–3. UNTAET consequently seeks to address interlocking deficiencies in health, education, nutrition, housing, public utilities, legal institutions and administrative expertise, through crash programmes on all fronts (United Nations 2000a). These are gradually increasing employment opportunities, but not yet rapidly enough to absorb many alienated youths. Establishing viable language strategies poses an immense challenge, with the Indonesian language spoken by 80 per cent of people, rejected for political reasons. Finally, serious problems have been reported for women who have suffered rape to be accepted by husbands who fled to or fought in the hills (Powell 2001).

An all local, thirty-three member, National Council was established on 14 July 2000, drawn from CNRT component parties, three other parties, major social and religious groups. Four of eight administrative portfolios were taken by Timorese, with finance, justice, police and political affairs held by UNTAET. Some harassment has been experienced by parties seeking to organise outside the CNRT umbrella and by some ethnic and religious minorities. One Catholic radio station's staff received death threats aimed at silencing political commentary. UNTAET has sought to disseminate civic and human rights education, working through NGOs and local community leaders in efforts to develop a culture of tolerance (United Nations 2000a).

The issue of reconciliation with the pro-integration minority influences both domestic politics and relations with Indonesia. Xanana Gusmao, while advocating reconciliation and a focus on future re-building,[29] reversed his earlier offer to discuss power-sharing. To be forgiven, militias must acknowledge their criminal actions to the people, from whom any true amnesty must come.[30] In responding to findings by Komnas HAM against Wiranto, Gusmao said he did not want revenge, but only to establish the truth.[31] Jose Ramos-Horta stated that all except militia leaders who continue to oversee terror campaigns may return without fear of reprisals (Miller 2000). Gusmao has since indicated his intention not to stand for election as President.

East Timorese leaders moved to normalise relations with Indonesia in direct discussions with President Wahid. In December 1999, Wahid allowed the opening of a CNRT representative office in Jakarta, overruling military objections. Apologies for past wrongdoing during a visit to Dili in February 2000 generated goodwill and respect among East Timorese, despite minor protests.[32] An eleven-point agreement with UNTAET was signed, providing for establishment of an Indonesian representative office in Dili, discussion of assets and claims on each side, refugees' status, demarcation of land and sea borders, trade and investment, socio-cultural and legal exchanges, cooperation in developing land, sea and air links, and continuing access to Indonesia for East Timorese students. Both sides promised to promote good governance, respect for human rights and fundamental freedoms, and to establish a border regime in Timor island permitting unimpeded passage of goods and people between the two countries, including a corridor connecting East Timor with the enclave of Oecussi.[33]

While the agreement may indicate a transformation in Indonesia's outlook, a high price for Jakarta's cooperation could yet be exacted. Some interpretations of 'reconciliation' with the pro-integration minority, including militias, could place intolerable strains on a fledgling government. Continuing Indonesian propaganda accusing UNTAET of favouring CNRT seems designed to pressure the UN into premature withdrawal, potentially weakening East Timor's capacity to function as an independent country.

Continuing militia presence in West Timor threatens East Timor's security through periodic cross-border attacks, and disinformation campaigns aimed at aggravating divisions among Timorese, and discouraging refugees from returning home. An East Timor defence force is to be set up to counter militia incursions, based on the former pro-independence army, Falantil. Support will come initially from Australia and Portugal, but other regional and international involvement is being sought (Garran 2000).

Former Indonesian Defence Minister Sudarsono, who acknowledged the probable role of Suharto loyalists and others seeking to destabilise President Wahid in supporting the militias, nevertheless believed that East Timor's leaders should make more substantial efforts to assure them of a future in an independent East Timor. This was necessary to overcome entrenched tribal, sub-tribal and family divisions detrimental to East Timor's long-term political health (Greenlees 2000a). Sudarsono's successor, Mohamad Mahfud, claims, without any tangible evidence, that East Timorese now wish to rejoin Indonesia. Repeated accusations that other states intend to turn East Timor into a client state may partly reflect Indonesia's own aspirations. But moves in this direction could produce the outcome it most fears, prompting East Timorese to again appeal for outside help. Any too interventionist stance by others could equally cause a turning back towards Indonesia. All parties will hopefully realise their stake in a viable and independent East Timor.

7 Australia, Southeast Asia and human rights

This chapter assesses trends in Australia's official human rights policies, contextualised in key fields such as defence, economic relations, aid, labour, regional and bilateral diplomacy. Although major focus is on regional relations, issues of compliance with UN human rights instruments will also be addressed. Civil society groups' outlooks emerge from debates on national and cultural identity, concepts of democracy, governance and economic development. Networking between Australian and Southeast Asian human rights NGOs have become integral to Australia–ASEAN relations.

External influences, identified in earlier chapters in terms of diplomatic and economic pressures, media commentary, critical reports by international human rights agencies, popular campaigns and compliance with UN regimes loom large in the politics of human rights in Southeast Asia. However, their sources in western countries were little explored. Consideration of the role of human rights in Australia's relations with ASEAN states will partly fill that gap.

These relations have their own unique characteristics, despite Australia sharing many western European and north American perspectives. Geographical proximity and networks of strategic and economic interest entail comparatively closer and more sustained engagement. Exposure to the region through media and public debate, though of varying quality, is correspondingly more continuous and intense in Australia. There is also relatively greater academic and educational focus on Southeast Asia.

ASEAN states are currently inclined to associate negative outside commentary directed towards them with Australia, throwing differences into sharper relief. Australia may also act as a convenient vehicle for resentment against more powerful western countries. Differences are not always expressed in human rights contexts, but may spill over into other fields, as illustrated by Malaysia's determination to exclude Australia from regional forums and trade arrangements. Value differences between states mostly remain latent, restrained by diplomatic norms of non-interference.

The first section of the chapter establishes the general diplomatic, security and economic context, comparing Australian and Southeast Asian priorities. It shows how successive Australian governments, while formally committed to UN regimes, have sought to contain human rights policies within a framework of national interest emphasising strategic and economic engagement with East and Southeast Asia. The second section connects issues of cultural identity, with discourse concerning Australia as 'part of Asia' and Asian values. Trends in public policy and opinion are then explored in various contexts embracing both civil-political and economic streams of rights, also revealing tensions between governments and civil society. An overview of Australia's compliance with UN regimes exposes philosophical and institutional barriers to full participation, reflected in a significant retreat by the current conservative government.

The latter part of the chapter contextualises Australia's human rights policies within the framework of bilateral relations with ASEAN states, excepting Laos and Brunei. A diffuse picture emerges, particularly when civil society networks are taken into account. Special attention is directed towards Indonesia, East Timor and Cambodia, where bilateral human rights engagement has been most substantial.

Overall, the chapter reflects key themes throughout the book, notably tensions between conforming with international human rights law, preserving state sovereignty and pursuit of national interest; balancing socio-economic with civil and political rights; interactions between democratic politics and human rights; the global context of local human rights development, and diplomatic complexities associated with bilateral engagement in this field. It also adds a further layer of understanding of the extent to which the UN system has been absorbed unevenly into governance and relations within the politically and culturally pluralist regional context of Australia and Southeast Asia.

Strategic context

Australia's geographical location ensures that its strategic priorities are heavily concentrated in East and Southeast Asia. This region buys over 50 per cent of Australian exports. Two-way investment flows have also grown rapidly. But Australian attitudes have adapted more slowly to changing realities.

Australian defence strategy seeks to reconcile maintaining ties with the US with strengthening regional security links (Commonwealth of Australia 1994). Priority is accorded to mobile and integrated defence systems geared towards 'strategic denial' of Australia's vast land mass to any invading force. Provision is also made for continuing contribution to UN peacekeeping forces, as in the recent case of East Timor. While any direct threat to Australia is unlikely in the near future, growing prosperity will increase regional capacity to deploy sophisticated weapons. Potential for instability arising from ethnic, religious and economic tensions has been increased by recent political and economic upheavals. Containing dangers from drug trafficking and other crime, illegal immigration, environmental and health threats also requires regional engagement through all available channels.

The ASEAN Regional Forum (ARF) provides a vehicle for security cooperation, embracing East Asian and ASEAN countries, Australia and New Zealand, the USA, India and Russia (Commonwealth of Australia 1997: 36–7). This large and perhaps deliberately unwieldy body has no human rights mandate (JSCFADT 1998*b*: 91–3). Most countries are reluctant to discuss each other's internal affairs even where regional stability is affected, as indicated in earlier consideration of Burma and Cambodia.[1] The ARF has nevertheless shown some capacity to raise sensitive issues, particularly at the margins of meetings.

Successive governments have identified Australian national interest with globalisation and free trade, despite public concern over employment and environmental consequences, and seemingly unilateral pursuit of these goals. While the 'Cairns Group' coalition of fourteen countries gained some concessions under the 'Uruguay Round', the newly established World Trade Organisation (WTO) has only partly slowed the flow of subsidised agricultural exports from Europe and the USA. The ASEAN Free Trade Area (AFTA), which extends preferential tariffs on an expanding list of items, also excludes Australia. While ASEAN countries claim no conflict in principle between regional economic cooperation and ultimate goals of international free trade, they assert the right to proceed according to their own pace and arrangements.

Maintaining US regional engagement remains central to Australia's strategic thinking. ASEAN opinions on the US role vary. While welcoming continuing engagement, particularly in northeast Asia, most countries are wary of any action which could be construed as intervention. This accords a good deal with the US' own outlook, favouring regional self-reliance.

Such considerations prompted Australia to play a leading role in establishing the Asian Pacific Economic Cooperation (APEC) organisation in 1989. This initiative was strongly supported by Singapore, anxious to encourage trade liberalisation, and Indonesia, which by the early 1990s was seeking a broader regional and global role (Suryadinata 1996).

Malaysia promotes an alternative proposal for an East Asian Economic Caucus (EAEC), to include all ASEAN countries, plus China, Japan, Hong Kong, Taiwan[2] and South Korea. Australia, New Zealand and the USA were to be excluded for perceived lack of identification with Asian approaches and concerns. Malaysia accordingly vetoed Australia's participation in the Asian delegation to the March 1996 Asia–Europe Meeting (ASEM) in Bangkok. The EAEC is envisaged as a cohesive East Asian community, whereas APEC is portrayed as a vehicle for American-style globalisation, with Australia as willing instrument. No other ASEAN country formally supported Malaysia's position before 1998. President Wahid has subsequently supported a re-vamped forum linking ASEAN with China, Japan and South Korea.

Rival concepts of regional cooperation highlight Australia's dilemma in reconciling Asian engagement with the American alliance as foreign and defence policy cornerstone. APEC provides scant compensation for Australia's continuing exclusion from core regional decision-making. Moreover, trade relations with the USA have become more competitive than cooperative, while exclusion of agriculture from US agendas reduces their value to Australia. Conversely, Australian criticism of US initiatives to impose human rights conditionalities, particularly on labour issues, have pleased ASEAN governments but disappointed human rights activists. They indicate Australia's search for both an independent role and inclusion in regional forums. In that context, APEC serves to blur sharp choices which Australia wishes to avoid.

Cultural and ideological context

Deepening engagement with Asia has intensified debates over Australian identity, reviving well-worn themes of reconciling European history with Asian-Pacific geography (Grant c 1988). Huntington's characterisation of Australia as a 'torn country' in civilisational terms, in attempting to become 'part of Asia' (Huntington 1996), strikes a chord with some conservatives. However, former Prime Minister Keating insisted that while close engagement was integral to its development, Australia was not and could never become 'part of Asia.' Its unique blend of characteristics and influences made it neither Asian nor European but Australian (Keating 1996). His successor, John Howard, sees no inconsistency between forging close relations with Asia and retaining strong ties with the USA and Europe (Kelly 1996).

Despite erratic funding policies, stark ignorance of Asian societies and minimal knowledge of Asian languages have been gradually addressed through various educational initiatives under the rubric of building 'Asia awareness' (JSCFADT 1998*a*: 147–58). This sought to bridge gaps between a growing Asian presence in Australia plus extensive interchange in many fields, with the seemingly entrenched Anglo cum European mindset underlying politics, institutions, scientific, legal and educational systems. But sudden discovery of Asia's significance by political and business leaders, combined with lack of basic 'Asia literacy', has resulted in serious errors and misreadings in Australia's regional dealings, with extreme swings in outlook from paternalism to deference, resulting in inability to bargain effectively on the basis of mutual knowledge and respect (Fitzgerald 1997).

A joint study by Australian and Asian scholars identified entrenched differences in approaches to conducting business, security and diplomacy, as well as more familiar differences over concepts such as freedom, authority and government. Regional cooperation across various fields has rendered many Australians more aware of their own value systems, emphasising individualism, egalitarianism and adversarialism (Milner 1996). There are also concerns about how far regional economic integration will entail harmonising political behaviour and institutions. Asian governments place a high premium on conflict management, and minimising differences likely to generate tensions in inter-state relations. Dr. Mahathir regularly raises this issue in order to maintain Australia's exclusion from Asian regional forums. Other countries take a more relaxed view in terms of ASEAN's own principle of respecting difference. Some commentators urge Australia to maintain its historical roots and identity, arguing that characteristics of respect for law, human rights and parliamentary institutions hold strong appeal for many Asians (Milner 1997: 44–5).

At a popular level, resistance to 'Asianisation' was linked to perceived over-emphasis on diversity and consequent loss of common values and sense of shared society (Milner 1997: 43). The promise by then Opposition leader John Howard to restore a sense of cohesive national community probably contributed to his electoral victory in March 1996. Pauline Hanson, elected as an independent member of the Australian Parliament in 1996 and founder of the One Nation party, reiterated this theme in cruder fashion, specifically attacking the alleged pace of Asianisation in Australia. Howard's slow response, which he justified in terms of both tactics and free speech, raised suspicions of a nexus with Hanson supporters. Her constituency soon expanded by tapping into social and economic discontent arising from globalisation. This discontent persists despite fractured support for One Nation.

Threats to Australia's regional diplomatic and business interests (JSCFADT 1998*a*: 159–60) eventually stimulated a vigorous campaign to repudiate Hansonism, particularly its racist and anti-Asian aspects. The episode illustrates underlying contradictions in relation to freedom of speech in Australia. It has also sharpened long-standing debates over issues of assimilation versus integration of non- 'Anglo-Celtic' minority groups. Broader issues of citizenship and nation-building, which most Australians are reluctant to address systematically compared with Southeast Asian countries' more articulate public strategies, are also at stake (Milner 1996: 224–83).

Australia articulates a broadly western outlook on human rights and democracy issues, based on its history and culture, adopting all major UN treaties and associated protocols. However, support for the UN represents a realist as much as an idealist stance. Despite modest expectations and assessments of the UN's capacity, Australia, as a small to middle power with no pretensions to major power status, identifies its interests with maintaining and extending structures of international law. This stance extends to trade policy, where open trade regimes are energetically pursued, even when reciprocity is not quickly forthcoming. However, when criticised for alleged breaches, the Howard government has played down principles of accountability and international law relating to human rights treaties to which it is a party, preferring to assert national sovereignty and Australian values.

Despite deviations in practice, principles of democratic competition, accountability, freedom of speech and association, open and impartially supervised elections, separation of powers, particularly in relation to the judiciary, and law-based as against personalised rule, are strongly upheld. However, consonant with commitment to social and economic rights, Australian governments intervene more strongly in regulating public health and safety, labour and environmental conditions than is normal in many ASEAN countries (Milner 1996: 44–68, 132–64).

Autonomy from the state, with no requirement for community and pressure groups to present their views in a 'constructive' and non-confrontational manner, are equally seen as essential to sustaining a strong civil society. As liberal democracy is commonly accepted as the only valid form of democracy, adjectives such as western or liberal are largely dispensed with. Conversely, other models of democracy with qualifiers such as Asian, Guided and Pancasila are seen less as variants than as sham democracies designed to disguise autocracy (Milner 1996: 148–53).

While Asian values are popularly dismissed as rhetoric for legitimising governments, influential groups are willing to accommodate them. Acceptance of Asian cultural relativism reflects a realist outlook on regional relations. Social conservatives and economic neo-liberals both appropriate elements of the Singapore model seen as supporting their position, although hard line civil libertarians reject even softer Asian civilisations variants.

Several submissions to a Parliamentary review (JSCFADT 1998*b*) noted potential for regional human rights dialogue to bridge gaps between artificial cultural and philosophical dualisms (JSCFADT 1998*b*: 6–13). The Australian Forum of Human Rights Organisations (AFHRO) called for human rights interpretations to draw on both non-western and western sources. Cultural differences should not preclude shared core values expressed through the UDHR. Camilleri considered polarity between Asian and western values exaggerated. Cultural and civilisational monopolies in formulating human rights should be rejected in favour of cultivating the universal within each culture. The Australian Council for Overseas Aid (ACFOA), the peak body for Australian overseas development and human rights NGOs, advocated dialogue as essential to overcoming mutual East–West stereotyping.

Views of Asian leaders, such as Anwar Ibrahim and Kim Dae Jung, and intellectuals such as Yash Ghai were widely cited to counter relativist uses of culture by Asian governments to deny universality and indivisibility of human rights. The Hong Kong-based Asian Human Rights Commission (AHRC)[3] saw the indivisibility principle as a powerful tool for transcending simplistic dichotomies between unrealistic universalism and paralysing relativism (JSCFADT 1998*b*: 13).

The Parliamentary Committee rejected calls for a review of the UDHR, recommending that Australia should only consider supporting a Universal Declaration of Human Responsibilities insofar as this complemented and did not derogate from the UDHR. ACFOA considered the timing of this proposal as dangerous in view of Mahathir's pronouncements, but acknowledged that dialogue could assist democratic progress (JSCFADT 1998*b*: 13).

Human rights policy trends

Australia did not formulate explicit human rights policies until the early 1990s. Their conceptualisation in both domestic politics and foreign policy lagged behind formal adherence to UN treaties, commonly characterised in terms of idealism as against realism and sense of national interest required in conducting foreign policy. A parallel dualism obtained in Australian aid policy, with humanitarian assistance commonly distinguished from economic development.

While acknowledging convergence between human rights advocacy and broad Australian values, realist commentary is often dismissive, warning against potential damage from attempts to impose external conceptions of morality. A report on *Australia and the Third World* (Harries 1979) concluded that as democracy was still a distant prospect in most countries, Australians should moderate their expectations and concentrate on supporting whatever incremental reforms might be possible. Strong, even authoritarian government was often desirable for the sake of national cohesion and social stability. Anticipating Asian values discourse, Harries insisted that no values were absolute (Harries 1979: 154–7). Lack of reference to UN regimes portrayed human rights as effectively outside normal systems of inter-state relations.

Change in Australia began during the 1980s. Anti-race and anti-sex discrimination legislation, complementary to UN treaties, gave human rights a higher domestic profile. NGO activity in overseas programmes and advocacy on official aid policy raised awareness of Third World issues. Labor's accession to government in 1983 was accompanied by growing activism in party branches on foreign policy, including human rights issues. Official emphasis on Southeast Asia was paralleled by community focus on human rights deficiencies. Growing strength of regional democratisation movements and the end of the Cold War reinforced these trends.

Harries (1979: 156–7) urged a sympathetic view of Third World stress on economic rights, without undermining national sovereignty. Conditionalities directing aid to the poorest should be avoided as misguided idealism and unwarranted intervention. Paul Keating, as Federal Treasurer and later Prime Minister, took a similarly upbeat view of economic growth as the key to overcoming poverty, but resisted linkage between development and human rights.

Complexities of incorporating human rights into Australian foreign policy-making led to establishment in 1991 of a new Human Rights Sub-Committee within the Parliamentary Joint Standing Committee[4] on Foreign Affairs, Defence and Trade (JSCFADT), to monitor annual Department of Foreign Affairs and Trade (DFAT) reports on the government's international human rights initiatives. Domestic compliance issues have featured in these reports from the outset. The Sub-Committee has become a focal point for interaction between the Australian Parliament and civil society on human rights issues. It also receives submissions from the Asian region. A full-time Secretary was appointed in 1995, but capacity to meet rising demands has been hampered by limited resources.

All Australian governments have experienced conflict in reconciling domestic human rights pressures with regional diplomatic realities. Of all Foreign Affairs ministers, Gareth Evans, appointed in 1988, was the most active in promoting the UN as a major instrument for international order and dispute resolution (Evans 1993) since Herbert Evatt, External Affairs Minister in the 1945–49 Labor government. To these must be added Gough Whitlam, Australian Labor Prime Minister from 1972–5, who still contributes regularly to public debate on human rights. Evans initiated a proactive role by DFAT, strengthening the Human Rights Section established in 1985, and introducing annual reporting to Parliament.

Reporting on UN treaty compliance was linked to an annually updated national action plan on human rights. The last plan was formulated in 1996–97. New arrangements announced in December 1998 envisaged future plans becoming 'more succinct and user friendly', improving coordination among government agencies and facilitating public input (DFAT 1999). Australia's plan reflected conclusions of a regional workshop on developing national action plans, held in Bangkok under UNCHR auspices in July 1999 (UNCHR 1999) with DFAT assistance. Lack of progress in reforming the UNCHR treaty committee system (Downer 1997a; 2000a) has intensified Australian indifference towards this process.

Though pragmatic in seeking cooperative regional solutions, Evans' internationalist agenda contrasted with Keating's determined promotion of Australian economic interests. Though not neo-liberal in a classical sense, Keating's economic philosophy was strongly oriented towards growth and open global markets. He sought to separate development, thus conceived, from anti-poverty programmes or civil and political rights conditionalities on Australian aid. A high Australian profile on human rights would disrupt his agenda of regional security and economic cooperation via APEC in which Australia–Indonesia cooperation would complement the leading role played by the USA, China and Japan.

The incoming conservative government in 1996 was under pressure to reassure Southeast Asian neighbours that it attached the same high priority to good regional relations as its Labor predecessor. Doubts were created by an apparent tilt back to traditional ties with Europe and the USA, Howard's ambivalent commentary on issues of race and multiculturalism and perceived inaction towards the rise of racism via the One Nation movement. While rebuttals and reassurances were formally accepted, one trade-off may have been a more circumspect approach to human rights, which also accords with Howard's personal outlook. Human rights references were excluded from a trade treaty with the European Union and delays in reporting to UN treaty committees accumulated (JSCFADT 1998b: 21–2, 99–101). Community pressure for stronger confrontation against governments violating human rights is opposed by conservative elements in the Cabinet and bureaucracy. But Howard's insistence on caution has been offset since the East Timor crisis by references to the former government's alleged 'appeasement' of Asian governments. Such statements have caused disquiet both in the region and Australia's foreign affairs establishment.

Alexander Downer, Minister for Foreign Affairs and Trade, has broadly continued Evans' efforts to integrate human rights into the foreign policy mainstream, reiterating Australia's support for principles of universality and indivisibility (Downer 1998c). To that end he encouraged a clearer anti-poverty focus in Australia's aid programme (Simons 1997). But he constantly urges avoiding lecturing-styles, liable to inflame national sentiment,[5] and concentrating on making a difference through practical cooperation. Institution building via technical assistance in legal, electoral and related fields, linked to programmes for improving governance, reduces the diplomatic heat associated with human rights issues. It also moderates charges of appeasement by domestic critics. This approach reflects Evans' belief that effective human rights policies could be pursued with relatively small cost to diplomatic relations, by quiet persuasion and cooperation rather than punitive sanctions or strident condemnation (Evans 1994: 260).

A coalition government White Paper (Commonwealth of Australia 1997) sought to integrate regional security, economic and human rights objectives with community-based 'Australian values' within a framework of 'national interest'. This concept was targeted at Australian domestic audiences, and consolidating domestic support for sustained regional engagement and associated, often unpopular policies of globalisation. Many human rights advocates nevertheless acknowledge that their concerns cannot be isolated from regional and national security frameworks.[6]

Key principles governing Australian foreign policy approaches to human rights, according to Downer, are based on concern for the treatment of individuals; their role in underpinning Australia's security and economic interests; Australia's support for the UDHR and other UN human rights instruments enshrining principles of universality and indivisibility (JSCFADT 1998a: 19–20). Unqualified rejection of racial discrimination is both a moral issue and fundamental to Australia's acceptance by, and engagement with the region where its vital security and economic interests lie (Commonwealth of Australia 1997: Clause 9).

It may be objected that if these propositions were true, UN treaties would be central to Australian law and administrative practice. In reality, they are incidental, with conservative politicians arguing that universal rights are redundant in view of Australia's 'excellent' human rights record. Similarly, state governments would be willing to pass legislation outlawing racial discrimination and Australia could withdraw its reservations on race relations issues.

Notions of governance underpinning both political and economic aspects of the government's 'practical' approach to human rights are open to objections that pursuit of technical and institutional change, without engaging underlying political culture, frameworks of power and authority, is unrealistic. Governance strategies also depend on a problematic nexus between democratisation and the rise of the middle class. While acknowledging the complexity of relationships between economic and political liberalisation, the 'national interest' White Paper urges pursuit of both as the best means to deliver comprehensive human rights.

Claimed complementarity between stated human rights priorities and Australia's foreign policy direction has encountered strong scepticism (JSCFADT 1998b: 21–5). The Australia Tibet Council considers that a 'Chinese Wall' has been erected between 'the whole dialogue, delivery and discourse of human rights and Australia's national interests.' AFHRO fears that regional advocacy will be undermined by refusal to accept the standard human rights clause in the European Trade Agreement. Community Aid Abroad (CAA) urges more critical appraisal of the socio-economic impact of trade liberalisation, particularly on women and children. James Dunn, former Australian Consul in Dili and veteran critic of East Timor policies, traces the role of 'quiet diplomacy' in marginalising universal human rights.

The shift from a multilateral to bilateral focus may have increased inconsistencies in applying human rights policies to different countries and issues. Whitlam described Australia's stance as one of constantly making bilateral protests to other countries but stalling on the most effective steps to bring human rights into a framework of international law (Kent 1997: 164). Amnesty International accused the government of undermining a consensus that had previously existed to pressure China at the UNCHR, and with finding bilateral dialogue more diplomatically congenial than sponsoring critical resolutions at the UN (JSCFADT 1998b: 27–31). Random linking and de-linking between human rights, security and economic policy, portrayed as a seamless whole in the 'national interest' White Paper, adds to this pattern of inconsistency, while 'pragmatism' and 'effectiveness' offer numerous escape routes from demands to implement international human rights law.

National human rights institutions

Australia has actively supported development of the Asia-Pacific Forum of National Human Rights Institutions (APFNHRI). In 1995 Brian Burdekin, an Australian former UNCHR Commissioner, was appointed to advise the UN Commissioner for Human Rights on developing national human rights institutions. The Human Rights and Equal opportunity Commission (HREOC) represents Australia in APFNHRI, providing its secretariat from aid funds. Training programmes for strengthening judicial processes and legal reform have been devolved to the Australian Legal

Resources group, an arm of the Australian Chapter of the International Commission of Jurists.

The Forum offers opportunities for informal and indirect engagement, compared with the limited direct scope available to DFAT. Its work will increasingly have an impact on Southeast Asian governments, for example, via plans to develop regional jurisprudence.[7] The capacity of national human rights institutions to embarrass their governments became evident in Australia when the Attorney-General proposed that HREOC seek prior approval of investigations. DFAT pointed out that this would breach the Paris Principles.

Defence cooperation

Defence cooperation provides indirect opportunities for human rights exchange (JSCFADT 1994: 67). Human rights components are included in all Australian Defence Forces (ADF) training courses, whether or not undertaken by overseas military personnel. A parliamentary review in 1994 recommended adoption of more detailed human rights training components, highlighting constraints imposed on military forces by international human rights treaties, and the need to subject uses of military force in civilian situations to legal due process (JSCFADT 1994: 78). International humanitarian law was subsequently built into both basic and specialist ADF courses (JSCFADT 1998*b*: 90–1).

The 1998 parliamentary human rights review recommended that sweeping uses of security legislation by ASEAN governments be raised in bilateral dialogues and at the UNCHR (JSCFADT 1998*b*: 79–82). Operational links with Southeast Asian military, especially Indonesia, were challenged as damaging to civil society both in Australia and overseas. Amnesty International argued that Australia should at least oppose security training likely to contribute to torture, disappearances and indiscriminate killings.

An earlier parliamentary review urged that defence related exports be scrutinised for consistency with international standards, particularly to countries persistently violating human rights (JSCFADT 1994: 81). Citing the supply of Steyr rifles to Indonesia, the 1998 parliamentary review committee called for clearer guidelines to prevent defence cooperation supporting internal security functions (JSCFADT 1998*b*: 87–91).

Labour

Labour human rights, which link civil and political with economic rights, offer a strategically important example of the indivisibility principle. They also provide a bridge between domestic and international processes. The International Labour Organisation (ILO) operates under a tripartite structure representing governments, employers and workers. Many ILO conventions closely reflect rights recognised in UN human rights instruments (JSCFADT 1994: 166–7). Despite dismal labour conditions across the world, formal adherence to ILO conventions appears to be slowly increasing, including in Southeast Asia.

Australia is represented on the ILO through the Australian Council of Trade Unions (ACTU) and Australian Chambers of Commerce and Industry (ACCI).[8] Compared with Labour's relatively proactive stance, the Howard government has distanced itself from ILO processes, reducing funding support as part of a shift from multilateral agencies. Funds were withdrawn in 1996 from an ILO training programme in Indonesia in which the ACTU was heavily involved.[9] Additional support was refused for a programme to combat child labour.[10] ACCI involvement is motivated by support for freedom of association in labour relations, although employer bodies are closely controlled by governments in several ASEAN countries. Australia forms part of the ILO's Asian regional group. Nevertheless, Australia's federal system and conciliation and arbitration-based industrial relations system tends to slow down ratification of several important conventions (JSCFADT 1994: 167).

An ACTU submission rejected requirements of rapid development and industrialisation as blanket justification for violating workers' rights. Thus in 1993, several ASEAN countries demanded immediate review and updating of ILO conventions to enable more realistic application of labour standards (JSCFADT 1994: 169–70). Nevertheless, experience in Indonesia convinced the ACTU that making ILO technical assistance conditional on achieving specific standards was counter-productive. Assistance could enable countries to build up labour standards prior to ratifying ILO conventions (JSCFADT 1994: 171).

Community Aid Abroad, which opposed the ACTU's collaboration with Indonesia's government controlled union federation, stressed obligations to respect ILO conventions and rights both in Australia and overseas. Australian companies operating overseas should encourage industry-wide voluntary codes, as introduced by the Australian Mining Industry, but based on ILO standards and providing for independent monitoring mechanisms (JSCFADT 1998: 108–9).

In response to the ACTU's call for an active, intermediary Australian role in upgrading social and human development aspects of APEC's work, increased support for the ILO was recommended, particularly in child labour programmes, together with a review of APEC's social and humanitarian role (JSCFADT 1998: 108–10). Such recommendations from a government dominated committee, though pleasing to many Southeast Asian NGOs and grassroots groups, seemingly opposed both official Australian policy and ASEAN's declared position. Nevertheless, many investors appreciate the capacity of well organised unions to improve productivity, occupational health and safety. Some countries have sought to tap Australian labour organising skills, though de-linked from political militancy. The Australian government could also exercise influence in this field via diplomatic networks linking regional labour attaches.

Aid programme

Although official discourse has been mostly framed in terms of promoting development rather than human rights, these are now included in governance, national interest and regional security agendas. Simons' framework replaced the earlier 'triple mandate' underpinning Australian aid set out in the Jackson (1984)

Report. This assigned equal weight between strategic and economic interests and humanitarian objectives to be served by aid, thus confusing design and implementation of programmes (Eldridge 1999). While Simons' anti-poverty focus was unequivocal, it is unclear how far it can be accommodated within neo-liberal orthodoxies dominating economic policy-making and the report itself. Economic rationalist perspectives nevertheless provided opportunity for a fresh look at programmes' efficiency and effectiveness, and a strong basis for rejecting special pleading by interest groups. While beneficial strategic and business outcomes for Australia were not rejected, they were not to represent basic aid goals.

The government's response effectively finessed Simons. While enthusiastically accepting the report's anti-poverty focus, the aid programme was to remain set within national interest guidelines defined in the 1997 White Paper. As these highlight Australia's regional security priorities and the business opportunities flowing from liberalising and globalising trends, the framework of the triple mandate is broadly maintained. Quite possibly, multiple objectives cannot be avoided, given the extent of conflicting domestic and external pressures (Kerin 1999). Nevertheless, the Simons review enhanced both the autonomy of aid administration and integrity of individual projects and programmes.

Six key principles officially underpin Australia's overseas development assistance (ODA), in pursuit of its anti-poverty objective. These are partnership with developing countries; rapid response to urgent needs and trends; improved definition and targeting; Australian identity, reflecting and projecting Australian values; an outward looking approach, drawing on best practice in Australia and overseas. Aid would focus on five key sectors supporting sustainable development, in which Australia is 'well placed to assist' – health, education, infrastructure, rural development and governance – defined as 'competent management of a country's resources in a manner that is open, transparent, accountable, equitable and responsive to people's need' (Downer 1997*b*). Gender and environment issues cut across all programmes. The geographic focus of Australian ODA on Papua-New Guinea, other Pacific countries and East Asia is indicated in the $1.5 billion aid budget breakdown for 1999/2000 in Table 7.1

Within 'East Asia' 86.8 per cent is allocated to Southeast Asian countries, as per Table 7.2. Assistance is also increasingly concentrated in the poorest regions within selected countries such as eastern Indonesia and southern Philippines.

From the aid programme's inception in 1950, successive governments have resisted demands for conditionalities based on egalitarian or pro-poor development policies, human rights performance or democratic political orientations (Harries 1979: 137–8, 154–7; JSCFADT 1994: 67). The prevailing view has been that such conditionalities would provoke nationalistic resistance damaging to Australia's broader regional interests, and that, as a relatively small donor, Australia can exert little influence alone. Assistance represented 0.25 per cent of Gross National Product in 1999–2000 (AusAID: 2000), only slightly above the continually declining Development Assistance Committee (DAC) country average, compared with ODA/GNP ratios of 0.34 in 1995–96 and a peak of 0.52 in 1974–75 (Downer 1996: 66).

The current programme focus nevertheless reflects domestic demands that scarce funds be targeted towards overcoming poverty and other human rights

Table 7.1 Regional distribution of Australian
bilateral and multilateral aid
1999/2000 (A$ m.)

Bilateral	
Papua-New Guinea	328.9
Pacific	136.9
East/Southeast Asia	421.4
South Asia	82.4
Africa and Middle East	84.6
Multilateral	
Emergency and Humanitarian	104.8
International Banks	225.6
International Development Organisations	93.4
NGO and Volunteer Program	42.1

Source: AusAID 2000.

Table 7.2 Country distribution of
Australian aid within East
Asia 1999/2000 (A$m.)

Indonesia	121.1
Vietnam	72.4
Philippines	61.8
China	55.5
Cambodia	36.8
Thailand	26.3
Lao PDR	20.8
Malaysia	3.4
Other & Regional	23.2
Total East Asia	421.4

Source: AusAID 2000.

deficiencies. Surveys consistently show that public support for the official aid programme, though broadly based, is also shallow (Simons 1997: 292–3), rendering it
vulnerable to budget cuts without risk of protest beyond recognised humanitarian
lobby groups. Support for overcoming poverty was also shown by private donations
to Australian NGOs. These increased from $89 to $165 million between 1988 and
1995, with an estimated 2.5 million Australians contributing (Simons 1997: 292).

The anti-poverty shift has not proved diplomatically difficult. Most ASEAN
states accommodate group and sectoral targeting within their overall strategies
and plans. Similar cooperation is evident in technical assistance and institution
building relating to civil and political rights. Projects of doubtful effectiveness
can usually be phased out smoothly, providing programmes are not axed abruptly,
as occurred in 1996 when support was withdrawn for infrastructure projects
under the Development Import Finance Facility (DIFF) programme, which added
an aid component to Australian-linked commercial ventures.

Assistance to national human rights institutions represents a 'flagship' for the growing governance component within Australian Agency for International Development (AusAID) bilateral programmes. This trend was accelerated by the regional economic crisis. Bilateral focus has been strongest in relation to Indonesia and Thailand, where the Centre for Democratic Institutions (CDI) cooperates with the Office of the Parliamentary Ombudsman, the Office of Judicial Affairs and the Thai Arbitration Institute. Establishment of the CDI in 1998 represented a major personal initiative by Alexander Downer. Its programme focuses on training and exchange relating to electoral, parliamentary, judicial and administrative institutions and processes. However, its mandate relates to governance rather than human rights (JSCFADT 1998*b*: 16–18, 123–4). Strong informal links with DFAT constrain CDI participation in any broader human rights dialogue.

Notions of governance fit well with national interest guidelines favouring problem-solving over strong human rights advocacy. However, its meaning is contested. Simons' definition (1997: 223) embraces government policies and administration, human rights, democratisation, the rule of law, civil society and participatory development. Greatest emphasis, particularly since the regional crisis, has been on improving economic performance, management and transparency. Though potentially supportive, governance and universal human rights are not equivalent, as rights are more multi-dimensional.

NGOs have been among the most articulate and well organised critics of the official aid programme. While supporting its developmental objectives, they stress participation and equity as central to both ends and means. They also urge that economic growth be integrated with programmes directly targeting the poorest groups. But despite many points of convergence, the language of human rights is not central to NGO discourse or agendas, with the notable exception of the Human Rights Council of Australia (HRCA), which promotes a 'rights way to development',[11] and the ACFOA Human Rights Office'.

Australian NGOs have become increasingly involved in designing and implementing programmes, with the percentage of official aid allocated via NGOs rising from under 2 per cent in 1985–86 to 7.4 per cent in 1995–96 (Simons 1997: 262–4). Annual consultations are held under joint AusAID and ACFOA auspices. The AusAID-NGO Cooperation Program (ANCP) provides for counterpart AusAID funding, on a 3 : 1 ratio, to programmes by accredited NGOs meeting relevant guidelines. Further support is provided by tax refunds on donations to recognised overseas development NGOs. Accredited NGOs, or their consulting arms, may tender to participate in official programmes.

Strong community links both within Australia and internationally remain NGOs' greatest asset. While such claims require careful scrutiny, their mobilising capacity depends on retaining substantial autonomy from governments and other powerful interests, as AusAID acknowledges. NGOs' continuing outspokenness and public interest lobbying capacity on issues ranging from child labour to East Timor belie fears that they will be silenced by funding and diplomatic pressures, faced in various forms by all publicly funded programmes.

Regional economic crisis

Australia responded to the Asian crisis on both bilateral and multilateral fronts. Focus on governance programs and sectoral priorities indicated earlier was intensified. AusAID sponsored an APEC survey of regional economic governance (Centre for International Economics 1998) and opened its Asia Crisis Fund to competitive bidding between country desks. Greatest concentration of programmes was in Thailand and Indonesia. Australia contributed one billion US dollars in loan funds to support IMF financial rescue packages in both countries. In July 1998, Australia raised its annual pledge to Indonesia via the World Bank sponsored Consortium Group for Indonesia (CGI) from $74 million in July 1997 to $120 million (Downer 1998*b*). These packages appear to have strengthened bilateral relations with Thailand (Alford 2000) but not Indonesia.

Compliance with UN treaties

Full understanding of issues here requires reference to their domestic context, which cannot be adequately treated in a broad regional survey. Nevertheless, domestic performance influences external perceptions and consequently the effectiveness of Australia's human rights advocacy. Legislative and bureaucratic initiatives associated with treaty ratification, for example, in the anti-discrimination field, build capacity for cooperation and advocacy overseas. Conversely, adoption of UN human rights treaties by ASEAN countries will over time sharpen peer review of Australia.

Australia has ratified all ten major human rights instruments listed in earlier surveys, though with important reservations to the ICCPR and CERD treaties. It sponsored or co-sponsored fifty-one resolutions on human rights at the April 2000 session of the UNCHR.[12] But Australia's federal system and, paradoxically, its Westminster-style parliamentary democracy represent significant barriers to full participation in UN regimes.

US-style constitutions accord their highest courts extensive powers of judicial review over both legislation and executive action. The US Constitution also entrenches some basic rights and freedoms reflecting universal human rights principles, thereby protecting individuals and minorities against discriminatory laws or abridgement of legal due process. In both Britain, which has no written constitution, and Australia, courts only limit executive action to the extent that this conflicts with statutory law. However, the role of adjudicating between the powers of Commonwealth and state governments accorded to the High Court within the framework of Australia's federal constitution, has opened up scope for interpretations based on international human rights law (Evatt 1994: 81).

The Australian High Court has upheld the supremacy of Commonwealth over state legislation in relation to international treaties, established in Sections 51 and 109 of the Constitution. However, extensive treaty ratification by Labour governments instigated conservative allegations both of weakening Australian sovereignty and ignoring the states, which carry responsibility for local enforcement. Adoption of the ICCPR First Optional Protocol was seen as detrimental to parliamentary sovereignty at both federal and state level, especially as states have no access to UN committees.[13] Such complaints overlook requirements to exhaust all domestic processes before approaching the UN. A Parliamentary Treaties Committee was subsequently established to monitor overall processes and give greater weight to states' opinion.

Charlesworth (1994: 21–3) believes that trust reposed solely in 'responsible government' to guarantee justice and individual rights is misplaced. Human rights law in Australia is 'haphazard and incomplete', with no rights entrenched constitutionally and their protection accorded a low legislative priority by state governments. The politics of federalism and traditions of legal reasoning have created a culture wary of rights discourse. English common law, derived from a corpus of context-specific case law and judicial interpretations, provides only incidental protection, and offers no systematic framework for establishing citizens' rights (Bailey 1990: 45–78). Australians' 'enduring suspicion' of entrenching rights constitutionally limits possibilities for adapting the Australian Constitution to international human rights law (Charlesworth 1994: 30–1).

A long-canvassed compromise would be a Bill of Rights, incorporating the core principles of all major UN instruments to which Australia is a party. This would provide a standard against which all legislation could be judged, encouraging emergence of a new jurisprudence linked closely to international human rights law (Alston 1994: 2–3). But progressively watered down versions of the Bill of Rights, first introduced in 1973, have failed to gain parliamentary assent. A 1994 parliamentary committee considered that Australia's accession in 1991 to the ICCPR First Optional Protocol made the matter more urgent (JSCFADT 1994: 37). But opponents continue to argue that a Bill of Rights would transfer policy decisions and debate to the legal sphere, thereby politicising the judiciary.

The 1986 Human Rights and Equal Opportunity Commission Act represented a partial substitute for failed efforts to establish a Bill of Rights (Charlesworth 1994: 29–33). The Act assigned HREOC responsibility for complaints, conciliation and general oversight in relation to the Racial Discrimination Act 1975, Sex Discrimination Act 1984 and Disability Discrimination Act 1992. These Acts give force to the ICCPR, the Convention on the Elimination of All Forms of Discrimination against Women, Convention on the Rights of the Child, Declaration on the Rights of Disabled Persons, Declaration on the Rights of the Mentally Retarded and ILO Convention 111 covering discrimination in employment and occupation (JSCFADT 1994: 50). Apart from ILO legislation, HREOC responsibility only applies to the federal situation. Its recommendations are not enforceable by courts (Charlesworth 1994: 37–8). HREOC's main impact has been in terms of promoting public awareness (JSCFADT 1998b: 120–1, 126–9).

Burdekin considers that Australia violates civil and political rights less than economic, social and cultural rights of aboriginals, people with disabilities and homeless persons. Human rights treaties are little established in Canberra's bureaucratic culture, apart from the Department of Foreign Affairs and Trade and the Attorney-General's Department (JSCFADT 1994: 51). Branding by Western Australia's Attorney-General of a report criticising Western Australia's jail conditions by the UN Anti-Torture Convention Committee as a 'blanket smear by a group of professional complainers' (O'Brien 2000) illustrates a similar outlook among state governments.

Policies requiring automatic detention of asylum seekers who lack legal identity documents breaches Article 31 of the Status of Refugees Convention, which stipulates that those who present themselves promptly to the authorities should not be penalised, nor their movements unnecessarily restricted pending determination of their status, or until they are admitted into another country. Systematic labelling of asylum seekers as 'illegal immigrants' is also unfair for the same reason. Those facing imminent danger may have been unable to complete complex processes or access Australian embassies in their countries of origin or in some third country where they lack secure temporary residence. Ironically, absence of national identity cards, opposed by both civil libertarians and conservatives during the 1980s, by complicating policing of illegal residence, has increased pressures for harsher control regimes.

The search for humane alternatives for supervising asylum seekers within community contexts has become more urgent following several riots at Woomera, a detention centre in a desert region of South Australia, and Port Hedland on Australia's northwest coast. The Department of Immigration and Multicultural Affairs (DIMA) has sub-contracted prison management to an American-controlled private prison company, which has been accused of suppressing evidence relating to alleged child rape (Plane 2000).

Article 2 of the refugees convention gives asylum seekers full access to courts and rights to legal assistance. The government has sought to limit such access, considering that it is used to extend appeal processes, allowing continuing residence to many whose cases are eventually rejected and taking up places of others waiting overseas. But detention, sometimes extended over several years, is itself a factor in causing delays, by concentrating detainees in remote locations and aggravating communications problems.

Despite these severe disadvantages, a large majority are eventually accepted as genuine refugees. But since 1999, assistance to those who originally entered Australia 'illegally' has been restricted, with bans on family reunion for at least three years.[14] *Prima facie* these restrictions breach Convention Articles 23 and 24 requiring equal treatment with nationals in public assistance, labour and welfare provision. The government nevertheless argues that harsh conditions are needed to discourage international 'people smugglers'.

The Refugees' Convention was established under conditions prevailing in post Second World War Europe. Fifty years later, many more asylum seekers are victims of civil war, ethnic upheavals, generalised repression and economic disruption, not covered by the Convention's core reference in Article 1 to well-founded fear of persecution for reasons of race, religion, nationality, social identity or political opinion (Millbank 2000). While the need for reform is widely recognised, human rights advocates fear that opening up the Convention may well result in further restrictions. Amnesty International also warns that 'persecution' does not specifically include torture or killing.[15]

Successive governments have sought to address changing conditions through the humanitarian component of the migration programme, but fear this will lose public support if numbers of onshore asylum seekers become excessive. Immigration Minister, Philip Ruddock (2001) has aggravated the problem by insisting on an inflexible overall quota of 12,000. Australia's situation is complicated by the failure of most transit countries in Southeast Asia to participate in the Convention. Ruddock proposes strengthened support via the UNHCR for holding refugees and negotiating a safe return home where possible.[16]

The Royal Commission into Aboriginal Deaths in Custody (RCADIC 1991), followed by the High Court judgement in Mabo v The State of Queensland in 1992 recognising native title to land, highlighted breaches of the ICCPR, CERD and the Rights of the Child Convention in Australia's treatment of aboriginal people. Mandatory sentencing of juveniles for property offences in the Northern Territory and Western Australia breach all three treaties, as illustrated by the death of a fifteen year old aboriginal boy imprisoned in Darwin. Mandatory sentencing has been criticised as pre-empting both judicial discretion and potential alternatives,[17] and, according to Commonwealth Education Minister, David Kemp, as interfering with children's education.[18]

Australia interprets Articles 19 and 21 of the ICCPR, guaranteeing rights to freedom of expression, assembly and association subject to preserving public order and morality, as encompassing Article 20 prohibiting advocacy of national religious or racial hatred, incitement to violence, hostility or discrimination. Reservation of Australia's right not to introduce specific legislation indicates that racist propaganda and incitement will be judged in terms of their impact on public order rather than as breaches of human rights.

The Racial Discrimination Act (RDA) was passed one month after Australia's ratification of the CERD treaty in September 1975, and further strengthened in 1992.[19] The RDA closely follows the treaty's wording and substance. Powers of reporting, conciliation and holding public hearings are granted to HREOC, with disputed recommendations adjudicated by the courts. Significant successes for complainants are reported in cases of overt discrimination (Race Discrimination Commissioner 1995: 33–53). But *ad hoc*, individualised, complaint-based mechanisms represent limited tools for dealing with entrenched racist discourses and structures (Thornton 1995).

The Racial Hatred Act 1995 declared racist speech unlawful.[20] The Keating government reluctantly accepted amendments by the Senate conservative majority removing criminal provisions. Offences under the Act provide grounds for civil action by aggrieved individuals, though not groups. Exemptions under Articles 18C and 18D for artistic representation and academic, scientific and journalistic commentary, based on fair and accurate reporting deemed in the public interest, and expressions of 'genuine belief', provide defences against such action. The Act thus falls short of standards required under Articles 4(a) of CERD and 20(2) of the ICCPR. Akmeemana and Jones (1995) urge the importance of acknowledging multiple forms of injury inflicted on victims of racial vilification, noting that Australian jurisprudence has little difficulty in accommodating injuries caused by defamation, blasphemy, obscenity, copyright, censorship, contempt of court or Parliament, or under consumer protection laws.

Australia's federal system further hinders resolution of issues relating to aboriginal rights. This obliged Australia, notwithstanding clear international law obligations, to declare that responsibilities for implementing the ICCPR would be distributed among Commonwealth, State and Territory authorities based on their respective constitutional powers and arrangements. Legislative powers granted to the Commonwealth government in a referendum carried overwhelmingly in 1967 were used by the Whitlam Labor government to grant land rights in the Northern Territory. However, apart from South Australia, state governments withheld necessary cooperation in many spheres.

The Koowarta v Bjelke Petersen case in 1982 validated the application of the RDA at state level, which the Queensland government had sought to deny (Race Discrimination Commissioner 1995: 48). The High Court's 1992 judgement in Mabo v Queensland set aside the infamous *terra nullius* doctrine, which declared Australia as owned by no one prior to European settlement. It also acknowledged, albeit in qualified form, the legitimate influence of universal human rights on common law by declaring *terra nullius* 'a discriminatory denigration of indigenous inhabitants ... frozen in an age of racial discrimination' (Charlesworth 1994: 28). The 1993 Native Title Act, which gave legislative effect to Mabo, evoked furious protest from pastoral leaseholders and miners concerned by uncertainty over future claims and requirements to negotiate with native title holders. Amendments in 1998, weakening and in many cases extinguishing native title, remain open to constitutional challenge as discriminatory in terms of the RDA.

The RDA also covers general discrimination based on ethnicity and national origin, and the rights to enjoy one's culture specified in Article 27 of the ICCPR. The Australian Law Reform Commission reviewed the role of law in a context of multiculturalism (Evatt 1994: 79–96). As with a parallel study of aboriginals, monocultural assumptions of Australian law came under challenge. The Commission recommended that, apart from cases involving harm to persons or property, legislatures should systematically review possibilities for exemptions from laws seen as interfering in groups' cultural and religious freedom. However, it recommended against separate legislation for marriage, family, property and the rights of women. It also condemned past policies enforcing removal of children from aboriginal families, as breaching ICCPR obligations to respect family life (Evatt 1994: 93).

The Howard government has sought to reduce its exposure to UN human rights regimes. Early in its first term, a parliamentary caucus of government backbenchers canvassed possible reservations to Australia's participation in the Rights of the Child Convention – a position eventually deemed too costly in diplomatic and political terms. The Prime Minister reacted to adverse treaty committee reports over mandatory sentencing by warning against UN interference.[21] Such populist national sovereignty rhetoric reflects that of neighbouring countries, with the difference that Australia is a high profile party to all major human rights instruments.

The dilemma is supposedly addressed by strident reference to 'Australian values'. These, rather than the formal wording of international treaties, are deemed sufficient to assert compliance with universal human rights principles, negating both the need or legitimacy of any formal UN role in Australian domestic processes. The implied contrast between Australian and Asian values in Howard's rhetoric also needlessly aggravates tensions with regional neighbours. But such dangers are ignored in face of the potential electoral power of some one million One Nation voters at the 1998 election (Milne 2000), reinforced by the timidity of the opposition Labor Party in this whole area.

Strong criticism of Australia's race relations performance by the CERD treaty committee (UNCHR 2000c) was described by the government as based on uncritical acceptance of the claims of domestic political lobbies', disregarding its own considered reports. Ironically, the government had made a virtue of NGO input into its reporting. The Foreign Minister announced a full Cabinet review of Australia's participation in the UN treaty committee system to bring pressure for long sought administrative change (Downer 1997a; 2000a). He further claimed that many countries' poor human rights performance negated their right to judge Australia's liberal democracy.

As only treaty participants are involved in monitoring processes, Australia's stance seems calculated to weaken both its international standing and the integrity of UN human rights regimes.[22] Additionally, women's groups were infuriated by refusal to ratify a new optional protocol to CEDAW, apparently responding to conservative charges of radical feminist dominance and liberally stretched interpretations of that treaty by its committee (Joseph 2000). Such exchanges no doubt cause wry smiles of satisfaction in Southeast Asian capitals.

Human rights in ASEAN–Australia bilateral relations

The Philippines

During the 1980s, domestic and overseas human rights activists cooperated closely in countering abuses by the military under President Marcos' and during the tense democratic transition under President Aquino. Diminished, though still significant reports of disappearances, violence, torture and illegal seizure of land (US Department of State 2000; Amnesty International 1997d) receive less regular international attention, which is reserved for regional rebellions, kidnappings or major political upheavals, such as the ousting of President Estrada. Outsiders play more background roles in relation to human rights, in light of vastly greater popular empowerment, while the Philippines' Commission on Human Rights increasingly represents a major reference source for international agency reports.

Australia–Philippines relations reflect this changing situation. Governance-oriented programmes via AusAID and CDI, and cooperation between national human rights institutions via the APFNHRI network, have replaced more direct human rights advocacy. Imprisonment of Australian priest, Fr. Brian Gore and fellow Irish Columban missionary Fr. Niall O'Brien, who supported the cause of Negros' sugar workers (McCoy 1984), sharpened many Australians' awareness of human rights and poverty issues. The case ultimately obliged the government to apply strong diplomatic pressure for Gore's release.

Official Australian concerns at that time centred on the potential for Marcos family corruption, military repression and human rights abuses to strengthen support for the revolutionary New People's Army, which would in turn threaten American bases at Clark Field and Subic Bay. US withdrawal, accelerated by the volcanic eruption of Mount Pinatubo and the end of the Cold War, was eventually negotiated without disruption to either national or regional security.

The Philippines' location in the South China Sea obliges it to operate within a changing East Asian power balance in which China will play a more forceful role. Despite some resentment at quarantine and other barriers to its primary products, Philippines' geo-political location between East Asia and the Pacific renders it supportive of flexible links between ASEAN and APEC favoured by Australia. But with Australian defence planning geographically focused on its immediate neighbourhood, bilateral relations currently focus on trade, governance and development issues.

The Philippine–Australia Dialogue was inaugurated in October 1997, bringing together a core of politicians, business people, academics and journalists to promote the bilateral relationship. Despite recognised commonalities and opportunities, trade and investment ranks low relative to other ASEAN countries (DFAT 2000c). Australia has avoided involvement in the upheavals surrounding the ousting of President Estrada, but was clearly more at ease with President Ramos' market oriented policies and cautious financial management, which it hopes will be resumed under President Arroyo.

On the socio-economic front, an important Dialogue outcome was a Memorandum of Understanding for Joint Action to Combat Child Sexual Abuse and Other Serious Crime. Australian aid is heavily concentrated in the southern Philippines, working with both NGOs and local government units in a region which has suffered decades of armed conflict. A Vulnerable Groups Facility targets women, children, rural and urban poor, indigenous and minority groups affected by the regional crisis and associated structural adjustment (DFAT 2000c).

Common language, religious and cultural affinities, strengthened by the presence of over 90,000 migrants of Filipino origin in Australia, have facilitated civil society links. Cooperation initiated during the struggle against Marcos' rule has continued through cross-denominational networks of East Asian churches, NGOs linked through ACFOA and the Hong Kong based Asian Human Rights Commission, and Filipino activist groups allied with the socialist left Resistance network in Australia. For the most part, except in times of political crisis or heavy military action, NGO cooperation centres on grassroots programmes and struggles, notably land and labour disputes. But Filipino groups neither need nor accept external direction in these fields.

Thailand

Thailand's relations with Australia have been positive. Strong pride in national identity has rarely taken an anti-western direction, as Thailand successfully avoided colonial rule. Desire for continuing US engagement is balanced against China's proximity and emerging strength, which also influences relations with Vietnam, Cambodia and Myanmar. The sensitivity of this balance, and Thailand's pivotal role within ASEAN weighs heavily in determining Australia's options. Thailand broadly shares the position of Singapore, the Philippines and Australia in promoting open global trade, including linking Australia and New Zealand with the ASEAN Free Trade Area. However, it is uncertain how far the new government elected in January 2001 will maintain these objectives. Trade, investment, tourism and educational links have recovered strongly since the 1997 economic crisis (DFAT 2000*d*). Support for civil and political rights is channelled through governance programmes via the CDI.[23]

Australian links with Thai civil society groups are less substantial than with the Philippines, due probably to lesser religious and language affinity and the more recent development of democratic movements. These received strong media coverage and popular support in Australia during anti-military struggles in 1992. However, military and commercial cooperation with the SLORC regime and Khmer Rouge elements have attracted strong criticism in Australia, as has perceived lack of support for asylum seekers from Myanmar. Earlier cooperation with the UNHCR in processing thousands of Indo-China refugees commanded strong respect from Australia, though partly offset by failure to control killings of Vietnamese boat people by pirates operating from Thailand's coastal villages.

While Thailand limits use of Asian values polemic, it remains sensitive to negative stereotypes of its society and institutions by foreign media, emphasising electoral corruption, drugs, child sex, prostitution and HIV/AIDs. Australian, Thai and regional NGOs increasingly cooperate in these sensitive areas, as do the two countries' police forces. Reciprocally, Thailand's media was the most outspoken among all ASEAN countries in goading the Australian government into action against One Nation. Thai commentary articulated both support for universal human rights values, crossing barriers of national sovereignty, and friendly concern lest Australia retreat from the region and slip back towards earlier racist and isolationist attitudes.

Singapore

Australia–Singapore relations have experienced significant change since the early 1990s. Improved rapport between political leaders, broad convergence in strategic outlook and economic interest, including strong two-way trade and investment (DFAT 2000*b*), has reduced the importance of cultural and ideological differences which coloured earlier relations.

Singapore's authoritarian style of government was the subject of much adverse media and academic commentary in Australia during the 1970s and 1980s. Singapore's leaders in turn counter-attacked perceived lax standards associated with liberal democracy, resulting social disorder, business and labour inefficiencies. Lee Kuan Yew's combative style of argument, which fitted well with Australian political culture, drew grudging admiration, reinforced by respect for Singapore's impressive economic achievements.

Though Lee remained unconvinced, Singapore elites' perceptions of Australia were changing by the early 1990s. A key reason was the liberalisation and globalisation of Australia's economy during the 1980s, resolving many of Singapore's complaints against trade barriers. Prime Minister Goh Chock Tong's consensus style coincided with urgency generated by Paul Keating for closer regional engagement. Australia also appeared more accepting of Asian links, human and cultural presence as part of its daily life. Singapore's frustrations at external trade growth being held back by slower developing ASEAN partners has coincided with Australia's search for inclusion in regional arrangements.

Relations with Australia have also assumed greater prominence, as Indonesia moves closer to Malaysia's position favouring more exclusive forms of East Asian cooperation. As partial insurance against often troubled relations with Malaysia and Indonesia, Singapore has strengthened defence cooperation, leasing and developing land in Australia for training purposes (Commonwealth of Australia 1994: 89). Bilateral free trade agreements are under negotiation with Australia, New Zealand, Canada and the USA. But despite strong efforts to diversify its options, Singapore has probably neither will nor capacity to fully break away from East Asian political and economic networks.

High strategic and economic stakes have diminished the role of universal human rights in bilateral relations. Australian media interest in Singapore politics is largely confined to five-yearly elections, with predictable commentary on predictable outcomes, plus periodic issues relating to media freedom and civil rights. This is more than offset by regular flow of positive economic news and analysis supportive of Singapore's regional situation. Australian activist groups focus on other countries committing extensive human rights abuses. The issue of capital punishment, previously a major source of friction, is now handled by routinised expressions of concern through diplomatic channels, based on information supplied by Amnesty International's Australian parliamentary group. Potential for future conflict deriving from latent value differences and pluralism of civil society groups nevertheless remains unpredictable.

Malaysia

Despite strong Australian efforts to talk them up (Downer 1997; DFAT 2000a), Australia–Malaysia relations remain at a low ebb. But differences over human rights represent only a proximate cause, used mainly as weapons of convenience. Apart from circumspect expressions of concern over Anwar Ibrahim's arrest and trial, Australia officially accepts Malaysian democratic processes at face value. Conflicting paradigms of regional cooperation constitute the basic cause of conflict, as Malaysia seeks to systematically exclude Australia from East Asian decision-making forums in areas vital to its interests. To this end, Australia is portrayed as culturally and politically outside Asia, and as 'little brother' to the USA.

Historically, the two countries, plus Singapore, have shared a broad and deep relationship dating back to World War II, especially in defence cooperation. Despite Indonesia's view of the Five Power Defence Arrangements (FDPA), involving Malaysia, Singapore, Britain, Australia and New Zealand, as anachronistic, colonial legacy, Malaysia sees it as non-threatening and in line with its multi-track approach of keeping options open within a general regional approach (Razak *et al.* 1995: 19–22). Enduring business ties have been established. Despite some slowing in investment following the regional economic crisis, trade rose in both directions during 1999, with Malaysia benefiting especially from its fixed low exchange rate (DFAT 2000*a*).

150,000 Malaysians who have passed through Australian educational institutions provide significant social contacts. Student intake has risen further since 1997, as exchange rate trends have rendered Australia increasingly competitive (DFAT 2000*a*). Strong educational ties were acknowledged by Mahathir's inauguration of the Malaysia-Australia Foundation, initiated by ex-Australian alumni.[24] However, Shamsul (1996: 54–5) suggests that non-Malays studying in Australia in dispro-portionate numbers, partly encouraged by their government, as an outlet to over-come exclusion at home by pro-*bumiputera* policies, may negatively influence Australian perceptions. Anti-discrimination advocacy by non-Malays fits naturally with western-style human rights discourse, but antagonises Malays, who will later dominate the bureaucracy and assert rights along more communitarian lines. Expressions of Islam which encourage self-segregation by Malay students in Australia reinforce such outlooks.

Earlier Australian complacency, based on shared British cultural and institutional inheritance, was eroded by Malaysia's East Asian links, the rise of Islam and cham-pioning of the Third World. By contrast, Australia has paid greater attention to Indonesia, where cultural and ideological differences more obviously threaten its geo-political interests. Conflict following Keating's reference to Mahathir's outlook on APEC as 'recalcitrant' (Searle 1996) energised efforts to rebuild relations. Even the Howard government's withdrawal of objections to the EAEC idea did not prevent Malaysia from vetoing Australia's participation in Asia–Europe security consultations and other regional forums. Attacks on Australia's regional role were intensified following the East Timor crisis, including personal denigration of Howard by Mahathir.[25]

Though partly deterred by the ferocity of Malaysian polemic, the limited impact of civil and political rights issues in Australia–Malaysia relations is also due to lack of active interest by Australian NGOs, and the Third World solidarity priorities of their Malaysian counterparts. As with Singapore, capital punishment is a source of continuing bilateral difference. Prime Minister Hawke's description in 1986 of cap-ital punishment as 'barbaric', was considered insulting by Malaysia, but otherwise diplomatic representations on this issue have been minimal.

Tension is aggravated by alleged negative stereotyping of Malaysia by Australian media in 'colonialist' terms, which fail to acknowledge its economic progress. The Malaysia-Australia Foundation has sought to counter 'negative' media coverage by bringing Australian journalists to Malaysia for greater exposure.[26] Environmentalist commentary on mining, logging and large dam construction is a further source of grievance, especially as Malaysian NGOs act as primary informants. Close links between Australian and East Malaysian activists at one stage resulted in demands for a ban on imports of rainforest products from both Malaysia and Indonesia.

Expulsion of several Australians, including the Catholic Bishop of Melbourne, attending a conference on East Timor in Kuala Lumpur in November 1996 were preceded by UMNO Youth attacks. The Australian government declined to protest on the grounds that Malaysia was exercising its sovereign rights.[27] This incident illustrates a continuing dilemma whereby Australia's efforts to identify with Asia can strengthen demands to conform with ASEAN norms (Crouch 1996*b*), providing a pretext for continuing exclusion of Australia from regional forums.

Indonesia and East Timor

Association with nationalist activists exiled from Dutch rule in Australia and trade union support for bans on Dutch military supply ships in 1945 initiated Australians' exposure to Indonesian politics. A sense of proxy involvement continued through the period of 'constitutional democracy', its overthrow by Sukarno, the rise and fall of communist influence during the 1960s, and the annexation of West Irian. Sharp opposition developed during the long period of military-led rule under President Suharto between successive Australian governments which defined cooperation with the New Order government as central to Australia's interests, and articulate civil society groups which abhorred its gross violations of human rights.

A review of Australia's defence capability (Dibb 1986) which asserted the geographically obvious proposition that any attack on Australia must come from or through Indonesia, raised diplomatic difficulties in implying even hypothetical future aggression. While Indonesian leaders seemed prepared to accept that no actual threat perception was implied, the report coincided with opinion polls in Australia indicating widespread perceptions of Indonesia as a probable future aggressor.

The Suharto government mostly ignored civil society criticism, though periodically banning Australian journalists. But the growth of democratic movements within Indonesia, and furious international criticism provoked by the Dili massacre in 1991 forced its government into a combination of internal reforms and external counter-attack along familiar nationalist lines. Relations with Australia nevertheless progressed well during this period, due to personal rapport between political leaders, which also created modest space for human rights exchange.

Over ten years of military cooperation with Indonesia culminated in the signing of a bilateral Security Agreement in 1995 (McBeth 1996). Indonesia's flexible interpretation of its 'free and active' principle of foreign policy (Sukma 1997) caused some surprise among regional neighbours. The New Order, though maintaining Indonesia's historical opposition to formal alliances, used this principle to accommodate military exchange with the USA and Australia.

Prior to Suharto's overthrow, Australia and Indonesia shared broadly compatible outlooks on regional security, with Indonesia strongly supporting Asian-Pacific regionalism, opposing reliance on geographically narrower East Asian frameworks. While ASEAN has provided the regional foundation for its foreign policy, Indonesia has always seen itself as a potential international player (Suryadinata 1996). It also has strategic interests in the Southwest Pacific, related to an emerging maritime emphasis in national defence policy, and diplomatic necessity to shore up support for Indonesian sovereignty over Irian Jaya.

President Wahid's priorities have focused on the return of East Asian investors, requiring confidence re-building among Chinese communities throughout East Asia. A re-defined EAEC, based on ASEAN countries plus China, Japan and South Korea assists this objective. This shift has been accompanied by strong tensions, at times bordering on hostility in Australia–Indonesia relations. As only Malaysia has so far defined East Asian cooperation in exclusivist terms, and as a rupture with Australia appears to run counter to Indonesia's strategic and economic interests, explanations must be sought in terms of domestic politics and ideology.

East Timor's secession was seen as both a blow to national honour and a threat to Indonesia's territorial integrity. Australia has been portrayed as supporting both trends, with Wahid at times giving credence to such sentiments. The conflict may prove harder to resolve in Indonesia's more volatile democratic environment, as bilateral relations now embrace civil societies in both countries. Violence in East Timor and across the archipelago weakened initially positive Australian responses to democratic and human rights reforms. Escalating conflict in Irian Jaya may evoke strong popular protest in Australia, leading to further tensions.

The two countries had earlier cooperated in achieving a political settlement in Cambodia, managing refugee flows from Indo-China and maintaining open sea lanes. Illegal fishing in northern Australian waters remains a source of difficulty, as has 'people smuggling' into Australia via Indonesia. Such problems, which penetrate deep into regional bureaucracies and local communities, are not easily amenable to inter-state diplomacy, especially in the currently troubled climate.

Despite commonalities in strategic outlook, the two countries have never established clear principles of equality and mutual respect for conducting relations. Indonesia's size, population, geo-strategic location and resource base weigh heavily in Australia's calculations, with air and sea communications and overall relations with ASEAN perceived as heavily dependent on Indonesian goodwill. This was expressed in a semi-official doctrine of 'asymmetry' whereby Australia is overwhelmingly more in need of Indonesia's cooperation than vice versa (Mackie 1974). This outlook was a major cause of Australian quiescence on human rights issues until at least the early 1990s.

More nuanced perspectives replaced asymmetry during the late Suharto years, as relations deepened and diversified, recovering from a low period during the mid-1980s.[28] Solid Australian assistance during the economic crisis, with parallel advances in democracy and human rights, seemed to have generated a more equal and relaxed environment. But upheavals in East Timor and consequent hostility to Australia by Indonesia's newly liberated media may indicate emerging populist versions of asymmetry.

Human rights issues, linked to repression of democracy, have been at the heart of bilateral conflict. East Timor reflected these tensions in extreme form. Distorted presentations of its culture and history up to the final withdrawal resulted in astonishment and resentment at Indonesia's rejection by both East Timorese people and the international community. High profile involvement by Australians in the ballot process and its aftermath made Australia an obvious target of both popular and elite anger.

Joint advocacy and programmes by Australian and Indonesian NGOs in both civil-political and socio-economic fields were extended during the late Suharto years, while the pro-democracy student movement in Indonesia enjoyed broad links in Australia. However, non-state support from Australia was stronger on radical participatory and political than social and developmental fronts, with mainstream NGOs looking more to the USA, Canada, Germany and the Netherlands for assistance. The leftist Action for Solidarity with Indonesia and East Timor (ASIET), was active in mobilising demonstrations in Australia, working closely with the Centre for People's Democracy (PDR) network – one of the few Indonesian groups to actively support East Timorese self-determination.

Under Suharto, the Australian government relied on 'quiet diplomacy', including representation on particular cases or issues and general dialogue via Indonesia's Department of Foreign Affairs. Senior Australian military were briefed to raise human rights issues with Indonesian counterparts. Parallel support was given to institutional strengthening, through cooperation between HREOC and KomnasHAM, exchanges in the legal, judicial and electoral administration and broader governance fields.

Australia retained good standing with Indonesia during President Habibie's early months, based on its solid support for economic and institutional re-building. But tensions over East Timor grew throughout 1999. A letter from Howard to Habibie in December 1998 has since become a focus of controversy. Responding to proposals to grant East Timor extensive autonomy, Howard apparently advocated a referendum with an independence option, but only after several years autonomy under Indonesian rule, in line with proposals by East Timorese leaders. But Habibie, preferring to settle the matter without delay, occasioned widespread surprise by offering an immediate choice between autonomy and independence. Habibie's close advisers later blamed Howard's letter for 'cornering' Indonesia at a time of political and economic weakness.

Official tolerance, and often encouragement of militia violence brought strong Australian public protest. Opposition foreign affairs representative, Laurie Brereton, demanded that armed UN peace keepers be present throughout the ballot. Howard claims to have put such requests to Habibie informally, but to have encountered categorical refusal. Although the process was firmly in the hands of the UN, the Australian government has been persistently blamed for insisting that the ballot continue and for concealing intelligence foreknowledge of TNI and militia plans in the event of a pro-independence outcome from both UNAMET and American allies. Official motivation, according to this thesis, supported by Paul Keating, was to present a deceptively optimistic picture of security in East Timor to the USA in order to exploit a window of opportunity to achieve independence under a transitional president (Kevin 2000). Others see Australia's behaviour as continuing diplomatic subservience to Indonesia. Both sets of arguments need to account for the internationally public nature of the referendum process by that stage, commitment by the UN, Indonesian anger when the ballot was twice postponed. Above all, East Timorese were determined to vote, fully knowing the dangers. Moreover, the USA scarcely lacks intelligence resources of its own. Evidence of official concealment is nevertheless compelling in light of continuing intelligence leaks.

Following the ballot, Australians and Indonesians experienced vastly different media coverage. Australians saw nightly pictures of burning, looting, forced deportation and evidence of an unknown number of killings. Attacks on UN personnel and property, foreign journalists, nuns and priests, Bishop Belo's diocesan complex and the International Red Cross compound created a sense that the militia and their TNI sponsors accepted no limits. The Australian government was immediately caught between demands for international and, if need be, unilateral Australian intervention and the reality that the UN would not move without a request from Indonesia, although it had never recognised Indonesian sovereignty over East Timor. Public anger in Australia boiled over during three weeks in September 1999 in demonstrations, boycotts, harassment of Indonesians and blockades of embassies and consulates. These dissolved quickly once the UN gave the green light and an international force, led by Australia, was rapidly deployed.

Indonesian television gave only limited pictures of destruction, which was attributed to 'civil war'. Australia became the target of sustained anger, fuelled initially by treatment of Indonesians in Australia, with burning of the Indonesian flag seen as an intolerable national insult. The Australian Embassy in Jakarta was constantly besieged, both by military and militia inspired and spontaneously angry student demonstrations,[29] with bullets fired through windows on several occasions. Some Australians experienced physical violence. Unexploded molotov cocktails were found at the Australian International School.[30] High level consideration was given to boycotts of textiles, wheat, sugar and other imports,[31] though these were not actively pursued.

The crisis caused suspension of several programmes, including joint military exercises, and abandoning the 1995 Security Agreement. Negotiated in secret between Suharto and Keating, this had always lacked popular legitimacy in Australia. Despite its lack of content, withdrawal from the agreement by Indonesia in September 1999[32] symbolised a major downgrading in relations.

Indonesian media commentary broadly followed the lines of division identified earlier.[33] *The Jakarta Post* and *Kompas* showed fair balance, but Australia was portrayed in some military and Islamic newspapers as an uncouth nation of ex-convicts,[34] responsible for torture, burning, murdering East Timorese citizens (militia) and firing on refugees.[35] Killing of an Indonesian policeman resulting from confusion over the border location with West Timor was portrayed as deliberate provocation.[36] Some security analysts, harping on religious and racial differences, suggested that Australia sought to establish East Timor as a client state, as a base for anti-Indonesian activity (Suryohadiprojo 1999). Abdurrachman Wahid expressed similar sentiments one week after the independence ballot (van Klinken 1999*b*).

Australia's Ambassador McCarthy argued that Australia had operated strictly within the UN framework and diplomatic norms, continuing to recognise Indonesian sovereignty prior to its handover, despite strong domestic pressures.[37] Australia had never pressed for an independence option, but merely supported Habibie's initiative. East Timorese made their own free choice. INTERFET had pursued the role assigned to it by the UN and had always sought to involve other ASEAN states. Public anger at the behaviour of the TNI and militias was genuine and understandable. Frank expression of opinion is an Australian characteristic, acknowledgement of which is necessary to cultural understanding. Property damage, violence and flag-burning against Australians in Indonesia had been on a far greater scale than vice versa. Nevertheless, all such actions were to be deplored. Australia's primary concern remained one of restoring relations.[38]

Difficulties here have been aggravated by both Wahid and Howard's personal style and outlook. Wahid pointedly sidelined Australia, visiting other countries across the globe. While both he and Indonesian diplomats hold out prospects for restoring positive ties, suggestions remain that some unspecified form of apology is required for 'insensitivity' and 'arrogance'. This stance reflects asymmetry doctrines, also fitting traditional behaviour by Malay and Javanese rulers in 'sulking' (*merajuk*), leaving those who seek restoration of favours to identify both cause and solution.

It is nevertheless accepted that relations with Australia may need to be temporarily downgraded to serve needs of Indonesian stability. As Wahid's core values have always centred on harmony and balance, his long-term objectives towards Australia are assumed to be similar. But opposition to restoring ties remains strong in many quarters. Though not sharing these views, Poerwadi (1999) considers that the Howard administration has yet to prove itself sympathetic to Indonesia, whether democratic or not.

Indonesia's negative outlook towards Australia contrasts with continuing deference towards the USA, which fully suspended military relations over East Timor (ETAN 1999*a*) compared with only partial suspension by Australia. Firm words from Washington, strongly urged by Australia, with Congressional threats to withhold assistance, were decisive in obtaining acceptance of UN peacekeeping forces and withdrawal by the TNI (Ellis 1999; ETAN 1999*b*). US and European journalists have been equally critical, though perhaps less ubiquitous than Australian counterparts.

Under the so-called 'Howard doctrine', East Timor and Australia's domestically popular military role in INTERFET reflected a turning point in Australia's relations with Asian neighbours, particularly Indonesia. Projection of Australian values would henceforth replace anxiety to avoid conflict at all costs. The idea of Australia playing regional 'Deputy Sheriff' to the USA attributed to Howard by *The Bulletin* magazine[39] caused a diplomatic storm, only partially calmed by a less than convincing denial after several days. Howard subsequently repeated the substance of this doctrine, claiming that Australia was 'at peace' with 'less frantic' regional relations pursued by earlier governments (Shanahan 2000).

Indonesians quickly translated Howard's language, suggesting equivalence between close relations and deference, into downgrading of relations, insensitivity and unfriendliness. The success of INTERFET forces and perceived triumphalism aggravated the media propaganda war on both sides. Indonesia lobbied strongly for Australia to be replaced as military commander following INTERFET's handover to UNTAET in February 2000. The UN acceded despite expressed preferences of East Timorese leaders.[40] This nevertheless removed one obstacle to restoring relations.

Earlier strong and diversified links (Sulaiman *et al.* 1998) provide a foundation for comprehensive re-building now required. The immediate need is for sustained low-profile, cooperative problem-solving, emphasising institutional strengthening in the human rights, judicial, legal and administrative fields. Persistence of KomnasHAM and human rights NGOs in building links with the UN system, including pursuit of domestically difficult prosecutions of crimes against humanity in East Timor, sustain hope that universal human rights will in future provide a common focus to Australia–Indonesia relations rather than a source of bitter conflict.

Myanmar

Australia has faced difficulties in reconciling its regional interests with support for international pressure on Myanmar to fulfil its human rights obligations. While rejecting 'constructive engagement', Australian governments have avoided direct confrontation with ASEAN's position, seeking to enlist its cooperation in encouraging change. Official strategies emphasise support for a strong UN human rights role; limiting aid to humanitarian assistance to displaced people from Myanmar in neighbouring countries, and grassroots activities via NGOs; urging influential, particularly ASEAN states to use their influence with the regime to promote change (DFAT 1998a). Australia also shares regional concerns at the growth in illegal drug exports caused by corruption and instability there.[41]

The Keating government suspended bilateral aid, apart from limited humanitarian support delivered through NGOs. The Howard government has demanded substantial progress in political and human rights as a condition of resuming aid. Defence exports and visits are banned. However, Australia has not supported economic sanctions. AusTrade visits were suspended, but the locally-staffed office in Rangoon operates under instructions of neither encouraging nor discouraging trade and investment (DFAT 1998a). Australian trade and investment are judged too small for any unilateral action to have a practical effect. In reality, both have continued to grow. Prospects for major increases in Australian food exports are under active review (Rural Industries Research and Development Corporation 1998).

ACFOA (1998a) sees the government's supposedly neutral stance as both encouraging trade and investment and consolidating the SPDC's income and position. The Council urges support for multilateral trade sanctions, UN resolutions and pro-reform activities by ASEAN NGOs. It also urges dialogue with Australian companies to discourage investment, boycott tourism, and local authorities to adopt 'selective purchasing policies', along lines pursued by the Sydney suburban Marrickville Council, discriminating against companies operating in Burma.

ACFOA's Human Rights Office established a 'Burma Project' in 1995, aimed at raising awareness in Australia and strengthening NGO regional democracy and human rights networks, through research, advocacy and campaigning. It has issued reports on forced labour (ACFOA 1998b), repatriation of Burmese refugees from Thailand and Bangladesh, prison conditions and tourism, also claiming success in persuading the Fosters company to withdraw beer sales in Burma.

Australia's sponsorship of human rights workshops in Rangoon in July and October 2000 was attacked by Opposition foreign affairs spokesman Brereton as giving legitimacy to an 'odious regime' (Sheridan 2000). Surprisingly, the SPDC announced its intention to establish a national human rights institution operating in accordance with the Paris Principles (Downer 2000b). Despite justifiable scepticism, Downer argues passionately that there is no alternative to engagement with Burma, in cooperation with the UN and ASEAN countries. His position was endorsed by Thailand's then Foreign Minister, Surin Pitsuwan, an outspoken democracy advocate, harshly critical of Myanmar's government (Sheridan 2000).

Apart from human rights training initiatives, the Howard government's Myanmar policies have been broadly similar to that of its Labour predecessor. Both have rejected US and European calls for economic sanctions and adopted a neutral stance towards promoting trade and investment. Both have emphasised multilateral and regional channels. But recent efforts by Downer to increase direct contact have been strongly attacked by the Labour opposition. The Labor Party's 1998 election platform promised, in the absence of progress on human rights and democracy, to impose sanctions, discourage travel and trade, including closure of the Rangoon AusTrade office, suspend visas for Burmese associated with the military regime, and downgrade diplomatic relations (Community Aid Abroad 1998). Any new Australian government will probably steer a middle course between the harder line approach of NGO activists and some western governments, and outright confrontation with ASEAN's position foreshadowed in Labor's 1998 platform.

Vietnam

Consistent with its neutral stance towards regional states of diverging political orientation, Australia has maintained cooperative relations with Vietnam. Human rights are included but do not feature prominently. Compared with the USA, which sustained economic and diplomatic boycotts until the mid-1990s, Australia recognised Hanoi in 1973, before Vietnam became united under communist control in 1975. Bilateral relations were frozen after Vietnamese intervention in Cambodia in 1979. But aid was channelled through UN agencies and NGOs. Cooperation has expanded on all fronts since the peace settlement in Cambodia in 1991, with regular exchanges between political leaders.

Australia's assessment conflicts with that of international human rights agencies in asserting that Vietnam is now willing to discuss human rights with both the UN and other countries, including technical and training assistance. In 1997, the Australian aid programme sponsored a human rights course in Hanoi, attended by communist party and Government officials. This was followed by a study tour in Australia, with ongoing plans for visits to national human rights institutions in the Asia-Pacific region, cooperative teaching, research and translation of human rights texts. DFAT also claims to have made representations on individual cases, and on the uses of national security laws to penalise peaceful expression of political and religious views (DFAT 2000e).

Vietnam was the third highest recipient of Australian aid in 1999, with around A$70 million concentrated in rural development and infrastructure, human resource development, health and governance. The My Thuan Bridge, opened in May 2000 over one arm of the Mekong River in southern Vietnam, links major rice growing districts of the Delta with Ho Chi Minh City. Two-thirds of its A$91 million cost was provided by Australia.

Vietnamese military officers undertake English language and other training at the Australian Defence Force Academy. A Police Liaison Office was established in the Australian Embassy in Hanoi in June 1998. Training and equipment support provided by the Australian Federal Police, aims to enhance narcotics enforcement capacities. In September 2000, the two countries declared their joint intention to combat illegal immigration and trafficking in women and children.

The Vietnam-born community in Australia of around 140,000, mostly post-1975 refugees, has not proved a serious impediment to good relations. While early arrival were ideologically hostile to communist rule, they lacked the influence of counterparts in the USA who had played more senior military and political roles in the former Republic of Vietnam. The advent of more open economic policies encouraged some expatriates to revisit Vietnam and seek business opportunities. Australian investment reached A$1.09 billion by January 2000, with 102 companies officially registered. However, strong Asian involvement and growth in US and European investment during the 1990s reduced Australia's relative position. Education and training was Australia's single largest export to Vietnam in 1999, estimated in excess of A$75 million, driven by emerging middle-class demand. Over three-quarters of around 4000 Vietnamese studying in Australia in 1999 were private students. Five hundred students received Australian Development Scholarships. The 1999 Law on Education opened new opportunities for collaboration with Vietnamese education and training institutions, including distance education (DFAT 2000*e*).

Australia's non-ideological relationship with Vietnam, driven primarily by strategic and economic interests, contrasts sharply with that of the USA. This is reflected in a low-key, non-confrontational approach to human rights, with social and economic aspects representing most substantive areas of cooperation.

Cambodia

Despite early establishment of diplomatic relations with Vietnam, Australia followed ASEAN, China and the USA in not recognising Hanoi-backed governments under Heng Samrin and his successor Hun Sen. But in 1981 it reversed recognition of the 'Democratic Kampuchea' coalition which held Cambodia's seat at the UN. Australia strongly opposed any Khmer Rouge role in government and promoted proposals for an international tribunal on crimes against humanity from an early stage. Many Australians were distressed by suffering caused to Cambodians by sanctions policies. These allowed humanitarian support, but not infrastructure and reconstruction assistance – a distinction not always strictly enforced in channelling official funds via NGOs and international humanitarian agencies.

Australian concerns for domestic public opinion and human rights, even acknowledging extreme violations under Pol Pot, challenged ASEAN's overriding priority of upholding national sovereignty principles. China asserted its strategic interests through military support for the Khmer Rouge. Achieving a peace settlement in Cambodia in face of these seemingly intractable forces consequently became a major priority for Australia.

Indonesia eventually provided a bridge with ASEAN. Once convinced that Vietnam had no plans to export communism, Indonesian military leaders chose to see its political system as a domestic matter and its rulers primarily as nationalists. Of all ASEAN countries, Indonesia was most wary of Chinese regional ambitions. It therefore sought to build bridges with Vietnam and by extension Cambodia. But its diplomatic leaders insisted that unity with ASEAN remained paramount.

Australia–Indonesia cooperation reached a high point in 1989 with an international conference in Jakarta, including the four Cambodian factions and all major regional and international players. While this narrowly failed to achieve agreement, it laid foundations for eventual agreement in 1991. Australia played a key role in each stage of drafting and negotiation (Evans and Grant 1991: 206–18). An Australian, General Sanderson, headed the forces of the United Nations Transitional Administration of Cambodia (UNTAC) established to implement this agreement.

Early initiative and sustained involvement have allowed Australia to carry weight with both UN and Cambodian administrations. While strongly supporting institutionalisation of democratic electoral processes, legal and judicial strengthening. Australia has been more inclined to accord legitimacy to the Hun Sen government, on the basis of recognising states rather than individuals or ideologies.

Australia contributed A$1.35 million towards elections in 1998, building on previous technical assistance provided through the Australian Electoral Commission (Downer 1998a). These funds also assisted the UN in monitoring the safe return of political exiles. An Australia–New Zealand (ANZ) delegation was active in the Joint International Observers' Group (JIOG) which co-ordinated the activities of groups from over thirty countries. JIOG/ANZ reports differed significantly from the dominant view in the US and among international human rights agencies, not so much on factual aspects, as the weight and interpretation placed on them.

The ANZ delegation considered the overall registration outcome representative and fair, although the appeals process was insufficiently transparent for the relatively few persons rejected (DFAT 1998b). It considered that allegations of widespread enrolment of ineligible Vietnamese citizens lacked substance, and was disturbed that valid registration of many Khmer citizens was disputed solely on grounds of Vietnamese ethnicity. Voting and local counting processes were acknowledged as overwhelmingly well conducted on polling day itself and the day following. However, levels of actual and attempted intimidation of voters and opposition groups in the weeks and months beforehand were unacceptable, with media outlets overwhelmingly dominated by the ruling Cambodian People's Party (CPP).

Credible evidence was found of systematic intimidation intended to raise fears of reprisal and weaken voters' belief in ballot secrecy. These crude efforts were deemed unsuccessful, due to extensive voter awareness campaigns by internationally recognised Cambodian NGOs and international observer groups. Also there was a majority vote for opposition parties. (DFAT 1998b: paras 30, 37, 39–40). The presence of these groups ensured the substantial accuracy of results, with relatively few attempts to interfere with the counting process. However, the JIOG issued an 'unequivocal' warning to the National Election Commission (NEC) that the sudden accreditation of large numbers of untrained national observers, with potential to crowd out international observers and established national observers, threatened the credibility of the entire observation process (DFAT 1998b: paras 41–2). JIOG demands were met in full.

The post-election situation was less satisfactory. The ANZ delegation considered that, while it did not distort the outcome, the complaints and appeals process was poorly organised, tarnished the NEC's earlier good reputation and weakened public confidence. The worst example was the Constitutional Council's refusal to address joint Sam Rainsy and FUNCINPEC party complaints over the formula for calculating parliamentary seat allocation, which those parties considered should have given them a combined majority. There were also credible accounts of intimidation, including death threats against opposition activists. A grenade attack at the NEC during a visit by Sam Rainsy claimed one life (DFAT 1998*b*: paras 89–91).

The ANZ delegation found that despite clear evidence of unacceptable intimidation, there was no significant fraud and that the Cambodian people ran a vigorous election campaign, were able to exercise their votes in secrecy and have them counted without serious distortion. Therefore the result of the election should stand. However, a minority report by two observers asserted that the various human rights violations, intimidations, distortions and irregularities prevented the election being declared free and fair, or credibly reflecting the Cambodian people's will. Its many positive features nevertheless represented a significant step towards establishing a system of truly representative government (DFAT 1998*b*: paras 78, 160–1).

In sharp contrast, Lorne Craner (1998), President of the International Republican Institute (IRI), argued that while Election Day itself impressed many observers, including IRI, the election overall fell below an acceptable standard. IRI concluded that accepting the Cambodian result would devalue the worth of elections in building democracies around the world, leaving dictators free to kill opposition members, dismantle opposition party infrastructures, appoint biased election commissions, intimidate voters, conduct questionable ballot counts and refuse recounts, yet still feel confident that the international community will certify the process, 'as long as Election Day looks good'. The US Congress should, therefore, continue to deny Hun Sen legitimacy and funds, and support the opposition as Cambodia's hope for democracy.

Such views have been strenuously attacked by Australia's Ambassador to Cambodia from 1994–97, Anthony Kevin (1998), who considers East European-style, 'fall of communism' scenarios as utterly misleading. Kevin sees the roots of conflict as lying between two unreconciled opposed views of history. Whereas the CPP sees itself and its Vietnamese allies as liberators from the genocidal Khmer Rouge regime, their opponents see the manner of this liberation as a cause of national shame. Each portrays the other as traitors and collaborators in league with either the Khmer Rouge or Vietnam; as self-seekers mobilising international pressure to deny Cambodians basic living standards, or as unreformed communists expropriating private property and suppressing national values and traditions. Lack of trust, de-humanisation and stereotyping of opponents has held back any sense of a shared civil society between the two rival political communities. Acceptance of each other's legitimacy is thus a pre-requisite for national reconciliation.

Sam Rainsy is a special target of Kevin's ire as the most skilled manipulator of western perceptions. Consequently, many Cambodians are confused and anxious, uncertain whether their election was fair or not, and misled by simplistic, self-righteous foreign interpretations of their own politics. International attempts continue, according to Kevin (2001) to label Cambodia as a 'rogue state' and Hun Sen as a 'war criminal', despite Prince Ranaridh's appointment as President of the National Assembly and Rainsy's acknowledged status as leader of a vigorous parliamentary opposition. Western democracy and human rights lobbyists, 'bitter at the failure of the 1992–93 UN project to transform Cambodia into a little Asian Switzerland', swell the refrain.

While eschewing Kevin's colourful language, the Australian government accepted the 1998 election outcome and consequently the current government's legitimate status. Overall, Australia has strongly supported reconciliation, political and legal institution-building, human resources and rural development. It participates actively in landmine clearance programmes and in promoting international agreement against their deployment (Downer 1997c). Australian governments have worked closely with the Cambodian Office of the High Commissioner for Human Rights (COHCHR). Pressure on Hun Sen during the 1997 crisis and for criminal trials of former Khmer Rouge leaders were directed towards achieving internationally acceptable outcomes in terms of human rights standards, while respecting Cambodia's national sovereignty. Australia's stance thus appears less at odds with ASEAN's position than with critics in the US Congress and international human rights agencies.

Conclusion

Development of Australian human rights policies encapsulates the dilemma of reconciling international human rights law with national sovereignty. Recognising that earlier approaches setting diplomatic 'pragmatism' against 'idealistic' human rights had proved unworkable, Australia has integrated them into its regional and bilateral strategies, within an overall national interest framework. Practical outcomes, in the language of Alexander Downer, nevertheless remain the primary goal.

Framing country plans and programmes has proved a sensitive exercise, primarily dependent on individual states' direction and priorities, their stance towards UN treaty regimes, and the strength and quality of civil society participation. While diplomatic conventions avoid confrontation over human rights, potential conflict based on normative and cultural differences remains latent.

Australian human rights involvement is not closely correlated with levels of cordiality or tension in bilateral relations. Thus Australia has been most active in Cambodia, Myanmar and Indonesia, where human rights violations are most pervasive. Diplomatic relations with Cambodia have been positive, range from cool to hostile with Myanmar, and from cooperative to confrontational with Indonesia. Conversely, there has been little human rights engagement with either Singapore, with which Australia has good relations, or Malaysia, with which relations have been strained over many years. Modest civil and political rights programmes have been established with Vietnam, Thailand and the Philippines, all of which have positive relations with Australia. Thailand and the Philippines, are moving in a strongly democratic direction, but Vietnam shows little sign of either democratising or integrating its plans with UN human rights regimes.

The pragmatic, bilateral focus of human rights policy under Howard, necessarily raises concerns that Australia is retreating from earlier high profile support for UN regimes. Selective application and prioritisation of human rights according to convenience often overrides universalist priorities. Cooperation with the UN has nevertheless remained strong in relation to Cambodia and Myanmar. While more variable in relation to Indonesia, the East Timor experience has necessitated closer cooperation. Indonesia's own plans project a similar direction. Australia has strongly encouraged development of national human rights institutions. These enjoy mutually supportive links with the UN, though partially constrained by governments.

Australia's partial retreat from UN systems is inconsistent with its official regional stance. Defensiveness against international criticism could lead to withdrawal from regional human rights engagement. This option would be looked on favourably by some analysts who consider that Australia can only influence ASEAN states' policies at the margins, but risks their displeasure or worse. ASEAN states have not expressed concern, and may well be reassured by assertions of Australian sovereignty. However, such sceptics mostly concede that human rights engagement serves to pacify Australian public opinion, which can do much to disrupt relations with Southeast Asia.

A more supportive view argues that Australia must add its weight to the efforts of others. Of all non-Asian voices on human rights, Australia is most deeply engaged with Southeast Asia. As a small to medium power, it poses no threat, and may be able to exert modest influence, particularly via personalised, non-public persuasion in areas of specialised cooperation. Though in no position to act as mediator, Australia may influence other countries' perceptions through media and academic commentary, development assistance and other international forums. This carries both opportunities and dangers.

Australia's most positive contribution could be to persuade ASEAN states of a shared stake in international law as counterweight to great power politics. However, this prospect is negated by notions of Australia playing roles of 'regional policeman' or 'deputy-sheriff'. Overly strident projections of 'Australian values' do similarly little to assist prospects for cooperation. Finally, the leadership cum advisory role projected for Australia by incoming US Secretary of State, General Colin Powell, carries potential for serious misunderstanding, particularly in relations with Indonesia (Stewart and Greenlees 2001).

Conclusion
Future prospects

This study has ranged widely across theoretical and practical contexts, exploring diverse understandings and applications of human rights in Southeast Asia. While issues of democratic transition and consolidation have featured extensively, the nexus between democracy, human rights and economic development is central to understanding regional human rights discourse. Principles of indivisibility between civil-political and economic-social rights bear strongly on prospects for eventual incorporation of universal human rights into ASEAN states' institutions and processes.

The regional economic crisis, whatever its causes, has represented an assault on basic economic rights of Southeast Asians. Triumphalist responses in some quarters, linked to promotion of neo-liberal programmes has allowed some revival of false labelling of human rights as western imposed. Governance agendas aimed at integrating political democratisation, accountability, market openness and well targeted anti-poverty programmes, have encountered similar responses.

Security and economic development dominate ASEAN states' national political agendas, while defence of national sovereignty is paramount in external relations. Universal human rights are consequently far from central to ASEAN states' concerns, and are to some extent seen as dysfunctional to them. Assessments in this study offer only modest encouragement to prospects for their institutionalising United Nations human rights instruments. Despite advances during the 1990s, participation in and compliance with UN treaties remains patchy and subject to the vagaries of domestic politics. A rhetoric of convenience, whether of Asian, western or Australian values has been developed to legitimise political interests. Asian values polemic appears more directed at western countries than specifically at UN human rights instruments. National sovereignty doctrines are routinely invoked against even the possibility of unwanted intervention, ignoring UN Charter obligations to uphold human rights.

The language of universal human rights nevertheless represents a pervasive counter-discourse to official agendas. Here Donnelly's paradox of piecemeal incorporation of the substance of UN human rights treaties into domestic law and practice without formal recognition as rights can assist understanding of reform processes in ASEAN countries. To the extent that UN human rights treaties represent the highest international levels of normative consensus at any given time, Southeast Asian countries remain aloof in varying degrees. Current gradual trends towards formal participation nevertheless show considerable advance compared with a decade earlier. Development of conscious links with UN regimes is crucial, as otherwise rights may later be withdrawn. Conversely, groups may demand rights not recognised in international treaties, consequently weakening their status.

Distinctions between liberal-democratic and communitarian understandings, in the sense of intrinsic as against state or society determined rights, provide a consistent guide for interpreting diffuse conflicts and issues. Discourse opposing Asian against western values provides parallel insights but confuses liberal democracy with unconstrained individualism and disregard for social responsibilities. Conflict between universalist and relativist understandings reflects these debates, which are also closely linked with issues of reconciling national sovereignty with international human rights law.

While post-modernist theory would claim that relativisation of values is enhanced by the global communications revolution, the search for viable systems of world order requires some minimum of commonly accepted behavioural norms. While geo-governance models require only transactional codes, universal rights are integral to humane governance models of globalisation. Though urging reform, pro-ponents of this school are strong advocates of the UN human rights treaty system. But in reaction to neo-liberal approaches which discount universalist understand-ings of economic and social rights, some interpretations of indivisibility border on communitarianism in their overly scrupulous refusal to privilege civil and political rights (Falk 1995: 105–16). David Held's model of 'international cosmopolitan democracy' avoids both extremes. The capacity for democratic politics and transna-tional movements to operate effectively across new sites of both global and local sites of contestation will nevertheless represent a major challenge.

Despite globalisation, nation-states remain a key frame of reference, as the only entities which can enact legislation and ratify treaties. Together with the UN, as the international forum of nation-states, these must, therefore, remain primary arenas for universal human rights advocates. At the same time, globalisation processes and advancement of international human rights law set limits to states' autonomy and immunity from external criticism based on national sovereignty. Closer interaction between domestic and international politics may not necessar-ily assist the cause of universal human rights. However, it weakens claims to absolute state sovereignty by challenging states' monopoly in conducting inter-national relations and so opening up space for human rights agendas.

Culturally particularistic approaches detract from searches for universally acceptable normative framework. The capacity of both individual states and the international community to accommodate cultural difference within universalist frameworks, as allowed in UN treaties, is essentially a matter of political will. Unfortunately much values polemic appears to operate on the principle of universalism for others, but relativism for one's own society.

Asian values cum democracy discourse is now largely confined to Malaysia and to a diminishing extent Singapore, where it has served important nation-building as well as politically and culturally defensive roles. An articulate counter-discourse of universal rights in Malaysia, based on principles of indivisibility, has been confused by differences between liberal-democratic and communitarian approaches among civil society groups. Asian values discourse has also been developed, *inter alia*, as a defence against external imposition of neo-liberal agendas which would exclude governments from active economic roles. More populist versions may be emerging, expressing resentment against increased external intervention following the regional economic crisis.

The growing salience of international human rights law and penetration of UN human rights regimes have induced new responses by ASEAN states. Several have recently developed human rights action plans, foreshadowing accession to more UN treaties. Establishment of national human rights institutions by states previously indifferent, if not implacably opposed to human rights agendas is also breaking new ground. However, ASEAN countries are also finding ways to accommodate external human rights pressures, including conformity with UN regimes, while maintaining the substance of national sovereignty.

Previous willingness to adopt new international instruments is in question as states become more vulnerable to pressures to ratify and implement them. Regional solidarity in resisting both UNCHR investigation of Indonesia's role in East Timor and criticism of China's human rights record illustrate this trend. Demands for consensus decision-making in UNCHR committees and protracted delays in approving new instruments to protect human rights defenders tell a similar story.

Defence of national sovereignty remains a consistent thread in the stance of nation-states towards UN human rights regimes. At one end of the spectrum, Cambodia, which has accepted a strong UN advisory presence, has proved versatile in pursuing its domestic agendas despite the overwhelming weakness of its economic and international position. Even the embryo state of East Timor chafes at the continuing necessity for UNTAET administration and international peacekeeping forces. The five permanent Security Council members have adopted various equally determined strategies in defending their national interests and sovereignty against intrusions by UN regimes.

National Human Rights Institutions (NHRIs) have been designated to promote awareness of universal human rights and participation in UN regimes, incorporating government and civil society roles. Despite structural and other weaknesses, NHRIs, building on less recognised work of NGOs and other activists, have contributed significantly to opening up many areas of human rights violation for scrutiny and bringing new pressures on governments. NHRIs' capacity to resist threats to their autonomy is enhanced by constitutional entrenchment, as in Thailand and the Philippines. Definitions of human rights in their statement of objectives are more closely linked with UN instruments than in those of Malaysian and Indonesian counterparts.

Capacity and will of civil society groups to promote human rights remains uncertain in the face of rapid change. While NGO participatory praxis broadly converges with universal human rights values, religious and ethnic assertions, and even routine political demonstrations have become violent and coercive. The gap between principles of tolerance and pluralism asserted by intellectual and religious leaders and grassroots practice (Agnivesh 2000) indicates the need to develop a popular and political culture supportive of universal human rights. Public education and media roles in presenting UN human rights principles and processes in western countries also need addressing.

Issues of democratisation have been at the heart of human rights debate in Southeast Asia, particularly among founding members of ASEAN. Indonesia, Thailand and the Philippines are each engaged in varying stages of transition and consolidation. The outlook in Indonesia remains perilous. Extensive popular mobilisation for democratic change has been accompanied by revival of primordial forces, reported to be instigated by military elements. Subordination of the military to civil institutions has yet to be firmly established. Major constitutional change has been achieved but remains incomplete, particularly in clarifying relations between President and Parliament. Functioning of newly established human rights courts remains hostage to political processes. On the ideological front, the balance between Pancasila, Islam and liberal democracy remains the focus of confusing struggle. Moreover, the loss of East Timor has inflamed nationalist sentiment in ways unhelpful to establishing a democratic civic culture. Indonesia has not yet seriously begun to address the destruction and violence it inflicted on East Timor, strengthening pressures for comprehensive international investigation and prosecution.

Democratic institutions in Thailand and the Philippines have been consolidated by strong constitutional reforms, including extensive human rights guarantees and associated legal arrangements. However, both countries' are threatened by extensive criminality, corruption of political processes and civic culture. Popular experience of the economic crisis has tended to associate advocates of accountability and transparency with pains of structural adjustment, opening the door for election of populist leaders such as Thaksin and Estrada. The latter facilitated rehabilitation of Marcos family associates and cronies. The Philippines is also threatened by both communist and Moslem insurgencies in Mindanao. But despite many irregularities and some serious violence, both countries have conducted several broadly 'free and fair' elections, resulting in several changes of government. Civic awareness and pluralist democratic culture is sustained by a profusion of NGOs and advocacy groups, especially in the Philippines.

'Semi-democracies' of Malaysia and Singapore have undergone relatively little change. Their economic performance, particularly in the case of Singapore, has given their governments high levels of legitimacy, although Malaysia experienced significant economic disruption post-1997. Singapore would credit policies described by critics as social engineering as producing the highest levels of inter-racial and religious cooperation in Southeast Asia. Malaysia has gone some way along that path, but communally based divisions remain deeply rooted. Independent civil society organisations are severely restricted in both countries, but have had some modest impact on public discourse and policy-making in Malaysia.

Malaysian politics appear to have currently reached an impasse, with power concentrated almost exclusively in the hands of the Prime Minister. Dominance of the opposition coalition by the Islamic Party has intensified the environment of illiberal democracy. In Singapore, in the absence of viable political opposition, the government seeks wider input into policy-making from citizens, channelled through established consultative structures. Possibilities for gradual democratisation from such 'blooming of many flowers' cannot be totally discounted.

Of the remaining ASEAN states, only Cambodia conducts seriously contested elections, albeit under strong pressure from the UN and western governments. But despite the necessity for formal coalition, Cambodian politics is dominated by the communist Cambodian People's Party. Laos and Vietnam remain under tight one-party communist rule. Brunei is autocratically ruled by hereditary sultans, seemingly by popular consent. Despite occasional shadow plays of dialogue with opposition leaders, in deference to UN overtures, Myanmar's brutal military rulers, supported by China, show no sign of loosening their grip on power. ASEAN's stance of 'constructive engagement' has provided them with a protective shield.

Australia has historically provided strong support to universal human rights and associated UN regimes. Its overseas assistance practice has also broadly reflected indivisibility principles. Integrating its geography and history is vital to Australia's future engagement with Southeast Asia. Institutionalisation of UN human rights regimes across the region would support this objective, not least because multilaterally-based mutual accountability processes would take much heat out of bilateral human rights exchange.

The issue of human rights cannot in any case be avoided in regional relations, as it goes to the heart of both Australia's and ASEAN countries' identities. While Australia's current stance emphasising 'practical' assistance finds broad regional acceptance, value differences linked to human rights issues may remain latent or be displaced into other fields. Thus Malaysia's determined exclusion of Australia from regional decision-making, justified on grounds of cultural and normative difference, derives primarily from rival models of economic and security cooperation. Australia's capacity to contribute towards regional human rights dialogue in the region has been sidelined, at least temporarily, by the Howard government's retreat from universal rights and counter-assertion of 'Australian values'.

The world, including Southeast Asia and Australia, remains far from accepting international human rights law as a common frame of reference. Progress towards this goal is by no means automatic. Recent developments indicate that regression into social disorder and warlordism remain equal possibilities. US disengagement may spur reduced cooperation in international institution-building, while reform of cumbersome UNCHR structures is an ongoing task. Nevertheless, participation in UN human rights treaties by ASEAN states broadly correlates with levels of democratisation, which is consolidating despite many convolutions. On balance, international human rights infrastructure appears to have reached sufficient critical mass to carry momentum for change forward in a region of the world which until recently has offered greatest resistance.

Glossary of Indonesian and Malay terms

Abangan	Native Javanese, following customary belief and practice
Al-haqq	Truth (Islam)
Aliran	Socio-cultural stream
Bumiputera	'Sons of the soil' (Malay race)
Bupati	District chief
Dakwah	Missionary activity
Fatwa	Pronouncements by Islamic clergy
Golkar	Functional groups (golongan karya)
Hadith	Sayings attributed to Prophet Mohammed
Haqq al-muraddah	Right to constructive criticism (Islam)
Hisbah	Commanding good and forbidding evil (Islam)
Hudud	Prescribed (Islamic) rules and penalties
Hukum	God's law (Islam)
Ijma	Consensus (Islam)
Ijtihad	Personal reasoning (Islam)
Jihad	Holy war or struggle (Islam)
Kasar	Coarse or rough
Keadilan	Justice
Kedaulatan rakyat	People's sovereignty
Laskar	(Non-state) militia
Merajuk	Express silent displeasure (by a ruler)
Mufakat	Consensus (Indonesia)
Musyawarah	Deliberation (Indonesia)
Napol	Political criminal (naripadana politik)
Nasibah	Sincere advice to rulers (Islam)
Orang asli	Native people of peninsular Malaysia
Pancasila	Five principles of official Indonesian state ideology
Pesantren	Islamic school
Pribumi	Native people
Rukun Negara	National harmony (Malaysia)
Santri	Literally, graduate of a pesantren … also a general term for pious or orthodox Moslems
Shariah	Islamic law
Shura	Consultation between rulers and people (Islam)
Sunnah	Authoritative sayings of Prophet Mohammed
Tapol	Political prisoner (tahanan politik)
Ulama	Islamic clerics
Ummah	Islamic community
Yang-di-Pertuan-Agong	King (Malaysia)

Notes

1 International human rights: Theory and practice

1 UN General Assembly document A/CONF. 157/23 of 12 July 1993. Online. Available.http://www.unhchr.ch/huridocda/huridoca.nsf/(Symbol)/A.CONF.157.23.En?OpenDocument cf. also DFAT 1993: 177–201.
2 Search the Commission website for operational details. Online. Available. http://www.unhchr.ch/html/menu2/2/chr.htm. cf. also DFAT 1993: 52ff.
3 Benedict Anderson (1983) coined the term 'imagined communities' as a collective term for groups aspiring to create nation states.
4 Resolution 41/128. Online. Available. http://www.unhchr.ch/html/menu3/b/74.htm (4 December 1986)
5 cf. e.g. Brandt 1980.

2 Human rights, democracy and development in Southeast Asia

1 cited in Neher 1995: 196–7.
2 Based on purchasing power parity, Brunei and Singapore ranked second and fourth in the world respectively in Real GDP per capita (UNDP 1999a: 134).
3 'Beware Asian backlash, Mahathir Warns', *The Straits Times*, Singapore: 5 June 1998, 37. cf. also Elliott and Brummer 1998.
4 'IMF bind can harm world, says Rubin', *The Straits Times*, 6 June 1998, 1.
5 Estimated by Vasil (1995: 2) at 77.7 per cent Chinese, 14.1 per cent Malay and 7.1 per cent Indian.
6 Health benefits are extended to temporary migrant workers, on whom the economy substantially depends to undertake lower paid jobs. Employers are responsible for CPF payments, housing and education where relevant.
7 'Public Debate and OB Markers. Realities of a Wired World', *The Straits Times*, 26 May 1999. (Extracts from an interview with Minister for Information and the Arts, George Yeo, with *Karyawan*, the publication of the Association of Muslim Professionals.)
8 Online. Available. http://members.tripod.com/-malolos/1987/toc.html
9 Comparable figures for Thailand are 2.9 and 1.3 per cent , with 2.4 and 1.7 per cent in Indonesia (World Bank 1999e).
10 One survey estimated their numbers as high as 16–18,000. cf. 'Agents for Change', *Far Eastern Economic Review*, Hong Kong: 8 August, 1991, 20–1.
11 'Two of a kind', by the Sunday Inquirer Magazine Staff, *Philippine Daily Inquirer Magazine*, 12 May 1999. cf. also Marfil 1999.
12 'Change no boost for democracy: SM', *The Straits Times*, 20 January 2001.
13 'The Decades Long Struggle in Mindanao', *Asiaweek*, 1 March 1999.
14 Available. Online (search from). http:www.parliament.go.th/16e/main-16e.htm
15 'Corruption Commission – This watchdog has fangs', 157(1), *Time asia*, Hong Kong: 8 January 2001. Online. Available. http://www.time.com/time/asia/magazine/2001/0108/ thai.elections_sb1.html

3 ASEAN and international human rights

1 The former Burma was re-named as Myanmar by the SLORC military junta in 1988. The National League for Democracy (NLD) does not accept this name change. The issue of which name to use is therefore integral to democracy struggles and associated discourse. However, there is no ideological consistency as Amnesty International uses 'Myanmar' and the Australian government 'Burma' in their public commentary. 'Myanmar' is mostly employed in this work, as the name is recognised by the United Nations and most states. 'Burma' is used when citing organisations employing this name.
2 These principles are reiterated in Articles 18(3) and 19(3) of ICCPR, but without reference to a democratic society.
3 General Assembly A/RES/53/144, 8 March 1999. Online. Available. http://www. unhchr.ch / huridocda / huridoca.nsf /(Symbol)/A.RES.53.144.En?OpenDocument
4 Online. Available. 1http://www.ifs.univie.ac.at/intlaw/konterm/vrkon_en/html/doku/ treaties. htm#1.0
5 For details regarding states' ratification of treaties in this survey, and associated reservations, understandings etc. cf. website links as per Table 2.
6 The official rate for the kyat was six to the US dollar in mid-1997 compared with the currency's market rate of 200 (Brandon 1998: 221).
7 BBC Online Network, 'World: Asia-Pacific Letters of surrender – full text', 26 December 1998. Online. Available. <http://news.bbc.co.uk/hi/english/word/asia-pacific/newsid_242000/242670.stm>
8 'Khmer Rouge trial formula approved', *The Australian*, 3 January 2001, 7.
9 'Law to try guerillas won't rock stability', *The Straits Times*, 4 January 2001.
10 'Suu Kyi set for deal with generals', *The Australian*, 2 February 2001, 8.
11 'EU extracts concessions from Burma', *The Australian*, 12 December 2000, 8.
12 'Mahathir arrives in Myanmar for talks with top general', *The Straits Times*, 4 January 2001.
13 cf. pp. 114–15.
14 cf. pp. 145–7.
15 cf. pp. 144–5.
16 cf. pp. 114–5.

4 ASEAN and international human rights

1 The civil service, military and police have followed an informal overall recruitment ratio of four Malays to one non-Malay.
2 *Far Eastern Economic Review*, 27 June 1991, pp. 16–17. Since the remaining 8.4 per cent was held by nominee companies, officially under Malay control, these figures may understate the Malay/non-Malay gap. Additionally, they only cover corporate equity, whereas most of the small business sector is in non-Malay hands.
3 The term 'orang asli' is applied to indigenous people of peninsular Malaysia. Native people of East Malaysia are known by their various tribal names – Kadazan, Dayak etc. The term 'pribumi' applied to non-Malay indigenes can signal differential treatment from 'bumiputera'.
4 Malaysian Bar Council sources.
5 'Exploitation of Foreign Labour Must Stop'. *Utusan Konsumer*, Penang: Mid-July 1994, 13.
6 *Utusan Konsumer*, September 1995, 6.
7 cf. e.g. Aliran Kesadaran Negara 1987.
8 Personal interview, Kuala Lumpur, May 1998.
9 Gurmit Singh, President of the Environmental Protection Society of Malaysia (EPSM), in an interview with the author in October 1995, cited projects relating to the Climate Change Convention, agreed in principle as part of the UN Conference on Environment and Development at Rio de Janeiro in 1992 but not followed up.
10 For example, the views of Marina Mahathir, the Prime Minister's daughter, who favours a more liberal outlook towards women, are influential in some quarters.
11 Interview with Irene Fernandez, October 1995.
12 cf. p. 34.
13 Personal interview, Kuala Lumpur, February 1996.
14 'Anwar's views same as mine, says Mahathir', *Star*, 8 May 1997.
15 Interview with Professor A. B. Shamsul, Kuala Lumpur, May 1998.
16 Address to International Conference on 'Jose Rizal and the Asian Renaissance', Putra World Trade Centre, Kuala Lumpur, 3 October 1995.
17 ABIM sources. cf. also Larif-Beatrix 1994.

18 'Mahathir warns Muslims against being Extremist', *The Straits Times*, 19 April 1997.
19 cf. p. 69.
20 The Gini coefficient declined from 0.501 in 1970 to 0.446 in 1990, rising to 0. 470 in 1997. The urban–rural income gap declined from 2.14 in 1970 to 1.7 in 1990 and the Chinese–Malay gap from 2.29 to 1.74 (Shari 2000).
21 'We overcame recession our way, says Mahathir', *The Sunday Times*, Kuala Lumpur, 18 July 1999.
22 'Mahathir thanks Chinese', *The Sunday Times*, 18 July 1999.
23 'Brace for a boom, PM tells Asians', *AP-Asia*, Tokyo: 4 June 1999.
24 AFP and BBC World Service, 28 February 1999.
25 Appeals based on rights to privacy were successfully lodged to the UNCHR, using the First Optional Protocol, against Tasmanian laws banning homosexuality.
26 'Anwar sentence sparks riots', BBC World: Asia-Pacific, 14 April 1999, 08:06 GMT.
27 *The Straits Times Interactive*, 17 November 1998.
28 'World Court Scrutinizes Malaysia', *The New York Times*, 25 April 1999.
29 'Azizah a puppet of Manila, says Mahathir', *The Straits Times Interactive*, 2 May 1999.
30 'World Court Scrutinizes Malaysia', *op. cit.*
31 'Anwar outraged over choice of new minister', *Hong Kong Standard*, 12 January 1999. Available. Online. http://www.hkstandard.com/online/news/001/asia/news002.htm
32 'Mahathir slams an ex-leader', *The Straits Times*, 2 May 1999.
33 Unpublished research by Dr. Loh Kok Wah, University Sains, Penang. For example, Chandra Muzaffar, standing for Keadilan, reduced the BN majority in Bandar Tun Razak (Kuala Lumpur) to 1224 from 14,735 in 1995.
34 Karpal Singh, who acted as part of Anwar Ibrahim's defence team, has since been arrested for alleged sedition.
35 'DAP's defeat shows need to rethink strategy', *The Star*, Kuala Lumpur: 1 December 1999.
36 'Malaysian opposition accused of sedition', *The Australian*, 16 March 2001, 7.
37 'Anwar activists arrested', *The Australian*, 12 April 2001, 9.
38 cf. e.g. exchange of letters between Lim Guan Eng and Chandra Muzaffar, *Commentary*, September 1999, 28, 10–12.
39 Laws of Malaysia Act 597.
40 cf. various commentaries in *Aliran Monthly*, Penang: 20(4), 6–14.
41 cf. pp. 145–7.

5 Indonesia: Democratic transition and human rights

1 'Involvement' was interpreted open-endedly to include membership of then legal mass organisations and even family relationships.
2 'Lahir, Gerakan Baru "Forum Demokrasi"', Jakarta: *Suara Karya*, 4 April 1991.
3 'Demokrasi tidak Terwudjud dengan Meredam Perbedaan', *Media Indonesia*, Jakarta: 31 March 1995.
4 'HAM, Demokrasi dan Republik', *Media Indonesia*, 9 December 1995.
5 'Parpol dan Golkar Belum Bisa Mandiri', *Kompas*, Jakarta: 19 September 1995.
6 Former Javanese empires of the 14–17th centuries CE.
7 Tanpa Emansipasi Rakyat, Perjuangan Demokrasi Sia-Sia', *Media Indonesia*, 20 March 1995.
8 'Demokrasi Bisa Tumpuh di Tanah Mana pun', *Kompas*, 5 April 1995.
9 Instruksi Mendagri No. 32/1981 required regular reporting by, guidance and monitoring of former prisoners by local authorities.
10 For example, membership of the Yogyakarta NGOs Forum grew from around ten to twelve in 1991 to seventy-four at the beginning of 1996.
11 Through repeal in January 1994 of decree 342 of 1986 (ICFTU 1995: 84).
12 The classic distinction by Clifford Geertz (1960) between 'orthodox' (*santri*) and 'nominal' (*abangan*) Moslems provides a continuing, though disputed frame of reference in this context.
13 cf. e.g. Geertz 1960; Mulder 1978; Hassan 1982; Felderspiel 1992; Madjid 1995; Ramage 1996; Schwarz 1999: 162–93.
14 *Pesantren* are Islamic boarding schools. Mostly rural-based and closely linked with local communities, they draw students from across Indonesia. *Pesantren* are headed by *kyai*, descended from their original founder, who are greatly revered. Many develop expertise in particular areas of Islamic knowledge – law, history, Arabic language etc. – attracting students based on personal interest. *Pesantren* also have a tradition of student self-management.
15 cf. p. 134.

16 A Dutch-linked secessionist attempt in the early 1950s still fuels nationalist suspicions towards Christians in the Moluccas, who are also resented by Moslems for preventing adoption of Islamic law when the Indonesian state was established in 1945.
17 In an interview with the author in November 1995, Wahid stated his desire for Moslems to enjoy freedom of choice to believe and practice Islam voluntarily.
18 cf. pp. 145–7.
19 *The Indonesia Times*, Jakarta: 15 October 1996.
20 'Partai Baru: Dari Bandung ke Surabaya', *Suara Independen*, Jakarta: No. 06/I/ December 1995, 11–12.
21 'Beberapa Tanggapan Atas Lahirnya KIPP', *Suara Pembaruan*, Jakarta: 16 March 1996, 1, 19.
22 *The Straits Times*, 15 April 1996.
23 Working Paper No. 5, 1992.
24 ACTU sources.
25 'Indonesia and the ILO Workplan: Indonesia-ILO (1994–99)', signed by Minister Abdul Latief Minister of Manpower, Republic of Indonesia and Mr. Heribert Maier Deputy Director-General, ILO Geneva, Jakarta, 3 May 1994.
26 For an extensive review of issues in this field see Bessell 1998.
27 'Skepticism confronts economic team', *The Jakarta Post*, 27 October 1999.
28 Peraturan Menteri Tenaga Kerja Nomor PER-05/MEN/1998.
29 'DPR protesters claim Golkar betrayed Habibie', *The Jakarta Post*, 23 October 1999.
30 'Millions live on under $27 a month', *The Straits Times Interactive*, 11 July 1999.
31 'IMF still insists Indonesia disclose PWC report', *The Jakarta Post*, 6 October 1999.
32 The Indonesian government estimates the cost at about US $67 billion, compared with the credit rating agency Moody's estimate of around US $100 billion – equivalent to roughly half of Indonesia's Gross Domestic Product (Khanna 1999: 96–7). cf. also (Hill 1999: 96–7).
33 'Opposition to state security bill gains momentum', *The Jakarta Post*, 23 September 1999.
34 'Government delays bill ratification', *The Jakarta Post*, 25 September 1999.
35 'PDI Perjuangan seeks to censure Amien', *The Jakarta Post*, 30 November 1999.
36 'East Kalimantan legislators join call for federalism', *The Jakarta Post*, 2 December 1999.
37 'Unitary vs federal systems sized up', *The Jakarta Post*, 8 December 1999.
38 'East Kalimantan legislators join call for federalism', *op. cit.*
39 'I quit, reform minister tells Gus Dur', *The Straits Times*, 4 January 2001, 1.
40 cf. e.g. 'West Papuans hoist Morning Star flag', *The Jakarta Post*, 2 December 1999.
41 Implementation of the division of Irian Jaya into three new provinces of West, Central and East Irian, announced on 27 July 1999, remains uncertain, though this is of less interest to the independence movement.
42 Online. Available. http://www.unhchr.ch/ html/menu2/indonesia.htm
43 *Suara Karya*, 9 January 1998. Carries full text.
44 MPR Decree III/2000 on The Sources of Law and the Hierarchy of Laws and Regulations, Article 1(3)(NDI:29).
45 cf. pp. 148–9.
46 Kepres No. 50/1993.
47 Law No. 39/1999.
48 Examples include riots at Democratic Party (PDI) offices in Jakarta on 27 July 1996 (ICG 2001*a*) and killing of over twenty people during a conflict with the Freeport mining company at Timika, Irian Jaya ... cf. 'Kesimpulan Komnas HAM – Ada Pelanggaran HAM Di Timika', *Suara Karya*, 23 January 1995.
49 For example, by an all party delegation from the German Parliament – "Parlemen Jerman Respek Atas Hasil Kerja Komnas HAM", *Suara Pembaharuan*, 22 March 1996, 1.
50 *Media Indonesia*, 7 and 8 January 1998.

6 East Timor, Indonesia and the United Nations

1 Kraince 1999b and *Republika*, 31 August 1999.
2 'UNAMET Diduga Lakukan Kecurangan ... Jamshed Marker: No Comment', *Republika*, 31 August 1999.
3 Laporan Perjalanan Pengungsi Timtim Jalan Berliku Menuju Atambua', *Republika*, 7 September 1999.
4 'Humanitarian group evaluates conditions in refugee camps', *The Jakarta Post*, 23 September 1999.

5 'East Timor refugees face health risks as rain nears', *The Jakarta Post*, 29 September 1999.
6 'Indonesia must continue to pay', *The Australian*, 30 March 2000, 7. (Citing an editorial in *The Jakarta Post* on 29 March 2000.)
7 'Killed UN staff fought Timor militia', *The Australian*, 12 January 2001, 7.
8 Resolution 1319 (2000) Adopted by the Security Council at its 4195th meeting on 8 September 2000. Online. Available. http://www.un.org/Docs/scres/2000/res 1319e.pdf
9 *ibid.*
10 'Jakarta to invite weapons auditors', *The Australian*, 9 October 2000, 6.
11 'Jailing of militia boss fails to silence critics', *The Australian*, 1 May 2001, 7.
12 'Presiden: Saya Bertanggung Jawab', *Republika*, 7 September 1999.
13 This difference is reflected in contrasting presentations by two major Jakarta dailies – *The Jakarta Post* and *Republika*, with the latter pursuing a vigorous nationalist cum Islamic line.
14 'Soal Timor Timur', *Republika*, 27 September 1999.
15 'Government pressed ahead with rights', *The Jakarta Post*, 6 October 1999.
16 'Ali Alatas: Resolusi Komisi Tinggi HAM PBB tak Mengikat', *Republika*, 29 September 1999.
17 'Question of East Timor', Letter from Secretary-General to UN General Assembly and Security Council, A/54/726, S/2000/59, 31 January 2000.
18 Letter dated 26 January 2000 from the Minister for Foreign Affairs of Indonesia to the UN Secretary-General. Tabled at General Assembly, Fifty-fourth session, Agenda Item 96 (A/54/727) and Security Council Fifty-fifth year, S/2000/65, 31 January 2000.
19 'Indonesia to cooperate with UN inquiry on East Timor', *The Jakarta Post*, 29 September 1999.
20 'Clearance given to question generals over East Timor', *The Jakarta Post*, 2 December 1999.
21 'Ali Alatas: Resolusi Komisi Tinggi HAM PBB tak Mengikat', *op. cit.*
22 'Bila Rekomendasi Komnas HAM Terbukti Presiden Minta Wiranto Mundur', *Republika*, 1 February 2000.
23 *ibid.*
24 'E. Timor probe faults Wiranto', *The Jakarta Post*, 1 February 2000.
25 'Bila Rekomendasi Komnas HAM Terbukti Presiden Minta Wiranto Mundur', *op. cit.*
26 'Akbar urges military top brass to resign', *The Jakarta Post*, 1 February 2000.
27 One of the latter was Moruk, murdered at Atambua on 6 September 2000.
28 cf. pp. 147–9.
29 'Xanana gets hero's welcome in Dili', *The Jakarta Post*, 23 October 1999.
30 'Xanana Tolak Berbagi Kekuasaan dengan Prointegrasi', *Republika*, 19 October 1999. *Republika* attributes Xanana's change of heart to time spent in Australia.
31 'E. Timor probe faults Wiranto', *The Jakarta Post*, 1 February 2000.
32 'Wahid forges deal with UN in Dili', *The Australian*, 1 March 2000, 8.
33 *ibid.*

7 Australia, Southeast Asia and human rights

1 cf. pp. 82–3.
2 Taiwan's inclusion precluded reference to 'countries'. ASEAN would not accord status to groups.
3 The Commission formulated an Asian Charter on Human Rights (AHRC 1997).
4 Initially 'Joint Committee …'
5 *The Age*, 7 November 1996.
6 cf. e.g. ACFOA submissions to parliamentary reviews (JSCFADT 1994: 53–4 and 1998b: 17–8).
7 cf. p. 87.
8 Brian Noakes, a senior ACCI executive, sits in his own right on the ILO's influential Committee on Freedom of Association.
9 cf. p. 131.
10 ACTU sources.
11 cf. pp. 29–30.
12 Online. Available. http://www.dfat.gov.au/qwon/000607_un_hr.html
13 cf evidence by Senator David Kemp (JSCFADT 1994: 58).
14 'Ruddock Announces Tough New Initiatives', MPS 143/99. Online. Available. http://www.minister.immi.gov.au /media_releases/media99/r99143.htm
15 'Ruddock redefining refugees', *The Australian*, 22 March 2000, 5.
16 *ibid.*
17 cf. e.g. Rintoul 2000 and letters page, *The Weekend Australian*, 18–20 February, 20.

18 'Sentencing a worse option: Kemp', *The Australian*, 1 March 2000, 6.
19 For a full text of the RDA see Race Discrimination Commissioner 1995: 330–76.
20 The Act makes no reference to religious hatred. A proposed constitutional amendment to outlaw religious discrimination was soundly defeated at a referendum in 1988.
21 'Don't tell us what to do, PM warns', *The Weekend Australian*, 19–20 February 2000, 9.
22 'UN attacks could "undo Timor work" ', *The Weekend Australian*, 1–2 April, 12.
23 cf. p. 173.
24 *The Star*, 15 September 1994.
25 'Mahathir to PM: Stay Home', *The Australian*, 17 May 2000.
26 *The Star*, 20 September 1994.
27 *The Australian*, 11 November 1996, 1.
28 *Australian Outlook* (1986) offers several articles covering bilateral relations issues from both Australian and Indonesian perspectives. cf. also Hardjono (1992).
29 'Protesters target Australian Embassy', *The Jakarta Post*, 23 September 1999.
30 'Molotov cocktails hit Australian school', *The Jakarta Post*, 5 October 1999.
31 'Stop Impor akan Berlanjut', *Republika*, 14 October 1999.
32 'Indonesia cancels security pact with Australia', ABC News, 16 September 1999. Available. e-mail. webserv7@YOUR.abc.net.au
33 cf. pp. 154–5.
34 'Nasionalisme Melawan Si Usil Aussie', *Republika*, 27 September 1999.
35 'Howard Akui Tentaranya Bunuh Warga Timtim', *Republika*, 8 October 1999.
36 *ibid.*
37 'RI-Canberra must cool things down', *The Jakarta Post* (Editorial and Opinion) 29 September 1999. (Article based on a paper presented by Australian Ambassador to Indonesia John McCarthy at the Indonesian Executive Circle on 23 September 1999.)
38 *ibid.*
39 'The Howard Defence Doctrine', *The Bulletin*, Sydney: 28 September 1999.
40 However, Malaysia was also denied command, at East Timorese request.
41 Approximately 80 per cent of heroin entering Australia comes from opium produced in Burma (DFAT 1998*a*).

Bibliography

ACFOA (Australian Council for Overseas Aid) (1998a) 'Council Resolutions – Burma', Canberra. Available e-mail: acfoahr@acfoa.asn.au
—— (1998b) 'Submission to the ILO's Commission of Inquiry into Burma's alleged non-observance of the Forced Labour Convention, 1930 (No. 29)', Canberra. Available e-mail: acfoahr@acfoa.asn.au
Acharya, A. (1995) 'Human Rights and Regional Order: ASEAN and Human Rights Management in Southeast Asia' in J. Tang (ed.), *Human Rights and International Relations in the Asia-Pacific Region*, London and New York: Pinter, 167–82.
Aditjondro, G. A. (1999) 'East Timor ABRI Inc.', *Sydney Morning Herald*, 8 May.
Agnivesh, S. (2000) 'Amman to Capetown: On the Interfaith Trail', *Commentary – International Movement for a Just World*, Kuala Lumpur: January, 32, 1–2.
Ahmed, S. (1995) '*Zina* and Rape Under the Syariah Criminal Code (II) Bill 1993 (Kelantan)' in Rose Ismail (ed.), *Hudud in Malaysia – The Issues at Stake*, Kuala Lumpur: Sisters in Islam, 13–21.
AHRC (Asian Human Rights Commission) (1997) *Our Common Humanity – The Asian Charter on Human Rights*, Submission to the Joint Standing Committee on Foreign Affairs, Defence and Trade, Thirty-Eighth Parliament, Human Rights Sub-Committee on 'The Effectiveness of Australia's Regional Dialogue on Human Rights Inquiry', Canberra: September, 1, 170–7.
Akmeemana, S. and Jones, M. (1995) 'Fighting Racial Hatred' in Race Discrimination Commissioner, *Racial Discrimination Act 1975: A Review*, Canberra: Commonwealth of Australia, Australian Government Publishing Service (AGPS), December, 129–81.
Alford, P. (2000) 'Thailand sings the praises of a steadfast ally', *The Australian*, Sydney: 6 March, 14.
—— (2001a) 'Thaksin sits tight as rivals scramble', *The Weekend Australian*, Sydney: 13–14 January, 10.
—— (2001b) 'Philippines asks: was that a coup we just had', *The Australian*, 22 January, 1, 6.
Ali, F. (1992) 'Catatan Kecil tentang Abdurrahman Wahid', *Media Indonesia*, Jakarta: 30 April.
—— (1995) 'Keharusan Demokratisasi dalam Islam Indonesia' in Nasrullah Ali-Fauzi (ed.), *ICMI Antara Status Quo dan Demokratisasi*, Bandung: Penerbit Mizan, 126–43.
Aliran Kesadaran Negara (1987) *Reflections on the Malaysian Constitution*, Penang: Aliran Kesadaran Negara.
Alston, P. (1994) 'An Australian Bill of Rights by Design or Default?' in Philip Alston (ed.), *Towards an Australian Bill of Rights*, Centre for International and Public Law, Canberra: The Australian National University and Sydney: Human Rights and Equal Opportunity Commission, 1–17.
Amnesty International (1997a) 'Kingdom of Thailand Human Rights in Transition', London: ASA 39/02/97, 19 May.
—— (1997b) *Myanmar – Ethnic Minority Rights Under Attack*, London: ASA 16/20/97, 22 July.
—— (1997c) 'Kingdom of Thailand: Erosion of Refugee Rights', London, ASA 39/03/97, September.
—— (1997d) 'Philippines: Killings and Eviction of Indigenous People', London: ASA 35/17/97, December.
—— (1998) '1998 UN Commission on Human Rights – Building on Past Achievements', London: IOR 41/01/98, January.
—— (1999a) 'Thailand: A human rights review based on the International Covenant on Civil and Political Rights', London: ASA 39/001/99, 20 January.
Amnesty International (1999b) 'ASEAN Labour Ministers meet where forced labour is commonplace', London: ASA 16/10/99, circa April.

Amnesty International (1999c) 'Kingdom of Cambodia – No Solution to Impunity: The Case of Ta Mok', London: ASA 23/05/99, 22 April.

—— (1999d) 'Malaysia Human Rights Undermined: Restrictive Laws in a Parliamentary Democracy', London: ASA 28/06/99, September.

—— (1999e) 'Aceh: End human rights violations and the culture of impunity', London: ASA 21/206/99, 26 November.

—— (2000a) 'Unsung heroines: the women of Myanmar', London: ASA 16/005/2000, May.

—— (2000b) 'Indonesia – Comments on the draft law on Human Rights Tribunals', London: ASA 21/25/00, June.

—— (2000c) 'Myanmar: Exodus from Shan State to escape forced labour', London: ASA 16/012/2000, July.

—— (2000d) 'Myanmar: Aung San Suu Kyi at risk', London: ASA 16/016/2000, News Service Nr. 169, 4 September.

—— (2000e) 'Myanmar: Positive development, but still concerns for safety', London: ASA 16/020/2000 – News Service Nr. 176, 14 September.

—— (2001) 'Indonesia: Struggle against impunity – one step forward, two steps back', London: ASA 21/008/2001. Online. Available. http://www.web.amnesty.org/web/news.nsf/ WebAll/971D155EF98 4609780256A380048B87B?OpenDocument (25 April)

Anderson, B. (1972) *Java in a Time of Revolution: Occupation and Resistance 1944–46*, Ithaca (NY): Cornell University Press.

—— (1983) *Imagined Communities – Reflections on the Origin and Spread of Nationalism*, London and New York: Verso.

APFNHRI (The Asia Pacific Forum of National Human Rights Institutions) (1998a) 'UN and National Institutions: What are National Human Rights Institutions?', Sydney: Human Rights and Equal Opportunity Commission (HREOC). Online. Available. http://www.apf.hreoc.gov.au/un_national/institutions/index.html

—— (1998b) 'Forum members'. Online. Available. http://www.hreoc.gov.au/members/ index.html (29 May)

—— (1998c) 'United Nations and National Institutions: Paris Principles'. Online. Available. http://www.apf.hreoc.gov.au/un_national/paris_principles/index.htm

—— (1998d) 'Summary of NGO Interventions and Recommendations, Jakarta: Third Meeting of the Asia Pacific Forum of National Human Rights Institutions', 7–9 September, Sydney.

Article 19 International Center Against Censorship (1995) *Pengadilan Pers di Indonesia – Kasus AJI dan Pijar*, London.

ASIET (Action for Solidarity with Indonesia and East Timor) (1996): 'Organising in Indonesia: An Interview with Dita Sari, Centre for Working Class Struggle', Sydney: August.

Aspinall, E. (1993) 'Student Dissent in Indonesia in the 1980s', Clayton (Vic.): Centre of Southeast Asian Studies, Monash University, Working Paper 79.

—— (1999) 'The 1999 general election in Aceh' in Susan Blackburn, *Pemilu: the 1999 Indonesian Election*, Clayton: Monash Asia Institute, Centre of Southeast Asian Studies, 29–42.

AusAID (Australian Agency for International Development) (2000) 'Aid Budget Summary 1999–2000', Canberra: Online. Available. www.ausaid.gov.au/publications/general/budget99/Budget99_Summary.html

Australian Outlook (1986), Canberra: 40, 3, December. (Issue on Australia–Indonesia Relations)

Bailey, P. (1990) *Human Rights – Australia in an International Context*, Sydney: Butterworths.

Bai-ngern, C. (1999) 'Thai Police Investigate Three Alien-Smuggling Gangs', *The Nation*, Bangkok: 9 June.

Bell, D., Brown, D., Jayasuriya, K. and Jones, D. (eds) (1995) *Towards Illiberal Democracy in Pacific Asia*, Basingstoke (UK): Macmillan Press.

Bello, W. (1997) 'From SLORC Critic to Apologist', *The Nation*, 15 September.

Bessell, S. (1998) *The Politics of Children's Work in Indonesia: Child Labour in Domestic and Global Contexts*, Monash University, Clayton: Ph. D Thesis.

Blackburn, S. (1994) 'Gender interests and Indonesian democracy' in David Bourchier and John Legge (eds) (1994) *Democracy in Indonesia*, Clayton: Monash University, Centre of Southeast Asian Studies, Monash Papers on Southeast Asia No. 31, 168–81.

Blackburn, S. (ed.) (1999) *Pemilu: the 1999 Indonesian Election*, Clayton: Monash Asia Institute, Centre of Southeast Asian Studies.

Blackburn, S. (ed.) (2001) 'Women and the nation', *Inside Indonesia*, Melbourne: April–June, 66, 6–8.
—— and Stensholt, R. (1999) *The Simons Report: Where to Now with Overseas Aid?*, Clayton: Monash University, Development Studies Centre, Occasional Paper No. 7, Monash Asia Institute.
Blay, S. (2000) 'Why West Papua deserves another chance', *Inside Indonesia*, January–March, 61, 16–17.
Bourchier, D. (1987) 'The "petition of 50": who and what are they?', *Inside Indonesia*, 10, 7–10.
—— (1996) 'Totalitarianism and the "National Personality": Recent Controversy about the Philosophical Basis of the Indonesian State' in Jim Schiller and Barbara Martin-Schiller (eds), *Imagining Indonesian Culture*. Athens: Ohio University Press, 157–85.
Brandon, J. (1998) 'The state's role in education in Burma – an overview' in Robert I. Rotberg (ed.), *Burma – Prospects for Democracy*, Washington DC: Brookings Institution Press, 233–45.
Brandt, W. (1980) *North-South: A Programme for Survival*, Report of the Independent Commission on International Survival (Brandt Commission), London: Pan Books.
Buchori, B. and Bahagijo, S. (2000) 'The case for debt relief', *Inside Indonesia*, January–March, 61, 20–1.
Budiarjo, M. (1994) *Demokrasi di Indonesia – Demokrasi Parlementer dan Demokrasi Pancasila: Kumpulan Karangan Prof. Miriam Budiardjo*, Jakarta: Penerbit PT Gramedia Pustaka Utama.
Budiman, A. (1999) 'The 1999 Indonesian election: impressions and reflections' in Susan Blackburn (ed.), *op. cit.*, 11–21.
Bull, H. (1977) *The Anarchical Society*, London: Macmillan.
Buriram, R. H. (2001) 'Bullets and Ballots', *Time Asia*, Hong Kong: 8 January, 157(1). Online. Available. http://www.time.com/time/asia/magazine/2001/0108/thai.elections.html
Camilleri, J. (1994) 'Human Rights, Cultural Diversity and Conflict Resolution', *Pacifica Review*, Melbourne: 6, 2: 17–41.
—— (1997) 'Submission to the Joint Standing Committee on Foreign Affairs, Defence and Trade', Thirty-Eighth Parliament, Human Rights Sub-Committee on 'The Effectiveness of Australia's Regional Dialogue on Human Rights Inquiry', Canberra: Submission No. 22, September, 1, 291–313.
Camilleri, J., Malhotra, K. and Tehranian, M. (2000) *Reimagining the Future – Towards Democratic Governance*, Bundoora (Vic): La Trobe University, Department of Politics.
Canuday, J. (1999) 'Millions lack food in RP's next food basket, says study', *Philippine Daily Inquirer*, Manila: 8 April.
Case, W. (2001) 'Malaysia's General Elections in 1999: A Consolidated and High Quality Semi-democracy', *Asian Studies Review*, Oxford: Blackwell Publishers, 25(1), March, 35–55.
Centre for International Economics (1998) 'APEC economic governance capacity building survey. An Australian initiative as part of APEC's response to the East Asian financial crisis', Report prepared for the Australian Government, Canberra: 30 October.
Cerny, P. (1996) 'What Next for the State?' in E. Kofman and G. Youngs, *Globalization: Theory and Practice*, New York: Pinter, 123–37.
Chan, Heng Chee (1976) *The Dynamics of One Party Dominance: the PAP at the Grass-Roots*, Singapore: Singapore University Press.
Chandler, D. (1998) 'Health in Burma – An Interpretive Review' in Robert I. Rotberg (ed.)' *op. cit.*, 247–65.
Charlesworth, H. (1994) 'The Australian Reluctance About Rights' in Philip Alston (ed.), *op. cit.*, 21–53.
Charoensuthipan, P. (1999) 'Stricter job rules set for employers – Threat of lawsuits if workers abscond', *The Bangkok Post*, 11 June.
Chee, Soon Juan (1994) *Dare to Change – An Alternative Vision for Singapore*, Singapore: Singapore Democratic Party.
Chenery, H. *et al.* (1974) *Redistribution with Growth*, New York: Oxford University Press for the World Bank and Institute of Development Studies (Sussex, U.K.).
Commission for a New Asia (1994) *Towards A New Asia, A Report of the Commission for A New Asia*, Kuala Lumpur: Institute for Strategic and International Studies.
Commonwealth of Australia (1994) *Defending Australia – Defence White Paper 1994*, Canberra: AGPS.
—— (1997) *In the National Interest – Australia's Foreign and Trade Policy White Paper*, Canberra: AGPS.
Community Aid Abroad (1998) 'Australian Federal Election Report: Human Rights in Burma', Melbourne: Online. Available. http://www.caa.org.au/current/election/burma.html

Cornia, G. A., Jolly, R. and Stewart, F. (eds) (1988) *Adjustment with a Human Face*, Oxford: Clarendon Press.

Craner, L. (1998) Testimony before the US House International Relations Committee, Subcommittee on East Asian and Pacific Affairs, 28 September. Available e-mail: Communication from khemarak@JUNO.COM to SEASIA-L@LIST.MSU.EDU re 'Kevin on Rainsy' (9 November).

Cribb, R. (ed.) (1990) *The Indonesian Killings 1965–1966*, Clayton: Monash University, Centre of Southeast Asian Studies.

Crouch, H. (1988) *The Army and Politics in Indonesia*, Ithaca: Cornell University Press, revised edition.

—— (1996a) *Government and Society in Malaysia.*, Ithaca: Cornell University Press.

—— (1996b) 'ASEAN way poses a dilemma for Australia', *The Australian*, 11 November, 13.

Daly, M. and Logan, M. (1998) *Reconstructing Asia – The Economic Miracle That Never Was, The Future That Is*, Melbourne: RMIT University Press.

De Vries, R. (1994) 'A Critique of Political Realism' in K. W. Thompson (ed.), *Community, Diversity and A New World Order*, New York and London: University Press of America, 227–47.

Diamond, L. (1999) *Developing Democracy – Towards Consolidation*, Baltimore and London: The Johns Hopkins University Press.

DFAT (Department of Foreign Affairs and Trade) (1993) *Human Rights Manual*, Canberra: AGPS.

—— (1998a) *Burma – Country Brief*, Canberra: Online. Available. http://www.dfat.gov.au/geo/burma/index.html (October)

—— (1998b) 'Joint Report of the Australian and New Zealand Observation Mission to the 1998 Cambodian Elections', Canberra: Online. Available. http://www.dfat.gov. au/geo/cambodia/cambodia_98_elections.html

—— (1999) 'National Action Plan on Human Rights', Canberra: Online. Available. http://www.dfat.gov.au/hr/nap/natact_plan.html

—— (2000a) 'Malaysia – Country Brief', Canberra: Online. Available. http://www.dfat.gov.au/geo/malaysia/malaysia_brief.html (January)

—— (2000b) 'Singapore – Country Brief', Canberra: Online. Available. http://www.dfat.gov.au/geo/singapore/index.html#brief (March)

—— (2000c) 'Republic of Philippines – Country Brief', Canberra: Online. Available. http://www.dfat.gov.au/geo/philippines/index.html#brief (May)

—— (2000d) 'Australia–Thailand Relations', Canberra: Online. Available. http://www. dfat.gov.au/geo/thailand/thailand_australia_relations.html (October)

—— (2000e) 'Vietnam – Country Brief', Canberra: Online. Available. http://www.dfat.gov.au/geo/vietnam/vietnam_brief.html (October)

Dibb, P. (1986) *A Review of Australia's Defence Capabilities: Report to the Minister for Defence*, Canberra: AGPS.

Donnelly, J. (1989) *Universal Human Rights in Theory and Practice*, Ithaca and London: Cornell University Press.

Downer, A. (1996) *Australia's Overseas Aid Program 1996–97*, circulated by The Honourable Alexander Downer M.P., Minister for Foreign Affairs, Canberra: AGPS, 20 August.

—— (1997a) 'Reinvigorating the United Nations: Reform, Rights and Reconfiguration', Statement to the 52nd General Assembly of the United Nations, New York: Online. Available. http://www.dfat.gov.au/pmb/speeches/fa_sp/unga3october97.html (3 October).

—— (1997b) 'Better Aid for a Better Future', Canberra: Online. Available. http://www.ausaid.gov.au/media/release.cfm?BC=Speech&Id=9468_5774_2981_3198_6381 (18 November)

—— (1997c) 'Australia pursues solution to landmines crisis', *Peace and Disarmament Newsletter*, Canberra: Online. Available. http://www.dfat.gov.au/isecurity/pd/ pd_march_97/pd_mar97_1.html (March)

—— (1998a) 'Australian Assistance for the Cambodian Elections', DFAT Media Release FA45, Canberra: Online. Available. http://www.dfat.gov.au/media/releases/foreign/1998/fa045_98.html (20 April)

—— (1998b) 'Consultative Group on Indonesia (CGI) Meeting', Media Release AA723, Canberra: Online. Available. http://www.ausaid.gov.au/media/release/ac72.html (31 July)

—— (1998c) 'Human Rights – A Record of Achievement', Speech to the Department of Foreign Affairs and Trade Consultations with Human Rights Non-Governmental Organisations, Canberra: Online. Available. http://www.dfat.gov.au/pmb/ speeches/fa_sp/980819-human-rights.html (19 August)

Downer, A. (2000*a*) 'Government to Review UN Treaty Committees', Canberra: DFAT Media Releases 24–30 March, Canberra: Online. Available. http://www.dfat.gov.au/media/ releases/index.html (30 March)

—— (2000*b*) 'Burma', DFAT Media Release FA 96, Canberra: Online. Available. http://www.caa.org.au/current/election/burma.html (24 August)

Downie, S. (2000) 'Cambodia's 1998 Election: Understanding Why It Was Not a "Miracle on the Mekong"', *Australian Journal of International Affairs*, April, 54, 1, 43–61.

Dworkin, R. (1977) *Taking Rights Seriously*, Oxford: Duckworth.

East, J. (2001) 'No let-up in Thais' gun-barrel politics', *The Straits Times*, Singapore: 3 January.

Edwards, G. (1996) 'Freedom of Expression and the Right to a Fair Trial in Malaysia: The Prosecution of Human Rights Worker Irene Fernandez', *Human Rights Solidarity AHRC Newsletter*, Hong Kong: Asian Human Rights Commission, 11 September.

Eldridge, P. (1985) 'The Political Role of Community Action Groups in India and Indonesia: In Search of a General Theory', *Alternatives*, NY and Delhi: 10, 3, 401–34.

—— (1995) *Non-Government Organizations and Democratic Participation in Indonesia*, Kuala Lumpur: Oxford University Press.

—— (1996) 'Development, Democracy and Non-Government Organisations in Indonesia', *Asian Journal of Political Science*, June, 4, 1, 17–35.

—— (1999) 'The Simons Report: a new beginning?' in Susan Blackburn and Bob Stensholt, *op. cit.*, 1–7.

Elliott, L. and Brummer, A. (1998) 'The IMF: one size doesn't fit all', *Guardian Weekly*, London: 12 July, 14.

Ellis, S. (1999) 'U.S. Expects Indonesia to Protect People of East Timor (Awaits results of UN survey before taking new steps)', *USIS Washington File*, Washington DC: (560), 7 September.

Emmerson, D. (1994) 'Region and Recalcitrance: Questioning Democracy in Southeast Asia', Berlin: World Congress of the International Political Science Association, August 21.

ETAN (East Timor Action Network) (1999*a*) 'Senate Foreign Relations Committee Passes Freeze on Military Relations with Indonesia – Normal Relations Must Wait at Least Until Resolution of East Timor Crisis', Brooklyn (NY): Online. Available. http://www.etan.org (September).

—— (1999*b*) 'Senate Passes Appropriations Bill Restricting U.S. Military Assistance to Indonesia Congress Sets Conditions Including Bringing Human Rights Violators to Justice, Return of Displaced Persons to East Timor', Brooklyn: Online. Available. http://www.etan.org (19 November)

Evans, G. (1993) *Cooperating for Peace – The Global Agenda for the 1990s and Beyond*, St. Leonards (NSW): Allen and Unwin.

—— (1994) 'Human Rights in Australian Foreign Policy' in Philip Alston (ed.), *op. cit.*, 257–65.

Evans, G. and Grant, B. (1991) *Australia's Foreign Relations In the World of the 1990s*, Melbourne University Press.

Evatt, E. (1994) 'Cultural Diversity and Human Rights' in Philip Alston (ed.), *op. cit.*, 79–105.

Falk, R. (1995) *On Humane Governance – Towards a New Global Politics*, The World Order Models Project Report of the Global Civilization Initiative, Cambridge: Polity Press.

Fan Yew Teng (2000) 'Disappointing Composition – A Critique of the National Human Rights Commission', *Aliran Monthly*, Penang: 20, 4, 13–14.

Fealy, G. (2001) 'Inside the Laskar Jihad', *Inside Indonesia*, January–March, 65, 28–9.

Feith, H. (1962) *The Decline of Constitutional Democracy in Indonesia*, Ithaca: Cornell University Press.

Federspiel, H. M. (1992) *Muslim Intellectuals and Development in Indonesia*, New York: Nova Science Publishers.

Fine, R. and Rai, S. (eds) (1997) *Civil Society: Democratic Perspectives*, London and Portland (Oregon): Frank Cass.

FitzGerald, S. (1997) *Is Australia an Asian Country?* St. Leonards: Allen and Unwin.

FitzSimons, N. (2000) 'West Papua in 1999', *Inside Indonesia*, January–March, 61, 18.

Fox, J. (2000) 'Was this revenge for death of priest?', *The Australian*, 8 September, 6.

Fukuyama, F. (1992) *The End of History and the Last Man*, London: Hamish Hamilton.

Garran, R. (2000) '$26m fund for Timor rebel force', *Weekend Australian*, 16–17 September, 33.

Geertz, C. (1960), *The Religion of Java*, London: Collier-Macmillan.

Gelbard, R. (1998) 'Burma: the Booming Drug Trade' in Robert I. Rotberg (ed.), *Burma – Prospects for Democracy*, Washington DC: Brookings Institution Press, 185–95.

Ghai, Y. (1995) 'Asian Perspectives on Human Rights' in James Tang (ed.), *Human Rights and International Relations in the Asia-Pacific Region*, London and New York: Pinter, 54–67.

Gill, S. (1998) 'New Constitutionalism, Democratisation and Global Political Economy', *Pacifica Review*, February, 10, 1: 23–38.

Grant, B. (c1988) *What Kind of Country?: Australia and the Twenty-First Century*, Ringwood, Vic: Penguin.

Greenlees, D. (2000a) 'Suharto camp accused of funding militia', *The Australian*, 14 September, 24.

—— (2000b) 'Jakarta for W Timor action', *The Weekend Australian*, 16–17 September, 33.

—— (2000c) 'The divide tearing Irian Jaya apart', *The Australian*, 28 November, 8.

Habibie, B. J. (1999) 'Accountability Speech by The President of the Republic of Indonesia Before the General Session of The People's Consultative Assembly Jakarta, 14 October 1999', *The Jakarta Post*, 15 October.

Hamid, Wan Hamidi (2001) 'New UMNO bid to restore Malay unity', *The Straits Times*, 4 January.

Hara, A. E. (1999) *The Claims of 'Asian Values' and 'Asian Democracy': Some Implications for International Society, with special attention to Singapore, Malaysia and Indonesia*, Canberra: Ph.D thesis presented to The Australian National University, May.

Hardjono, R. (1992) *White Tribe of Asia: An Indonesian View of Australia*, Clayton: Monash University, Hyland House.

Haris, S. (1994) *Demokrasi di Indonesia*, Jakarta: Social and Economic Research, Education and Information Institute (LP3ES).

Harries, O. (1979) (Committee on Australia's Relations with the Third World) *Australia and the Third World – Report of the Committee on Australia's Relations with the Third World*, Canberra: AGPS.

Harris, D. R. (ed.) (1995) *Prisoners of Progress – A Review of the Current Indonesian Labour Situation*, Leiden: INDOC-FNV-INFID.

Hassan, M. H. (1982) *Muslim Intellectual Responses to 'New Order' Modernization in Indonesia*, Kuala Lumpur: Dewan Bahasa dan Pustaka.

Held, D. (1995) *Democracy and the Global Order – From the Modern State to Cosmopolitan Governance*, Cambridge: Polity Press.

Hewison, G. (1996) 'Political oppositions and regime change in Thailand' in Garry Rodan (ed.), *Political Oppositions in Industrialising Asia*, London/New York: Routledge, 72–94.

Hill, H. (1999) *The Indonesian Economy in Crisis*, St. Leonards: Allen and Unwin.

Hitchcock, D. I. (1995) *Asian Values and the United States: How Much Conflict?*, Washington DC: The Center for Strategic and International Studies.

Howard, R. E. (1990) 'Monitoring Human Rights: Problems of Consistency', *Ethics and International Affairs*, 4, 33–51.

HRCA (Human Rights Council of Australia) (1998) *The Rights Way To Development Manual For a Human Rights Approach To Development Assistance*, Marrickville (NSW): Andre Frankovits and Patrick Earle for The Human Rights Council of Australian Inc., May.

Human Rights Watch (1999a) *Human Rights Watch Report 1999 – Thailand*, Washington DC. Online. Available. http://www.hrw.org/hrw/worldreport99/asia/thailand.html

—— (1999b) *Human Rights Watch Report 1999 – Vietnam*, Washington DC. Online. Available. http://www.hrw.org/hrw/worldreport99/asia/vietnam.html

—— (1999c) *Human Rights Watch Report 1999 – United States of America*, Washington DC. Online. Available. http://www.hrw.org/hrw/worldreport99/usa/index.html

—— (1999d) *Human Rights Watch Report 1999 – Indonesia and East Timor*, Washington DC. Online. Available. http://www.hrw.org/hrw/worldreport99/asia/Indonesia.html

—— (1999e) *Human Rights Watch Report 1999 – Burma*, Washington DC. Online. Available. http://www.hrw.org/hrw/worldreport99/asia/burma.html

Huntington, S. P. (1968) *Political Order in Changing Societies*, New Haven and London: Yale University Press.

—— (1991) *The Third Wave: Democratization in the Late Twentieth Century*, Norman: University of Oklahoma Press.

—— (1993) 'The Clash of Civilizations?', *Foreign Affairs*, 72, 3.

—— (1996) *The Clash of Civilisations and the Remaking of World Order*, New York: Simon and Schuster.

Husaini, A. (1996) *Habibie, Suharto dan Islam*, Jakarta: Gema Insani Press.

Hutchcroft, P. (1998) 'Sustaining Political and Economic Reform' in D. G. Timberman (ed.), *The Philippines*, New York: Asia Society and Singapore: Institute of Southeast Asian Studies, 23–47.

Hutchison, J. (1993) 'Class and State Power in the Philippines' in K. Hewison *et al.* (eds), *Southeast Asia in the 1990s – Authoritarianism, Democracy and Capitalism*, Sydney: Allen and Unwin, 192–212.

Ibrahim, A. (1996) *The Asian Renaissance*, Singapore and Kuala Lumpur: Times Books International.
ICFTU (International Confederation of Free Trade Unions) (1995) *Annual Survey of Violations of Trade Union Rights 1995*, Brussels.
ICG (International Crisis Group) (2000a) 'Indonesia's Crisis: Chronic But Not Acute', Jakarta/Brussels: ICG Asia Report No. 2. Online. Available. http://www.crisisweb.org (31 May)
—— (2000b) 'Indonesia: Keeping the Military Under Control', Jakarta/Brussels: ICG Asia Report No. 9. Online. Available. http://www.crisisweb.org (5 September)
—— (2000c) 'Indonesia: Overcoming Murder and Chaos in Maluku', Jakarta/Brussels: Online. Available. http://www.crisisweb.org (19 December)
—— (2001a) 'Indonesia: Impunity Versus Accountability For Gross Human Rights Violations', Jakarta/Brussels: ICG Asian Report No. 12. Online. Available. http://www.crisisweb.org (2 February)
—— (2001b) 'Indonesia: National Police Reform', Jakarta/Brussels: ICG Report. Online. Available. http://www.crisisweb.org (20 February)
—— (2001c) 'Indonesia's Presidential Crisis', Jakarta/Brussels: ICG Briefing Paper, 21 February.
Ichyo, M. (1995) 'Debates on Human Rights Must Remain Free of State Discourse', *AMPO Japan-Asia Quarterly Review*, Tokyo: 26, 2: 48–51.
ILO (International Labour Organisation) (1995) 'Complaint against the Government of Indonesia presented by the International Confederation of Free Trade Unions (ICFTU) and the World Confederation of Labour (WCL)', Geneva: Case No. 1773, ILO hearings March–April.
International Law Book Services (1992) *Legal Profession Act 1976*, Kuala Lumpur: MDC Publishers Printers Sdn Bhd.
—— (1994) *Laws of Malaysia – Industrial Relations Act, 1967 (ACT 177) and Rules and Regulations As At 10th April 1994*. Kuala Lumpur: MDC Publishers Printers Sdn Bhd.
—— (1995) *Laws of Malaysia – Trade Unions Act Regulations (includes all amendments up to April 1995)*, Kuala Lumpur: MDC Publishers Printers Sdn Bhd.
Ismail, R. (ed.) (1995) *Hudud in Malaysia – The Issues at Stake*, Kuala Lumpur: Sisters in Islam.
Jackson, G. (1984) *Report of the Committee to Review the Australian Overseas Aid Program*, Canberra: AGPS.
Jannuzi, F. S. (1998) 'The New Burma Road' in Robert I. Rotberg (ed.) *op. cit.*, 197–208.
Jayakumar, S. (1996) 'Towards a United Nations for All its Members', New York: Speech by Minister for Foreign Affairs, Republic of Singapore, to the 51st United Nations General Assembly, 26 September 1996.
Jayasuriya, K. (1995) 'The Political Economy of Democratization' in Daniel A. Bell *et al.*, *op. cit.*, 107–33.
Jellinek, L. (1999) 'The new poor', *Inside Indonesia*, January–March, 57: 4–6.
Jenkins, D. (1984) *Suharto and His Generals: Indonesian Military Politics 1975–1983*, Ithaca: Cornell University Press.
Jesudason, J. (1993) *Statist Democracy and the Limits of Civil Society in Malaysia*, Working Paper No. 119, Singapore: Department of Sociology, National University of Singapore.
Jesdapipat, S. (1997). Available e-mail: Communication from Sitanon Jesdapipat sitanon@tei.or.th to aprenetlist@nautilus.org (5 June).
Johanson, V. (1999) 'Human rights and the general election 1999 in Aceh' in Susan Blackburn (ed.), *op. cit.*, 43–51.
Jomo, K. (1994) *Trade Unions and the State in Peninsular Malaysia*, Kuala Lumpur: Oxford University Press.
Jones, D. (1995) 'Democracy and Identity' in Daniel A. Bell *et al.*, *op. cit.*, 41–77.
Joseph, R. (2000) 'Treaty Monitors Act More Like Dictators', The *Australian*, 11 September, 31.
JSCFADT (Joint Standing Committee on Foreign Affairs, Defence and Trade) (1994) *A Review of Australia's Efforts to Promote and Protect Human Rights*, Canberra: Parliament of the Commonwealth of Australia, November.
—— (1995) *A Report on Human Rights and the Lack of Progress Towards Democracy in Burma (Myanmar)*, Canberra: The Parliament of the Commonwealth of Australia, October.
—— (1998a) *Australia and ASEAN: Managing Change*, Canberra: The Parliament of the Commonwealth of Australia, March.
—— (1998b) *Improving But … Australia's Regional Dialogue on Human Rights*, Canberra: The Parliament of the Commonwealth of Australia, June.
Just World Trust (1999) 'Memorandum On The Proposed Malaysian National Human Rights Commission', *Commentary – International Movement for a Just World*, Penang: July, 5–8.

Kahin, G. (1952), *Nationalism and Revolution in Indonesia*, Ithaca: Cornell University Press.

Kalyanamitra (1986) 'Pembantu Rumah Tangga', *Dongbret*, Jakarta: 2 April.

Kamali, M. (1994a) 'The Islamic State and its Constitution' in Norani Othman (ed.), *Sharia'a Law and the Modern Nation-State – A Malaysian Symposium*, Kuala Lumpur: Sisters in Islam, SIS (Malaysia) Berhad, 45–66.

Kamali, M. (1994b) 'Freedom of Expression in Islam', Kuala Lumpur: Berita Publishing Sdn. Bhd.'

Keating, P. (1996) *Australia, Asia and the New Regionalism*, Singapore: Institute of Southeast Asian Studies, Singapore Lecture Series.

Kelly, P. (1996) 'An Australia in transition not turmoil', *The Australian*, 27 November, 15.

Kent, A. (1997) 'Human Rights' in F. A. Mediansky (ed.), *Australian Foreign Policy: Into the New Millennium*, South Melbourne: Macmillan, 162–79.

Kerin, J. (1999) 'New players and old in the aid decision making process' in Susan Blackburn and Bob Stensholt, *op. cit.*, 57–62.

Kevin, A. (1998) 'Cambodia's misunderstood crisis', Melbourne: Speech delivered by Ambassador Anthony Kevin at the Australian Institute of International Affairs, 16 November. Available e-mail: Communication from mvick@CHMAI.LOXINFO. CO.TH to SEASIA-L@LIST.MSU.EDU (2 December)

—— (2000) 'Machiavellian diplomacy reaps a bitter harvest', *The Australian*, 1 April, 13.

—— (2001) 'Firm but finer hand on Cambodian reins', *The Weekend Australian*, 13–14 January, 9.

Khanna, V. (1999) 'Views and Opinions', *Business Times Online*, Singapore: 20 September.

Khoo, Boo Teik (1995) *Paradoxes of Mahathirism – An Intellectual Biography of Mahathir Mohamad*, Kuala Lumpur: Oxford University Press.

Kothari, R. (1984) 'The Non-Party Political Process' in H. Sethi and S. Kothari (eds), *The Non-Party Political Process: Uncertain Alternatives*, Delhi: Lokayan, 18–46.

Kraince, R. (1999) 'Jakarta Pro-Reform "Provocateurs." ' Available e-mail: Communication from <rk257386@OAK.CATS.OHIOU.EDU to SEASIA-L@LIST. MSU.EDU (25 September).

Kwik, Kian Gie (1996) 'Ada Kecenderungan Menunda Investasi Sampai 1998', *Ekonomi & Bisnis*, Jakarta: Online. Available. http://www.idola.net.id/tempo/anggota/mingguan/ ed2401/ekbis2.htm (9 August)

Lao Human Rights Council Inc. (1999) 'Letter to The Honorable Harold H. Koh, Assistant Secretary of State, Bureau of Democracy, Human Rights and Labor, U.S. Department of State', Washington, DC: Lao Human Rights Council Inc., Available e-mail: laohumrights@earthlink.net (13 January)

Larif-Beatrix, A. (1994) 'The Muslim State: Pursuing a Mirage?' in Norani Othman (ed.), *op. cit.*, 33–44.

Lawson, S. (1996) 'Cultural Relativism and Democracy: Political Myths about "Asia" and the "West" ' in R. Robison (ed.), *Pathways to Asia: The Politics of Engagement*, Sydney: Allen and Unwin, 108–28.

Lim, A. (1999) 'Co-opt people, ideas at all levels, urges BG Lee', *The Straits Times*, 30 March 1999.

Lim, P. (1999) 'Human Rights Watch Decries Anwar Sentence', Singapore: Available e-mail: Communication from alsona@PACIFIC.NET.SG (15 April).

Lintner, B. (1998) 'Drugs and Economic Growth' in Robert I. Rotberg (ed.), *op. cit.*, 165–83.

Lowry, R. (1996) *The Armed Forces of Indonesia*, Sydney: Allen and Unwin.

Mackie, J. (1974) 'Australia's Relations with Indonesia: Principles and Policies', *Australian Outlook*, Pts. I and II, 28, 1 and 2, April and August.

Macuja, J. (1992) 'The Mass Movement and the 1992 Elections', Baguio City: Cordillera Studies Center Issue Paper No. 2.

Madjid, N. (1995) *Islam Agama Kemanusiaan*, Jakarta: Yayasan Wakaf Paramadina.

Mahathir, M. (1970) *The Malay Dilemma*, Singapore: D. Moore for Asia Pacific Press.

—— (1986) *The Challenge*, Petaling Jaya: Pelanduk Publications.

—— (1995) 'Islam Guarantees Justice for All Citizens', in Rose Ismail (ed.), *op. cit.*, 63–76.

—— (1999) 'World Analysis – a case study for a country under economic stress', *Mainichi Shimbun*, Tokyo: Online. Available. http://www.mir.com.my/lb/econ_plan/contents/press_release/capital.htm (National Recovery Strategy) (2 August, 1999)

Mahbubani, K. (1993) 'The Dangers of Decadence – What the Rest Can Teach the West', *Foreign Affairs*, 72, 4.

—— (1998) *Can Asians Think?*, Singapore and Kuala Lumpur: Times Books International.

Manderson, L. (1980) *Women, Politics and Change: The Kaum Ibu UMNO, Malaysia 1945–1972*, Kuala Lumpur: Oxford University Press.

Marfil, M. P. (1999) 'Estrada lambasts newspaper owners', *Philippine Daily Inquirer*, 23 April.

Mason, M. (1998) 'Foreign Direct Investment' in Robert I. Rotberg (ed.), *op. cit.*, 209–25.

Massakh, B. (1995) 'Harus Diwaspadai, Demokrasi Jangan Sampai Merosot', *Suara Karya*, Jakarta: 10 April.

McBeth, J., Vatikiotis, M. and Rees, J. (1996) 'Personal Pact', *Far Eastern Economic Review*, Hong Kong: 28 December 1995–4 January 1996, 19.

McCoy, A. (1984) *Priests on Trial*, Ringwood (Vic): Penguin Books Australia.

Millbank, A. (2000) 'The Problem with the 1951 Refugee Convention', Canberra: Parliament of Australia, Parliamentary Library, Research Paper 5, 2000–1, 5 September.

Miller, J. (2000) 'East Timorese Leader Urges Swift Return of Refugees'. Available e-mail: Communication from john@etan.org to SEASIA-L@LIST.MSU.EDU (23 March)

Milne, G. (2000) 'Hanson Spectre Bedevils Howard', *The Australian*, 11 September, 31.

Milner, A. (ed.) (1993) *Australian–Asian Perceptions Project, Working Paper Number Six – 'Perceiving Democracy'*, Sydney: Academy of the Social Sciences in Australia and The Asia-Australia Institute, The University of New South Wales, August.

—— (1996) *Australia in Asia – Comparing Cultures*, Melbourne: Oxford University Press.

—— (1997) 'The Rhetoric of Asia' in James Cotton and John Ravenhill (eds), *Seeking Asian Engagement – Australia in World Affairs, 1991–95*, Melbourne: Oxford University Press, 32–45.

Morgenthau, H. (1973) *Politics Among Nations*, New York: Knopf.

Mulder, N. (1978) *Mysticism and Everyday Life in Contemporary Java*, Singapore: Institute of Southeast Asian Studies.

Mutalib, H. (1993) *Islam in Malaysia*, Singapore: Singapore University Press.

Muzaffar, C. (1986) *Islamic Resurgence in Malaysia*, Kuala Lumpur: Penerbit Fajar Bakti Sdn. Bhd.

—— (1993) *Human Rights and the New World Order*, Penang: Just World Trust.

—— (1995a) 'Human Rights and Hypocrisy in the International Order' in Chandra Muzaffar (ed.), *Dominance of the West Over the Rest*, Penang: Just World Trust, 83–109.

—— (1995b) 'Human Rights, the State and the Secular Challenge', *AMPO Japan-Asia Quarterly Review*, 26, 3: 47–53.

—— (1999a) 'The People's Verdict', *Commentary – International Movement for a Just World*, May, 24, 11.

—— (1999b) 'One Man's Obsession', *Commentary – International Movement for a Just World*, May, 24, 12.

Mysliwiec, E. (1988) *Punishing the Poor – The International Isolation of Kampuchaea*, Oxford: OXFAM.

Nair, S. (1997) *Islam in Malaysian Foreign Policy*, London and New York: Routledge.

Nanuam, W. (1999) 'Army lays claim to 50 channels – Concerns aired over national security', *Bangkok Post*, 6 May.

Nasution, A. B. (1994) 'Human Rights and the *Konstituante* Debates of 1956–59', in David Bourchier and John Legge (eds), *op. cit.*, 43–9.

—— (1995) 'Pelenggaran HAM Terjadi Akibat Sistem Pembangunan', Jakarta: *Republika*, 16 December.

Navarete-Recina, A. (2000) 'The Philippines Commission on Human Rights' in S. Rachagan and R. Tikamdas (eds), *Human Rights and the National Commission*, Kuala Lumpur: HAKAM (Persatuan Kebangsaan Hak Asasi Manusia), 75–84.

Nazri, S. (1995) 'Anwar talks on advantages Muslims in the region have', *New Straits Times*, Kuala Lumpur: 27 September, 1–2.

NDI (National Democratic Institute for International Affairs) (2000) 'Road to Constitutional Reform: The 2000 MPR Annual Session', Jakarta/Washington DC: Online. Available. http://www.ndi.org (October)

Neher, C. and Marlay, R. (1995) *Democracy and Development in Southeast Asia – The Winds of Change*, Boulder: Westview Press.

Noer, D. (1991) 'Mendayung di Tengah Karang: Pikiran dan Politik Perjuangan Bung Hatta' in Fauzie Ridjal and M. R. Karim, *Dinamika Budaya dan Politik dalam Pembangunan*, Yogyakarta: PT Tiara, Wacana Yogya untuk Yayasan Hatta, August, 267–307.

Nusantara, A. (1995) 'Perlindungan hak Berkumpul Masih Rendah', *Merdeka*, Yogyakarta: 14 December.

O'Brien, N. (2000) 'UN Handed Evidence of Jail Torture', *The Weekend Australian*, 18–19 November, 8.

O'Donnell, G. (1973) *Modernization and Bureaucratic Authoritarianism*, Berkeley: University of California, Institute for International Studies.

Ott, M. (1998) 'From Isolation to Relevance. Policy Considerations' in Robert I. Rotberg (ed.), *op. cit.*, 69–83.

Othman, N. (1994) 'Umma and Citizenry: Civil Society in the New World Order' in Norani Othman (ed.), *op. cit.*, 81–6.

Padman, P. (1998) 'Impact of current economic woes tops UNDP agenda', *New Straits Times*, 15 May, 10.

Parekh, B. (1997) 'Rethinking Humanitarian Intervention', *International Political Science Review*, 18, 1: 49–69.

Pereira, B. (1998) 'I might lie if asked to, says witness – NST'. Available e-mail: Communication from: Roland Takeshi roland@PPP.NASIONET.NET to SEASIA-L@ LIST.MSU.EDU (6 November)

Philpott, S. (1999) ' "We are rich but we are dead": Irian Jaya and the 1999 Indonesian general election' in Susan Blackburn (ed.), *op. cit.*, 63–71.

Plane, T. and Chan, G. (2000) 'Woomera in Crisis – Sex claims made earlier than July', *The Australian*, 24 November, 6.

Poerwadi, N. (1999) 'History binds RI and Australia', *The Jakarta Post*, 13 October.

Powell, S. (2001) 'Rape: just another weapon of war', *The Weekend Australian*, 10–11 March, 20–1.

Race Discrimination Commissioner (1995) *Racial Discrimination Act 1975: A Review*, Canberra: Commonwealth of Australia, AGPS, December.

Rachagan, S. and Tikamdas, R. (eds) (2000), *Human Rights and the National Commission*, Kuala Lumpur: HAKAM.

Rajamoorthy, T. (1995) 'Double Standards, Selectivity and Western Domination' in Chandra Muzaffar (ed.), *Dominance of the West Over the Rest, op. cit.*, 73–82.

Ramage, D. E. (1996) *Politics in Indonesia: Democracy, Islam and the Ideology of Tolerance*, London: Routledge.

Ramos-Horta, J. (1994) 'Text of 1994 letter by Nobel Peace Prize Laureate Jose Ramos Horta to Indonesian President Suharto 31 March 1994', Geneva: 31 March. Available e-mail: Communication from etio@ozemail.com.au to apakabar@clark.net (14 October 1996) (Under heading 'Nobel laureate writes President Suharto')

Razak, A., Baginda, A. and Mahmood, R. (eds) (1995) *Malaysia's Defence and Foreign Policies*, Petaling Jaya: Pelanduk Publications.

RCADIC (Royal Commission into Aboriginal Deaths in Custody) (1991) *National Report*, Canberra: AGPS.

Reform Movement (1998) 'Anwar's Letter From Sungai Buloh'. Available e-mail: Communication from islah_reform@hotmail.com to BICNews@MailingList.net (5 November)

Reeve, D. (1985) *Golkar of Indonesia: An Alternative to the Party System*, Singapore: Oxford University Press.

Reid, A. (1974) *Indonesian National Revolution 1945–50*, Hawthorn (Vic): Longman.

Richardson, M. (1998) 'Under Protest', *The Australian*, 10 July, 32.

Richburg, K. (1998) 'Malaysian Trade Minister Makes Fun of Secretary's Action', *Washington Post Foreign Service*, 16 November, A15.

Rintoul, S. (2000) 'Three strikes and you're dead', *The Australian*, 18 February, 19.

Robison, R. (1996) 'Looking North: Myths and Strategies' in R. Robison (ed.), *op. cit.*, 3–28.

Robles, R. (1997a) 'Army and police "kings of crime" ', *South China Morning Post*, Hong Kong: 8 May.

——(1997b) 'Outrage follows killing of journalist', *South China Morning Post*, 4 June.

Rodan, G. (1996) 'State-society relations and political opposition in Singapore' in Garry Rodan (ed.), *Political Oppositions in Industrialising Asia*, London/New York: Routledge, 95–127.

Rodan, G. and Hewison, K. (1996) 'A "Clash of Cultures" or the Convergence of Political ideology?' in R. Robison (ed.), *op. cit.*, 29–55.

Rood, S. (1998) 'Decentralization, Democracy and Development' in D. G. Timberman (ed.), *op. cit.*, 111–36.

Rosenberg, D. (ed.) (1979) *Marcos and Martial Law in the Philippines*, Ithaca: Cornell University Press.

Ruddock, P. (2001) 'Minister Warns that Illegal Arrivals Threaten Australia's Humanitarian Program', Minister for Immigration and Multicultural Affairs Media Release 046/2001. Online. Available. http://www.minister.immi.gov.au/media_releases/media01/r01046.htm

Rural Industries Research and Development Corporation (1998) 'Gaining an export foothold in Myanmar', (Summary of report by S. Bhaskaran and S. Fahey, published by the Corporation entitled 'Agrifood Sector in Myanmar – Market Review and Analysis of Trends') Canberra: Online. Available. http://www.rirdc.gov.au/pub/media_releases/ 21oct98.htm (21 October)

SAHRDC (South Asia Human Rights Documentation Center) (2000) *Komnas HAM – The Indonesian National Human Rights Commission: The Formative Years*, New Delhi: Online. Available. http://www.hrdc.net (November)

Said, E. (1995) *Orientalism: Western Conceptions of the Orient*, London: Penguin Books (Re-printed with a new Afterword).

Sajoo, A. (1994) *Pluralism in Old Societies and New States – Emerging ASEAN Contexts*, Singapore: Institute of Southeast Asian Studies.

Samudavanija, Chai-Anan (1994) 'Thailand: A Stable Semi-Democracy' in L. Diamond *et al.*, *Political Culture and Democracy in Developing Countries*, Boulder: Lynne Rienner, 305–46.

Santoso, A. (1996) 'Immature political elite slows reforms', *The Jakarta Post*, 11 March, 1.

Sasono, A. (1994) 'Politik Partai "ICMI" Politik Islam', Jakarta: *Trotoar*, 47, 5.

Schwarz, A. (1999) *A Nation in Waiting* (2nd edition), St. Leonards: Allen and Unwin.

Searle, P. (1996) 'Recalcitrant or *Realpolitik*' The Politics of Culture in Australia's Relations with Malaysia' in R. Robison (ed.), *op. cit.*, 56–84.

Seow, F. T. (1994) *To Catch a Tartar: A Dissident in Lee Kuan Yew's Prison*, New Haven, Yale University Southeast Asia Studies.

Severino, Jean-Michel (1998) 'Indonesia's Road to Recovery', Opening Statement to the Consultative Group for Indonesia by Vice President East Asia and the Pacific, The World Bank, Paris: 29 July. Online Available. http://www.worldbank.org/html/extdr/ offrep/eap/jmssp072998.htm

Shamsul, A. B. (1996) 'Australia in Contemporary Malaysia's Worldview' in Z. Marshallsay (ed.), *Australia – Malaysia Relations – New Roads Ahead*, Melbourne: Monash Asia Institute, 1996, 46–74.

Shanahan, D. (2000) 'All warm and fuzzy over Asia', *The Australian*, 6 March, 14.

Shari, I. (2000) 'Financial Crisis and its Social Implications', Canberra: The Australian National University. Paper presented to 2nd Australia – Malaysia Conference on 'Malaysia after the Financial Crisis and General Elections: Economic, Social and Political Implications', 24–26 May.

Sheridan, G. (2000) 'Engaging Burma is "best way"', *The Australian*, 21 December, 6.

Simons, P. (Chairman, Committee to Review the Australian Overseas Program) (1997) *One Clear Objective – Poverty Reduction Through Sustainable Development*, Canberra: Report of the Committee of Review, AusAID, April.

Simunjuntak, M. (1994) *Pandangan Negara Integralistik*, Jakarta: PT Pustaka Utama Grafiti.

Singh, S. (1995) '11 New Conditions for Foreign Workers', *New Straits Times*, 8 October.

Sinjal, I. (1991) 'Masalah Keterbukaan dan Demokrasi Pancasila', Jakarta: *Suara Pembaruan*, 5 January.

Spaeth, A. (1996) 'The Split Peace Prize Pair', Time, New York: 148, 19, 21 October.

Spegele, R. (1996) *Political Realism in International Theory*, Cambridge: Cambridge University Press.

SPRIM (Indonesian Peoples' Solidarity Struggle with the Maubere People) (1995) 'SPRIM Position Paper 2/2', *Aksi News Service*, Sydney: ASIET, 1 August.

Steinberg, D. (1998) 'The Road to Political Recovery: The Salience of Politics in Economics' in Robert I. Rotberg (ed.), *op. cit.*, 269–86.

Stewart, I. (2000*a*) 'Malays split on policing of Islam', *The Australian*, 4 October, 6.

—— (2000*b*) 'Race first, politics second in Malaysia', *The Australian*, 29 November, 8.

—— (2001) 'Malay rally heightens racial tensions', *The Australian*, 6 February, 8.

Stewart, C. and Greenlees D. (2001) 'US Steps back on Jakarta', *The Australian*, 19 January, 1.

Stiglitz, J. (1998) 'The Role of International Financial Institutions in the Current Global Economy', 27 February, Chicago: Address to the Chicago Council on Foreign Relations. Online. Available. http://www.worldbank.org/html/extdr/extme/jssp022798.htm

—— (1999) 'Participation and Development – Perspectives from the Comprehensive Development Paradigm', Seoul: Comments by Senior Vice President and Chief Economist, 'International Conference on Democracy, Market Economy and Development', The World Bank, 27 February. Online. Available. http://www.worldbank.org/html/extdr/extme/js-022799/index.htm

Streeten, P. (1981) *First Things First: Meeting Basic Human Needs in the Developing Countries*, Oxford University Press for the World Bank, New York.

SUARAM (Voice of Malaysia) (1994) *Malaysian Charter On Human Rights By Malaysian Non-Governmental Organisations*, Petaling Jaya, December.

Sudradjat, E. (1995) 'Jangan Jatuhkan Orsospol Tertentu', *Kompas*, Jakarta, 6 May.

Sukma, R. (1997) 'Bebas-Aktif Foreign Policy and the "Security Agreement" with Australia', *Australian Journal of International Affairs*, July, 51(2), 231–41.

Sulaiman, I., Sofyan, G. and Smith, S. (1998) *Bridging the Arafura Sea: Australia–Indonesia Relations in Prosperity and Adversity*, Canberra: The Australian National University, Asia Pacific School of Economics and Management, Asia Pacific Press.

Sumarno (1999) 'Politisasi Timtim', *Republika*, 15 September.

Suryadinata, L. (1996) *Indonesia's Foreign Policy Under Suharto – Aspiring to International Leadership*, Singapore: Times Academic Press.

Suryohadiprojo, S. (1999) 'Implikasi Hasil Jajak Pendapat Timtim', *Republika*, 7 September.

Talwar, M. (1997) 'Indonesia's National Human Rights Commission: A Step in the Right Direction?', Washington DC: The Center for Human Rights and Humanitarian Law, Washington College of Law, American University. Online. Available. http://www.wcl.american.edu/pub/humright/brief/v4i2/indo42.htm

Tamthai, P. (2000) 'The National Human Rights Commission of Thailand' in S. Rachagan and R. Tikamdas (eds), *op. cit.*, 95–101.

Tang, J. (ed.) (1995) *Human Rights and International Relations in the Asia-Pacific Region*, London/New York: Pinter.

Tanter, R. and Young, K. (eds) (1990) *The Politics of Middle Class Indonesia*, Monash Papers on Southeast Asia No. 19, Clayton: Centre of Southeast Asian Studies, Monash University.

Thillainathan, R. (2000) 'Malaysia and the Asian Crisis – Lessons and Challenges', Canberra: Paper presented to 2nd Australia – Malaysia Conference, *op. cit.*

Timberlake, I. (2000) 'E Timor toll put at 2000', *The Australian*, 22 December, 6.

Thompson, K. (1994) 'Understanding Political Realism' in K. W. Thompson (ed.), *op. cit.*, 249–64.

Thong-Bee Koh, T. (1993) 'Does East Asia Stand for Any Positive Values?', Singapore: *International Herald Tribune*, 11–12 December.

Thornton, M. (1995) 'Revisiting Race' in Race Discrimination Commissioner, *op. cit.*, 81–100.

Toha-An Nee (1995) 'Workers detained in hell holes: Tenaganita', *The Sun*, Kuala Lumpur: 28 July.

Tu Weiming (1989) *Way, Learning and Politics: Essays on the Confucian Intellectual*, Singapore: Institute of East Asian Political Economy.

—— (1997) 'Towards a Global Ethic: Spiritual Implications of the Islam-Confucianism Dialogue' in Osman Bakar and Cheng Gek Nai (eds), *Islam and Confucianism – A Civilisational Dialogue*, Kuala Lumpur: University of Malaya Press for the Centre for Civilizational Dialogue, University of Malaya, 19–34.

UNCHR (United Nations Commission for Human Rights) (1998*a*) 'Situation of human rights in Cambodia, Report of the Special Representative of the Secretary-General for Human Rights in Cambodia, Mr. Thomas Hammarberg, submitted in accordance with Commission resolution 1997/49', New York: Fifty-fourth session, Item 17 of the provisional agenda, E/CN.4/1998/95, 20 February.

—— (1998*b*) 'Asia Pacific Governments and NGOs: Opportunity for Dialogue', UN Commission on Human Rights Session on Regional Arrangements in the Asia Pacific (sic), Geneva: 24 March.

—— (1998*c*) *Report of the United Nations Special Rapporteur on Human Rights Conditions in Burma on the UN General Assembly's Third Committee*, New York: November.

—— (1998*d*) *Year Review of the Implementation of the Vienna Declaration and Programme of Action*, New York: Interim report of the United Nations High Commissioner for Human Rights, Fifty-fourth session, 16 March – 24 April, Items 3 and 21 of the provisional agenda.

—— (1999) 'Workshop on the Development of National Plans of Action for the Promotion and Protection of Human Rights in the Asia-Pacific Region, Bangkok, Thailand, 5–7 July 1999', New York: Online. Available. http://www.unchr.ch/html/menub/ bgkcncls.htm

—— (2000*a*) 'Situation of human rights in Cambodia: Report of the Special Representative of the Secretary-General for human rights in Cambodia, Mr. Thomas Hammarberg, submitted in accordance with resolution 1999/76', New York: UN Economic and Social Council, Fifty-sixth session of the Commission on Human Rights, Item 19 of the provisional agenda, E/CN.4/2000/109, 13 January.

—— (2000*b*) 'Report of the International Commission of Inquiry on East Timor to the Secretary-General'. New York: Online. Available. http://www.unhchr.ch/huridocda/huridoca.nsf/(Symbol)/A.54.726,+S.2000.59.En?OpenDocument (January)

UNCHR (2000*c*) New York: Committee for the Elimination of Racial Discrimination (CERD), Hearings on twelfth periodic report by Australia (document CERD/C/335/Add.2), 21–22 March. Online. Available. http://www.unhchr.ch/tbs/doc.nsf/(Symbol)/CERD.C.56. Misc.42.rev.3.En?Opendocument

UNDP (United Nations Development Program) (1999*a*) *Human Development Report*, New York and Oxford: Oxford University Press.

—— (1999b) 'Mitigating the Human Impact of the Asian Crisis: The Role of UNDP', New York: United Nations Development Programme. Online. Available. http://www.undp.org/rbap/Reports/Mitigating.pdf (September)

United Nations (1993a) 'Asian Preparatory Meeting for the World Conference on Human Rights Opens in Bangkok', Bangkok: United Nations Information Service, Press Release No. G/10/93, 29 March.

—— (1993b) 'Vienna Declaration and Programme of Action', New York: UN General Assembly, A/CONF.157/23 of 12 July. Online. Available. http://www.unhchr.ch/huridocda/huridoca.nsf/(Symbol)/A.CONF.157.23.En?OpenDocument

—— (1993c) 'National institutions for the promotion and protection of human rights', New York: UN General Assembly, A/RES/48/134, 85th plenary meeting, 20 December.

—— (1999a) 'Agreement between the Republic of Indonesia and the Republic of Portugal on the question of East Timor', New York: Report by the Secretary General to the UN Security Council and General Assembly, 5 May (A/53/951-S/1999/513).

—— (1999b) 'Question of East Timor – Progress report of the Secretary-General', New York: UN General Assembly, Fifty-fourth session, Agenda item 96, 13 December 1999, A/54/654.

—— (2000a) 'Report of the Secretary-General on the United Nations Transitional Administration in East Timor (for the period 27 January–26 July 2000)', New York: UN Security Council, S/2000/738, 26 July.

—— (2000b) 'Militias Root Cause of Problems for UNTAET and Indonesia in East Timor, Secretary-General's Special Representative Tells Council', New York: UN Security Council, Press Release SC/6938, 29 September.

US Department of State (1999a) '1998 Country Report on Economic Policy and Trade Practices – Thailand', Washington DC: 31 January.

—— (1999b) 'Country Report on Human Rights Practices for 1998 – Indonesia', Washington DC: 26 February.

—— (2000) '1999 Country Reports on Human Rights Practices – The Philippines', Washington DC: 25 February.

van der Kroef, J. (1988) 'The Philippine Vigilantes: Devotion and Disarray', *Contemporary Southeast Asia*, 10, 2: 163–81.

van Klinken, G. (1999a) 'A dark scenario', *Inside Indonesia*, Digest 82, 6 September. Online. Available. http://www.insideindonesia.org/digest/dig82.htm

—— (1999b) 'What Jakarta's papers say about East Timor', *Inside Indonesia*, Digest 83, 8 September. Online. Available. http://www.insideindonesia.org/digest/dig83.htm

Vasil, R. (1971) *Politics in a Plural Society: A Study of Non-Communal Political Parties in West Malaysia*, Kuala Lumpur/New York: Oxford University Press.

—— (1995) *Asianising Singapore – The PAP's Management of Ethnicity*, Singapore: Heinemann Asia.

Vatikiotis, M. (1996) *Political Change in South-East Asia – Trimming the Banyan Tree*, London: Routledge.

Vincent, R. (1986) *Human Rights and International Relations*, Cambridge: Cambridge University Press.

Wahid, A. (1995) 'Intelektual di Tengah Eksklusivisme' in Nasrullah Ali-Fauzi (ed.), *ICMI Antara Status Quo dan Demokratisasi*, Bandung: Penerbit Mizan, 70–5.

Wahjono, S. and Padmo (1991) 'Demokrasi Politik Indonesia' in Fauzie Ridjal and M. R. Karim (eds), *op. cit.*, 227–66.

Wanandi, J. (1992) *Human rights and Democracy in the ASEAN Nations: The Next 25 Years*, Jakarta: Centre for Strategic and International Studies.

Warren, C. (1990) 'The Bureaucratisation of Local Government in Indonesia', Working Paper No. 66, Clayton: Monash University, Centre of Southeast Asian Studies.

Weingast, B. (1997) 'The Political Foundations of Democracy and the Rule of Law', *American Political Science Review*, 91, 2.

Weiss, L. (1998) *The Myth of the Powerless State*, Cambridge: Polity Press.

Williams, M. (1996) 'Rethinking Sovereignty' in E. Kofman and G. Youngs (eds), *Globalization: Theory and Practice*, New York: Pinter, 109–22.

Woodley, B. (2000) 'Murdered staff chose to stay despite threats', *The Australian*, 8 September, 6.

Woollacott, M. (1998) 'Asia's masses shift against the West', *The Guardian Weekly*, London: 12 July, 1, 4.

World Bank (1999*a*) 'A World Free of Poverty', Bangkok: 21–22 January, Chairman's Communique, Regional Meeting on Social Issues Arising from the East Asian Economic Crisis. Washington DC: Online. Available. http://www.worldbank.org/html/ extdr/extme/pc012699.htm

—— (1999*b*) 'Malaysian Country Assistance Strategy Reviewed by World Bank', Washington DC: 31 March. Online. Available. http://www.worldbank.org/html/ extdr/extme/ps033199.htm

—— (1999*c*) '$1.1 Billion in Loans Approved for Indonesia', Washington DC: 20 May. Online. Available. http://www.worldbank.org/html/extdr/extme/2198.htm

—— (1999*d*) 'What is the Social Crisis in East Asia?', Washington DC: 24 June. Online. Available. http://www.worldbank.org/eapsocial/whatis.htm

—— (1999*e*) *Social Indicators*, Washington DC: Online. Available. http://www.worldbank.org/ poverty/eacrisis/indicat/index.htm#sic

—— (1999*f*) 'Donors Pledge Continued Support for Economic Recovery of The Philippines', 22nd Consultative Group meeting for the Philippines, Tokyo 24–25 March. Washington DC: Online. Available. http://www.worldbank.org/html/extdr/extme/ 2125.htm.

Yamamoto (1995) *Emerging Civil Society in the Asia Pacific Community*, Singapore: Institute of Southeast Asian Studies.

YLBHI (Foundation of Indonesian Legal Aid Institutions) (1995) *Catatan Keadaan Hak Asasi Manusia Di Indonesia 1994*, Jakarta.

Zainuddin, D. (1998) 'Take cognisance of internal weaknesses', *New Straits Times*, 29 May, 12–13, 19.

Index